DRACULA IS DEAD

How ROMANIANS Survived Communism, Ended It, and Emerged since 1989 as the New Italy

SHEILAH KAST   JIM ROSAPEPE

bancroft press

Published by Bancroft Press ("Books that enlighten")
P.O. Box 65360, Baltimore, MD 21209
800-637-7377
410-764-1967 (fax)
www.bancroftpress.com

Cover and interior design by Tamira Ci Thayne, Crescent Communications
www.tsgcrescent.com • 814.941.7447
Maps by Tracy Copes, Daft Generation • www.daftgeneration.com
Authors' Dustjacket Photo by Carolyn M. Brenner

ISBN (10 digit): 1-890862-65-7
ISBN (13 digit): 978-1-890862-65-7
LCCN: 2009931827

SUBJECTS/TOPICS OF BOOK: Public Affairs/Current Events/Travel
Printed in the United States of America

First Edition

1 3 5 7 9 10 8 6 4 2

For our friend Valentin George,
who saw what Romania could become
and devoted his life to achieving it
(1/22/1970—12/19/2002)

ROMANIAN
LANDS
DURING THE
SEVENTEENTH
CENTURY

The changes—and continuities—of European history are evident in this map. With numerous border changes over the centuries, Transylvania, Wallachia, and Moldavia made up the "Romanian Lands" four hundred years ago—and they do again today. The empires of the Ottoman Turks, the Austrians, and the Poles are long gone. But their homelands remain, though they do not border Romania anymore.

Praise for DRACULA IS DEAD

"If they gave out gold medals for books, *Dracula is Dead* would get one. It's a fascinating, long overdue, and timely look at Romania, giving readers an unparalleled view of my country's many, many layers."—NADIA COMĂNECI, OLYMPIC CHAMPION AND GYMNASTICS COACH

"To understand how Eastern Europeans moved from Soviet satellites to NATO allies, *Dracula Is Dead* is a great place to start. Sheilah and Jim know the region well. Their insights are relevant to nations from the Baltic to the Black Sea." —U.S. HOUSE MAJORITY LEADER STENY HOYER; FORMER CO-CHAIR, U.S. HELSINKI COMMISSION

"If you buy only one book about Romania, *Dracula is Dead* should be the one. Culture, religion, war, humor, kings, Communists, kids, IT nerds, gypsies—and Dracula—they're all here, seen through the eyes of two keen American observers and storytellers."—SAM DONALDSON, ABC NEWS CONTRIBUTOR AND ANCHOR

"Romania is a living legacy of Rome, as well as a great American ally. Jim and Sheilah are outstanding guides to this country, which is both familiar and exotic."—MADELEINE K. ALBRIGHT, U.S. SECRETARY OF STATE, 1997-2001

"Vivid travelogue, gripping memoir, and accurate analysis, this book is a compellingly insightful look at the dilemmas entailed with Romania's embrace of democracy. Sheilah Kast, the indefatigable journalist, and Jim Rosapepe, the astute diplomat-politician, take readers on a marvelous journey through Romania's history, geography, culture, and habits of the heart. Highly recommended to all those who want to understand the human underpinnings of the struggle for freedom in East-Central Europe."—VLADIMIR TISMĂNEANU, PROFESSOR OF POLITICS, UNIVERSITY OF MARYLAND; AUTHOR, *STALINISM FOR ALL SEASONS: A POLITICAL HISTORY OF ROMANIAN COMMUNISM*

"What a great read! With the eye of the journalist and the ear of the politician, Sheilah Kast and Jim Rosapepe make their Romanian experience so absorbing that you'll want to jump on the next plane to go see for yourself. But I refuse to believe that Dracula is really dead."—COKIE ROBERTS, AUTHOR, SYNDICATED COLUMNIST, AND SENIOR POLITICAL ANALYST FOR ABC NEWS AND NPR

"I chose fiction to convey the chaos and connections of Chicago politics. Sheilah and Jim found chaos and connections and much more while uncovering the real story of Romania—exploding the myths and filling in the rest of the story. You'll be fascinated by what they found."—SCOTT SIMON, HOST, NPR'S WEEKEND EDITION SATURDAY; AUTHOR, WINDY CITY

"You don't have to be Italian American to understand why Sheilah and Jim call Romania the New Italy—Latin language, dazzling creativity, roots in the Roman Empire. They show you the Romania you don't know, the place you'll want to visit."—BILL NOVELLI, FORMER CEO, AARP; AND AUTHOR, FIFTY PLUS: GIVE MEANING AND PURPOSE TO THE BEST TIME OF YOUR LIFE

"This book puts a three-dimensional face on a country most Americans know only through legend. At last, the appeal, the wonderful reality and the fascinating interplay of the past and the present make Romania a place which belongs on everyone's "must see" list. Tourism or business, there is hidden treasure here!"—LESLEY ISRAEL, FORMER PRESIDENT, NATIONAL CONFERENCE ON SOVIET JEWRY

"Post-communist Romania was lucky to have a bright couple who were genuinely fascinated by the country, an ambassador who asked questions, and a journalist who dug deep. The portrait they have drawn of a vibrant and warm nation should overthrow many of the negative clichés that have persisted in our media. Travel with them in this eye-opening book, and you may feel the urge to go there yourself."—ANDREI CODRESCU, NPR COMMENTATOR AND AUTHOR, THE POSTHUMAN DADA GUIDE: TZARA AND LENIN PLAY CHESS

"Hungarians knew Transylvania long before Bram Stoker created Dracula. This intriguing book shines a spotlight on the Hungarian heritage—and current struggles—in 21st-century Romania. Agree or disagree, it's thought-provoking reading."—HELEN SZABLYA, HONORARY HUNGARIAN CONSUL, SEATTLE, WA, AND CO-AUTHOR, THE FALL OF THE RED STAR

"Dracula is Dead is just the right metaphor. This interesting and entertaining book, with Sheilah's journalistic acumen and Jim's inside knowledge, takes readers behind the myth and the fiction to today's real Romania."—PROFESSOR RADU FLORESCU SR., HISTORIAN AND CO-AUTHOR, IN SEARCH OF DRACULA

CONTENTS

"We're waiting for you"

Kiss my hand!

Wave it or wear it?

Fast track to high tech

Why Orthodoxy is important in Romania

How Orthodoxy survived Communism

The religious revival since 1989

Oh, please pardon my English

The spies and the spied-on

All politics is local

Something to chew on

Surviving urban renewal, Ceauşescu-style

Nixon, Castro, and Pillar 23

A Romanian view of Americans abroad

Let's drink to that!

God's love, good doctors, and anti-retrovirals

Generation X in the Balkans

Standing in line for no reason

Post-Cold War frostbite

Rome vs. Romania: 1054 and all that

Pope John Paul II and us

The Pope and the Patriarch

Welcome to Romania

Resting in peace

We're not on Plymouth Rock anymore

PREFACE

Our first winter in Romania

Before the 1989 collapse of Communism in Eastern Europe, neither of us had ever been to Romania. Sheilah had a chance to visit briefly, as a reporter, seven years later, but Jim had never set foot on Romanian soil before stepping into the job of U.S. ambassador in early 1998.

It wasn't because we lacked passports or feared foreign lands. Jim was born in Italy. Sheilah had studied in France, and both of us had traveled a good bit abroad, in Asia as well as in Europe. But other than Jim's eight months of infancy in Rome and Sheilah's summer in Paris, we had never lived abroad before going to Romania.

However, we had worked and traveled in the region. As a White House correspondent for ABC News, Sheilah had covered President Ronald Reagan's trips to Moscow and Berlin and first lady Hillary Clinton's 1996 trip to Central and Eastern Europe, including Romania. On the morning of August 19, 1991, Sheilah was the sole ABC News correspondent in Moscow reporting on the attempted coup against Mikhail Gorbachev—the attempted coup that led to the breakup of the Soviet Union that December. That same month, with Jim along for the

Christmas holiday, she went to Georgia to cover the violent overthrow of that new republic's first democratic government. After dashing across a no-man's land, Sheilah interviewed the beleaguered president in his basement bunker in the Georgian parliament building. It was on January 1, 1992, the day the U.S. recognized Georgia and the fourteen other republics as independent of the Soviet Union.

Jim, then a Maryland state legislator and investor, shared Sheilah's interest in the collapse of Communism in the Soviet bloc and became active in the region as well. He was an election observer in Croatia. He invited leading Soviet democrats to testify in Annapolis, Maryland's capital city. He chaired the new Sister State Committee, promoting exchanges between Maryland and the Leningrad Oblast in Russia. In 1995, President Bill Clinton asked him to join the first board of the Albanian American Enterprise Fund, set up by the U.S. government to invest in business development in that poorest of former Communist dictatorships in Europe.

But how did all this lead Jim to become ambassador? Here's the background: Jim has known President Bill Clinton and Vice President Al Gore since the early 1980s. He had worked on both their 1992 and 1996 campaigns, primarily organizing support in the Italian-American community. He told the White House he was happy to remain on the board of the Albanian fund, but would also be interested in a full-time job on the ground in Eastern Europe or the former Soviet Union, if he could make a difference in helping their transition from Communism. The obvious option, given Jim's public service and business experience, would be an ambassadorship.

He knew it was a long shot—there were few embassies, and many interested and qualified candidates. But what was the likelihood that another Democratic president whom Jim knew would be elected any time soon? Like most Democrats, Jim's win-loss record for presidential candidates had not been good in the preceding decades.

Months passed with no obvious interest from the White House. Then, during a dinner at the Italian Embassy in Washington, Jim ran into John Podesta, a friend of twenty-five years and President Clinton's chief of staff. John pulled Jim into a corner.

"I want to ask you something," Podesta said. "Are you really interested in an ambassadorship?"

Jim's initial thought was that his friend was trying to soften the news that an embassy post was not in his future.

"Yes," Jim replied, "but I understand there's lots of competition."

"There is, but you're on a short list," Podesta said. "You need to get your résumé and go see Marsha Scott at the White House—she's handling ambassadorships."

Hmmm, Jim thought. *This might just be possible after all.*

Two days after his legislative session ended in April, Jim went to the White House, résumé in hand. In Marsha's office, he sat ready to explain his interest and answer any questions.

"I appreciate your coming in," she said. "The president would like you to be ambassador to Romania."

What? Jim thought. *Did I miss the start of this conversation?*

"That sounds great," was the best response he could produce.

"Good," Marsha said. "Keep this to yourself for now. We'll be talking a lot over the next few months."

She was referring to the White House vetting and Senate confirmation processes.

Jim walked out of the White House and called Sheilah.

She was as astonished and pleased as Jim was. But there was a complication.

Just a few months earlier, Sheilah had been recruited away from ABC News by *Business Week* magazine and public TV to host a new weekly show—*This Week in Business with Sheilah Kast*. It was the business version of PBS's *Washington Week in Review*, produced by WETA. At the time she accepted the job, we'd concluded that nothing would come of Jim's interest in full-time diplomacy.

Sheilah found herself firmly in the middle of a feminist's dilemma. Half her friends said, "It's great Jim has this job, but you can't give up your career!" The other half said, "It's nice you've got this television show, but you really should be with your husband at a special time like this."

Our compromise turned out to be an extreme case of commuter marriage. In the year following his Senate confirmation, Jim returned to the U.S. several times to accompany Romanian officials, or to visit Romanian-American communities. Sheilah made eight round trips to Romania, flying out after taping her TV show on Friday and returning the following Wednesday to work on the next week's show.

Midway through Jim's first year in Romania, it became clear to her that Jim was having way too much fun by himself in Romania, and she didn't want to miss it. *We only have one chance to represent the United States.* So Sheilah gave *Business Week* and WETA-TV notice, left the show at the end of 1998, and moved to Romania with her eighty-nine-year-old mother.

For the final two years that Jim was ambassador, we traveled the country, both together and apart. This book is the product of our unique look at Romania, and of our continuing involvement there. Both of us maintain close ties to the friends we made there, and Jim visits a few times a year as a board member of several regional investment funds.

Our experience was a little different than "a year in Provence" or twelve months "under the Tuscan sun." When you're the U.S. ambassador or "Mrs. Ambassador," you see the country from a different angle than you would otherwise. Part of that comes with diplomacy—not the ceremonial dinners and such, but the opportunity in a free country like Romania to go almost anywhere and talk with almost anyone.

Professional diplomacy is a lot more like journalism than many people in either profession might acknowledge. Foreign Service officers, and non-career ambassadors like Jim, spend a huge portion of their time learning and listening, and then writing up what they've learned in "cables," as the State Department quaintly calls the daily memos each embassy sends to "Washington" (the metaphor that appropriates the name of the whole city to mean U.S. government headquarters).

The big difference between journalism and its diplomatic cousin is that cables are largely secret—neither the people written about nor the average American gets to read them. The results of this secrecy are predictable: Some actual secrets are reported and kept, some errors of fact and interpretation are never corrected because of lack of scrutiny, and most interested Americans rarely hear or see the information collected in their name and paid for with their tax dollars.

Normally, much of what diplomats learn is kept secret, retained in their heads, or shared publicly only in professional memoirs or academic treatises.

This book is different.

We traveled all over Romania. Jim visited all forty counties, most of them more than once, and Sheilah went to some spots that Jim did not. We saw more of Romania and of Romanians—from the mines to the software labs, from the monasteries to the hospitals—than most foreigners and even many Romanians have.

Because of Jim's political experience, we conducted town meetings in villages and cities that had never seen a U.S. ambassador. We invited ordinary Romanians to our house—the Ambassador's Residence—by the thousands. When the Romanian American Enterprise Fund (RAEF) asked us to host a dinner for its board, we upped the ante and suggested inviting *all* the Romanian small business owners to whom they had made loans. That night, our backyard was filled with Romanian entrepreneurs.

Working with the U.S. Consulate, we threw going-away parties for Romanian students who decided to study in the U.S.—with a pitch to come back to Romania, where we saw so much opportunity for them. And we hosted a backyard barbeque for hundreds of credit union managers from all over Romania—mostly women—who had kept the credit union system alive for working people during the Communist years and were now working with the U.S. Agency for International Development (USAID) to modernize their organizations.

Jim loved visiting factories and hiking across farms. (Sheilah was less entranced by the chicken-rendering plants.) In every town we visited, we tried to meet with all American citizens, to hear their concerns and their insights into Romania. On New Year's Day, we threw an open house for all American citizens in Romania, partly for fun and partly to meet more of them so we could learn about their experiences.

Why did we spend so much time with Americans around the country—people like Romanian-Americans who had returned to retire or to start small businesses, Peace Corps volunteers teaching high school English, or church and charitable workers helping orphans and the disabled? Weren't we supposed to be talking with Romanians and other diplomats?

We did that, of course, but Jim's fundamental view was that he worked *for* Americans—they paid his salary, just as Maryland taxpayers now pay his state senate salary. They had the right to talk with the U.S. ambassador, so his policy was to see every U.S. citizen who asked for a meeting. And, more broadly, Americans living in, and even visiting, Romania were a valuable source of information and insight for the Embassy. They could help us see through the blur of living as public officials in a nice neighborhood in the nation's capital.

We tried to minimize the filter. Jim was guarded by a security detail for only about a month of his tenure. He drove himself around Bucharest and its suburbs whenever possible, much to the astonishment of Romanians and Americans alike. And Sheilah often traveled on her own, either in her own used car or by train.

Nonetheless, Romanians knew who we were and that we represented the U.S. government. That didn't always elicit the most candid conversations. Ordinary American citizens, on the other hand, lived all over Romania—in villages and small towns, as well as in Bucharest. They had no diplomatic license plates on their cars, and worked and played with Romanians as people, not as government officials. Thus, they knew and understood things about Romania that were not obvious to those of us in the capital's diplomatic bubble. And they evaluated what they learned through their American eyes and American values.

By listening to these Americans, some of whom are quoted in this book, we learned a great deal.

Jim's political and business experience also meant he could, and loved to, talk with Romanian politicians, business people, and labor leaders as peers. He felt their pain when their poll numbers dropped, their stock prices slid, and their members were laid off. And he admired their persistence and commitment to making a success of their country—and of their own parties, unions, and businesses. Jim's interactions with cultural figures were less rewarding, at least for them. Given the big role the U.S. plays in any country, Jim as U.S. ambassador was both an observer of, and a participant in, major issues affecting Romania directly and indirectly.

Sheilah had unique access as well. She was invited to be a part of health fairs, seminars, and galas, and to attend recitals, observe artists at work, and judge essay contests. A professional interviewer of her experience and predilections could only dream of doors opening up and down society as easily as they did for her in Romania.

Romanian journalists, another great force-multiplier for someone who wants to understand a nation, treated her as one of their own, talking with her as they wouldn't with Jim. With lower public visibility than Jim and no official government responsibilities, she could go places and speak with people where his notoriety would overwhelm or intimidate. At the same time, as the wife of the ambassador and not a working journalist during her years there, she could learn things and get to know people in ways which would be much more difficult had she been wearing a press tag.

As we began to consider this book soon after returning home to America, the differences between Jim's and Sheilah's professional approaches became clear. To Jim, what he remembers is what he remembers. In politics or business, what he remembers may be wrong, in whole or in part, but as he sees it, information is always imperfect. What's important is whether the conclusions drawn from those memories are correct—whom you can trust, whether that idea worked out the last time it was tried, why people believed what they believed.

None of this is "truth" in a metaphysical sense. At its best it's a fragment of truth, but it's definitely what Jim thinks he knows. That was the book Jim had in mind.

But Sheilah, the journalist, reasoned, "If we were going to write a book, we should have been taking notes from day one. How can we rely on our slowly fading memories? How can we know we'll quote people correctly?"

We decided to conduct the interviews we hadn't done. We knew the stories we wanted to share and we knew the people who would tell them. All we had to do was go back to Romania and ask them to tell us again—this time on tape. Graciously, all but two of the Romanians we asked to sit for taped interviews agreed to do so. The major interviews in this book are all the products of those taped sessions, done over the past several years. In contrast to our interpretations, they allow a variety of Romanians, from the Patriarch of the Orthodox Church to recent IT graduates, to tell their own stories and share their own insights.

Not all the dialogue is from tapes, however. Shorter vignettes and those which did not lend themselves to replays are based on our best memories. If we misunderstood by a wide margin, we apologize in advance and look forward to being corrected.

Another big challenge was figuring out whose "voice" the book would be in—Jim's, Sheilah's, both, or neither? There's no question that this book is the product of our common experience, endless conversation, and shared values. But Jim didn't drive Sheilah's car or have a fractured ankle treated at the Maramureş hospital. Sheilah wasn't briefly barred from Turkey because she left her tourist passport in her hotel room. You've been reading our decision. When we're writing about the two of us, "we" means both of us, "Jim" means Jim, and "Sheilah" means Sheilah. It feels a bit strange to write in the first and third person simultaneously, but we hope it works.

Of course, this book is not encyclopedic. It is not a guidebook, but rather a look at a country and a people through American eyes. This is what we saw and what we think is useful to understand about Romania as it concludes its second decade after the fall of Communism.

One tiny caveat: Even for political junkies, it may be hard to immediately grasp the references here to Romanian political parties, not least because leaders move from one party to another and the parties themselves change names much more often than we're used to in the U.S. Here's the crib sheet:

- The major party on the left, led originally by Romania's first post-Communist president Ion Iliescu and in 2009 by former Romanian Ambassador to the U.S. Mircea Geoană, is now called the Party of Social Democracy. Its initials have changed from PDSR to PSD. We'll use the latter throughout the book.

- Major parties on the center/right during the past twenty years have included:

  * The National Liberal Party, which was the party of the center/left before Communism, went into opposition in 2009. We'll refer to it by its initials PNL.

  * The National Christian Democratic Peasant Party was the party of the center/right before Communism and was strong in the late 1990s when we were there, but it has not been able to elect any members of parliament since then. Its initials are PNŢCD.

- The major center party, led by Traian Băsescu until his election as president, is the Democratic Liberal Party. Previously, it was called the Democratic Party. We'll use with PD-L, its current initials.

- The Hungarian party, which as an ethnic party covers the ideological spectrum and wins the overwhelming majority of votes of Hungarians in Romania, is known in Hungarian as the RMDSz (*Romániai Magyar Demokrata Szövetség*) and in Romanian as the UDMR (*Uniunea Democrată Maghiară din România*). We'll refer to it as UDMR.

Just as Stalin committed the Soviet Union to "Socialism in one country," this book tells the story of post-Communism in one country. Much of what's interesting is unique to Romania—the Latin island in a sea of Slavs—but much of it is also relevant to nations from the Czech Republic to Kyrgyzstan and Stalin's Russia in between. After all, Romania is the fourth-largest former Communist country in the world—the only ones larger are Russia, Ukraine, and Poland. (Once when Jim made that point, a fellow diplomat responded, "What about China?" Jim reminded him that China still is a one-party, Communist-ruled country, even if it is much more open than it was under Mao. It's a complicated world. Sometimes even the pros have trouble keeping up.)

Many of Romania's most difficult challenges in the twenty years since the fall of the Berlin Wall in Germany and the fall of the Ceauşescu dictatorship in Romania have been similar to those encountered throughout the former Soviet bloc. Privatization of property; creation of a multi-party political system; relations with Russia, Western Europe, and the United States; the decline of living standards for many and new opportunities for others; the public re-emergence of religion; and managing ethnic conflict in an open society—this is the story of all 350 million people in two dozen countries.

Because we traveled so much around Romania, and because we know the country is much more diverse than Bucharest, we've organized the book around our travels. After the three introductory chapters, Chapter 4 starts in Bucharest—"the Paris of the East," as it was called between the wars.

Then, in Chapter 5 we move to communities around Bucharest, north to Lake Snagov and south to a Gypsy village and the Boy Scouts. We celebrate Christmas in the stunning Transylvanian Alps, which have formed the most important border in Romania's history.

In Chapter 6, starting at Peleş Castle in the mountains, we meet King Michael, the "good king" who overthrew a fascist dictator at age twenty-two and remains involved in his country as he approaches age ninety.

On the other side of the mountains, in Chapter 7, is Transylvania, the home of Dracula, Romania's large Hungarian minority and much more.

In Chapter 8 we head south again, to Wallachia, the historical heart of Romania south of the mountains. This includes Oltenia, where residents like to compare themselves to Texans.

Chapter 9 takes us to the northern edge of Romania—Maramureş, home of the Merry Cemetery and birthplace of Holocaust witness Elie Wiesel.

We go east in Chapter 10 to Bucovina and Moldavia, which border Ukraine and Moldova, the latter a country which used to be part of the Soviet Union and, before that, part of Romania.

Chapter 11 takes us south again to Dobrogea, to the Danube River and the Black Sea, sometimes called Romania's only good neighbor—besides Serbia.

Chapter 12 is called "Back to Europe" because the Banat and Crişana, the regions that border Hungary and Serbia on Romania's western edge, are the most physically, culturally, and economically integrated into Europe. Europe being Europe, isolationism is not an option for Romanians.

Chapter 13 explains what it's like "living in the Balkans, in the shadow of the Kremlin."

Finally, Chapter 14 pulls it all together. Just twenty years after the fall of Communism, why does Romania work?

The book is a series of vignettes—what we heard, what we learned, what we thought.

Like all Americans, we were fascinated by the stories of the Communist period—what didn't work, but also what did; why and how people left Romania during those forty-two years, and why other people stayed, even those who could have left; and how some people remember those years with horror, while others have more mixed memories.

One of the odder questions we occasionally get from Americans who don't know much about Romania is: "Is it still a Communist country?" The question is a bit behind the curve, but more important is the way it defines the nation by its political system. That's understandable for the Cold War generation of Americans. For decades, the world did seem, at least to Americans, as if it were divided between the Free World and the Communist world.

But as America learned in Vietnam, that's not the way most people around the world see their own countries. Romanians know the difference between freedom and Communism—much better than Americans do, frankly—but they never defined their country solely by its transitory political system. Romanians saw—and see—their country as unique, and with ample reason: their Latin-based language, their Roman and Dacian heritage, their Christian Orthodox religion, their location in southeastern Europe, their humor, their cuisine, their foreign-language talents, and their engineering skills, among others. Communism, we learned, is not at the heart of their identity. As Romanians periodically reminded us, they hadn't chosen Communism; it had been imposed on them by the Soviet army.

Come with us, then, as we lead you past the misconceptions and show you the fascinating Romania we experienced.

Sheilah Kast and Jim Rosapepe
College Park, MD
August 1, 2009

ROMANIA's REGIONS

CHAPTER 1:
LISTENING TO ROMANIANS

Credit: *Emanuel Tânjală*

Jim listening to very young Romanians

Short of knocking on doors or chatting at the supermarket, a town meeting is the best way to learn what's on the minds of ordinary people, and to make clear to them you care about *their* concerns, not just those of the big shots—the ones the Romanians call "the big potatoes."

Jim hatched a plan for a series of town meetings with ordinary Romanians around the country. We had a sign made for one of the embassy vans that said, "America Listening to Romanians." In a society only a decade removed from a police state, the sign might have been interpreted as an unfortunate reminder of sadder days. But the fact that our van pulled into school yards and village squares in broad daylight bespoke the difference between democracy and dictatorship.

Most days on the road, we took part in seven or eight events, from informal walking tours of markets to question and answer sessions in dusty villages. Few of these communities had ever been visited by a U.S. ambassador. Unlike Romanian officials, we controlled no highway funds or farm subsidies, so our visits weren't important in any material sense. But the U.S. ambassador is a minor celebrity in Romania. A poll taken near the end of Jim's term reported that about two-thirds of Romanians, including half of all peasants, knew his name.

People turned out for our town meetings. The crowds ranged from dozens to hundreds. Typically, we'd conduct these sessions in a community hall or village square. The mayor would introduce us, and Jim would make a few opening remarks. Usually, he'd open with, "Bună ziua, Rădăuți!" ("Hello, [insert name of town]"). Sheilah, not thinking Jim would actually do it, had suggested this, parroting "Good morning, Vietnam!" But it turned out to be his biggest applause line.

Jim would thank everyone for coming, and then ask the crowd a little about themselves.

"How many children are here? Raise your hands." Hands pop up followed by applause.

"How many parents?" Hands shoot up, with more applause.

"How many grandparents?" More applause.

"How many great-grandparents?" Fewer hands, but much smiling and applause.

Then Jim would ask if any of them had ever been to the United States. Occasionally, a few hands would go up.

"Do you have friends or relatives in the U.S.?" he'd ask. In almost every town, no matter how small or isolated, a few people would raise their hands. So he'd ask, where?

"Toronto," came the first reply in one town.

"Great. How about in the United States?"

"Montreal."

"That's great, too," Jim replied. "Anyone else know people who live in the United States?"

"Vancouver."

Jim surrendered. Much to the chagrin of our Canadian friends, some of the folks in small-town Romania were a little hazy on the border between our countries. But on with the show. Jim would say we were there to learn about "your town and your concerns and to answer your questions." Jim would relate a little of what he'd seen in Romania. Generally, it was an upbeat message about progress and hope for the future.

Early in his first trip, without thinking too hard about it, Jim decided to mention the European Union and Romania's hope that it would soon be invited to join. The crowd exploded in tumultuous applause. *Interesting.* So he mentioned the EU in the next few towns that day. Same response. No fool, he made it a standard part of his introduction.

More important, that experience made the whole tour worthwhile. We learned in those villages what we never would have learned in Bucharest—about the EU, and most important, about Romania.

At least in Romania, the EU is not just a free-trade zone or job-creation project for retired European politicians and bureaucrats. To poor Romanian peasants, it's a vision of what they had too little of in the last century or any other: peace and prosperity.

When Eastern European peasants give an American ambassador an ovation simply for mentioning that their country will join the EU, it's clear they have a vision of what they want to make of their country, and it gives an insight into how they've done it in the twenty years since the fall of Communism in 1989.

CHAPTER 2:
THE ROMANIA YOU DON'T KNOW

Name almost any country in the world, and you're conducting an instant Rorschach test.

China? Crowded, bustling, exotic.

Haiti? Poor, dangerous.

Italy? Food, wine, churches.

These are all stereotypes based on what's shown on television, what's learned in elementary school, and what's heard from friends who have visited.

Mention Romania to most Americans and the Rorschach results are predictable: Dracula, orphaned kids, dictatorship. A few Olympics fans may mention gymnastics and Nadia Comăneci, the great Olympic champion, and some tennis players will remember Ilie Năstase or Ion Țiriac. But that's about it.

We know this because, over the last decade, we've talked about Romania with thousands of Americans, some who have visited and most who have not.

What's striking about Americans' snapshot of Romania, except for the one held by sports fans, is that it's negative—not hostile, just negative.

Dracula, orphans, dictatorship.

OK. Americans are hostile to dictators, but not to their victims.

Dracula is a curiosity.

Orphans are objects of sympathy, as so many Americans have demonstrated.

Strobe Talbott, who reported for *Time* magazine in the 1980s, told us that, when he visited Romania during those years, he was only half-kidding when he warned other foreign reporters, as Dante advised in *The Inferno,* "Ye who enter, abandon all hope."

Sounds like a great place for a summer vacation.

Of course, the snapshot is wrong.

In fact, twenty years after the fall of the Berlin Wall, Romania is a vigorously democratic country with well-educated young people, remarkable foreign language skills, a rapidly modernizing economy, a fascinating history that bridges east and west, hospitality that borders on the manic, strong religious faith, and ethnic relations that are a model for more troubled regions. And Romanians love Americans.

The real Romania is what we saw during our time there and since. That is what our book is about. It draws on the experience of our daily lives, direct involvement with major players in its transition from Communism, and interviews with extraordinary people, young and old.

We visited orphanages, and the many places Dracula seems to have slept. We also visited Romanians who lost their homes to the Communist regime and those who got from it their first chance to go to college.

In many ways, Romania is the new Italy. It's a relatively large European nation; with nearly twenty-two million people, it's the seventh-largest country in the European Union. It's Latin, with Roman ruins, government corruption, world-class creativity, a zest for life, and vivacious, attractive people. Driven by the ambition of its people and the EU, Romania's economy grew rapidly, as Italy's did in the decades after World War II, until the worldwide recession of 2009.

It's true that Dracula, fictional though he may be, is from Transylvania, the western region of Romania that borders Hungary. It's true, too, that, because of President Nicolae Ceauşescu's catastrophic economic and natal policies, Romania's orphanages were grim and overflowing when Communism imploded in 1989. And it's true that the personal dictatorship of Nicolae and Elena Ceauşescu, in contrast to nations run by faceless Communist leaders, branded Romania in Western eyes.

But there was much more to Romania, even before Ceauşescu was overthrown.

Unlike those of its neighbors in the Balkans, Romania's language and culture are Latin. They call themselves Romanian for a reason.

Theirs is one of the five Romance languages and, like the others, they trace their roots to the Roman Empire. In the second century, Emperor Trajan conquered the native Dacian population of what's now Romania. Showing the ethnic equanimity that reflects their better angels, Romanians later named their national car the Dacia, and their founding heroes are both Trajan and Decebal, the defeated king of the Dacians. What other country honors equally the losers as well as the winners of their founding struggle?

In the early twentieth century, Bucharest, Romania's capital city, was the boom town of southeast Europe. Called "the Paris of the East," it boasted art nouveau architecture that's still visible today. Greek, Turkish, Jewish, Armenian, and American business people flocked to Romania, making it the biggest oil producer in Europe and the fifth-largest grain exporter in the world. Romania's Queen Marie was the Princess Diana of her day, such a celebrity she was greeted with a ticker-tape parade when she visited New York in 1926. Artists like Brâncuşi were known the world over.

Like Italy's, Romania's political geography was split for centuries between Germanic culture (Austria in both cases) and Mediterranean influences (the Normans and Spanish in southern Italy; the Ottoman Turks in southern and eastern Romania, as well as Greeks and Byzantines).

Because of changing borders and immigration, Romania has ethnic and religious diversity on a grand scale. Its Hungarian minority, a million and a half people, is the largest in Europe, but most Americans have never heard of them because they live in peace with their Romanian neighbors. Germans were another big ethnic minority—hundreds of thousands traced their ancestors to thirteenth-century settlers—until most of them left in the late twentieth century through negotiated exits, not ethnic cleansing.

Nearly half of Romania's eight hundred thousand Jews were murdered during the Holocaust of World War II. Most of the rest left the country as the Germans did in the 1970s and '80s, with exit visas sold by Ceauşescu. Today, almost five percent of Israel is Romanian.

Unitarianism was founded in Romania. Many of the Americans we encountered in Transylvania were Unitarians visiting their sister congregations in Hungarian villages.

We got a good glimpse of the complexities of Christianity in Romania when Pope John Paul II came to Bucharest in May 1999, the first visit of a Roman Catholic pontiff to an Orthodox country since the Schism of 1054. His trip had to be negotiated with the Orthodox Church, as well as with the Greek Catholic Church. The latter follows the rituals of the Orthodox, including allowing priests to marry, but pledges allegiance to Rome. The Greek Catholics, or Uniates, were created when Orthodox bishops, faced with pressure from Austria's Roman Catholic emperor in the seventeenth century, decided to switch rather than fight.

Then there was the king. To Americans whose founding fathers earned their title by firing the king of England, Romania's recruitment of a twenty-seven-year-old German prince to become their king in the 1860s seems a little odd. But the role of his heir, twenty-two-year-old King Michael, in switching Romania from Nazi Germany's side to America's in 1944, was historic. The fact that King Michael, after years in exile (some of them earning a living as a test pilot), has lived to see the restoration of democracy, if not a constitutional monarchy, in Romania is stunning, if not unique.

When we were in Romania, the heads of both houses in the parliament, the patriarch of the Romanian Orthodox Church, and the leader of the organized (though now small) Jewish community were all men in their eighties. Like King Michael, each of them had been professionally active before Communism. During Communism's forty-two-year run in Romania, these leaders survived in different ways: the senate president was a forced laborer on the Danube canal, the patriarch a rising leader in a compromised church, and the leader of the Jewish community a practicing physician. While we were there, a miners' union leader protested a seventeen-year prison sentence for attempting to overthrow the newly democratic government. The chair of the House noted dryly that he had survived his seventeen-year imprisonment

(1947-64) and figured this guy would, too.

Part of the reason the American snapshot of Romania is negative is that in the last decade of Communism, the 1980s, the reality inside Romania was undeniably negative. To pay off the country's foreign debt, Ceauşescu exported food and rationed electricity. The people's standard of living plummeted. To maintain control, the totalitarian state tightened its grip. While Solidarity was organizing in Poland, Goulash Communism was opening up the Hungarian economy, and *glasnost* was becoming the watchword in Gorbachev's Soviet Union, in Romania, the Securitate, the nation's secret police, maintained rigid control.

The result was that Romania came out of Communism in 1989 in much worse shape than other countries in Central and Eastern Europe. The economy, which had been bigger than Greece's before World War II, was now one-sixth its size. There was no Vaclav Havel or Lech Walesa to symbolize democratic aspirations, unify anti-Communist forces, or win the enthusiasm of the leaders and publics of Western Europe and the United States.

Romanians, including some who now live in America, compounded the problem. In our experience, they are much more likely than Americans, Poles, Chinese, Hungarians, and just about everyone else we've ever met to talk their country down. They don't speak much about Dracula or orphans. But corruption, disorganization, and lack of respect outside Romania—these are their complaints, and they are not unfounded. When he was hospitalized, a friend told us his mother was confused, trying to figure out how big a bribe to give each Romanian staffer (doctor, nurse, technician) to make sure they'd take proper care of him.

During World War II, the great American anthropologist Dr. Ruth Benedict was asked by the U.S. government to write a profile of Romanian culture. In words which could have been written today, she said:

"The entire openness of all Romanians about corruption is more striking than the admitted venality . . . [The Romanian] prides himself on insight more than on what most other European nations define as virtue. He accepts the fact that people will try to 'get theirs' and sees no reason at all why that should sour him on life."

Romanians don't like the corruption around them, but often seem resigned to it while talking about it incessantly.

As for disorganization, one diplomatic colleague told us, "Like my own people, I find the Romanians stronger on spontaneity than discipline. And as the Italian ambassador to Romania, I myself am caught between two spontaneities!" Now, twenty years after the collapse of Communism, Romania's spontaneity has paid off, just as Italy's did in the twenty years after World War II.

Democracy, while flawed, is alive and well in Romania. Even while we were living there, politicians' major concerns were fundraising, press coverage, and poll ratings.

Twenty years ago, Ceauşescu's giant state companies were overstaffed. When Communism finally fell, millions of workers were moved out—people who, as Romanians told us, "had sacrificed to build Communism, [and] were now sacrificing to destroy it." Without much help from the West, Romania muddled through.

They privatized their apartments, with the result that Romania today has a rate of home-ownership much higher than the U.S.—95 percent, compared to 68 percent in the U.S.—with much less mortgage debt.

They returned plots of land to millions of families who had owned them before Communism. Thus, for years after the fall, most families would feed themselves from what they raised, even if they lived in cities.

And Romania promoted early retirement on a massive scale. The bad news was that workers in their fifties and even forties were forced out of work and left to live on their small pensions. The good news was that, with no debt on their homes and small plots on which to raise food, they could survive as the economy reoriented itself to the twenty-first century.

For much of the last decade—until the worldwide slowdown in

2008—Romania's biggest economic problem was a labor shortage. The carmaker Renault makes its popular Logan in Romania, and ships it all over the world. European and American manufacturers—from big firms like Alcatel, Siemens, and Ford, to family-owned companies from Italy—are making Romania the workshop of Europe. Microsoft, Hewlett-Packard, and dozens of IT companies are profiting from Romanians' longstanding software skills. When we were there, Romania was graduating software engineers at a much higher rate than the United States.

Even before joining the European Union in 2007, Romanians, capitalizing on Latin culture and language, had flocked to jobs in Spain and Italy, sending more than six billion dollars a year back to their families, building new homes, and outfitting them with new washing machines, ovens, and televisions.

Contrary to the standard American snapshot, Romania today is a major European country with a remarkable history and a more remarkable future.

CHAPTER 3
BEYOND COMMUNISM

"WE'RE WAITING FOR YOU"

VĂ AȘTEPTĂM. AT FIRST, we didn't know what to make of this Romanian phrase, though it popped up often during conversations with Romanians. Usually cheery, sometimes warm, and occasionally business-like, it means, "We're waiting for you."

Initially, we translated the phrase literally, and firmly planted it in the context of our brisk North American lives. During Jim's first months as ambassador, when Sheilah wasn't yet living in Romania but visiting for a few days each month, a Romanian might phone her ahead of a visit to plan some activity, and the call would end with, "We're waiting for you." When she was in-country, a perfectly pleasant meeting or chance encounter would end with, "I'm waiting for you."

Sheilah racked her brain. Had she promised to do something and then forgotten? Was she supposed to be somewhere? Because she wasn't in Romania full-time then, she felt pressured by the phrase, as if she were not meeting expectations—as if they expected her to be there, or they disapproved that she wasn't.

Then someone explained that vă așteptăm is not a demand, but an embrace. It just means, "We look forward to being together again. Things are better when you're with us. It will be nice when we're all together." Vă așteptăm is a micro-daydream of how happy we'll be the next time we meet. During conversations in America, we found ourselves thinking we lacked a quick way to convey the same happy anticipation. We could use a phrase like that here.

Romanian is a Romance language. It picked up a fair amount of Turkish during centuries of Ottoman domination, and it has also borrowed from its Slav and German neighbors, but its core is Latin. "Goodbye" is la revedere—"until we see each other again"—similar to the Italian l'arrivaderci and the French au revoir. A plaza in Romanian (*piaţa*) sounds exactly like it would in Italian, *piazza*. "You're welcome" in Romanian is the charming *cu plăcere*, translated literally as "with pleasure."

The transitive verb "to wait for," *a aştepta*, comes from the Latin. But in Romanian, the recurring use of *vă aşteptăm* goes beyond an accident of language. It reflects the tradition of a country that, for centuries, has longed to be connected to the West, while thwarted by the constraints of geography and poverty, Ottoman rule, Nazi fascism, and Soviet Communism. Like many societies, Romania treasures the traveler for the connection he brings to the larger world.

The phrase *vă aşteptăm* looks toward a bright future time in the company of someone else—a friend, a visitor, a stranger. It is hopeful, but seems a bit tentative, not the confident hope exuded by Americans. Americans tend to *assume* that life will get better. Generation after generation, that has been the American experience. Such optimism is part of what Romanians seem to like about Americans.

An American can't spend more than a few days in Romania without hearing a native say, with a smile, "We've been waiting for you for sixty years."

Romania started World War II on the side of the Germans and switched sides in 1944. They hoped that when the Axis powers lost and the Allies won, it would be American troops instead of Russian soldiers who would occupy Romania. It didn't work out that way, and after the war the United States didn't challenge Russian domination in most of Eastern Europe.

Romanians had seen American planes fly over their land during World War II. American pilots repeatedly bombed the oil fields around Ploieşti, north of Bucharest, to keep Hitler from getting his hands on that oil. For years after the war, some Romanians continued to watch the skies, looking for the Americans would come again, hoping that America, the champion of liberty, would take a military stand against the evils of Communism.

We discussed those years with Mircea Ionescu-Quintus just after he finished his term as president of the Romanian Senate. More than a half century earlier, before the Communist takeover in 1947, he had been a young leader in the PNL and was jailed for his politics.

Ionescu-Quintus recalled the rumors flying—"the idea that the Americans would come to re-establish the independence of the country. It was a belief that nobody believed. It was a very beautiful dream. Nobody really believed that the Americans would come, but they wanted to believe."

As a political prisoner laboring on the Danube Canal, Ionescu-Quintus expected that Communism would outlast him. Eventually, Romanians stopped looking up to the sky. Even before the 1956 uprising in next-door Hungary, which brought no American response, and the Prague Spring in 1968, which also brought no U.S. action, most Romanians had figured out that we Americans weren't coming to their aid. We asked dozens of Romanians, "Why do you smile when you say you've been waiting for the Americans?"

It's still a good question.

KISS MY HAND!

A PROVERB WE HEAR often in Romania is "Kiss the hand you cannot bite." The saying shows up elsewhere in the Balkans and in the Middle East, and we were told it had worked its way into Romanians' thinking during the centuries of Ottoman domination. Smiling submission, even if you're seething inside, is one way to keep the master from exercising all his terrible power. The proverb is a chilling tribute to hypocrisy, but because Americans are not in the habit of kissing any hands, whether or not they can bite them, the saying at first struck us as disconnected from twenty-first century reality.

But the old custom of hand-kissing is still good manners in Romania. Those who do it are more likely to be repressing a smile than repressing hostility. Men greet women by kissing their hands.

The first few times, the hand-kissing threw Sheilah for a loop. In America, when she extends her hand to a man, she expects him to shake it. In Romania, she was not expecting him to take her hand, rotate it to be parallel to the ground, raise it to his lips with a bow, and land a kiss on it. At first, the ritual took her breath away. She felt swept up in a novel from another era, as if her footman were just around the corner with her horse and carriage. If the man added a slight smile or eye contact in that half-second before the kiss, the ritual was completely irresistible.

Once she got over the sheer romance of the hand-kissing tradition, she started wondering whether it were a paternalistic throwback to a time when women didn't run businesses, own property, or have much independence. She raised that question with Viviana Palade, the young woman who was Jim's Romanian language teacher.

It was hardly an egalitarian custom, Vivi acknowledged—men kiss women's hands, but not the other way around. Still, she said, women have more control than it might appear. Vivi asserted that it's up to the woman whether the gesture ends up as a handshake or a hand-kiss, and she demonstrated how. Vivi gently stretched her hand forward, fingertips in a delicate curve toward the floor—a clear invitation, she said, for a Romanian man to kiss the hand. By contrast, when she thrust her hand forward, perpendicular to the floor, with thumb pointing upward, it was much more likely that a man would shake rather than kiss.

This was plausible, but, as it turned out, far from inevitable. The nuances of the angle of approach are lost on some Romanian men, who simply clutch a lady's hand, position it before their mouths, and plant their lips upon it. It can be a lot like being trapped on the dance floor with an over-enthusiastic waltzer. If a graceful hand-kiss evokes the elegance of an eighteenth-century ballroom, a clumsy one suggests the equivalent of a middle school prom. Many professional women told us they're tired of the hand-kissing habit—that it seems too personal in a modern professional setting, and you don't know where those lips have been recently, or what germs might be lurking behind them. A kiss is still a kiss, they suggested, even when it's on the metacarpals.

Vivi and other ladies told us the custom is entirely generational: Young Romanian men don't kiss women's hands, but older men do.

That's another way of saying the ritual is dying out.

Happily, there's a parallel tradition that captures much of the romance of the physical act of hand-kissing, with none of its drawbacks. In settings where men don't kiss a woman's hand, they *say*, "I kiss your hand." The Romanian phrase *sărut mâna* seems to be the standard greeting of man to woman, in all settings. Sheilah first encountered it her second day in Romania, strolling through our new neighborhood. She felt competent to set out on her own because she knew how to say "good day"—*bună ziua*. It slowly dawned on her that the tall young Romanian soldiers stationed with rifles outside various diplomatic residences (Romania at that time had a universal draft, and guarding embassies was a good use of conscripts' time) were not saying *bună ziua* back as she passed. She worried that she was breaking some rule, until she learned they were saying *sărut mâna* ("I kiss your hand").

Honoring the tradition in word rather than deed (or as Sheilah's mother used to say, "Let's not and say we did") keeps it alive, and opens it to both genders. The only hand a Romanian woman ever kisses is that of a priest. But as a mark of respect, a woman can say *sărut mâna* to an aged person of either sex. And women of all ages use the phrase with each other as a way of expressing deep gratitude. When Sheilah's friend Hermina pours her a glass of iced tea on a hot day, Sheilah rewards her with a fervent, *sărut mâna, doamnă*. Because it's rooted in the so-long-ago, it hints at near-sacred gratitude. It would be nice to have a phrase that could be used the same way with friends in the United States.

Cheek-kissing seems less fraught with overtones than hand-kissing. It's quite common to greet someone you've met before with a kiss on both cheeks, or a brush on each cheek. Often, the lips don't fully land, but just pucker in the air.

Cheek-kissing gives men another way of expressing who they are, as well as what the relationship is. A Romanian man who's focused on being a player in the Western world is less likely to kiss the cheeks of a Westerner; a Romanian who's deeply into his heritage is more likely to. It often signifies affection, but men don't have to be close friends to kiss cheeks. A kiss on each cheek is likely to be evoked by a moment of some emotion or excitement—say, at a celebration, or after achieving a political milestone. It was normal for Jim and Mircea Geoană, who was then Romania's ambassador to the U.S., to shake hands, but they kissed cheeks the first time they saw each other after Romania was admitted into the North Atlantic Treaty Organization (NATO).

Generally, though, the kissing is stylized. It's almost a way of putting boundaries around emotions—a peck on this cheek, a peck on that cheek, perhaps a brief embrace. But the hugs that mean something are the hugs that last a few seconds—the hugs of comfort at a funeral, the hugs of joy at a wedding, the hugs of reunion after an absence. They convey real emotion, and they're outside the bounds of this ritual.

WAVE IT OR WEAR IT?

A FEW MONTHS AFTER President Clinton asked Jim to become ambassador, but before he was on the job, Clinton visited Romania. Just days before, Clinton had been in Madrid at the NATO summit which voted in the alliance's first new members from the former Soviet bloc—Poland, Hungary, and the Czech Republic. Romania, along with Slovenia, wanted to join in that first round. But the decision was "no for now."

From Madrid, the president flew to Warsaw, where he was greeted by thousands of cheering Poles. For a country divided and dominated by the Russians beginning in the eighteenth century, becoming America's military ally was the Polish dream of generations come true.

To show the Romanians that their dream of NATO membership was deferred but not dead, Clinton went on to Bucharest. The president wasn't sure what to expect. After all, as the press had correctly reported in Madrid, the United States was the country that had blocked Romania's invitation.

When he arrived in Piața Revoluției (the Plaza of the Revolution) in the center of Bucharest, Clinton was shocked. More than two hundred thousand Romanians were waving American flags. It was the largest crowd Clinton had seen up to that time anywhere in the world.

By the time he left office in 2001, it was still his second-largest crowd.

Credit: Getty Images

Credit: Time & Life Pictures / Getty Images

After the December 1989 Revolution, Romanians cut the Communist insignia out of their flag to symbolize the end of the Ceauşescu regime. Romanian Senate President Petre Roman gave President Bill Clinton such a flag when Clinton visited Bucharest in July 1997. Though Romania had just been denied entrance into NATO, Clinton drew the second-biggest crowd of his presidency.

Also waving in the sunshine that day were red, yellow, and blue Romanian flags. Some of them had large holes in the center, making them look like striped rectangular donuts. They symbolized the overthrow of the Ceauşescu regime. During the Revolution of December 1989, anti-Communists cut the Communist coat of arms from the center of the socialist republic's flag and waved the residue as their new banner. It was one of those *empty* revolutionary flags that Petre Roman, then president of the Romanian Senate, gave to the U.S. president, who unfurled it to huge cheers.

The visit, all of a few hours, was a success for both the United States and Romania. In the faces of two hundred thousand Romanians, President Clinton saw commitment to being America's ally. And Romanians saw the United States as serious about welcoming them into the alliance, even if it would take a few more years.

Seven months later, Jim arrived in Bucharest. Within days, the new ambassador was reminded of Clinton's visit. Romanian newspapers were reporting that Petre Roman had received a thank-you note from the White House. What attracted media attention was not the note's timing, but its content. The letter referred to the Romanians' warm welcome, and Roman's memorable gift of a "flag or poncho."

Ouch!

One newspaper headline shouted, "Clinton Can't Tell Romania's Flag from a Mexican Poncho!"

Obviously, some junior White House staffer—Clinton had kept his campaign pledge to reduce the size of the regular White House staff—was not fully conversant with recent Romanian history, but he or she knew what a poncho looked like.

The good news was that Roman reacted with grace, not outrage. He told Romanian television viewers that, regardless of the U.S. president's confusion, he would be "very happy if President Clinton wore the blue, yellow, and red flag of the Romanian Revolution on his shoulders."

Romanians are used to Americans knowing a lot less about them than they know about us. And mistaking a symbol of democracy for a poncho is far from the most dangerous mistake the United States has made in the world.

FAST TRACK TO HIGH TECH

SHEILAH FIRST MET CHARLES Lewis at an event in Washington before she moved to Romania. He had a memorable way of introducing himself.

"I'm Charles Lewis, and I'm with the U.S. Department of Justice."

Even if you don't have a guilty conscience, you hold your breath after an opening line like that.

"Nice to meet you," Sheilah cautiously replied.

"My family and I are moving to Bucharest. I'm going to be working with your husband at the Embassy," Charles continued.

So it was good news after all.

Charles turned out to be one of the best U.S. government representatives we met. He'd been an assistant U.S. attorney in south Texas for decades. The State Department had sent him to Romania the previous year to teach Romanian prosecutors American approaches to criminal prosecution. It was a program known inside the State Department as "drugs and thugs." Charles actually had gone after drugs and thugs, particularly along the Mexican border. In his line of work in the United States, he needed bodyguards a lot more than Jim did in Romania.

The U.S. government loves training programs. They're inexpensive, easy to describe in reports to Congress, and "quantifiable" (e.g., 443 prosecutors from seven countries completed three courses in Fiscal Year 2010). How effective short-term classes designed in Washington really are is another question.

One of the classes Charles taught during his earlier visit to Romania was on how to prosecute check-kiting. It was a half-day course.

"The two dozen prosecutors listened intently," Charles told Sheilah. "Some took notes. For most of the class, no one asked a question. I figured that could have been because my presentation was so clear and thorough.

"Finally a hand went up. 'What's a check?' asked one of the Romanian prosecutors."

What's a check? Charles repeated in his own mind. *We may have a problem here.*

"It turned out that nobody had told me, including whoever in Washington designed the course, that Romania didn't have checks," Charles explained. "Their economy operated mostly in cash, with electronic transfers just beginning to play a role. They went from cash to electronics, skipping the stage of paper checks.

"The class had been silent because many had no idea what I was talking about, but all but one student were too polite to expose how little I knew about their country."

WHY ORTHODOXY IS IMPORTANT IN ROMANIA

EIGHTY-FIVE PERCENT OF ALL Romanians express attachment to the Romanian Orthodox Church. Not all of them, of course, are active churchgoers, but about half the country is. Those are very high numbers.

Americans are so accustomed to the separation of church and state that it takes a little effort to absorb all the implications of the Orthodox Church being a *national* church. That doesn't just mean the government helps pay the cost of building churches, or that there's likely to be an icon hanging over the desk of the assistant cabinet minister in his government office.

It also means that the church is tied up in the Romanian identity. And it means the church and the state accept the idea of state authority over the church.

Many see the church as compromised during Communism. To a degree that is hard to know, it was infiltrated by the Securitate. Either the Securitate actually installed some of its own in various church positions or vetted the men who filled those positions.

As a result, two decades after the demise of Communism, many from the urban middle class are still critical of the church. In rural areas and small towns, the church has much stronger adherence, and its most ardent followers are the older generation, including those who formed their attachment to the church before World War II.

Many younger cosmopolitans exude skepticism about the institution, which has shaped so much of their country's history. At a relaxed dinner with a half-dozen Romanians who all speak better English than we do, and several other languages to boot, we mentioned that we were to interview the Patriarch in a few days. They loaded us up with questions they wanted us to ask the man who had headed the Romanian Orthodox Church since Communist days:

- "Ask the Patriarch if he believes that without reform, the Orthodox Church has a chance to survive."
- "One of the main spiritual exercises is confession. Why did he oppose the law opening the [Securitate] files about the clergy?"

"The Romanian people have a lot of faith in the church, but not in its patriarch. Ask him why."

The man we were going to see, Teoctist, had been elevated to Patriarch in 1986, when no one thought Communism would ever implode, much less in three years. He surely had heard already all the questions our friends had posed. In the wake of the 1989 revolution, amid allegations that the church's relations with the Communist regime had been far too cozy, Teoctist offered his resignation. But his fellow churchmen stood by him, and after lying low for a few months, he came back into public life as Patriarch.

The Patriarch had a well-developed sense of public relations.

He was in his mid-eighties when Jim was ambassador, but Teoctist never failed to appear at the big Fourth of July party at our Embassy residence. No matter how hot the July sun, he was always fully bedecked in white robes and gold chains, smiling serenely.

After floods devastated Romania one spring, International Orthodox Christian Charities (IOCC) organized relief efforts. Their supplies were stored at the back door of the Patriarchy, the relatively small building that is the church's national headquarters. In hopes of encouraging Romanians themselves to contribute to the relief effort, IOCC invited the media to cover the trucks as they were being loaded with supplies for distribution. Because Jim had encouraged the organization to set up operations in Romania, the U.S. ambassador was pleased to show up in casual clothes to help pitch boxes of supplies into the trucks. Equally visible in all the coverage (and no, he was not dressed in casual clothes) was the Patriarch, smiling and blessing the supplies being sent on their way.

Critics viewed the church as compromised by the decades of Communism, but Teoctist's message was that the church had been purified. Five years after the Revolution, he told an interviewer, "God permitted Communism so that it could be conquered by faith."

He didn't go quite that far the day we walked up the cobblestone hill of the Patriarchy to speak with him. The Patriarchy building is no Vatican City. It's a modest two-story structure at the edge of a courtyard with a seventeenth-century church in the center.

Romanian Orthodox Patriarch Teoctist chatting with Jim at the U.S. Embassy's July 4 celebration, with translation help by Alfred Fusman

A PATRIARCH'S VIEW OF HISTORY

AT A HEAVY WOODEN table in a dimly lit conference room, we sat with the aging chief bishop and with the bearded young priest who interpreted for us—his grasp of English was easily as rich and idiomatic as the young skeptics with whom we had dined two days earlier.

Teoctist was eager to resume constructing a framework for our view of Orthodoxy in Romania.

"Before the Communists, the church was free and enjoyed quite a rich life, within the context of democracy and the bourgeoisie, which was the mark of the times," Teoctist recalled. The church was independent, making its own decisions in a pluralistic democracy. But from a spiritual perspective, things were, in Teoctist's view, too comfortable.

"As for the affirmation of the gospel principles, which should be part of the life of the faithful, I could say that that quality was not as high as it was even during the dictatorship time—that is, the struggle somehow brought us up," he told us. "It is a paradox: Under persecution, you bring out all that is good in you."

We thought we heard the Patriarch use the Romanian word "sleep," *dormit,* to describe the church's discipline and missionary activity between the world wars.

"I personally lived through that period. I was a pupil, then student, then deacon serving the church. I started in a special theological seminary for monks."

Teoctist credited the first patriarch of the Romanian Orthodox Church, Miron Cristea (1925-1939), with not only founding seminaries, but also reaching out to the Greek Catholics in Transylvania and responding to an invitation from the archbishop of Canterbury to take part in a meeting in England in 1936.

"That was a novelty in terms of relations with other churches." Teoctist had reason to know—in his ninth decade when we spoke with him, he had seen almost the entire trajectory of the Romanian church. When he was born in 1915, the tenth of eleven children of the Arapaşu family in Botoşani, one of the poorest areas of the country, the church in Romania did yet not have its own patriarch. That didn't happen for another decade, when Miron was elevated. In those days, Teoctist told us, the church was poor. He recounted his teenage years as a novice at the Sihăstria Voronei Hermitage, not far from the famous painted monasteries in northeastern Romania.

"In our rooms, we used wood for heating, but we had to cut it and prepare it ourselves. We were preparing our papers and reading with petrol, no electricity, and we were also responsible for taking care of that. The glass which was used for the lamp was not very strong, so quite frequently, if the glass was broken during the evening, there was no more preparation for the next day! Although the idea behind the setting up this school was very important, the church had no funds, and no possibility of getting funds, to operate it."

But, Jim asked, what about the vast stretches of land and forests we'd heard the Orthodox Church owned before Communism? Teoctist was eager to tell us that was a *lifetime* before Communism. He said the state took the church lands in 1863.

"The Church became poorer and poorer beginning with this secularization of its properties," Teoctist said, and the arrival of a German-born King, Carol I, accelerated the decline. True, Carol brought a German spirit of discipline and democratic principles from Prussia, but he also brought his Roman Catholic faith, which put pressure on the Orthodox Church.

"And then, too, the political parties which brought Carol to Romania represented the generation of the Luminists in France—that is, the rationalists, followers of Voltaire, Leibniz, Spinoza, or the so-called French school on the ideas of freedom and democracy. But religion was somehow left behind."

That excursion through history left us both a bit breathless, but Teoctist had more to share.

"Even after the unification of Transylvania with Romania at the end of World War I, the royal dynasty was not so favorable toward the Orthodox Church. The governments of the time were somehow libertine and talking about freedom, in spite of the fact that, as lords, they themselves used to own churches and monasteries and large plots of land. And consequently, the church remained quite poor.

"All these, one after the other, were events which were quite unhappy for the Church. In the 1940s, there was the nationalist movement, the Iron Guard, then the occupation by Russia. The Western powers left us with the Russians, and consequently Romania remained isolated from the outside world. Then the Communists came, and we had the Bolshevik influence."

Teoctist reiterated his version of his church's perseverance through the political turmoil:

"There was the Communist dictatorship that we had to go through, and afterwards the big changes after the Revolution, and now we're going through a different type of change—democracy and pluralism, which is very different from what we had before: dictatorship and cult of personality. Now, it's this confrontation between ideas. The difference is extraordinary."

And what about the Church's influence in society, Jim asked, in the newly democratic Romania compared to before World War II? We were surprised by the Patriarch's answer: that the Church exerts much more sway now.

"Incomparable. At that time, it was a little influence—just a very little influence on the society in the thirties and forties. Today, with all humility, the opinion polls give us more than ninety percent popularity. And, of course, one can see the impact.

"I believe that this is a reflection of the years of dictatorship, when the Orthodox Church and its patriarch, in spite of the views of the Western world, were quite dynamic and very lively. And that is in spite of the fact that the Church was not allowed to take care of her orphans, children in difficulties, old people, handicapped, and so on."

Unasked, the Patriarch launched into a chronicle of how much worse it could have been. "Compared to what happened in Russia, where the churches were closed down and the priests put in prison, or in Bulgaria, where funerals or weddings could not take place in churches, in Romania, during this dictatorship time, all the Romanian churches were open, and the patriarch of the time took care of the theological schools, so all the parishes would have their own priests. And the monasteries remained open—and more than that, the artistic historical monuments."

Teoctist noted that it was the Communist government, in the early- and mid-fifties, which invested in restoring the painted monasteries in

Moldavia, a poor area of eastern Romania.

"The state authorities would look the same way at the Făgăraş citadel or the Putna monastery—one a lay monument, the other a church monument. For them, though, they were the same." That is, both were part of Romania's cultural heritage.

As an example of how oppression energized his church, Teoctist cited new business opportunities: "Because the Communists were not allowed to go to church or to have shops with church objects, the church organized itself with its own workshops to make religious objects, candles, anything that was needed for the life of religion. Before, the church hadn't had its own factories.

"As you know, our religious worship is very rich in terms of objects—vestments, the church building, the church bells. Everything is very complicated, so you need a lot of *stuff*—icons, church calendars. Each one of the faithful has to have in his home a church calendar so he would know all the feast days of the year. He and his family have to know which saints who are celebrated on such and such a day."

Teoctist said the church's trade in catechetic symbols was just one of the rights spelled out in the church constitution approved by the parliament of the new Communist government in 1948.

"For example, each parish should have a pastor, and the monasteries should have their monks and nuns. The number of high school-level seats for theological education was fixed at that time, as well as three faculties of theology at the university level."

Teoctist said the Orthodox Church supervised the religious curriculum in these public schools, and as earlier governments had done, "the Communist state continued to pay the salaries of the priests and the professors of theology, on the faculties and in the seminaries, though of course at a lower level. The Church had a right to provide more money—to supplement it. The organization of the Church at the time was very lively, very dynamic."

This same 1948 Church constitution is remembered bitterly by the Uniates, the so-called Greek Catholics who practice an Orthodox liturgy but profess allegiance to the Pope in Rome. This was the legal framework that folded *their* church into the Orthodox. Over the decades that followed, the constitution was used to justify repression, imprisonment of Greek Catholic bishops and priests, and the deaths of scores of them. The rift between the Greek Catholics and the Romanian Orthodox had erupted centuries ago in Transylvania, and Teoctist had a lot to say about it. But it didn't dampen his approval of the 1948 law with which the Orthodox Church cooperated.

The Greek Catholics and Roman Catholics had only themselves to blame that they didn't cooperate when the Orthodox did, Teoctist said.

"When the new authorities came into power, representatives of all the religious denominations met. They decided that they should enter into this new system. And the new authorities asked all these religious denominations to present their own statutes in order to approve them. The Roman Catholics and the Greek Catholics did not do that.

"From the outside, the enemies of the Orthodox Church would look at this constitution of the Church as a sort of Communist law," Teoctist acknowledged. He contended that if critics looked more deeply, they would see that it protected the church.

"If one would look at what it means, all the stipulations in this document were favorable [to the church], starting from the parish level all the way to the patriarchal level. It's important that the authorities in charge of control and surveillance—at the Ministry of the Cults at the time—were keeping the activity of the Church under observation. When someone from this Ministry of Cults would ask a priest, 'Why are you doing this?' the priest would just point to the constitution—a law which, because it was approved by the State authorities, was a valid code throughout the country."

We did not debate the point, but asked Teoctist, "How can the dispute over church properties between the Orthodox and the Greek Catholics be resolved?"

"The resolution cannot come from the outside," he said. "They have freely expressed their view. As much as we love the Greek Catholics, we cannot force the believers to agree. The generation of

1948 is no longer the new generation. The Church remains, the village remains, but the people are different.

"We cannot throw two thousand Orthodox out of the church just to give the church to fifty [Greek Catholics]. It is not possible, because the Orthodox Church is not like the Catholic Church: The lay people have a large role in running the parish. They have taken care of the church, they have repaired it, and they have kept it running."

Teoctist described himself as both "optimistic" and "realistic" about relations between his church and the Uniates, but that day, he stressed the latter.

"We have to be realistic," he said. "Even the Pope has this realistic view: If the believers do not want to go back, how can we force them to be believers again? The Pope was here, during your time. He came in under exceptional circumstances. I was in Rome last summer. We recommended together that all these different issues be dealt with through dialogue.

"In theology, in international relations, this Catholic system to take away parts from the big Christian churches and to bring them under the Pope's jurisdiction has brought a lot of difficulties. These difficulties are proving to be a heavy burden on our relations with the Catholics. In all these national churches, except the Anglicans, they have taken away parts. With the Orthodox and the others, they created parallel churches.

"Under the popes in Transylvania during the Hapsburgs, the Orthodox were not officially recognized. But they were given the promise that, if they came under the jurisdiction of the Pope, they would have the same rights as the Catholics. As long as this Greek Catholic Church will exist, I think there will always be tensions."

How Orthodoxy survived Communism

Jim asked why Communist Party officials in Romania allowed the Orthodox Church more leeway than their counterparts did in Russia or Bulgaria.

"First of all, the Romanian Communists were native Romanians,"

Teoctist answered. "Except for Ana Pauker, who was a Jew, and another Jew, Vasile Luca, who studied in Moscow and came to Romania together with the Russians, all the other so-called Communists were workers, so-called proletariat, known for their worker's activities."

As an example of why the Communists were sympathetic to the Orthodox church, Teoctist told us the story of Gheorghe Gheorghiu-Dej, the railroad worker who would go on to rule Romania as Communist Party secretary after World War II. He had been put on trial by the anti-Communist government in 1933. Workers, including Gheorghiu-Dej, were accused of shooting at churches and other buildings during a union protest. Gheorghiu-Dej called a priest as one of his witnesses; there was no objection from the prosecutor, who was sure the priest would back the political authorities of the time. But Teoctist, who was ordained a monk that same year, recalled, "Since it was a democratic time, the trial was open to international observers. When the priest came to the trial—these are the words from the priest, Alexandru Neacşu—he said, 'I'm the priest of that church. I saw what happened. And since I am before God, I cannot say anything else but the truth. In the church, it was the policeman who actually fired the shots.'"

It was not the testimony the judge was expecting to hear, but he had to take it into account. Presumably, when Gheorghiu-Dej was running Romania decades later, he remembered how the testimony of a priest lightened his sentence—or was often reminded of it by Church officials like Teoctist.

Gheorghiu-Dej and his successor, Ceauşescu, were generally viewed as much more nationalistic than other Eastern bloc Communist leaders. In 1958, Gheorghiu-Dej succeeded in convincing Moscow to withdraw its occupying troops. In the spring of 1968, Ceauşescu was so cool to the Soviet crackdown in Prague that Romania and the United States feared the Soviets might invade Romania as well.

We were often told by Romanians of brutal tactics by Russian soldiers who occupied their country in 1944—descriptions of soldiers helping themselves to food, jewelry, sexual encounters, and pretty much anything else they wanted. That picture was remarkably similar to one painted sixty years earlier of Russian conduct in World War I.

"The older Romanians who remembered World War I," Frederick Hunt, a foreign service officer who served in Bucharest from 1939 to 1941, said in an oral history, "remembered that the Germans were so much better than their Russian allies. The Russian allies were in there, and they raped the women and they drank all their wine. Then, in 1917, when the political commissars came down and told the Russian soldiers to quit, it left gaps in the Romanian line, which permitted the Germans to come in. The Germans were very proper. The one thing the Romanians held against the Germans was that they made everybody clean the snow in front of their house."

But Teoctist's memory of World War II was different. The Russian soldiers were Orthodox believers, even if the USSR was shutting down churches. To Teoctist, they were less obnoxious than the German soldiers who had walked Romania's streets during Hitler's occupation.

"I was deacon here at this cathedral at the time," Teoctist said. "I used to see how the Germans entered and smoked inside the Church in a very despicable way. When they spoke to the priests, they did so in demeaning words." Teoctist described the contrast when the Nazis were chased out. "[When] the Russian Army occupied Bucovina, the Orthodox eastern part [of Romania], they would take care of the monasteries and the churches, and would not destroy them. Some of the soldiers were very faithful, even though they did not know the Romanian language. When they would see a priest, they would ask for a blessing. Some of them were making the cross like us [in making the sign of the cross, Orthodox believers tap the right shoulder first, then the left; Roman Catholics go left to right], and they were entering the church with a different demeanor. Of course, the people knew that in Russia, the churches were destroyed or closed. Still, that created a certain opinion, a view of the Orthodox people in Romania that the Russians were faithful."

As we began to leave the Patriarchy, we lingered a few minutes with Teoctist and our priest-interpreter in the somber foyer. High up on its walls are murals depicting uniformed, seventeenth-century Austrian soldiers on horseback vanquishing Romanian peasants, and presumably forcing them to convert. Peering up through the shadows, we gained a new awareness of how deep the rupture between Eastern and Western Christianity has been in Romania, and how extraordinary it was that this Patriarch had embraced the pontiff of Rome here in Romania.

We thanked the Patriarch. "May God bless you," he said. Then, he added, "Don't forget about us, because there are still many people who look at us with different eyes."

THE RELIGIOUS REVIVAL SINCE 1989

YOU MIGHT BE SURPRISED at how many young people and families you will see at church in Romania. Sunday services last for hours, and there is no shame in coming late, or leaving early, or both. On big feast days—Easter being the biggest of all—there are huge crowds at church. For the Holy Saturday vigil service, which is a magnificent tumult of chant and incense, with glowing wax tapers in the hands of the faithful, the crowd is much bigger than any church could possibly hold. That's all right, because for a large part of the service, the priest is outside among the people, circling and blessing them. In Bucharest, and probably other cities, teenagers attend in groups or with their boyfriends and girlfriends, as if on a date.

The Orthodox services we attended were magical, not in the sense of hocus-pocus, but in the sense that some people find a good opera or a rock concert magical. The music transports you to another place. That's primarily because Orthodox priests can sing—really well. It's one of the criteria on which seminarians are chosen. If a young man can't carry a tune in a robust voice, he's not going to make it in the seminary. When several priests sing polyphony together at a big ceremony, it's really luscious. It makes the Roman Catholic masses we're used to in North America seem as simple as a Quaker meeting.

Simplicity is not what the Orthodox liturgy is all about. Though simplicity of spirit shines in the lives of monks and nuns who fast and deny themselves, simplicity of décor is a non-starter in Orthodox churches. Every square centimeter on the walls and carpets is covered with frescoes, gilt, or carving. Some of the older monasteries, especially in the north, are also frescoed outside. Inside, most Orthodox churches are dark, with candles or small electric lights straining to pierce the gloom and the candle soot that has settled on the frescoes over the years.

Like many religions, the Orthodox Church tries to make God's presence vivid in the minds of believers, and uses physical objects to do that. Candles carry special meaning. At the back of nearly every church, is at least one aging woman, usually clad in black from the kerchief on her gray hair down to her shapeless skirt, selling candles. People buy several, and place them in front of the church's special icons in frames and on tables around the church. It's sort of prayer on autopilot: Even after you've left the church, the candles flicker on, sending your supplications to heaven, renewing your entreaty to the specific saint depicted in that particular icon.

"Depicted" may be too weak a word. An icon is considered more than a pretty or dramatic picture of the Deity or the saint in question, and is felt to actually anchor some of that spirit on earth. One believer told Jim he considered icons special windows that connect him to God and the saints. And one of the nuns who came to Washington, D.C. to demonstrate the art of icon-painting at the Smithsonian Folklife Festival said she thinks of her painting as "a conversation with God."

Romanians are especially proud of what they consider a specialty: icons painted on glass. Over and over, we were told that this technique is "specific Romanian" (although Jim's Ukrainian assistant, Elena Kuzina, and others might not agree). The artist layers the paint on the glass that will be the back of the icon, which means she must begin with the details that will appear up front, and build back to the broad sweep of background. Sheilah never saw an icon on glass without thinking of that line about Ginger Rogers—that she did everything Fred Astaire did, but backwards in high heels. These icons follow very stylized patterns and are often naïf in style.

The church is probably the best classroom in which to learn the Romanian approach to connections—indeed, that's probably where most Romanian children learn the technique. You don't just flounce into church and ask God directly for what you want. You make your supplication to his mother, the Virgin Mary, or to God's friends, the saints. And you don't come empty-handed. You bring a gift—flowers, or a candle, or a donation to the church. For big requests, you slip a gift to the priest to persuade him to pray on your behalf. And then he places your petitions before God's family and friends. "A prayer without a gift," it's said, "is a dead thing."

Religious baksheesh has a long and honorable history in Romania. To communicate thanks to God, princes built a church after each military victory, and the gift in turn was depicted in a fresco at the back of the church. That's the spot where the benefactor, usually surrounded by his wife and kids, and often holding a scale model of the very edifice in which you're standing, is captured in paint and plaster for posterity, lest his beneficence go unnoticed.

There's a robust history of trading money for indulgences in the Roman Catholic Church, too, so we weren't shocked to encounter parallels in Romania. But as Americans thoroughly comfortable with church and state moving in separate spheres, we found it harder to absorb the involvement of government and public institutions in actually building churches.

Nor, as Roman Catholics, are we fazed by hierarchy. But, as Americans, we are used to a democratic style around it. In Romania, the deference paid to priests by the laity seems boundless. Most jarring to Jim was the practice of lay people kissing the hand of the priest. True, in America, priests and lay Catholics kiss the hand of a cardinal or archbishop as a sign of respect. But when that happens, the ecclesiastic usually outranks the layman in age as well as church office.

By contrast, in the Orthodox church, rank trumps everything. The oldest, frailest, whitest-haired grandmother bows her head to press her lips to the hand of the youngest priest. To Jim, this was deeply anti-democratic—the old-fashioned hierarchical church in the flesh!

Oh, please pardon my English

THE BIGGEST CHALLENGE TO learning Romanian while living in Bucharest is not the difficulty of the language. It's that so many Romanians speak such excellent English. As a conversation starts, both participants do the mental calculation: *We can conduct this dialogue in nuanced English, or in rudimentary Romanian.* The temptation to speak like adults nearly always proves too great. Another conversation unfolds in English, and another chance to practice Romanian is lost.

Sheilah began to realize how pervasive Western languages are the first time she went to pump gas into her car at a shiny new Petrom station in north Bucharest. Slowly, she studied the signs on the pump. She had learned that *fără* means "without," and noticed that *plumb* looked a lot like the symbol for "lead" on the periodic table of elements she learned in high school chemistry. She was just concluding that *fără plumb* means "no lead" when a young construction worker from the site next to the station vaulted the fence, inquired in pretty good English whether he could help, pumped her gas, and disappeared back to his workplace, almost before she could thank him.

In surveys, Romania often shows up as the most multilingual country in Europe. Four out of ten Romanians can speak a foreign language; of those, one-fourth can speak English. The second most frequently used and studied language is French, followed by German, Italian, Hungarian, Spanish, and Russian.

Actually, Romanians have more reason to speak German than English, because of the history of Saxons in Transylvania, and more reason to speak French, because of their long connection to that Latin country. We lost count of the conversations in impeccable, measured, idiomatic English that ended with the Romanian apologizing with a deferential shrug, and maybe a little bow. "Oh, please excuse my English—it's not nearly as good as my French." Or "my German."

The apologetic speakers were not, by and large, language specialists. They were engineers, journalists, nurses, clerks, students, waitresses—people across society, more from the middle class than from among workers and peasants, but not only in the elites. And no, they weren't mocking us. Unlike the majority of Americans, who see mastering a second (or third, or fourth) language as well-nigh impossible, Romanians think it's normal, and even necessary.

We asked a lot of Romanians where that attitude came from. Many of their answers linked it to Romania's long craving to be part of the West, as well as the opportunity that Communism presented for intellectual pursuits. During the decades when television was a growing distraction in the West, it didn't air many hours in Romania, and most of what was on the air was not very tempting. That left time to attend concerts and opera (at subsidized ticket prices), read books, and learn languages.

In fact, some of what was on the television screen helped with language study. Such Western movies and TV programs as the regime allowed generally kept their original soundtracks, with Romanian subtitles added. Lots of Romanians reminisced to us about watching the TV series *Dallas* during the 1980s, their ears absorbing Texan English while their eyes could scan a Romanian translation on-screen.

Even today, unlike the rest of Eastern Europe, when television channels in Romania air western fare, it's with subtitles rather than dubbing—because that's what their viewers prefer.

Romanians hold the study of foreign languages in such esteem that there's a proverb that holds, "Tell me how many languages you speak, and I'll tell you how much of a person you are." (Spune-mi câte limbi vorbești, ca să-ți spun ce fel de persoană ești.) That makes it all the harder to understand the run-in Lia and Dorel Jurcovan had with the Securitate, Romania's secret police under the Communists.

When we met the Jurcovans, they were running a great little pizza parlor in Timișoara, the city in western Romania where the Revolution started in December 1989. But before the Revolution, Lia had worked at a computer research institute. It was heavily monitored by the Securitate "because they said the Americans would come steal our secrets, which was stupid, because we were copying the American computer systems."

One day, the chief of the Securitate assigned to her institute approached her with a weighty question: "I have news that you and your husband are teaching your four-year-old daughter English. Why is that? You probably want to leave the country."

Lia still looked exasperated as she recalled the exchange years later. "It was very hard for me to find a smart answer. Why am I teaching my daughter English? For me, it was so obvious—this was a window for her knowledge, for everything.

"Both my husband and I speak several foreign languages, which was bad enough." They looked at each other and laughed. "We were speaking French and German. We tried to teach our daughter English, but not because we want to leave the country. We just want her to *know*. It was so difficult to explain that I couldn't find the words. And I knew, from that moment on, that we would be blacklisted."

Sure enough, the following year, all of Lia's colleagues were allowed to make a trip across the border to Budapest—but not Lia. "They never explained why. They just said, 'Everybody is OK—not Jurcovan.' But I knew why: It was because I was teaching my four year old English."

But Lia and Dorel had the last laugh. Partly because of their prodigious language skills, when protests grew into a revolution in the streets of Timişoara five years later, they became the point of contact for many Western reporters.

"I couldn't have imagined that the Revolution would happen in five years, or that in five years, I would be talking with Irish television," Lia told Sheilah. "Oh my God, we spent our first free New Year, 1990, in this room with Irish TV and [a] French channel. They went live, with all the satellite equipment on our balcony. They became our new best friends—here were twenty-four people in a small room, but it was the best time of our lives, despite almost nothing to eat, and despite the fact it was a time of great political stress and resulting food shortages. The French brought oranges and French chocolate, and the Irish team brought Irish whiskey. So we had the best New Year's Eve, eating oranges and chocolate and drinking whiskey!"

In a free Romania.

THE SPIES AND THE SPIED-ON

IT'S NO SURPRISE THAT the relationship between the minders and the minded during Communism was often complex. We heard secondhand about the evening when a dissident suffered a flat tire while returning home. As the story goes, the Securitate team tailing him at a discreet distance waited a while, then drove up close, hopped out, and changed the tire for him. It had become clear that their work wouldn't end that night until the tire got changed.

Andrei Pleşu, the hyper-articulate foreign minister during our years in Romania, had been under Securitate scrutiny for years because of his extensive, frequent, and candid contacts with the West. There were plenty of frustrations and humiliations—and eventually he was banished to a museum near Bacău—but Pleşu remembers an occasional benefit of being tailed.

One time, he told us, he and a friend wanted to order beer in a beer garden. "We asked them [the secret police], 'Are we allowed to?' And they said, 'Yes, but we must come with you. We will not stay at the same table, but we will be around.' Okay. We go there, we ask for a beer—there was no beer, of course. And then my friend just tells the waiter, 'Ask those gentlemen at that table about some beer.' Maybe the waiter didn't understand. He went to the other table, there was some talk, and in the end the waiter brought us some beer." Pleşu mimed the smirk, the raised eyebrow, and the circled thumb and forefinger the Securitate team flashed them when the beer arrived.

Of course, the surveillance covered not just Andrei, but his wife Catrinel, a writer and editor. And the Securitate took no pains to hide it—the openness of the stakeouts was probably part of the strategy.

Catrinel told us it got to be tiresome—the clicks on the phone line, and always a car parked in front of their house. One day, she recalled, a neighbor came to the door with news that the market around the corner had received some eggs. *Eggs!* Very hard to come by. So Catrinel threw off her apron and trotted off to the store with her neighbor. Behind her, she heard the doors of the Securitate sedan springing open, and the guys struggling to give chase on foot. Catrinel said she called over her shoulder, "We're just going to buy eggs!" And the Securitate guy said, "We want eggs, too!" So they all ended up in the same line together.

Walking back, catching her breath, and shielding her prized eggs—five of them, stuffed in hands and pockets—Catrinel recalled her surprise that the Securitate guys had to queue up for eggs like everyone else. "Why do you do this, if you don't at least get eggs?" she asked. And one of them shrugged, and said, "Hey, it's a job."

When Pleşu became culture minister in 1990, one of his former watchers came to his office, brought him a present, and wished him well in his new job. The man seemed proud that the professor he had spied on was now a cabinet minister. It reflected well on him as a spy—he'd been assigned to keep track of such an important person.

ALL POLITICS IS LOCAL

FORMER U.S. HOUSE SPEAKER TIP O'NEILL was well-known for telling new House members, "All politics is local." The point was simple. People live in their own communities and expect their elected officials to pay attention first to them.

When we visited Baia Mare, one of the two cities in Maramureş in northern Romania, our gracious host was Mayor Cristian Anghel, an English-speaking, Western-oriented man who was also president of the Romanian Association of Mayors.

When he drove us back to the airport, we all noticed a group of elementary school children who seemed to be on a field trip visiting the airport. Like children around the world, they were fascinated by a model plane hanging from the ceiling in the center of the waiting area.

As soon as he saw the children, Anghel transferred his attention to them. He became totally absorbed, introducing himself to them, making sure they met the mayor. They were as delighted by the encounter as he was. Ambassadors come and go, but these kids were constituents.

Tip O'Neill was right, even about Romania.

SOMETHING TO CHEW ON

ONE EVENING, WHEN JIM was having dinner in a Bucharest restaurant, he struck up a conversation with his waitress. She was eighteen, and had just moved from Piatra Neamț in northeastern Romania to Bucharest in hopes of winning admission to the university. She had not scored high enough on the entrance exam for her first choice, so she was working until she could apply again.

Evidently, Jim's questions about her background and plans struck her as extensive, if not downright excessive.

"You know," she said in reasonable English, "Aries Oatlay said that 'curiosity is the appetite of the mind.'"

Great line, Jim thought, but he hadn't heard of the author. "Who is that?" he asked.

"Aries Oatlay."

"Why don't you write it down?" he suggested.

"A-R-I-S-T-O-T-L-E," she wrote.

"Oh yeah, of course, Aristotle," he said. How could he have forgotten?

Jim tried to think of high school waiters and waitresses he'd met in the United States who quoted Aristotle. He's still thinking.

BUCHAREST, ROMANIA's CAPITAL

CHAPTER 4
LIVING IN "THE PARIS OF THE EAST"

SURVIVING URBAN RENEWAL, CEAUŞESCU-STYLE

BUCHAREST CAN BE AS magical as a visitor lets it be. Its narrow streets and broad avenues cover many centuries of history. On some can be found a residue of beauty, on others a backlog of human misery. It's all there. You can focus on what grabs your heart (or mind).

What charmed us most was the air of faded elegance suffusing so many neighborhoods: stately nineteenth-century villas with French doors, ornate carvings, and clamshell porticos, often with peeling paint or cracked walls; intriguing streets whose cobblestones were not up to the punishing traffic they take today; and delightful parks with neglected plantings and rusting wrought-iron fences.

We could daydream that we were living in another era, and the occasional horse-drawn cart clopping on the cobblestones would support our dream. But people live in those villas, navigate those streets, and bring their children to those parks.

Faded elegance is only part of Bucharest. It's the part that would have been urban-renewed away in a vibrant economy during the second half of the twentieth century. But in an economy stagnant during forty-two years of Communism, a lot was left untouched.

There would probably be even more neighborhoods of faded elegance except that in the 1980s, the dictator Nicolae Ceauşescu took it in his head to build the biggest, most imposing building he could conceive of to be the seat of his government. For that and its supporting structures, he condemned block after block near the Dâmboviţa River, sometimes giving people only a few days to vacate homes their families had lived in for generations.

Though the government had already nationalized these homes, the blow was felt intensely by the homeowners. So many Romanians could talk of the pain to their family—the aunt who went stark, raving mad, or the grandfather who suffered a heart attack on the spot. People were generally relocated to the depressing ten- and twelve-story blocks of too-small apartments built beyond downtown Bucharest. The move meant cramming people in, and selling or giving away family heirlooms.

It most cases, it also meant abandoning the family pet on the streets, because there wasn't enough room in the new apartment. We were told repeatedly that the packs of stray dogs that bedeviled Bucharest's streets until a few years ago dated from Ceaușescu's building projects.

Ceaușescu's urban renewal also obliterated nearly all of what had been the capital city's Jewish quarter, as well as many historic Christian churches. At the time of the Revolution in December 1989, Ceaușescu's monstrous building, the Palace of the People, was not quite finished. (Reportedly, Ceaușescu and his wife had repeatedly changed their minds about one room or another, requiring a lot of tearing down and rebuilding.) Except for those assigned to work on the building, Romanians didn't know much about what was inside—the acres of marble, the hand-loomed rugs and drapes, the elaborately carved doors. Every item—every amazing weaving, every intricate inlay—had been quarried, gathered, cut, crafted, and worked on in Romania.

For several days after the Ceaușescus fled Bucharest, but before some new system of security was established, Romanians wandered through the massive building. They walked around dumbfounded to see the project on which Ceaușescu had been spending one-third of the nation's income at a time when Romanians were going without enough to eat and were shivering in dark rooms on cold nights without heat. The daze did not prevent a few enterprising Romanians from "liberating" items not nailed down or too massive to move, or so we were told.

NIXON, CASTRO, AND PILLAR 23

"THE MOST IMPORTANT THING that happened in Romania after the Revolution was the fact that Americans started coming," Emil Constantinescu, then president of Romania, told us one afternoon.

"It is true they came too late, with a small delay of forty or fifty years. But because we Romanians have a history of two thousand years, we are used to waiting. So we didn't find this fact very dramatic," he continued. "These American people were either coming with a certain mission or they were coming to meet us, the Romanians. We were also interested in getting to know them."

To an outsider, it never seemed as if Emil Constantinescu was having much fun as president. He didn't seem to thrive on the job the way a natural-born politician would. In that way, he reminded us of Jimmy Carter—not physically, except for the somewhat high-pitched voice. Constantinescu is taller than Carter, with a slender face, a goatee, graying hair, and great posture.

But like Carter, Constantinescu conveys enormous confidence in his own rightness of purpose. He projects vision, honesty, courage— and a limited appreciation for the nitty-gritty of politics. He does *not* come across as one of the boys.

Maybe it's all those years in front of a college classroom. Constantinescu's roots are firmly in academia: He trained as a lawyer, but switched to geology to avoid the kind of political compromises, and perhaps boredom, he felt would have been required of a lawyer during Communism. By 1990, he was head of the geology department of Bucharest University.

"If not for the West promoting the myth of Ceauşescu's independence, he would have been overthrown much earlier, and the sufferings of the Romanian people would have been less—and not only during the Communist period," he mused during another conversation with us after completing his term as president.

"The effects of the American policy that misanalyzed Ceauşescu have continued until now. This also is a feature of the psychology of the Romanian people. Their collective memory is that whatever comes from the West is good, and whatever comes from the East is bad. Romanians are constantly living under the stream of integration into Europe and the Western world, and Ceauşescu used this trump card with maximum shrewdness."

Take President Richard Nixon's state visit in August 1969.

"Ceaușescu received Nixon in a sensational way," Constantinescu told us. "In other countries, I understand tomatoes were thrown at him, but in Romania, there was a grand reception. And Nixon felt that this reception had nothing in common with the Korean kind."

In other words, Nixon thought his reception in Bucharest was spontaneous, and not engineered by a dictator. After a day and half, Nixon declared that of all the sixty countries he had visited, "there has been none that has been more memorable than the visit to Romania."

John Florescu, an American of Romanian-French origin, was born and raised in Boston, and often visited Romania with his historian father. John recalled that the United States had landed men on the moon just two weeks before Nixon made his entrance in brilliant sunshine before crowds at Otopeni airport. He had visited Romania before, as a private citizen after his term as vice president, and he'd given Ceaușescu just five weeks to put this state visit together. The dictator sent workers into overdrive to make a good impression—overnight, gardeners were furiously sprucing up the airport, speed-potting flowers and bushes.

As vibrant as the daylight was, it couldn't illuminate all the hidden reasons for the trip—such as Nixon's deliberate aim of annoying the Soviets in Moscow by showing off U.S. connections in Eastern Europe, or the back-channel role Romania was playing in opening relations between the United States and China. What *was* clear, John recalled, was the warmth of the crowd as Nixon and Ceaușescu left the airport.

Florescu, a teenager at the time, told us, "Nixon freaked Ceaușescu out by stopping the motorcade at several points as he journeyed out, campaign-style, into the throngs, probably six rows deep. The crowds were much bigger than those that greeted [French President Charles] de Gaulle just one year earlier—even though the Franco-Romanian tie was supposedly so much deeper."

Florescu remembered Nixon stopping at a housing project and at a surprisingly well-stocked outdoor market (from which the produce and butchered meat, flown in from Western Europe for the occasion, was crated up and sent back minutes after Nixon walked through).

Meanwhile, in the center city, the presidential visit was shaping up like any other dreary official occasion for a young geology professor named Emil Constantinescu.

"We were obliged to go—Ceauşescu was requiring us to go with our colleagues from work," Constantinescu told us. "There were special spots where you had to stand, depending on whether you were a historian or a worker. They put numbers on the pillars so your group could find your location. Ours was number twenty-three—not just for Nixon, but for everybody! Number twenty-three for all receptions, whether it was Nixon or Mobutu [Sese Seko], and even for the National Day celebration!

"At these receptions, you had to stand next to your pillar and not move. For ten years, you knew you had your own pillar where you were supposed to go."

But that day, Constantinescu said, there was an amazing transformation.

"Once everybody got to their places, and Nixon appeared in his car, the sympathy the people showed was extremely sincere and honest. And Nixon felt that. You cannot fake something like that. You can take people to their spots, and show them what to do, and give them banners. We had to move the banners up and down. We were given little cards with a few lines of the slogan we had to shout. And we were not allowed to shout anything else but what was on the little note. When Nixon came as president for the first time, all this organization turned into a message of sincere sympathy. He was the first American president on an official visit to Romania. When people crossed the security lines, he could see that from the car, and he was genuinely moved."

Seated at the dining table of his modest home, Constantinescu told us Fidel Castro had a very different experience when he visited Bucharest three years later.

"He wanted to meet with the students, so a meeting was organized for the Polytechnic. Students and teachers from all schools and universities were taken there. Ceauşescu and Castro were expected to arrive at ten o'clock, so we were woken up at five in the morning, and we gathered in the yard of the Polytechnic. They closed the doors so nobody could get out, and blocked the doors with Securitate troops," Constantinescu recalled.

"Castro and Ceauşescu were two hours late. So, during this period, we had to do rehearsals: 'Ceauşescu! Fidel Castro! Ceauşescu! Fidel Castro!' And we were sitting down, and then standing up again. But then Ceauşescu and Fidel Castro came into the alley, standing in an open car. The students were intelligent, so without previous discussion, they turned completely and glacially silent. Nobody moved. Nobody uttered a word. And only at the end, after a police car came at the end of the entourage, was there any shouting—and that was to greet the policemen.

"Fidel Castro understood this very quickly. He reproached Ceauşescu, and cut short the visit by one day. Then the strangest thing happened: The access of the students at Fidel Castro's departure, at the relevant pillars, was forbidden. From that moment on, we were no longer allowed to go there! Some people went there without knowing what had happened, and they were sent away by the Securitate. Ever since that day with Castro, only workers and civil servants were required to come to the parades. Once the students got this treatment, we professors were saved, too. Ceauşescu said, 'I don't want to see these people anymore.'"

Was there any punishment?

"No, because they understood that students can act in an unpredictable way. They decided to deal only with those people whose jobs depended on their behavior."

A ROMANIAN VIEW OF AMERICANS ABROAD

THE GEOLOGY DEPARTMENT CONSTANTINESCU would eventually chair is located right on the corner of University Square, overlooking the place where gunfire and demonstrations took place in December 1989, and where negotiations were conducted immediately following the Revolution. So he was in the middle of everything, right at his base in academia. He was one of the founders of the Civic Alliance, pushing, along with other intellectuals, for free and democratic elections.

Because Constantinescu was on the "to-visit" list of so many Westerners after the Revolution, we asked him what Romanians thought of Americans.

"In general, our opinions are good, because we wanted to see the Americans in the right way. We were very ready to like them, and it was very difficult for any American to contradict this impression.

"But after five or six years of getting to know the Americans—in Romania, the USA, Europe, and throughout the world—I can say that I managed to see them as part of two very different categories. Some of them, either through education or their own beliefs, think that the whole world has to be organized according to the American system, which is the only good system of organizing, and that the world is only going to be a happy place when it resembles America—in whole, and in every way, down to the smallest details. These people are only happy with airports if they look like the ones in the Midwest United States. And they consider a country civilized only if it has highways, even though they cannot see any development from the highways. If they see warehouses at the entrance to a town, as well as billboards, and can go to a McDonald's once they reach town, and get a scotch on the rocks at their hotel, they think they're in a good place and are happy. Like a snail, they carry all their habits with them. And whenever things are not exactly this way, they withdraw a little and pull back into their shell. This is not good.

"The second category of Americans I have met are completely different. These are people who preserved something of the old America. They don't come from the America of the downtown or of the malls. They come from the America of the pioneers. They live in cities, and they might do their shopping at malls, but they wish to do something different when they travel. These people have experienced in Romania and other former Communist countries the forgotten sensation of discovery, of discovering new territories. Only this time, they were not going into territories with no civilization. On the contrary, they were going into their own past and into the origins of civilizations.

"These Americans are, first of all, curious people, because they want to know about something different. And what is even more important about their mentality is the fact that they understand there can be people who are different from Americans, who will probably also speak a different language than English. To find out there are different cultures and different habits is, they believe, a good thing. They don't want to bring everybody the American way of life. They want to find something new.

"But here something specific about the American people enters. And this is related to America's type of culture. They don't limit themselves to contemplating. They are not tourists, dreamers, or writers. They roll up their sleeves and start to work. And they begin to do not whatever comes along, but the most difficult things. And this is the greatest surprise for these old countries and especially for the countries in southeastern Europe: They give the people they meet the gift of team spirit, which they learned in school, at the university, or in the neighborhood. These Americans love those whom they encounter, and even if in the beginning they look strange, they end up being loved by them. I'm very happy for having had the chance to meet such Americans."

The birth pangs of democracy in Romania did not keep Constantinescu from spending part of 1991 as a visiting professor at Duke University. Back in Bucharest, he continued to combine politics and academics: In 1992, he became rector of the University. He also ran for president, and lost.

Constantinescu was taken seriously by political conservatives—for example, by diplomats from Western Europe and by Republican members of the U.S. Congress, like Representative Frank Wolf of Virginia and Representative Chris Smith of New Jersey, and Ronald Reagan's ambassador to Romania, David Funderburk, who publicly blew the whistle on Ceaușescu's cruelty and stupidity in the early 1980s.

White House photo

President Constantinescu, Romanian Ambassador to the U.S. Mircea Geoană, President Clinton, and Jim in the White House in 1999

Constantinescu understood English fairly well, and could speak well enough in casual conversations. For more serious topics, he was more comfortable with an interpreter. At dinner that night, his daughter Norina was drafted for that duty.

Constantinescu has an academic's flair for imposing a structure on the randomness of life. That's what academics do, especially scientists like Constantinescu—observe a confused world and come up with a theory that explains it, or at least describes it. Constantinescu is skilled at such formulations, talking in paragraphs and sometimes in chapters.

Early in the NATO action in Kosovo, he declared, "For the first time in history, we're going to be on one side for the entire war." The press tends to love such sweeping statements, as do outside audiences (like diplomats). They don't play as well with fellow politicians in the trenches.

As president, he seemed obsessed by the power of the old Securitate-business crowd which has dominated much of Romania's economic life since 1989. He talked about it in a way we seldom heard from other politicians, mixing analysis with outrage. He was right. Not all of the Securitate alumni were brutal thugs. Some were among the most ambitious and able Romanians of their time. When the system changed in 1989, they seized the moment—and a lot of state property. To anticommunists who feared a rear guard action to protect totalitarianism, they were a threat which never materialized. To academics like Constantinescu, they were special interests lining their own pockets and blocking modernization.

He also directed some of his irritation at American business interests looking for special deals from the Romanian government. When he visited the Untied States in 1998, his speech to the U.S. Chamber of Commerce included a denunciation of companies with bigger net worths than Romania's entire gross domestic product looking for sovereign government loan guarantees. On another occasion, he had similarly withering words for the U.S.-Romania Action Commission, a bilateral group aimed at improving the business and development climate in Romania. The president had been out inspecting flood damage all day. The whines from the business group that evening did not sit well with him. He essentially told them to "suck it up"—not at all what the group's chair, former United States Defense Secretary William J. Perry, expected to hear.

LET'S DRINK TO THAT!

ALMOST AS SOON AS Jim started learning what worked and what didn't within the Romanian government, he kept encountering the Court of Accounts. Generally, it was the answer to the question, "Why won't such-and-such an official make a decision on this privatization or that contract?" Everyone seemed afraid that the Court of Accounts would come after them. It sounded a lot like government auditing agencies in the United States—sometimes promoters of good government, other times just tools for bureaucrats to fight innovation.

This Romanian agency wasn't on the list of courtesy calls to be paid by a new United States ambassador, but it sounded more important than a lot of the others. So Jim asked his staff to set up a meeting.

About 11:30 a.m., he arrived at the office of the chairman, who greeted Jim's team warmly and ushered them into his office. He sat on one side of the table. Jim, Michael Spangler, the embassy's opera-loving economic officer, and Marina Niculescu, a highly motivated, experienced Romanian embassy staffer, sat on the other. The table was set as if for lunch.

Jim has never been a great fan of protocol, so he was anxious to start talking about the Court—how it worked, what it did, and why everyone was so afraid of it.

The chairman was no technocrat; he was a politician with a background in accounting. As he explained later in the conversation, he had served in the first post-Communist parliament. As the parliament was writing the constitution and restructuring the government to put it more in line with democratic models, he took the lead in creating the Court of Accounts—in his words, the Romanian version of the U.S. Congress's Government Accountability Office (GAO).

In a bureaucratic sense, he was right. But, as he also pointed out, the Latin version of government audit agencies—Romania has one of only nine in the world—is much more intrusive on the decisions of individual officials than is the U.S. version, thus the shock and awe the Court inspired in Romanian bureaucrats.

But it would take a while to learn all this. First, the chairman offered his guests whiskey. *Oh,* Jim thought, *that explains why there's a collection of small glasses at each of our places.*

Jim cheerfully declined, pointing out that it was still morning.

"Ah," the chairman said. "You want țuică!"

With that, he jumped out of his chair and rushed to a large cabinet behind him.

Jim likes plum brandy, but that wasn't why he had declined the whiskey. As he was searching for a way to set his host straight, the chairman pulled open the door, revealing one of the more impressive collections of liquor Jim had ever seen in a government office.

"I made this țuică myself," he crowed. "It's from Sibiu, where I come from. Very good."

He circled the table, filling a glass at each place.

"Please," he said, "try it."

It was one thing to turn down whiskey—Jim doesn't really like whiskey, and more important, whiskey isn't the Romanian national drink, wrapped up in national pride and identity. And whiskey wouldn't have been brewed by the host himself. Jim's defenses dissolved.

"This is great," he said, sipping the chairman's pride and joy.

"You like it? Please drink the rest. There's more." His tone was reassuring, and Jim had no doubt there was plenty more where that came from.

With that, the conversation proceeded. The chairman talked about his visits to the GAO in Washington, where Jim's father Joe had worked in the 1970s, and why the chairman wanted to make the Court work well. All in all, it was an interesting and useful visit.

As his guests got up to leave, the chairman asked them to wait a minute while his assistant prepared gift bags for us—books on the Court and on his home of Sibiu, as well as large plastic bottles of his home-fermented brandy.

When Jim got back to the embassy, he put the bottle in the refrigerator near his office, and just as quickly forgot about it.

Months later, he was meeting in his office with Roda Tiniș, the telecom expert from the U.S. Commerce Department. She started choking, and seemed to need water, so Jim rushed to the refrigerator, found a bottle, and poured a cup for her.

She took a big gulp, after which her face turned red and her eyes welled up, and she spat out the țuică.

God's love, good doctors, and anti-retrovirals

Dr. Victor Babeş Hospital for Tropical and Infectious Diseases sits on a perpetually congested high-speed, multi-lane boulevard, just a few miles east of Bucharest's center. But once inside the hospital gates, the sprawling campus feels surprisingly bucolic. In summer, its trees buffer the noise of the whizzing traffic outside. A brick driveway leads to one of the white-painted buildings, with lots of windows and bright letters above the door that spell out the name of the pediatric AIDS unit.

It's a considerably more upbeat place than during the last months of the 1980s, when doctors and morticians at Victor Babeş already had begun to piece together the news the rest of the world would not learn until Ceauşescu's regime collapsed: A full-blown HIV-AIDS epidemic was sweeping through Romania's state orphanages. Some of the hundreds of infected infants were being brought to this hospital, and many were never leaving.

Romania's orphanages were so crowded because Ceauşescu was determined to grow the country's workforce. His 1966 decree banning contraception and abortion declared, "Giving birth is a patriotic duty." He required each married woman to bear at least four children; that was later upped to five. In some workplaces, gynecologists made surprise examinations to ensure that all pregnancies were carried to term. But by the 1980s, as Romania grew poorer and poorer and its people starved, some families could not afford to feed the children they were required to bring into the world. Many took them to orphanages—and left them.

But the orphanages were poor, also. Without enough money to feed all their hungry mouths, they turned to administering "micro-transfusions," on the tragically mistaken theory that injections of blood from a (presumably) healthy person would boost an infant's nutrition level and health. Romania was not then screening blood and blood products for viruses like HIV—that would not start until the year after the Revolution. And the orphanages did not even have clean syringes for the injections.

So, between 1986 and 1991, ten thousand children were infected with HIV-AIDS.

The story that has gotten much less attention is that most of those infected children have lived. UNICEF reports that about 7,000 of them are entering, or have entered, adulthood. They are coping not only with HIV, but often with poverty and prejudice. Worse, they have poor job skills, primarily because they had not been expected to live long enough to need a job.

How have they made it this far? Mary Veal, an American social worker who has been working with these kids since they were toddlers, credits it to "God, anti-retrovirals, and our good doctors."

During the 1990's, nearly two-third of all the pediatric AIDS cases in Europe were in Romania. The pediatric AIDS unit at Victor Babeş, the small non-profit Mary Veal works with, as well as many other volunteer groups and many other hospitals around the country, scrambled to support the young patients and their families, but saw too many of them die.

In the spring of 2001, Veal told Sheilah she and the hospital were scurrying to change sleeping arrangements for live-in patients, having realized that, because of their varying ages, all the youngsters couldn't be allowed to sleep in the same ward. "No one dreamed they would reach their teens, that they would think romantic thoughts or dream their future fantasies," Veal said.

It was around that time that a donor helped the non-profit hire a young psychologist to hold group sessions with the girls, and separate ones with the boys, to talk about whatever they wanted to talk about.

"The first hour, the girls talked about everything, from sex and gays, to penises (what do they do?) The girls' average age was 12, and it was like the conversation never slowed," Veal said. "They were so relieved to able to talk to somebody."

Veal slipped into one of the early sessions. "They were asking about babies, and how they get born. It was so cool. And at the end, this new girl—God, I love her, she's a great kid—asks, 'What's an abortion?' This is Romania. [Ceauşescu's ban on abortion was one of the first orders reversed in 1990.] She's heard about it on TV, and she's heard the staff talk about it. So, Cristina, the psychologist, told her what an abortion is, and that some people think it's a good thing and some people think it's not.

"And she looked over at Ioana, a little girl who was homesick, and tears were running down her face. Cristina had to stop and comfort her, because she thought it was just so terrible.

"But these are things that kids could ask. They're going to ask why they're getting hair under their arms—nobody has told 'em. And while this was all going on, the boys, who are a lot harder for Cristina to handle, are in the hallway and so anxious for their session to start that they've got their noses pressed against the window, pointing to their wrists, like, 'It's *our* time, it's *our* time!'"

In the early years, the small non-profit that Mary and her Romanian colleague Ana Filip ran was called Nobody's Children (*Copiii Nimănui*). Now, reflecting the surprising vitality of the kids and families it serves, it's called Hope for Health (*Speranţă pentru Sănătate*).

Hope for Health tries to hold things together for these families. Sometimes, it supplements groceries, or buys school supplies or toys or clothes, or co-ordinates social services. Very often, it buys vitamins and medications families can't afford. "How do you keep the child in the home [and not in an orphanage]?" Mary asked rhetorically. "You keep them in the home by having a support system. You can't expect people to do this on their own. It's really, really hard."

Sometimes poverty and poor nutrition and too little heat in the winter defeat the best efforts of doctors, drugs, nurses, and volunteers to keep them alive.

Anti-retroviral drugs make a huge difference. Despite budget stresses, disorganization, and limited social services, Romania has done a better job than many countries in making anti-retrovirals available to poor people with AIDS. In 2004, government health officials told *The New York Times* that three-drug anti-retroviral cocktails were available to everyone who needed them. The resulting headline proclaimed: "Romania Declares Victory in Fight Against AIDS."

Not really, Mary told Sheilah. "No one anywhere in the world has won the fight against HIV/AIDS." She and Ana see young patients who face such prejudice that they don't even apply for benefits in their village, fearful that their neighbors will find out about their illness.

Plus, many of these kids have grown without proper schooling, job skills, or even life skills because of the stigma of HIV/AIDS.

From Victor Babeş Hospital, Hope for Health gets a simple, sunlit office. It subsists on private donations and small grants, all of which are budgeted and accounted for. Sometimes, someone slips Mary some cash so she can buy something not in the budget—sweets for the kids, make-up for a teen-aged girl, flowers and a coffin for a funeral. She calls it her "jeans pocket" money.

Mary Veal keeps her network clued in to how things are going through occasional e-mails like this one:

> Ana went to a village this morning to help with the burial expenses for Marian, a very poor 21-year-old victim of AIDS. The family could not afford the wooden coffin, so we helped them pay for what was needed. Ana brought the flowers to cover the grave, along with candles. But the coffin rested on an earthen floor in a two-room dwelling, primitive and cold, on this early spring day.
>
> This young man leaves behind him a family, foreshadowing what we know will be very much a part of the future here. His beloved Petruţa clung to Ana, both of them crying, and when Ana offered the sedative that our doctors recommend in such times, she cried even more and refused it, saying, 'I want to feel it all.' She is so young, so full of love, and so completely devastated. She told Ana she didn't want to live any longer, but Marian had made her promise to take the anti-retroviral treatment, so she could live to raise their son, nearly 2 years old now, thankfully negative and healthy.
>
> A few months ago, Ana took Marian on an outing, afraid it would be his last Christmas. Then in January, he turned 21, deep in depression and so very ill. He told Petruţa that if he spent his birthday in hospital, it would be a sign he would never have another birthday. Unfortunately, he was right.
>
> But I remember so clearly that birthday, how we bought a cake and new pyjamas, and Petruţa organized his friends in hospital, and even his son was there at that time…and for a few moments, Marian

was happy.

The doctors tried everything, and our trips to the pharmacy for special medicines were endless. Likewise, we bought anything he could eat, which was so very little, and at the end, when he went home to die, he ate nothing at all, and refused all medicine. He was so very weary of the painful struggle, and ready to die.

Petruța's own immunity level is low, her doctor told us, and these past weeks of constant, dedicated care have taken their toll, physically and mentally. We have to give her emotional, social, and medical support now so she can cope.

This story is so different from those I have written about in the past, when it is parents mourning their children, but in the future, there will be more stories such as this one. Ana and I are profoundly affected by this death, and by Marian and Petruța's love for one another. We thought their story should be shared with all of you.

Peace,
Mary
13.03.09

GENERATION X IN THE BALKANS

TO THIS DAY, THERE are Romanians who believe Ambassador Rosapepe spoke Romanian pretty well.

They are wrong, but not for any lack of trying by his competent, energetic, and creative language teacher, Viviana Palade. She did her valiant best with a not-very-gifted student.

In elementary, junior, and senior high school, Jim had studied French for a total of nine years. He took two years of Latin. He had been born in Italy. Both of his parents and his older sister spoke Italian. But with him, almost none of it stuck.

The State Department offered Jim instruction in the Romanian language as soon as he was selected ambassador to Romania. But in the midst of wrapping up his business and his duties as a state legislator, as well as digging into the issues he would face as ambassador, language lessons didn't seem like the best use of his time. He arrived in Bucharest having learned only a handful of phrases and memorized a few more for Romanian TV interviews.

The night before we entered Romania for the first time, he was on the phone in our Vienna hotel room, comparing notes with Steve Strain, the embassy's public affairs officer in Bucharest. The arrival of a new American ambassador the next afternoon was bound to draw press coverage, and Jim wanted to be sure that if he said in Romanian, "I come with an open mind and an open heart," it wouldn't be heard by Romanian journalists as, "I'm showing up with a hole in my head and an aortal leak." (The arrival turned out fine.)

John Klipper, the Romanian-born American businessman who chaired the Romanian-American Enterprise Fund, introduced the new ambassador to a young female employee of the Fund who moonlighted as a language instructor. She was as beautiful as her name—Viviana. And her grasp of the American language, idioms and all, was perfect.

After two years of Vivi's efforts, Jim made progress. He could chit-chat (briefly and superficially) in Romanian, he could understand newspaper articles about topics he was familiar with and, most important, he could memorize or read short statements in Romanian and drop them into television and radio interviews. This was a useful job skill because, as his television-correspondent wife pointed out to him, what TV producers want are sound bites. If you give Romanian TV producers sound bites in Romanian, that's what they'll put on the air.

It worked—too well, as it turned out. After several months, Romanian TV viewers and radio listeners had heard so many Romanian sound bites coming out of Jim's mouth, they assumed he was fluent. He'd travel around the country, and some would chatter away to him in Romanian until he had to confess, "I'm not a Romanian speaker. I just play one on television."

Language can be a window into a nation's personality, as Jim learned through Vivi's coaching. Compared with English, the Romanian language is circuitous. Ideas are often implied rather than stated directly. Such indirection seems to fit the way Romanians communicate—one could debate whether they shaped the language or the language shaped them. Working with Vivi on speeches he planned to give, Jim learned it often took many more words to make his point in Romanian than in English. And occasionally, when he drafted something especially blunt, Vivi would protest, "You can't *say* that in Romanian!"

We watched Vivi explore some of the possibilities of the changing Romanian economy, such as filing on-camera reports about Romanian culture for an English-language TV show geared to expatriates. We also watched her fall in love with a charming Irishman, John Ball. Early one spring in 2000, we went to their late-afternoon wedding in the Orthodox Biserica Albă (White Church) in downtown Bucharest, and then to the dinner and reception in a nineteenth-century mansion that doubled as a club for oil company executives.

Compared to some of the village weddings we would later attend, which were family celebrations, this party was full of young, good-looking, elegantly dressed cosmopolitans. Vivi was stunning in white satin and lace, John in formal evening clothes. There was lots of pop music as well as traditional tunes. The evening proceeded in a rhythm any Romanian would recognize: an appetizer, then time to dance; a fish course, more dancing; salad, then a few dance tunes; roast beef, more music. Everyone was prepared to dance the night away.

Except us. This was the first wedding we had attended in Romania. Because the festivities had started at 4 p.m., we assumed they'd wrap up in no more than six or eight hours later. We will always remember Vivi's amazed expression when we gathered our coats to leave just before midnight.

"You're leaving *now*?!" she asked incredulously. She must have thought that all her attempts to clue us into Romanian language and customs had gone for naught. No one but the oldest fogy leaves a Romanian wedding until the wee hours.

Within a year, Vivi had left the Enterprise Fund and struck out on her own as an entrepreneur. She started a business to teach languages to people who need language skills in their business or profession. She called it WordLand International.

One of the niches she found were Romanian executives who wanted to quickly acquire enough English to handle a negotiation themselves, instead of relying on an assistant.

"The guys prefer to use their hands a lot with a little bit of negotiation in English, rather than having the assistant with them," she explained. So she scheduled short courses to fit their schedules, centering on the specific vocabulary they would need in their particular business.

Another niche was older Romanian managers who know their business cold, but lacked the English skills their younger colleagues had. They didn't want to be embarrassed when making a big presentation.

When WordLand was about a year old, and Sheilah asked what had been the biggest challenge, Vivi sounded like many an American entrepreneur.

"The hardest thing was finding the instructors I could trust to unhesitatingly send out to clients," she said. "It took month after month after month of training. And even then you still don't know. What if it's just another investment, and not the right one? You train the people and you waste your time and your resources to do that and you still don't know if, after three months, they will tell me, 'Okay, thank you very much, goodbye, it was very nice meeting you.'"

Vivi said Romanian labor law didn't allow her to add any restrictions to her contracts with instructors, such as a non-compete clause that would have prevented instructors she trained from setting up their own businesses. She just had to risk it. Sheilah asked whether Vivi had had to rely on connections to cut through red tape to get her business going.

"Connections in the sense of Romanian *pile*?" she asked. Romanians use *pile*, the same word for "nail file," to describe contacts and maneuvers that "file down" bureaucratic resistance. "Everybody [from abroad] I talk to these days says, 'It's exactly the same as in our country.' All the Americans I talk to say that if they want something, they have to go to someone they know there, and it works better.

"For example, some American told me, if you want to get the repairman to fix the phone, you make a call, and if you don't know the rules, you talk to the operator and you ask to send someone to fix the phone, but they don't send anyone. If you call and say, 'I want to talk to your boss,' and you talk to the supervisor, you get your phone fixed in five minutes. This is the secret. This sounds exactly like Romania. If you know how to make a point, you get what you want.

"I don't need connections. If I stand in a line for a good reason, I don't mind. I have my own set of rules. I don't want to pay extra for something I can get on my own."

But at the same time, Vivi says some of her American clients are frustrated with the attitudes they encounter in daily life in Romania.

"They are so depressed about what's going on in Romania and the way they are treated. They come to us and say, 'Guys, I can't stand it anymore. The people are so unhelpful.'

"For example, a man goes to the store, where he points to something, and the clerk, pretending she can't understand him, asks, 'What?' in Romanian. Then a young person appears and says, 'What can I do for you?' Even if it's in Romanian, the young one understands, but the old one doesn't."

Why are younger workers motivated in a way older workers are not?

"You never know," Vivi mused. "Self-motivation, usually. Not outside factors. They just think, 'You never know who that person might be whom I'm helping, and what may happen as a result.'"

STANDING IN LINE FOR NO REASON

VIVI WAS HALFWAY THROUGH high school when Communism collapsed in Romania. Now, she looks back on what she calls "a national, systemic disorganization" during Ceauşescu's regime.

"I guess the lack of order is very Communistic. I guess they wanted us to be disorganized. Everybody acted like sheep, going from the left to the right, and going to queues and yelling at each other, 'Hey, meat is coming!' and moving from one queue to the other, to get meat, cheese, whatever.

"There were even fake queues. There was even a joke about it. An old lady feels sick while walking in the street. She leans against a wall, and within ten seconds, two hundred people are behind her in a queue. A young boy comes to the queue and asks what they are selling, but nobody knows, which wasn't very unusual. You could stand in a queue and know nothing about what they were going to sell, because it would just grab you. Forget about thinking; they keep you standing in the queue and you don't think. So the boy goes to the old lady in front and asks, 'Hey, granny, what are you doing here?' And she says, 'I felt sick and leaned against the wall.' He says, 'If you felt sick, why didn't you leave?' She says, 'What? When I'm the first one in line?'"

If older shopkeepers in Bucharest appear to be sullen, maybe it's because they lived through more years of such tactics than Vivi did. Or maybe because, unlike Vivi, they didn't have a grandmother who often told her grand-daughter about a pre-Communist state of affairs called *vremuri normale*—normal times. What did "normal times" mean to Vivi?

"*Vremuri normale* is something like, you go to the market and you can get tomatoes, cheese—real cheese, not like in Communism—meat, everything for a different price, and you don't have to stand in a queue forever. To me, *vremuri normale* is when everything is settled. I can still remember my grandmother talking about the big oil companies, shoe factories, and textile plants, and private people owning them. The laborers were very serious. For fifteen years, or forty years, they were still there delivering good service.

"I think stability is, in a phrase, *vremuri normale*. That's exactly what everybody wants now, but it's sort of impossible because the conditions change from today to tomorrow—they just change nonstop."

There's a big difference between a society like Russia's, where

Communism stretched through seven decades, and Romania's, where it lasted only four. Romanian grandmothers could paint a picture of "normal times" for a generation, like Vivi's, that would grow up to be entrepreneurs.

POST-COLD WAR FROSTBITE

THE WEATHER IN BUCHAREST is pretty much like the weather in Washington, D.C., except it's hotter in the summer and colder in the winter. By his first Thanksgiving in Romania, Jim had already experienced one snowfall. That's when Sheilah and her mother came to visit.

About a week later was December 1, Romania's national day, which marks the unification of Transylvania with Romania at the end of World War I. Technically, it's the equivalent of our July 4, but lacks the emotional punch and recreational opportunities of our holiday. Before 1989, the national day was celebrated on August 23, the anniversary of Romania's 1944 overthrow of the Antonescu regime and the end of its alliance with Nazi Germany.

Whatever the weather, diplomats are expected to show up for official ceremonies celebrating the national day. As it approached, Jim kept asking his staff if they'd learned what events were planned and which ones he was expected to attend. This being Romania, the details did not appear until the day before December 1.

The schedule was this: First, at 9 a.m., a wreath-laying at the Tomb of the Unknown Soldier; then a series of speeches in the Parliament building; and finally, a review of the troops in the piața in front of the Parliament. All three events were expected to be over by early afternoon.

And the forecast was for frigid weather. The outdoor activities would be very cold.

Always unclear about the demands of protocol, Jim asked his deputy, Mike Einik, a smart, down-to-earth foreign service officer with broad experience in Eastern Europe and Russia, if there was any reason not to bundle up. Assured that "dignified but warm" was acceptable, Jim went to work in his closet.

Two components were key: One was his tan Nanook-of-the-North down jacket that made him look a little like the Pillsbury Doughboy. The other was a pair of boots lined with the thickest wool socks sold in Maryland. These were the boots he had bought at REI in College Park before his first trip to Moscow in December 1990. They look larger than life, or at least larger than Jim's feet. When he went to see the vice-rector of Moscow State University during that trip, the professor eyed him from top to bottom and asked, "Do you wear boots like that in the United States?" Jim had to admit he didn't, and that his expectations of Moscow cold turned out to be excessive.

But for December 1 in Bucharest, Jim wasn't taking any chances. As he stood for an hour that morning with his diplomatic colleagues waiting to lay the wreath, he knew he had not made a mistake. It *was* very cold.

The next event was at the Parliament building, where it was very hot. The jacket came off, but the boots remained.

Jim moved outside to the reviewing stand for diplomats and military attachés to view the parade of Romanian soldiers and weapons. Jim saw many of his fellow ambassadors, but also noticed that several seemed to be missing. This should have alerted him, but he ignored the signs.

Within about half an hour, the parade began—tanks, planes, armored personnel carriers, one after another. Various countries, not including the United States, had sent contingents. The military band music was terrific, and the parade of weapons was interesting. Jim's defense attaché, Air Force Colonel Tom Geary, gave him a running commentary on the weaponry's strengths and weaknesses.

But it remained extremely cold. The jacket was doing its job, but Jim's fingers were freezing, as were his feet. In fact, they were beginning to feel a little numb.

Finally, after noon, the parade was over. Jim found his car and his driver, Panait Dumitrescu, a man with the remarkable ability to drive fast, creatively, and safely, all at the same time. The streets were filled, as well as the sidewalks, and traffic slowed to a crawl. That was no problem for Jim, now comfortable inside the heated car. But for the multi-car security team of the Israeli ambassador, who was right behind Jim's car, it seemed to present a major annoyance. They honked, they screamed, and they honked again. They did not want to drive five miles an hour in a crowd.

Finally, the crowd parted, Panait speeded up, and so did the Israeli convoy.

By the time he got home, Jim was warmed up—everywhere but in his left foot. It still felt somewhat numb. He didn't worry about it until the next morning, when much of it was still numb.

This was enough to send Jim to see the embassy nurse. A dark-haired woman in her thirties, Glenda Siegrist had about the best bedside manner of any medical professional he had ever met. You not only felt better afterward, but you knew going in you'd feel better at the end of the appointment.

He told her his story and asked, "So what do you think?"

After poking around his foot a bit, she said, "You have frostbite."

"What do you do about it?" he asked.

Jim's niece Allison Bodwell with picture of Vlad Ţepeş (aka, Dracula)
at the chapel at Snagov Lake where he is said to have been buried

"Nothing," she replied. "It may go away in a few years—or it may not."

"Will it get worse?" he said.

"Probably not, but if your foot gets cold, it will freeze again," she said.

The accuracy of her diagnosis was confirmed about a month later, when Sheilah's brother Ken and his family visited over Christmas. We took them to visit an island in the middle of Lake Snagov, where Vlad Ţepeş (a/k/a Dracula) is rumored to have been buried in a small church. The good news was that the lake was entirely frozen, and we could walk across it to the island. The bad news was that walking across a frozen lake on a frostbitten foot tends to re-freeze the foot.

Not a smart move, Jim concluded.

When December 1 came around the next two years, the Romanian government skipped the usual long parades. And even it hadn't, the effects of global warming seemed to have kicked in by then.

ROME VS. ROMANIA: 1054 AND ALL THAT

BECAUSE POPE JOHN PAUL II played such a visible role in promoting the peaceful collapse of Communism in Eastern Europe, many assume that will be his major political legacy. It may be, but there is another important one—his effort to heal the breach between Catholicism and Orthodox Christianity.

Among most Americans, the Schism of 1054 is about as well-remembered as the year Mohammed migrated to Madinah (622 A.D.). But in Europe, this history is better known and has continuing relevance. The war between Croats (Catholics) and Serbs (Orthodox) in the early 1990s is simply the most tragic recent example.

The potential clash between Christian and Islamic civilizations has understandably dominated public attention since September 11, 2001. But the author of the clash theory, the late Dr. Samuel Huntington, focused as much attention on the potential divide between Orthodox Christians and Western Christians.

"Where does Europe end?" he asked. "Europe ends where Western Christianity ends and Islam and Orthodoxy begin." Huntington argued that's the middle of Romania, where the mountains separate Transylvania from the rest of Romania.

Pope John Paul did not agree. He launched an ambitious initiative to bridge the gap, which included visiting countries with Orthodox majorities—something no pope had done in one thousand years.

His breakthrough came in Romania in June 1999, when we were there.

POPE JOHN PAUL II AND US

OUR OWN EXPOSURE TO the Pope during his Romanian visit included watching the Popemobile coming down Kiseleff, the boulevard by our house. Sheilah, her mother, and our niece Samantha went outside to wait for him. They waved. He waved.

That night, President Constantinescu held a reception for the Pope at Cotroceni Palace, Romania's White House. Various "big potatoes," including diplomats, were to be invited, but it wasn't clear until that afternoon whether spouses like Sheilah would be on the list.

Even by Romanian standards, the reception was remarkably disorganized. The Pope and the president were milling around up front. We were milling around in the back. There was no receiving line.

Sheilah was worried because she had forgotten Catholic grade school admonitions that women should wear black and cover their heads to meet the Pope. Nearly every diplomatic spouse was attired in black—even their hose and pumps were black, so the somber hue extended to their toes. Sheilah had worn tweed, and was feeling conspicuous. What a relief it was to spot the blonde wife of the Danish ambassador in a bright red outfit! She said that when her husband suggested black, she had retorted, "Oh, the cardinals wear red." But then, she's not Roman Catholic. Sheilah is.

It turned out that we didn't get close enough to the Pope at Cotroceni to talk to him. In fact, we could barely see him over the crowd—the dais at one end of the room wasn't high enough to compensate for his stooped posture. He spoke, and his comments were translated three separate times into three separate languages—Romanian, French, and English.

The next day, Sheilah went to the Pope's Mass at the Catholic Cathedral of St. Joseph (Catedrala Sf. Iosif) in downtown Bucharest. It was packed. People were bracing themselves in arches, leaning on one another's shoulders for a better view, and tucked into every available spot, even behind pillars. This Mass gave Roman Catholic priests and nuns in Romania their best chance to get close to the Pope. Sheilah could feel their intense desire to be in his presence.

On the third and last day of the Pope's visit, there were several huge outdoor gatherings. We went to the joint celebration on the big field next to the massive Palace of Parliament built by Ceauşescu. Pope John Paul II took part in an Orthodox service that Sunday morning, and in the afternoon the Patriarch came to the outdoor Roman Catholic Mass.

Prime Minister Radu Vasile and Chris Crabbe, the energetic and engaged U.K. ambassador, arrived together, looking a bit underdressed for the occasion. It turns out they had come straight from a soccer game.

Catholic bishops were arrayed behind the Pope on the left; the Orthodox clergy sat behind the Patriarch on the right. The headgear was different, but the basic fashion statement on both sides of the dais was the same: lots of brocade, gold chains, and bejeweled crucifixes. The crowd was waving small gold-and-white flags with the papal insignia, and small blue, yellow, and red Romanian flags. After the Mass, the Pope and Patriarch hugged and the Pope announced that he had invited Teoctist to visit him in Rome.

At one point, in response to something the Pope said, a group of young clergy started chanting, "Unity, unity, unity." At that moment, the Orthodox hierarchy seemed distinctly uneasy. In the naïve ecumenical spirit of people like us, unity sounded like a great idea. But in the context of the Uniate Church's competition with the Orthodox, and the fact that they are unified with Rome and the Orthodox Church is not, it was a strong political message.

THE POPE AND THE PATRIARCH

THE POPE'S VISIT TO Romania in 1999 was a breakthrough in ecumenical relations of continental, if not worldwide, significance.

After the 1989 fall of Communism, the Romanian government sent repeated invitations to Pope John Paul II. They saw a visit as a way to strengthen ties with Western Europe, accelerating their entrance into NATO and the European Union.

But for a decade, the Romanian Orthodox Church had objected, just as Orthodox churches from Russia to Greece had.

Patriarch Teoctist told us the Pope was wise to wait until the invitation came from both the church and the state.

"I visited the Pope the first time in 1984. The second time was in January 1989 on my way to India. The Romanian ambassador to Rome found out about it, came to the airport, and said I was not allowed to visit the Pope. I told the ambassador, 'You should take care of your diplomatic problems. These are church problems I have to take care of.'"

Teoctist slept that night as a guest of the Vatican.

"Even before 1989, we had very good relations. I was a member of the leadership for the Conference of European Churches, and we came together many times with the churches in Europe, including the Vatican. We are accustomed to their theology and their way of thinking."

Then, we asked, why didn't Teoctist agree to the Pope's visit before 1999?

"There was violence taking place against the Orthodox in certain parishes—you know, occupying the churches," he answered. "There was no opposition to the Pope's visit in principle. But we wanted to solve our own problems before the visit would take place. That wouldn't occur until the dialogue with the Greek Catholic Church here was set up."

In Teoctist's view, it was the Greek Catholics who resisted the start of a dialogue after the 1989 Revolution. Others say the Orthodox Church feared that a visit from the western pontiff would strengthen the Uniates' hand in any negotiations. But Teoctist told us he had always looked forward to a rendezvous with the Pope.

"We saw that welcoming the Pope here was a way of gaining something for the Church and for the country, because the country had been isolated."

The stalemate broke in 1999, when then-Prime Minister Vasile, a convert to Catholicism and a skillful politician, began working with then-President Constantinescu to cut a series of deals.

Courtesy of Bogdan Aurel Teleanu, Romanian Patriarchy

Pope John Paul II and Patriarch Teoctist celebrating together in Bucharest in 1999, the first visit of a Roman Catholic pope to an Orthodox country since the Great Schism in 1054

The Vatican agreed to encourage the Uniates to negotiate property issues with the Orthodox Church. The Pope agreed to visit only Bucharest, and not go to Transylvania, where the Greek Catholic Church is centered. And the Romanian government agreed to help build a new Orthodox cathedral in Bucharest.

Over three days in June 1999, the Pope wowed Romanians. Thousands packed the Catholic and Orthodox cathedrals to see him. At an open-air service, he hugged the Patriarch and invited him to visit Rome. Jim's language tutor Vivi marveled at the Pope's deft pronunciation of Romanian. Most important, Romanians, some of whom may have wondered if he was coming to undermine their Orthodox Church, felt his respect and brotherly love.

We asked the Patriarch how he viewed his people's reaction.

"*Foarte bine!*" was the way Teoctist summed it up for us. "Very good!

"The intelligentsia, the personalities from the cultural world, everyone looked at it favorably. The Romanian Academy courageously declared the Pope a member of the Academy. And that was because the visit was well prepared in advance.

"The results were more than good in all different aspects of life—in church life, in theological life, in social life. Everywhere I went after that—to Venezuela, the United States, Canada, Italy, Germany—I sensed it. Whatever we do in the church, we do it in the spirit of serving the unity of the Church of Christ. Disunity, even from the social or family point of view, is a sin, because it's the result of the devil's work. Unity is only Christ's work through the Holy Spirit. He created this unity through His incarnation. Taking our own image, he united the heavens with the earth. Therefore, whatever is done for brotherhood, for equilibrium, for unity, is done in the spirit that all may be one."

Within just a few years of his Romanian visit, the Pope preached in Armenia, Bulgaria, Ukraine, and Greece—all countries with Orthodox majorities.

Romania and Bulgaria joined NATO and, in 2007, the EU. Other Orthodox countries—Serbia and Macedonia—are in the queue to join both, and Ukraine and Georgia have asked to join as well. These are the political legacies of Pope John Paul II's leadership. He helped defuse a potential clash of civilizations.

But the legacy is not just political.

"Christ does not want us to be disunited, in conflict with each other," Patriarch Teoctist told us. "He wants us to be brothers. We as churches have to be an example for peoples."

Pope John Paul II could not have agreed more.

WELCOME TO ROMANIA

IF THE ORTHODOX CHURCH teaches the importance of relationships, the first baptism Sheilah attended in Romania underscored that lesson on several levels.

First came the rumors that our Kenyan-born butler, Julius Nzungi, and his Romanian wife, Jenica, were planning to name their new baby daughter after two of the women he worked for—Sheilah, the temporary mistress of the ambassador's residence, who is American, and Gabriella Sorgente, the manager of the residence, who is Italian.

The scuttlebutt was that the baby's name would be Sheila Gabriela. Sheilah was skeptical. For one thing, it seemed odd that Julius wouldn't have mentioned such a plan, especially because it might be construed as blatantly sycophantic. More important, it seemed like a heavy burden to lay the name Sheila on a Romanian kid. It's a perfectly fine Gaelic name, and has served Sheilah quite well (even though she's of German heritage, not Irish). But "sh" and "ei" are not found in the Romanian language, and the sounds of the syllables mean something else entirely: "She" would be spelled "şi" in Romanian, with a tail on the "s" to make the "sh" sound. That word means "and." "La" means "to."

Why would Julius and Jenica want to name their new daughter something that sounds like "And to"? It could be he just liked the sound of it, it could be (albeit less likely) he considered Sheilah a good role model for his daughter, or it could be he was thinking of the previous ambassador—wealthier than we—who had generously underwritten the private school tuition of Julius's older daughter Priscila. It could be that it never hurts to have a namesake relationship. Sheilah didn't ask, and Julius didn't say.

The Gabriela part made much more sense, because the only difference between the Italian version and the Romanian version is one "l."

So, it was only half a surprise when Julius presented Sheilah an invitation to the baptism of his daughter, Sheila Gabriela. It would take place in less than a week.

The ceremony unfolded in a small, dim Orthodox church. We should say "ceremonies," because two separate, unrelated families scheduled a baptism at the same time. Everything the priest did for and to Sheila Gabriela, he then did for or to the other infant. Both mothers looked a little tired, though dressed in their best. Both sets of godparents seemed excited, and took their responsibilities—holding candles, reciting prayers, and pronouncing names—quite seriously.

After many prayers and chants, the mothers and godmothers took their cue to disrobe the babies. With a flourish, the priest picked up tiny Sheila Gabriela, held her high, with one hand under her tiny tush, and totally plunged her in a huge basin of water. She didn't cry. He lifted her high, wet and naked, in this cold church, and prayed for what seemed like an hour but was probably half a minute. Then he again immersed her in the basin, prayed again, and handed her to her godmother. Never a peep or a squeal from Sheila Gabriela.

Turning to the other family, the priest held their naked daughter high, plunged her into the basin, and all hell broke loose. That baby yelled and screamed and splashed and struggled, and did all of that louder and harder the second time.

There was a brief lull in the service while mothers and godmothers dressed their infants in pristine baptismal dresses, and then there were more prayers and chants to wrap up the service.

After the service, on the porch of the church, Julius introduced Sheilah to the priest, who insisted on running to fetch an icon to give her as a gift. A few days later, she got a call from the priest about a cousin seeking a visa to the United States She explained that she couldn't help—an explanation that never seemed to make sense to Romanians, for whom connections make the world go round.

RESTING IN PEACE

ROMANIANS SEEM TO APPROACH funerals differently than Americans do. That's not to say that their sorrow is deeper—who can know that?—but they tend to express it more openly and more vociferously. At funerals, Romanians don't just weep—they wail and moan. This is not a time to keep a stiff upper lip.

While living in Bucharest, we attended the funerals of the family members of two of our friends—Vivi Palade lost her father in an accidental fall from a building, and our chef, Mihai Ghiţă, lost his beautiful fourteen-year-old daughter Cristina to cancer.

The Romanian funeral reaches into the neighborhood, both before and after the service. For Cristina Ghiţă's funeral, we and other mourners went to the family's apartment, where her body had been prepared. The coffin was carried down to the street and placed in a hearse, which inched toward the church, scores of friends following on foot for several blocks.

We had seen such sad processions often in Bucharest, but this was the first time we walked in one, so we felt firsthand the connection it gives to the grieving family. It's a tradition that has migrated from the country's villages into its towns and cities.

After the church service, mourners followed the hearse to the cemetery. At the graveside, the priest said more prayers. In Romania, there's a cemetery tradition of giving alms to the poor, with the expectation that they will pray for the soul of the departed, which is an invitation for beggars to make themselves available. At the cemeteries we visited, there was no shortage of mendicants willing to accept alms.

There's also a tradition of distributing to mourners and beggars a kind of porridge with nuts and dried fruit. Sheilah was told it symbolized the eternal feast the departed is hoped to be enjoying in heaven. That same kind of porridge is shared with friends on All Souls Day, which is celebrated on November 2.

Funerals are fairly expensive—not just the embalming, which is sometimes skipped in favor of a quick burial, but also the cemetery plot. And then there's the cost of the wake. Because the family of the deceased doesn't invite friends to a wake—they just come—the family has to be prepared with food and drink for anyone.

One of Sheilah's Romanian friends told her about her sister, who knew she was dying and begged to be buried in the ground, not cremated. So Sheilah's friend took on extra, funeral-related debt and required several years to pay it off. Another friend who had the option to escape Communism and work in the West told us that one of the reasons he stayed in Romania was to be sure that his older relatives—aunts and uncles—got a proper burial.

There's another aspect of funerals that you don't see in the United States, but is often evident in Romanian cities—round-the-clock funeral assistance. Yep, 24/7 mortuary services. If you need a mortician in the middle of the night, just call.

WE'RE NOT ON PLYMOUTH ROCK ANYMORE

IN ROMANIA'S CONTINUING QUEST to understand all things American, the nation's interest in Thanksgiving seemed to grow year by year. The third Thanksgiving we lived in Romania, we began and ended the day on live television, telling viewers how easy it is to cook a turkey—highly ironic, because neither of us is great shakes as a chef. Both TV anchors asked what the holiday means, what the menu is, why turkey, any special recipe for it, what other traditions, what about the Canadians, etc.

The morning show on Antena 1, which we did together, was a big production. It was hosted by a genial young musician named Horia Brenciu. Like most television anchors and interviewers in Romania, he does a lot of his own producing (arranging interviews, planning the questions, ordering the logistics, etc.) and speaks very good English, but, of course, needs to speak Romanian on TV for his audience. On cheerful, fast-paced shows where information is secondary to entertainment, by the time a question is asked and translated, the host is ready to move on after very brief answers given in English, which are then translated. The key concept is to smile a lot and not worry too much about what you say.

So after we'd talked about Pilgrims and Indians and family feasts for a few minutes, we assumed we were moving to a new topic when

Horia asked us for a typical Romanian name. We looked at each other, and came out with "Radu." Immediately, an attractive production assistant appeared on the set to hand Horia a large wicker basket.

Inside, with a big red bow around his scrawny neck and his legs tied together beneath him, was a live turkey. Horia bestowed on him the name we had chosen. We were pretty sure Radu had been sedated, but we still felt very sorry for him. The conversation continued, Horia was happy, and we smiled a lot while keeping an eye on Radu in his basket on the table in front of us. His wattle throbbed to his racing heartbeat. Then his eyes closed for a long time, and Sheilah thought, *This little bird is so scared, he's about to have a heart attack and die on national television.* This sequence, including her apprehension, repeated itself several times. Radu didn't make a peep.

Toward the end of the segment, when they played some music on a toy nearby, Radu perked up and tried to stand. This is a tough maneuver when your legs are tied, and he did not succeed. But at least we figured he was not on the verge of death.

As we said our on-air goodbyes, Sheilah thought they wouldn't *really* give Radu to us, but they did. What could we do but accept, and smile?

Out at the car, Jim's driver was all set to put the turkey-in-a-basket in the trunk, but Sheilah was sure he'd panic in the dark. So she held the basket on her lap as we drove over the potholes, and Radu alternated between wide-eyed observation and close-eyed stress. When we got home, he flapped about as we approached the door, so Sheilah set the basket down outside the kitchen door and went to find help.

When Sheilah encountered the unflappable butler Julius a few minutes later, she explained that we'd been given a turkey, to which Julius calmly replied, "Oh, the one by the door," as if there's a live turkey with a red bow in a basket at the door every day.

We untied Radu and he started strutting. He was really quite elegant. After he wandered around bleating for a few minutes, we carried him into the big garden and put out water and cornmeal, which he didn't touch all day. At nightfall, Mihai chopped up an apple—presumably, Radu was the only turkey in Romania with a professional chef preparing his food. Mihai wanted to clip his wings so he couldn't fly away (actually, turkeys can't fly). In any event, our friend Hermina argued he was too smart to leave such comfortable digs.

Radu spent most of the next afternoon burrowed inside a bush. We assumed this meant he was cold, but Hermina insisted that turkeys "in the village" live outside all winter. Of course, Hermina was also assuming that, at some point, we would give the word to Mihai to transform Radu into dinner, which we had no intention of doing.

But the next day, we weren't quite sure what to do with him. Sheilah e-mailed the head of GSO, the buildings section of the embassy, who put her troops to work constructing an impressive turkey residence to shield Radu from the cold. By the time it showed up the following day, though, Sheilah had concluded that Radu was not cut out to be a resident of the terrace. Though he seemed to ignore whatever food we laid out for him, he left multiple telltale reminders of his presence wherever he strutted. In short, he was making a mess.

We moved his splendid new residence down to the lower patio, a bit away from the house, but still near grass and the few roses that were still in bloom. Then we laid trails of dried corn leading to his new residence, so he'd get the idea. He didn't. He continued to hang around the terrace, making the occasional mournful noise. At times, he would look expectantly at the French doors.

On the third day, Sheilah figured it out: He wasn't looking *in* the window; he was looking *at* the window. Staring at his own reflection, he evidently thought it was another turkey. In other words, Radu was lonely! That clinched it. Sheilah phoned a friend whose Romanian cousin-in-law on the farm had taken her live turkey off her hands the previous Thanksgiving. That turkey, it was claimed, was still enjoying a happy retirement in the country.

"Amy," Sheilah said, "when can Cousin Doru come for Radu? No strings attached. I'm not insisting that he can't turn Radu into a protein source. I just don't want to know."

Another typical Thanksgiving in Romania.

AROUND BUCHAREST

CHAPTER 5
A DRIVE IN THE COUNTRY

WHERE ARE THE SPEED CAMERAS?

NORTH OF BUCHAREST, BUT close enough that weekend getaways are common, rise the Carpathian Alps. The drive north, across the flat plains punctuated by the lights of the oil refineries in Ploieşti, brings the mountains into view. The road starts ascending.

On one trip there with friends from the United States, the driver of our van was, to put it diplomatically, making good time. It clearly distressed one of our guests.

"We're going very fast," the guest said. "Can you ask him to slow down?"

"Don't worry," Jim replied. "He's an excellent driver, and everybody drives fast here."

Our friend was not comforted.

As our van moved from the flat land to the mountain road, we slowed a little, but the road also narrowed. In a few minutes, our friend pulled Jim over to the left window and said, "Look at that." He pointed to a car on the far side of the downhill lane. The car was vertical, not horizontal, sticking out the roof of a house.

Jim asked the driver to slow down.

ARE YOU A FOOTBALL FAN?

SHORTLY AFTER HE BECAME prime minister, Radu Vasile invited Jim for a Saturday morning at his villa on Lake Snagov. Accepting seemed like a great idea. He might or might not have something specific on his mind, but it was obviously a nice way for Jim to get to know him better.

To get there, you drive due north on the main road to the mountains and to Transylvania. Leaving Bucharest is like leaving any big city for the suburbs, and then for the countryside. One minute you're surrounded by high-rises and pedestrians, and then, suddenly, while traffic remains dense, the buildings become shorter and the foot traffic is mostly people walking to bus stops. Despite the boom in car ownership since the fall of Communism and the rise in living standards, working people still use public transportation most of the time in Bucharest. Buses and trams are always full and crowds line every bus stop.

Once you drive past Otopeni Airport, you know you're not in the city anymore. There's green on both sides of the road, mostly trees but also some open fields. There are occasional gas stations and cafés. The land is so flat and Romanians drive so fast that it takes only about thirty minutes to reach the turnoff to Snagov. Almost immediately, you're on a two-lane road, winding through several villages.

Lake Snagov is the summer mecca for Bucharest's elite. It's like the Chesapeake Bay for Washingtonians or Long Island's South Shore for New Yorkers. It's surrounded by large homes built before and during Communism—and even larger ones built since then. Sailboats compete with motorboats for the waterways. In the middle of Lake Snagov is the island with the Orthodox church where Vlad Țepeș, Dracula, is said to have been buried.

Jim reached the prime minister's villa about 10:30 a.m. It seemed anything but pretentious—low trees, and a driveway leading to a two-story house with a large yard. Once used by the Ceaușescus, it was now a state protocol house, available to the prime minister because of his office, much as Camp David is used by the president of the United States. A second house, looking like a new version of a large peasant farmhouse, was off to the right.

Vasile, wearing his signature black turtleneck, greeted Jim at the door.

Radu Vasile looks like Marcello Mastroiani—maybe not quite as tall, but dark, mustachioed, dashing if not traditionally handsome, and very sure of himself. Female students, we were told, made a special effort to enroll in his economic history classes when he was teaching at the Academy of Economic Studies, which is sort of Romania's Harvard Business School.

The real attraction might have been something else, one of his best male students told us. During the last decade of Communism, he used economic history as a way to acquaint students with market economics.

Vasile is energetic and sarcastic, with a wicked sense of humor. As academics go, he's informal in dress and speech. He speaks a more colloquial Romanian than, say, former president Constantinescu, or so we're told—we cannot judge ourselves. We *do* know he is fearless about speaking English, even though his English is not perfect. He and Jim never used a translator, and trust us, it wasn't because Jim was speaking Romanian or French. Not only is Vasile not troubled by his minor blunders in English, but his charm is such that they don't even seem to be mistakes, and they grow on you. Ten minutes into any conversation with him, one of us might be saying, "I must to make a phone call," or "I don't discuss about that issue."

When we first met Vasile, he was a heavy smoker. When he was preparing for his first ever trip to the United States in 1998, his biggest worry, he told Jim, was not the round of high-level meetings he'd have. He was confident of his ability to handle those. But how would he survive them without being allowed to smoke? "Does everyone in America really stand outside buildings to smoke?" he asked us one night at dinner. "That's what we see on TV." He may have pictured himself between meetings at the White House stepping out on the South Portico to take a few puffs. That changed when he had a heart attack in 2000—immediately, he swore off smoking.

As Jim entered Vasile's house, they exchanged kisses on both cheeks and walked to the living room, which was decorated in what we'd call Ceauşescu Realist Style—light-brown wooden walls, large chairs, and sofas with the thickest cushions Jim had ever seen. Sitting down in them was kind of fun.

Dominating the room was a TV set, though not a huge one. A European football game was on. Vasile offered Jim a drink, and they settled into their big cushions to watch the game.

After about ten or fifteen minutes, Jim's concentration began to wane. He wondered when Vasile would say something—about the game, the country, the weather, anything.

After a half hour, Jim took the opportunity to ask for another drink. This momentarily broke the monotony. Vasile got up, walked over to the bar, got Jim a refill—and then sat back down to watch the game.

It's not that Jim doesn't like soccer. He played it as a kid. Unlike baseball, it's fast-moving. But watching it is always more interesting when you know the teams and the language.

After about an hour, Jim decided to take matters into his own hands. He started asking the prime minister about current political issues. Talking politics with Vasile was always a joy because Vasile enjoyed doing so.

In contrast to President Constantinescu, who reminded Jim of Jimmy Carter, Vasile was more Lyndon Johnson—a backroom operator who put energy into figuring out what the other players wanted and what could result in a deal, but always with a plan in his head to bring big change to his country. He's not at all naïve about what that takes—he has a keen understanding that people don't do things for you because they want to help you, but because it benefits them. So, of course, Constantinescu and Vasile, products of the same political forces, drove each other crazy and weren't shy about making that clear, even to the U.S. ambassador.

Vasile didn't seem to mind Jim interrupting the game. He answered each question—and then went back to watching the game.

Over the next few hours, there were a few breaks in this routine. Vasile's son dropped in to say hello, but not to join them in watching the game. Jim refilled his drink a couple of times more. Vasile's wife Măriuca came by and there was brief discussion of lunch. But she did not join them to watch the game.

Finally, at about 2 p.m., they moved to the dining room for lunch with Vasile's wife and son. Mrs. Vasile had recently spent several weeks in Canada with Romanian friends who live there. One of her major impressions, or at least the one that made the biggest impression on Jim, was that Canadians routinely *schedule* visits with their friends, or at least they call ahead before dropping by someone's home. They don't just drop by without warning, as Romanians often do. Măriuca found such social planning not just odd, but cold.

At lunch, Vasile, now temporarily separated from the football match, spoke expansively about his political challenges. He had a game plan, and he was going to use his few years of maximum power to implement it. He wanted to shift Romania to a modern market economy, with business in private hands. Up to that point, the only significant privatizations had been the sale of apartments to their residents at nominal prices and the return of small farm plots to their original owners. Most consumer prices, other than energy, had been freed from government control the year before under his predecessor—action that caused a recession. But nearly all the major industrial firms—what Central Bank Governor Mugur Isărescu dismissively called the "white elephants"—were still owned by the government.

Jim had assumed that at some point Vasile would bid him a gracious goodbye. As much as he had enjoyed himself and felt as if he was doing his job, Jim was getting anxious. He had a late afternoon commitment back in Bucharest and it hadn't occurred to him that this visit would run through the afternoon.

To Jim's surprise, Vasile asked if he'd like to join him at a Romanian football game that night at a Bucharest stadium. And then Măriuca asked if he'd like to stay for dinner.

Ouch! On the one hand, the prime minister of Romania was asking him to spend more time with him. Obviously, he should say yes. That was his job. On the other hand, could he take any more silent viewing of European football? Vasile clearly did not think of TV football primarily as background noise for serious conversation or even chit-chat.

So Jim said, "It's a very kind invitation, but I have to be back in Bucharest for a meeting this afternoon."

"*Nici o problemă!* Just go to your meeting and come back," Vasile said. "We'll have dinner and then go to the game. It won't start until 8:30 p.m. or so."

Jim was trapped.

"That sounds wonderful," he responded.

When he returned to Snagov from Bucharest about 5:30 p.m., he found Vasile on the tennis court adjacent to a house down toward the lake. Dinner followed, and then, about 8 p.m., they were off to the game.

It was the first time Jim had ridden with a Romanian official. With the prime minister's police escort, they sped along the two-lane road from the villa to the stadium. Jim calculated that the ride would be his last chance of the day to learn more from Vasile. If he was glued to the TV football games, he no doubt would be entranced at live stadium events.

Word was that Vasile had once debated University of Maryland Professor Vladimir Tismăneanu on Romanian radio. Tismăneanu argued that, even with all the problems it generated, Ceaușescu's forced industrialization had, on balance, benefited Romania by modernizing its economy.

Jim told Vasile that made sense to him. Steel mills, oil refineries, and chemical plants were built and the workforce had been largely converted from peasant agriculture to industrial skills: engineering, which is today in great demand worldwide; and assembly, which has become a great competitive strength for Romania and the rest of Eastern Europe. The major modernization of the economy took place under Communism, not before and not after.

"No, no, no," Vasile replied. Western Europe industrialized during the same decades without Communism, he said, and is much richer today. Over-investing in heavy industry and under-investing in the rest of the economy, which Ceaușescu clearly did, couldn't possibly have been good for Romania.

Ever the economic historian, he was describing what they call "opportunity cost." If the same billions Ceaușescu spent trying to build six steel mills the size of the ones in Gary, Indiana had been invested in consumer products, financial services, and advanced technology, Romania would not be one of the poorest countries in Europe, Vasile contended.

Jim got his point. More than that, he was impressed with Vasile's intellectual intensity. Vasile was not going to try to change the economy to please the World Bank, the International Monetary Fund (IMF), the EU, and the United States. He had a vision he was going to fight for.

As we saw clearly throughout the rest of his eighteen months as prime minister, Vasile saw himself as a player in history. When things were going well, *and* when they weren't, Vasile felt as if he was making a historic impact on his country.

He forced the closing of Bancorex, the huge state bank that had run up billions of dollars in losses since 1989 because of sweetheart loans to well-connected ex-Securitate officers and others. He pushed through Romania's first major privatization—the sale of Romtelecom, the landline phone monopoly, to a consortium of the Greek phone company and GTE from the United States. He put then-transport minister and future president Traian Băsescu in charge of the World Bank's economic reform program. And, in the fall of 1999, he appointed a new, market-oriented board of Romania's central bank. Most of what the West calls economic reform, Vasile made happen in Romania. He did all this in the middle of the worst recession in Romania's recent history.

Arriving at the stadium, Vasile and Jim went up to a VIP booth, which was not that different from one you'd find in an older stadium in the United States. They sat down with about a dozen Romanian big shots, a few of whom Jim knew. Everyone was very friendly and cheerful.

All Romanian football teams are sponsored by one or another major institution—the railroad company, a branch of the military, etc.

The game had already started. There was a bit of small-talk in Romanian, but the guys were mostly watching the game.

As 9:30 p.m. approached, Jim's mind raced back to the morning spent watching football in silence. It wasn't much better in the stadium ten hours later. But this time, he wasn't alone—the box was filled with enthusiastic fans.

Jim probably could have slipped out unnoticed. He considered doing so, but it didn't seem very diplomatic. Still, mostly from boredom, he was getting sleepy. Snoozing in the prime minister's box probably wasn't a good idea, either.

So Jim just said to Vasile, "This has been a wonderful day. Many thanks, but I think I'll be going home."

That was fine with Vasile. He stayed for the rest of the game, while Jim headed down the stairs and home.

SHEILAH'S RENAULT MEETS ITS MAKER

TWO OBVIOUS PERKS OF being ambassador are the embassy car and the embassy driver. The ambassador is always on duty and constantly traveling the city and the country on business. Understandably, State Department rules are clear that, while the ambassador's family can ride in the car with him or use it for an official function, spouses are on their own for personal transportation.

But far from being thrilled to be a passenger, Jim was a stereotypical American male—fearful of separation from his own wheels. He spent a fair amount of energy wriggling out of being driven around.

Within days of arriving in Bucharest, he told the embassy staff that he wanted to drive himself as much as possible, as soon as possible. His security officer, a highly competent and motivated professional, was not impressed. After all, Jim didn't speak the language, he didn't know his way around town, and U.S.-Iraq tensions were high in the wake of stepped-up U.S. flights to enforce the Iraqi no-fly zone. Not a great time to have a U.S. government official wandering around a strange territory, unable to communicate, the security officer argued.

Jim bided his time. In February, United Nations Secretary General Kofi Anan went to Iraq, met with Saddam Hussein, and left telling reporters the talks had been constructive and helpful. That night, on CNN, Jim saw the White House spokesman say that tensions had cooled. The next morning, Jim called the security officer.

"Saddam Hussein says there's not going to be a war," he told her. "Kofi Anan says there's not going to be a war with Iraq. Bill Clinton says there's not going to be a war with Iraq. Can I start driving myself home at night on Friday?"

After consulting with her supervisors back in Washington, she agreed. For the next three years, Jim drove himself whenever possible.

Sheilah, on the other hand, would have been delighted to have someone drive her—not for the prestige of it, but the sheer practicality. She has no sense of direction. She gets lost going around the block—and that's in cities with definable square blocks. Throw in meandering alleys, cobblestones, and signs posted in evolved Latin, and it was not a promising travel environment for her.

Still, she knew she'd need to get around, so as soon as she decided to move to Romania, she put out feelers about purchasing a used car. Suggestions filtered in for high-end European cars with sun roofs and low mileage; it was hard to convey that Mrs. Ambassador was looking for a really cheap used car, because it didn't match what people expected Mrs. Ambassador to drive. Eventually, she got word that the director of the Peace Corps contingent in Romania, who would be leaving for another post in a few months, was interested in selling his Renault.

"It's a stick shift," he said.

"No problem," she said, "I like sticks."

He also warned her that the gas gauge didn't work. "No problem," she said to herself. "I can just keep track of how many liters I put in."

"It's a really old car," he told her. "1987."

"No problem," she said. "My car at home is a 1987. More important is the number of miles on it. Is this odometer on its first time around?"

"I have no idea," he said. "But I want you to be comfortable with it. Have a mechanic check it out. By the way, the Renault speaks German."

What a symbol of how the EU and NATO have brought six decades of peace between France and Germany!

It wasn't until a few months before we were to return home that Sheilah realized her education in Romanian red tape had barely begun. She started to spread the word that she was willing to sell—cheap—this great Renault that had a few dents but was running well. No takers. She put notices on bulletin boards, and in the embassy newsletter, and mentioned it to friends. Soon, she learned that, because the Renault had spent its entire time in Romania in the possession of diplomats, no one had ever been required to pay the value-added tax (VAT) on its sales price. Anyone other than a diplomat who bought it now would owe the entire *original* VAT, which was far more than the sedan's depreciated value.

This greatly reduced the car's potential market. Notices in other embassy newsletters produced no interested parties. As our departure date grew closer, Sheilah explored the idea of donating the car to a charity. Before leaving the country, she returned its diplomatic license plates to the embassy and left the car with a friend who tried to find it a home. Everyone has heard the tales of nonprofits set up in the early nineties for the express purpose of acquiring cars for their founders. So the Romanian rules are very strict about charities accepting donated cars without paying taxes on them.

Three months later, *after* we left Romania, the cold truth stared at Sheilah: She could not even *give* this car away without paying the VAT. All she could do was destroy it. Peppy and articulate as it was, the Renault was headed for the crusher. Various Romanian friends clucked their tongues and whispered that perhaps the problem could be solved with a gift or gratuity to this or that official. But Sheilah had no wish to go that route, and no idea how to pull it off even if she did.

On her next visit to Romania, she asked friends to find out what she would have to do to legally un-register the car. The process involved signing some papers, getting the appropriate stamps, and borrowing the license plates back from the embassy. Early one morning, Gabriella

Sorgente, the warm and well-organized manager of the ambassador's residence, joined her as they rendezvoused with a young man in the scrap metal trade. He drove his own car, and they followed in the Renault, out of the city, down country lanes, over the railroad tracks, and then, with a sharp left, into a bustling junkyard.

Sheilah's Renault receiving its last rites

The German-speaking Renault was by far the classiest car in sight, though that was hardly a high standard. Two men lounging near the heaps struck up a conversation with our young escort, who explained why Sheilah was junking this obviously functional sedan. There was brief flurry of interest, as if the two were brainstorming how they could conquer the VAT problem that had defeated her. But then they went back to lounging. She drove the car onto the metal platform of a huge scale. Then, she and Gabriella climbed into the trailer that functioned as the junkyard office. A cheerful brunette who had met Sheilah and Jim at a wedding party (to which they had been invited on the spot) took her car papers, affixed another stamp, and paid her the calculated value of the Renault's metal. Forty dollars in Romanian lei—that's what her trusty traveling companion had come to.

Inasmuch as junkyard workers had already pulled the seats out of the Renault, it was all over but the crushing, which she didn't want to see. Gabriella snapped one last picture of the car, and they left.

How the Boy Scouts survived Communism

Not quite twenty miles south of the capital, on the way to the Danube Delta, lies a patch of what's left of the dense forest that used to cover southern Wallachia. This was Romania's forest primeval, offering concealment to medieval soldiers, and a hideout for highwaymen and other outlaws. It was in this forest in 1461 that Vlad the Impaler defeated the Ottoman forces who had come to depose him, and in the Romanian tradition he founded a monastery there. As Romania became part of Europe's breadbasket in the nineteenth century, millions of trees were felled to clear land for farms, and early in the twentieth century, Romania's Boy Scouts took on a project to plant new trees in the Comana nature park, to keep it going.

Nicolae Decuseară was nine years old when he became a Boy Scout. That was in 1928—right in the middle of what he called the glory days of scouting in Romania.

Decuseară still has a picture of the uniform made for him by his grandfather. His father was also a scout. Decuseară remembers memorizing the Boy Scout creed, and learning to pitch a tent and take care of himself in the woods. When he was twelve, he rode his bicycle from his home in Bucharest to Sibiu, a distance of about 170 miles, for the National Boy Scout Jamboree, which included the Scouts' own brass band.

Crown Prince Michael, just a year younger than Decuseară, was a scout himself. The titular commandant of Romania's Scouts, Michael joined in some of their hikes and jamborees. In the glory years between 1913 and 1937, Decuseară said, Romania had one hundred thousand scouts, boys and girls combined.

All that changed when Decuseară was a teenager. In 1937, King

Carol II replaced scouting with his own youth movement. When Communism came, all alternative youth programs except its own Pioneers were abolished.

As Decuseară tells it, Romania's new powerbrokers—many of whom had not grown up in Romania—deeply distrusted scouting for two reasons: because it was an international network headquartered in London, it was perceived as capitalist; and even more important, Decuseară says, because scouts professed a belief in God.

At age eighty, he cited the Scout Creed he memorized as a kid:

"'The boy scout always keeps his word.' If only this article would be respected in our country, we would be beside friends. It is not followed, but the Boy Scouts do follow it!" he asserted. Even in translation, Sheilah could hear the fierce pride in his voice. "The second article is to put the interests of the country and the community before himself. The last article is that the boy scout does his best to do a really good deed every day. The permanent love for the one next to you is profoundly Christian, and a very important article: Boy scouts believe in God."

As Sheilah spoke with him six decades after scouting was suppressed, Decuseară was still exasperated that the Communists saw all that as subversive—to him, it was so clear that these were "not some frivolous virtues, but really, strictly necessary so that the person would be useful to the society."

Decuseară's grandfather, a village teacher, had been a leader among the scouts who worked as sanitarians during World War I, transporting the wounded, helping turn around the railroad cars that brought troops to the front, working the telegraph system, and cutting wood in the forest for fuel. After World War I, a statue in honor of these scouts was erected in the town of Tecuci in Moldavia. Under Communism in the 1950s, the statue was pulled down.

Decuseară described the decree against scouting as a secret letter from a government minister in 1944. Activities were limited to just a few trips, and soon even those stopped.

But a few hundred scouts across the country, in what Decuseară called a "spontaneous" action, decided to keep meeting. They called themselves "former" scouts.

"We were just small groups. We went to the mountains on trips. We didn't wear uniforms, and we wouldn't sing any Boy Scout songs, even though they had some really wonderful songs. Our goal was to keep the flame of Boy Scouts alive.

"Or, we would go to church and commemorate the boy scouts who had died during the war, the First World War. When the Communists would ask, 'Why are you going to honor the memory of these guys?' we would say, 'They were the heroes of Romania.'"

The "former scouts" put notices of their meetings in newspapers, and allowed anyone to come. So they expected to be infiltrated by members of the Securitate, and they were.

"We had our own antennae," Decuseară told Sheilah. Sometimes, they called their gatherings a party, and held them at the home of Professor Alexandru Daia, an Eagle Scout who was the Scouts' under-ground leader during the Communist years. They put wine on the table and some of the scouts pretended to be drunk, to throw off sus-picion. Decuseară said they never recited the scout pledge, and they never talked politics.

Some tried to keep up personal contacts they had with scouts in Communist countries like Poland, where scouting remained legal. A few new "former scouts" were added over the years, vouched for by parents or relatives.

"The important thing is that, in this way, there were five hundred boy scouts between forty and sixty years old [when Communism ended in 1989]. Daia was almost ninety then. He died in 1993— two years after petitioning to make Boy Scouts legal again."

Decuseară's career during Communism was as a hydro engineer, working on the huge Iron Gates generating plants that supplied much of Romania's electricity. Even with the suspicions of the Securitate, he said, he did not believe he was held back by his underground activity as a scout. On the contrary:

"I was successful in my career because I applied the Boy Scout law. I was not a member of the Communist Party, but I was the leader of one of the biggest construction sites in the country—because the government knew that with Decuseară on the job, the work would get done."

You can count on a boy scout, even if you don't know he's a scout.

Decuseară is proud of the Iron Gates, and his role in building them. The Russians were smart about hydroelectric power. But beyond hydro, Decuseară said he and other engineers and technical experts believed the system they worked in wasn't creating valuable technologies—it was stealing what it could from capitalist companies. During all those decades, Decuseară said he did not expect the Communist system to last.

The former scouts played no role in the 1989 Revolution, Decuseară said. "Our principle was that everybody would do what their heart would tell them to do."

But Decuseară and his peers believed scouting had a big role to play in what he called the "hour of moral decay" that confronted Romania after 1989.

"It's the wildest part of capitalism," he explained. "The principle of the young people is to do everything for their own benefit. It's an exaggeration of selfishness. We are exactly the opposite. We always believe that honorable people will keep their word and that they will put their country's interests before their own. They would be the ones to rebuild the moral part of this country. And we believe strongly that the crises—economic, financial, technological, political, and social— have a main reason, a main cause, that has to do with morality."

As soon as he could after the Revolution, Professor Daia petitioned to have scouting made legal again. Young scouts and old met at the old elementary school in Bucharest called "The Stork's Nest." They resumed camping trips and planting trees. Within a decade, there were ten thousand scouts in Romania, fifty-three percent of them girls.

And connections with scouts from other countries were eagerly made. We got our first tip about the underground history of Boy

Scouts in Romania when a group of American and Romanian scouts camped out on the grounds of the ambassador's residence. The overnight stay had been organized by Carolyn Johnson, an American Foreign Service officer. When she wasn't busy as the embassy's energetic political counselor, she was a mother of two boys, and a scout leader.

Today's Boy (and Girl) Scouts in Romania

On May 21, 1996 in Tecuci, Moldavia, the Scouts dedicated a new statue to scouts who died in the World Wars.

"The Boy Scouts gathered, kilo by kilo, the bronze and copper to build the statue again," Decuseară told Sheilah. "We wanted to teach our scouts to be economic in every way, and not to just throw their money—or any resource—around."

Planting trees in the Comana Forest teaches the same lesson.

"Every year, we gather to put trees in the soil. This year, we just planted the forty-seventh hectare in the forest. We show our boys the Comana Forest, where some oaks are now seventy years old. And we say, 'I planted this when I was nine.'"

Houses of aluminum foil

To most foreigners, Teleorman is one of the most obscure counties in Romania, even though it's within an hour of Bucharest. It's a little like suburban New Jersey for New Yorkers, or Delaware for Washingtonians. You know it exists, but you never go there; you only pass through it. And that was our experience.

It's a rich agricultural area, and we visited once or twice with local farmers and students. But mostly, we passed through on the way to Craiova or to the Danube.

On one of those trips, we suddenly understood why so many Romanians see *Roma* (gypsies) not as an oppressed underclass, as do so many foreigners (including us), but rather as an exotic, but rich, subculture.

On the way back from town meetings in Oltenia, we passed through a small town. The main street was dominated by huge houses, outfitted with baroque features glistening in silver. It was what Disney World would look like if all the fairy tale buildings were decorated with aluminum foil. Perhaps they just used silver paint.

"What is this?" Jim asked our Romanian traveling companions.

"It is a Roma village," we were told. Many people live in each house. But they are not poor.

Most Roma don't live in such style. Most live in the outskirts of cities in neighborhoods without paved roads or decent plumbing. Too few of their children go to school, and too many fall into crime. But you wouldn't have known that driving through the town.

Christmas in the Carpathian Alps

We decided to spend our first Romanian Christmas in the mountains.

We were still learning how and why Romania had remained a deeply religious nation despite four decades of Communism.

The Communist Party frowned on attending church, but many did so anyway. Roda Tiniş, the U.S. embassy's near omniscient expert on telecom, told Jim about attending secret Greek Catholic services as a child in Transylvania. Even the dictator Nicolae Ceauşescu, whose brand of nationalism made life harder in Romania than it was anywhere else in Eastern Europe, tolerated party members taking part in church weddings, burials, and baptisms. He himself attended the Orthodox funeral of his father in 1972 at the village church of Scorniceşti. Of course, after his own departure from life in December 1989, even more people began to show up at church.

So Romanians never forgot how to celebrate Christmas. Even during Communism, in big towns and small villages, Moş Crăciun (Old Man Christmas) made the rounds on Christmas Eve, bringing gifts for boys and girls who had been good, and sticks or stones for the naughty.

Romanians love Christmas trees. But there's no specialized tree industry to breed the dense branches and perfect shapes Americans expect. Even city dwellers often go to the country to cut their own trees—and are happy to come back with a scraggly evergreen even Charlie Brown might disdain.

Christmas in Romania is not as commercial as in the United States, and the shopping season doesn't last two months. Gifts are modest and often homemade.

Decorations and shopping don't start in earnest until a week or so before Christmas, about the same time people start gathering for parties. These parties are remarkable for the food—*sarmale* (little cabbage rolls) and wonderful sweets—and for the Christmas music, from haunting lullabies to foot-stomping jigs. They add to the beauty of the repertoire by organizing beautiful voices—young men studying to be Orthodox priests fan out in small groups to share their talents with revelers, and collect tips for doing so.

Experiencing all this for the first time was wonderful—even more so as our extended family assembled for Christmas in Transylvania. The Carpathian Alps are tall and rugged. People come from everywhere in Europe to ski here, attracted by the beauty of Switzerland at Eastern European prices.

There was just one tiny complication: For the first and only time during our stay in Romania, the U.S. ambassador was being shadowed by bodyguards.

Before that, Jim mostly tramped around Romania with no bodyguards or security of any kind. It fit his style, and frankly, as popular as the United States is among Romanians, it didn't require any special courage. Besides, it seemed to confirm what Romanians like best about Americans, as well as confirming something positive about their own country.

But at this particular time, a threat had been heard somewhere in the region, so the embassy and the Romanian government agreed it would be prudent to set up a security detail. It involved a lieutenant who rode in the embassy car with Jim and his driver, plus a team of three officers in a chase four-by-four with a revolving blue light on its roof. The primary inconvenience of this set-up was that Jim had to plan his movements at least a quarter-hour in advance, to give his security team time to get into place. Even that posed no big problem, and they were all nice guys with good senses of humor. We enjoyed their company.

This step-up in security happened to take place just as Sheilah was moving to Romania with her eighty-nine-year-old mother, and as Sheilah's brother, his wife, Jim's sister, and five nieces and nephews from both sides of the family were visiting for the Christmas holidays. Because they hadn't spent enough time in Romania to have any expectations on the matter, we tried to act as if it were perfectly normal for Jim to be trailed by four big guys with guns of various calibers. Sheilah's nieces and nephews thought it was cool.

A few days before the two of us could leave, our families went up to Sinaia, a gingerbread resort in the mountains which had been the summer resort of Romania's kings. By the time we joined them, Sheilah's brother Ken had heard about a village where you could take torch-lit sled rides into the hills to dine at a quaint restaurant.

Sounded great! After a day of snowy alpine vistas and historic castles, the family convened at twilight. As Jim's security team eyed the torches a little nervously, the family arranged itself five each on two sleds. These were not the sleighs you see in a Currier and Ives print. These were more like rough benches positioned lengthwise along runners. You straddled the bench, arranged a woolen blanket around your lap and legs, and held on to the person in front of you, unless you were the front rider, in which case you tried to find a grip on the bench so you wouldn't be tempted to grab the horse's tail.

It turned out the security officers were not the only ones nervous about the torches. One of the horses apparently took a dislike to the idea of flames on a stick, and made a sharp U-turn to head back to the stable. But long sleds on runners can't make U-turns. Instead, they flip over and dump their riders into the snow. That's what happened to half our family, with the added excitement of sparks flying in all directions. Our nephew Christopher still has scars on his scalp, and singe-holes in his sweater, from the turnover.

Eventually, the five of us who had *not* been upended persuaded the other five they were not as bruised, burned, and battered as they felt, and the hostlers found a more stable sled for them. We dispensed with the torches and set out.

It was a breathtaking experience to forever hold in our hearts: snow falling upon deep snow . . . lights twinkling in the windows of tiny houses we passed . . . the steady rhythm of sleigh bells beating against the horses' chests . . . immense fir trees staring down on us . . . echoes of our own laughter and caroling . . . and, casting an eerie glow over it all, the revolving blue light of our security SUV.

Skiing under Communism

For Americans, particularly those of us who had not been to Romania before 1989, it's normal to ask what life was like under Communism. Our mental pictures of Romania in that era are so different from our own experience in the United States that our curiosity is understandable. When we asked Romanians this question, we generally expected to hear about the problems—the climate of fear, the long lines to buy food, the energy and lighting blackouts. We heard a lot of that, from both Romanians and Americans who had been there in the last years of the Ceauşescus.

That's why Valeriu Stoica and his wife got our attention one day at lunch. Jim asked them what it was like for them personally before 1989. What were some of the biggest changes for them after Communism fell?

"We get to ski a lot less now," was Valeriu's immediate reply. He smiled and added, "We really like to ski."

Both Valeriu and Cristiana are lawyers. They are a power couple: When we met them, he was Romania's justice minister and she had a private practice. They were no apologists for Communism. He was the number two leader of the PNL, one of the most anti-Communist parties in Romania. But before 1989, they had been academics. And like many college-educated Romanians during those years, they had avoided politics by burrowing into the academy.

For those like the Stoicas who could do that, the Communist years were not all bad. They lived in Bucharest and worked at the university. The Carpathian Alps were within easy reach.

"We could go skiing because we had the time," she said. "We had more time for everything, particularly our families. Now, we're working much harder."

Under Communism, there was no way for most people to turn time into money. So they took time for their families, for reading, for friendships. They weren't working twelve-hour days or commuting for months to Italy, Spain, or London to make money to send back to their families, as so many Romanians do now. So they were with their families, their parents, and their children—a lot. It was the upside of a low-productivity economy.

"Now I'm putting a lot of time into politics," Valeriu said. "In a market economy and a democracy, we're busier. Not much time for skiing."

ROMANIAN BORDERS 1859

CHAPTER 6
THE GOOD KING

THE KING AND QUEEN WOULD BE PLEASED TO COME TO LUNCH

ROMANIA'S CARPATHIAN ALPS INVITE comparisons to Switzerland's, so we shouldn't have been surprised when, a bit farther up the mountain, enfolded in the tall fir trees above Sinaia, we encountered a Bavarian *schloss* with fairy-tale turrets and tall spires.

Peleş (PEL-esh) Castle and its surroundings are breathtaking. Its exterior is built in grand German neo-Renaissance style. Inside, we wandered through some of its 160 gloriously diverse—and, let's be frank, occasionally over-the-top—rooms. There's the impressive armory on the ground floor, stuffed with suits of armor, small canons, swords, and early firearms. That's just a prelude to a series of reception rooms, dining chambers, halls, studies, and nooks and crannies adorned in styles ranging from Gothic and Florentine to German Renaissance and Turkish, and many in-between. Nothing is too much—we saw whole rooms of furniture in deepest carved ebony, ceilings in tooled leather, and walls covered in mirrors or mother-of-pearl, walnut, and oak.

Peleş, the name of the small river that runs nearby, is an archaic word that used to mean *tassel* or *fringe*. For the last century and a half, though, the word has represented, in broad brush, the colorful characters, connections, and idiosyncrasies of Romania's royal family. The prince who started this monarchy back in the nineteenth century began building the summer palace when he had been on the job for just nine years.

We arrived in southeast Europe more than a half century after Romania's king had been banished. But that's not to say Romania had no king. Although Michael of Romania lived in exile during Communism and some years after, the connection between him and many of his former subjects was never broken. Even before we knew the exciting story of his life—on the throne at age five, deposed three years

115

later, back on the throne when he was barely nineteen, a kind of war hero at age twenty-two, and forced into exile at gunpoint three years after that—Sheilah was enchanted by the oil portrait of the tall, handsome prince hanging in the royal compound at Peleş. In that picture, there's a boyish crinkle at the edges of his eyes that she found hard to forget.

We met King Michael a few months later. He and Queen Anne were in Romania for events marking the tenth anniversary of the 1989 Revolution. We invited them and their oldest daughter, Princess Margareta, to lunch at the ambassador's residence. More than a half century after that portrait at Peleş had been painted, we had no trouble recognizing the boyish glance, or the friendly crinkle around the eyes.

At lunch at the Ambassador's Residence, Prince Radu (the King's son-in-law), Princess Margareta, Jim, King Michael, Queen Anne, and Sheilah

Just past his seventy-eighth birthday, the king was still tall and erect. He had grown hard of hearing, and that may be why he seemed to regard the world as a bit of puzzle—he looked around intently, as if something didn't quite make sense but would soon. He didn't speak much, and when he did, he spoke very softly and not very distinctly.

Straining to listen, we realized that an only child raised to be a king grew up with people listening hard to him. He didn't have to speak up to get attention.

His wife Anne, a princess of the royal family of Bourbon-Palma, carried the conversation. She was as energetic and vivacious as he was reserved. They have five daughters who never had a chance to see Romania until they were adults, after Communism fell in 1989.

WANT AD FOR A MONARCH

HOW DOES ROMANIA EVEN come to have a king? It's an improbable story.

Americans are so steeped in a national narrative that involves getting rid of a king, it's hard for us to comprehend why Romanians went out looking for one in 1866. One important factor to understand is that, after centuries of wars and occupations, Romania in the mid-nineteenth century was developing a national consciousness. Just a few years before, in 1859, leaders found a way around the pressure that Russia and the Ottoman Turks were exerting in order to keep Romania fragmented: The assemblies of Wallachia, in southern Romania, and Moldavia, in the east, threw their support behind the same leader, Alexandru Ioan Cuza. That effectively united the area along the Danube River, which is a big part of the country. (In the west, the other big component of what makes up Romania today, Transylvania, was still part of Hungary.)

Cuza and his allies made some big changes, including sweeping land reforms aimed at abolishing serfdom and nationalizing vast lands held by the Orthodox Church. The Agrarian Law of 1864 was meant to make each peasant the owner of his own plot of land. But that was not what the wealthy landowners had in mind. They forced Cuza to abdicate in 1866.

That's when the Romanian power structure looked to the West for a leader—someone who could bring stability and connections. The first offer went to Philippe Sommes, the Count of Flanders, brother of King Leopold II of Belgium. He turned it down. So did a second prince. Third choice was twenty-seven-year-old Prince Karl of Hohen-zollern-Sigmaringen, a Prussian cousin of Kaiser Wilhelm I. The Catholic prince knew little about Romania, but he agreed to be its king. To accept, he had to sneak across Austria and enter Romania incognito. In the plebiscite that set up his throne, nearly all of 686,193 votes cast were in his favor.

The Romanian elites expected that a monarch of foreign origin could rise above factionalism and be less interested in acquiring personal wealth than one of their own. By most accounts, King Carol I delivered. He was a sober, diligent, and industrious monarch. He brought German managerial skills to reorganizing the Romanian army. When the Romanians and the Russians confronted the Ottoman Turks at Plevna, Bulgaria in 1877, Carol led their combined armies to victory, essentially pushing the Turks out of the Balkans. The Treaty of Berlin the next year confirmed Romania as the second independent nation-state in the eastern half of Europe, after Greece.

Michael, whose perpetual calm is almost surreal, grew animated in telling us about his great-great-uncle's battlefield exploits 125 years earlier: "He won our war of independence in Bulgaria, beating the Turks. Yes, the Turks capitulated to Carol the First!"

Near the end of Carol I's nearly half-century reign, Romania was enjoying much faster economic growth than most of Western Europe. In the decade before World War I, Romania was starting to export large quantities of oil, and was one of the world's biggest exporters of wheat and corn.

The growing economy exacerbated inequalities. A middle class was starting to form, but four out of five Romanians were peasants. Most could not read or write, and while they might have title to the land they worked, they were required to pay dues or rent on it. By the beginning of the twentieth century, most were paying twice as much rent as their parents had thirty years earlier, and for many, the rent had risen three- or five-fold. In the spring of 1907, the aggrieved peasants erupted in a violent rebellion. It started in the east, in Moldavia, and spread south to Wallachia. By the time the state regained control, thousands had been killed.

Carol I spent the last two years of his life debating whether to enter World War I. His family connections to Germany made him reluctant, but Romania had formed a secret alliance with the Central Powers (Germany, Austria-Hungary, and Italy) twenty years earlier. Until Carol's death on October 10, 1914, Romania maintained an armed neutrality. That was to end with the next king.

Carol died without a son. He and his eccentric wife, Elisabeth Pauline Ottilie Luise zu Wied, who was born a German princess, had just one daughter, Little Maria, who died of scarlet fever at age four. For the rest of her life, Queen Elisabeth of Romania dressed in white mourning, meaning diaphanous dresses with veils and tiaras, when she wasn't swathed in some traditional Romanian folk costume.

Queen Elisabeth comes down to us through the decades as a bit of a ditz. There's a story of her waving her embroidered handkerchief at a herd of cows—she was so nearsighted, she had mistaken them for a cluster of subjects by the side of the road. But Queen Elisabeth was a certified celebrity in her own right, as an author widely published under the name Carmen Sylva. In addition to emotive poems, she wrote short stories and nursery rhymes, some based on Romanian legends. She founded social support programs, organized orphanages, and established schools for the blind.

After Carol died, his nephew Ferdinand, another German prince imported to the Balkans and the younger son of Carol's brother Leopold, mounted Romania's throne. Ferdinand brought Romania into the war on the side of the Allies in 1916. Up to that point, Ferdinand's major claim to international fame was having married (in 1892) the beautiful and charming Marie Alexandra Victoria.

Marie of Romania was an international celebrity. On her father's side, she was the granddaughter of Queen Victoria; on her mother's side, she was the granddaughter of the Russian tsar.

She was enormously popular, despite her extravagances. A biographer wrote that she showed up in Paris as one of Romania's delegates to the 1919 peace talks after World War I with sixty gowns, thirty-one coats, twenty-two furs, twenty-nine hats, and eighty-three pairs of shoes. She considered her glamorous image to be part of her negotiating strategy, and it proved successful. She persuaded French Prime Minister Georges Clemenceau and the other powerbrokers to take Transylvania from Hungary and give it to Romania. Romania came out of the Paris parlay with its territory and its population more than doubled—it had acquired not only Transylvania, but Bucovina to the north, Basarabia to the east, and southern Dobrogea to the south.

Not every provision of the 1920 Treaty of Trianon is Marie's handiwork. But nearly one out of six Romanians had died during World War I, and those still living were happy to praise her for this new Greater Romania.

Two notes here about that royal summer palace in Sinaia:

1.) Until Marie worked her magic at the Paris peace talks in 1919, the royal summer retreat was almost an outpost. Sinaia is just twenty-three miles from Braşov, the edge of Transylvania and what was then the frontier with Hungary. It took serious planning to visit in those days—King Carol used to take a huge entourage, including drivers, cooks, maids, and government aides, for a month at a time.

2.) During most of the decades of history we've just galloped through, Peleş Castle was still under construction. Carol began the work in 1875, nine years after he came to Romania. Parts of it were finished during the nineteenth century. But about four hundred craftsmen continued to labor on its grandiose rooms, finally finishing mere months before King Carol I died in 1914. Romanians are proud that it was the first castle in Europe to have central heating and electricity.

As princess, Marie did not get on very well with her in-laws, and could not stand Peleş Castle. So, in 1899, her father-in-law generously ordered up another summer castle for Ferdinand and Marie, just a few hundred yards up the mountain. That summer retreat, called Pelişor (Little Peleş), was built in a mock German medieval style, and Marie decorated the interior in Art Nouveau pastels.

Ferdinand and Marie had six children—the first Hohenzollerns to be born on Romanian soil. The eldest was named Carol after his great-uncle, and could not have differed more in temperament. He was headstrong, selfish, and sexually adventurous, which earned him the nickname "The Bad Boy of the Balkans." Three times he renounced his rights to the throne; twice he changed his mind.

At age twenty-four, Carol II deserted his military unit to elope with a Romanian woman, Ioana "Zizi" Lambrino. The Romanian Supreme Court voided the marriage, but he fathered a son, and controversies over the annulment and the child would continue to swirl into the next century, long after Carol, Zizi, and even their son Mircea had left this earth.

Carol returned to Romania and, two years later, tried to make a go of this monarchy business by marrying a thoroughly appropriate bride, Princess Helen, daughter of the exiled king of Greece. They had a son in 1921, and named him Mihai, in honor of Mihai Viteazul, "Michael the Brave," the seventeenth-century prince who united much of what is now Romania. Almost immediately, Carol started an affair with a promiscuous Jewish divorcee, Elena Lupescu. He eloped to Paris with her in 1923, again renouncing the throne.

CROWN PRINCE PROMOTED, DEMOTED, PROMOTED AGAIN

THEN CAME THE KICKER in the melodrama of Carol II's personal life. He'd positioned his two-year-old son Michael as next in line to become king. Sure enough, when King Ferdinand died of cancer in 1927, his grandson Michael, a five year old with chubby cheeks, charming dimples, and a bewildered smile, was crowned king. He asked his mother, Helen of Greece, why people were calling him "Your majesty." She told him, "It's just another nickname, darling."

The boy king relied heavily on his mother. Actually wielding power was a regency composed of the patriarch of the Romanian Orthodox Church, the chief justice of the highest court, and Michael's uncle Nicholas, another prince with an eye for fast women.

Queen Helen's protective attitude toward her son became a wedge between him and his grandmother, Queen Marie. In 1930, Queen Marie went to the country rather than celebrate Independence Day in the capital, writing in her diary, "I had no heart to drive through the streets beside a fat, overeducated, unresponsive little boy who . . . is almost . . . a stranger."

Queen Marie was joyful when, less than one month later, Carol II returned to Romania to reclaim the throne. Romania, like all other nations, was struggling with the economic crisis of the Great Depression, and various factions agitated for a stronger monarchy than the dysfunctional regency, so nine-year-old Michael was demoted to crown prince. But much more crushing to Michael is what happened to his mother Helen: Carol removed the crown prince from his mother's care, isolated Helen from the rest of the royal family, spied on her, and eventually sent her into exile. Michael's Aunt Ileana (who ended her life as abbess of an Orthodox convent she founded in Pennsylvania) would later quote Michael as saying, "When I needed a father, I had a mother. When I had a father, I needed a mother."

We spoke with King Michael at his home in Versoix, Switzerland, in 2003. He reminisced about the education his father organized for him.

"He made a special school for me—it started with about twelve boys, on the grounds of the palace," the king recalled. "And each boy was from a different social level. One was the son of a simple peasant, another was the son of an automotive mechanic, another was the son of an intellectual [a lawyer], and another was the son of an industrialist. Twelve different levels, and from different parts of the country—it put me in very close contact with the various social levels, in addition to the various parts, of the country."

He told us about the field trips the boys would take each summer, to different regions of Romania, and the history he learned during those trips.

"Many were living in quite prosperous conditions," Michael recalled, "because our standard of living in 1938-39 was the same as France and Belgium. The peasants themselves were fairly rich. They had their land, and produced quite a lot. We were part of the granary of Europe at that time."

Romania's economy may have been doing well, but its society was being torn apart. A fascist movement called the League of the Archangel Michael was gaining strength. The violent core of that movement, called the Iron Guard, blamed Jews for many of Romania's ills. At first, King Carol II tolerated the League and even the Iron Guard in their attacks on Jews and their murders of political figures during the early thirties. But when he found himself unable to control the politics, Carol II declared a royal dictatorship in February 1938, dissolving all political parties but one. The following year, he clamped down on the Iron Guard and had its leaders arrested. After they were sentenced to prison terms, he had them killed. In retaliation, the Iron Guard murdered his prime minister, and Carol responded by murdering 252 more members of the Iron Guard and stringing their corpses up in public squares.

Romania's political turmoil intensified as Hitler marched through Europe. France, Romania's strongest Western ally, fell to the Nazis in May 1940. In June, a non-aggression pact, which Hitler had worked out with Stalin the year before, took away most of the territory of Greater Romania that Queen Marie had won after World War I. The USSR annexed the eastern and northeastern parts of Romania—northern Bucovina and Basarabia, which was to become the Soviet Republic of Moldova. The southeast tip of Romania, Southern Dobrogea, went back to Bulgaria. Most painful of all, Hitler and Mussolini forced Carol to turn over northern Transylvania to Hungary.

Decades later, Michael described the situation to us with stunning, though typical, understatement: "The eastern province was gone—north of Transylvania, also. Europe was already burning, so to speak. And people in Romania started to blame my father for a lot of the things that went on. The ten years that he was here, the country went up very high culturally and economically. Politically, it started going bad with all these things happening."

The last straw, as Michael recalls it, was that in a country increasingly under the thumb of Hitler, Carol II lived brazenly with a Jewish mistress. Threatened with revolution and German intervention,

Carol dissolved Parliament, suspended the Constitution, and gave his prime minister, Marshal Ion Antonescu, sweeping powers, which Antonescu immediately used against him. Michael remembers being in his father's office on the night of September 5, 1940, when a military courier came from Antonescu with a letter demanding Carol's abdication.

"So the thing was, my father found himself in a situation that he couldn't cope with anymore," Michael told us. "So he just had to accept. And then I found myself like a fish out of water, without knowing all these things were going on."

Carol II left Romania the next day with his mistress Lupescu and nine railroad cars of cash and state treasures. Michael was not quite nineteen years old. He never saw his father again.

PLOTTING A COUP WHEN YOU'RE THE KING

"ON THE MORNING OF the sixth of September, they called me to quickly take the oath," Michael said. Waiting there were Antonescu and the Patriarch of the Romanian Orthodox Church with a Bible, as well as the minister of justice and the justices of the Supreme Court.

"I was in a daze. After that, luckily, Antonescu did get my mother to return. He sent a telegram asking her to come to me [from her exile near Florence, Italy]. So she arrived at the beginning of October 1940."

Whether by plan or happenstance, the schooling of the Crown Prince, which had grounded him so well in Romanian language, attitudes, history, and culture, had included nothing about the country's politics. "I was completely kept away from any sort of political information," Michael told us. "I had no education about the political part of the country—none! I used to hear about it on the sidelines—we knew what was going on, of course—but to actually make anything of it, no. I think it might have been my father's idea . . . So, when all these things started happening, I mixed in it without knowing quite how and why and all the rest of it. Very difficult."

And things were happening very fast. In November 1940, Antonescu proclaimed himself "Conducător," the Romanian version of Hitler's title "Fuhrer." He did little to stop the orgy of violence against Jews and liberals by the Iron Guard elements in his government. To ensure a stable ally, Hitler pressed Antonescu to curb the Iron Guard. That provoked an armed uprising and the slaughter of 120 Jews in Bucharest in January 1941.

"It happened at the end of 1940, the very beginning of 1941," King Michael recalled. "The Iron Guard got quite a few of the Jews in Romania, up in the north. Not just the Jews—they took our politicians, our statesmen, and they hung them on hooks, tore their hair out, shot them." The king's grim account trails off. Ion Antonescu, he said, "sort of let it happen, until there was a rebellion." Antonescu used the army to quell the rebellion in forty-eight hours. That, King Michael recalls, kindled a shift in policies.

"After that, he started a little bit to change [with] the influence that my mother, myself, and the Church had on him to go easy on the Jewish question. It wasn't one hundred percent, but it was something."

Michael told us about meeting during the early 1940s with Romania's chief rabbi, Alexandru Shafran.

"He used to come quite often to see me, and explain what was happening, and what he thought was going to happen. I called my mother into one of these meetings, and they talked together. She was appalled, and she said, 'If you don't do something, you will go down in history as Michael the Horrible.'" Michael said she took the same message to Antonescu: "She said, 'This can't go on anymore. You have to stop or change something.' He had quite a bit of respect for her. So, somehow, something did get through."

Queen Helen, who died in 1982, was later honored as a "righteous gentile" at Israel's Holocaust memorial, Yad Vashem. Despite her efforts and those of her son, more than two hundred thousand Romanian Jews and gypsies were sent to Transnistria, where many died. Still, in southern and Eastern Romania, three hundred thousand avoided camps and massacres, more than anywhere else in occupied Europe.

The king told us that in his first months back on the throne, he didn't realize the strength of Antonescu's ties to Hitler. "The incredible thing was that he [Antonescu] declared war on Russia without me knowing anything about it," Michael told us. "My mother heard the news on the BBC that morning, as the war started. About six o'clock in the morning, she came into my bedroom and said, 'Listen!' We were all taken aback. So I called up my prime minister, who was Mihai Antonescu [a distant cousin of the marshal], and I said, 'What the hell is going on here?' He said, 'Yes, it's true. I studied the situation in the newspapers.'"

That was June 22, 1941. We asked the king why he thought Marshal Antonescu had done it, and Michael displayed his usual detachment. He pointed to Russia's occupation of Romania's eastern provinces:

"As far as I can make out, because I never discussed all that with him, it had to do with patriotism. These were our provinces . . . After the Russians took our provinces of Basarabia and northern Bucovina, the Hungarians took northern Transylvania, which was something that went down very hard with the Romanian people . . . All our political parties and the population were fully in agreement that we should get these provinces back. We couldn't do that alone. That's why Antonescu went and allied himself with the Germans. But they all hoped to limit the conditions, [so that] we'd get to the frontier and not one step farther."

Instead, Romania's army took Odessa and joined in the German attacks on Sevastopol and Stalingrad.

Michael said he then "put the question" to Antonescu: "'What are we doing there in Russia?' Antonescu said, 'I am sure that by going east, we're going to get back Transylvania. Hitler promised.'" The King said there was no written agreement between Romania and Germany on that point, but that Antonescu told him that "he, as an officer, had given his word, and [that therefore he] had to go along without asking . . . His word to Hitler was more important than what was happening in the country."

It proved to be a case of costly loyalty. At Stalingrad, during the last months of 1942, Romania lost eighteen divisions fighting the Russians, nearly two-thirds of the forces it had posted to the eastern front.

During his first two years on the throne, Michael told us, he did not have any contact with the Allies.

"But then, as things started going bad in Russia, we decided that this was not our war. This had nothing to do with us, and we had to find some way to get out." He remembers commentators on BBC Radio and Voice of America badgering him, 'Get out, get out. If you don't, you won't be able to show your face in the world.' I said, 'Fine to get out, but how do we do it?' To that, I never got an answer."

But the young monarch didn't give up on back-channel communications with the Allies, though he was pretty sure Antonescu's spies knew about them. The king told us he sent messengers to British and American contacts outside Romania—"representatives [authorized] to speak in my name and in the name of the opposition parties," the PNL and the PNŢCD. Still no answer. So, the king told us, the head of the PNL, Constantin Brătianu, "sent another message that explained exactly the group we had and what we were trying to do, and that's when we got a reply. It said, 'We will not talk with you until you bring the Communists and the Socialists into your group.' And then we understood," the king told us. "It very much looked as if that message came from Moscow. And that's what we had to do, finally.

"I wouldn't say that America and Britain were thinking quite like that [to include Communists and Socialists in Romania], but Stalin was pushing. Why it was accepted so widely, I still don't quite get. And then in 1943, we said, 'There's disaster in Russia. We have to do something urgently . . . and we could guarantee a certain part of [our] country free of the Germans, on the condition that they send in a massive airlift.' We never even got an answer about that."

In retrospect, the king told us, he could see that Stalin did not want Romania cutting a deal with the Western Allies. The contacts with the Allies that continued through 1943 and into 1944 were spotty. Meanwhile, King Michael was consolidating the elements of a conspiracy of his own. He had to move on it carefully, because Antonescu had chosen most of the royal aides, the servants at the royal palace, and even members of the cabinet. So, the king "huddled" with military and political people in settings that would thwart Antonescu's eavesdropping—at parties, for example, or late in the evening. The king said several of the Army's generals were loyal to him, and brought him intelligence, as did the head of the code office at the Foreign Office.

Antonescu was probably not as suspicious as he should have been. The king remembers the wartime dictator as very stubborn, even when his analysis was wrong.

"You know what the French say—'as the father, so the son.' Antonescu had the mentality that I was going to follow in the footsteps of my father," Michael told us. "He could not get it into his head that I was different." The young king was not a playboy, and not focused on personal wealth, as his father had been. As Michael said with a sad smile, Antonescu didn't get the psychology right.

"And he didn't want me interfering. In 1943, at Christmas or New Year's, I'd given one of my [public] messages, and said something to the effect that, 'after the war,' or 'the war would end soon.' The German minister objected. Antonescu was very angry about that, but it had already been done."

Antonescu and his German allies had reason to be upset. From their perspective, the war was not going well. By late summer 1944, Russian troops had reoccupied northern Basarabia, and were headed toward Iaşi, in northeastern Romania. King Michael decided it was time to act, though he wasn't sure what support he could expect from the Allies.

"We hoped and we imagined there would be a difference between the Russians and the Americans. But we couldn't know it." The king paused. "We were, I must say, extremely lucky, because the Germans pulled two Panzer divisions from Romania about the beginning of August. That let us breathe a little."

Still, nearly fifty-five thousand German troops remained on Romanian soil, with almost none of Romania's own troops present, except some raw recruits with a few months' training, Michael recalled. What the twenty-two-year-old king had in mind—to seize power from Antonescu and switch sides in the war—was risky. It almost didn't happen.

"The whole thing was planned for the twenty-sixth of August. One of the general staff officers, who was with us in this coup, began telling the units outside to start coming into Bucharest slowly and gently. But then, accidentally, my doctor in Sinaia was visited by a brother of someone on Antonescu's staff, who stayed at the doctor's house—I was at the summer palace in Sinaia at the time. My doctor told us the telephone rang, and he went to pick it up, and this other fellow picked it up at the same time. The doctor didn't say anything, but he heard that Antonescu was going to the front for an inspection on the twenty-fourth."

It was clear that if King Michael didn't act right away, he'd lose his chance.

"So we nearly panicked. I got a call from one of our people in Bucharest. Then we dashed down to Bucharest—I left my mother in Sinaia. In the meantime, I had sent a telegram—I put it out myself, in military terms, to General [Henry] Maitland Wilson, who was commanding Allied forces in Italy. I said, 'In view of the important events in Romania, we need massive bombardment' at points I specified."

Here was the king of Romania, telling the Allies precisely where to bomb his own country and people. Allied air attacks had started a few weeks before—Americans bombed the oil fields near Ploieşti during the day while the British made more tactical strikes at night. After he hustled back to the capital about August 20, the king recalled, "I went shooting ducks south of Bucharest as a sort of diversion."

The new plan was for the king to call Antonescu in on the twenty-third, just before he was to head to the front, and demand a report from him. Also present would be the new prime minister, who was loyal to the king, and a military attaché who had served with Antonescu. In the next room waited three non-commissioned officers and a captain of the guard, and beyond them waited another aide de camp. The king and his co-conspirators had worked out a code—certain words the king would say if Antonescu did not agree to break Romania's ties to the Nazis.

"Antonescu came late, as usual," Michael remembered. "We started talking . . . We discussed and discussed. Finally, I said, 'Look, we have to get out of the war, and I'm asking you to do so.' He said, 'No! I've given my word to Hitler, and this is not my choice.'"

That was it. The king enunciated the pre-arranged code: "'I'm very sorry, but you don't leave me anything else to do.' So at that moment, these three [officers] came into the room, got hold of him, and took him away. He was furious—and red in the face. He being the big leader, how could this happen to him? I didn't like that attitude. I walked out—we didn't get on well together, but this latest development was still not quite proper. It was unpleasant." Sitting with us in the elegant parlor of Villa Serena, the king screwed up his patrician features at the memory of the long-ago unpleasantness. He continued the story:

"Before going upstairs, [Antonescu] turned around, spat on his captors, and said, 'Tomorrow morning, you'll all be hanging in the public square.'"

The king didn't stick around to find out if that would actually happen. He remembers his staff telling him, "'You've got to get out of here, because there's going to be a reaction,' which actually happened. I left about two o'clock in the morning and drove past Craiova [west of Bucharest]. I heard one airplane go by—when I looked up, it was a P38 Lightning [a U.S. reconnaissance plane] going toward Bucharest. I said to Mircea Ioaniţiu, my secretary and my friend, 'I'll bet he's going to those places I gave him in my telegram.' And that turned out to be right."

"THEN THE RUSSIANS WALKED THROUGH"

AS THE KING LOOKED back on the coup from the vantage point of six decades, he described it as "touch and go. Afterwards, I was quite sure that the [German] Gestapo and our Secret Service knew that something was up. But what they did not realize is that it was going to be mostly a military thing." The king said that not a single Romanian soldier defected when he ended his country's military alliance with Germany.

The German troops fought back. "They bombed the palace, they ruined our house, and they started to come in from Otopeni [north of Bucharest, where the airport is]. And there we were lucky—we had an anti-tank gun, and with it [our side] happened to hit a [German] tank just in the middle of a bridge, so it blocked the road. When the American bombers came, they dropped their bombs in the middle of the concentration of German troops and equipment. An officer who happened to be there with our troops said he'd never seen such a mess."

Before fleeing the royal palace in Bucharest the night of the coup, the king had issued a declaration of war on Nazi Germany. Doing so brought with it a drama of its own.

"When I made my proclamation, the Communist man in our group was [Emil] Bodnăraş. He was very highly placed in the Communist Party. He came to the office where I was trying to do things, and he walked right up to me and said, 'What have you done?!' You've ruined us!'"

Six decades later, the king could still remember how, pumped with the adrenalin of his triumph, the charge took him aback.

"I didn't know what he meant. But much later I understood. What we did on the twenty-third of August was what the Poles did in Warsaw. If you remember, there was an uprising. And though the Russians were just outside Warsaw, the Germans massacred the lot. Then the Russians came in and did their dirty business. When we did this, they told the Russians to slow up their advance. The plan was that we would be crushed and the Russians would take over. When this same man went to Moscow, some big fellow there told him, 'What the hell have you been doing? You've ruined our plan! You've messed up our plan.'"

It obviously delights the king to have tormented the Russians, even if briefly. He delivers a thoroughly Romanian analysis of what the Soviets called the liberation of Romania from the Nazis in 1944:

"Then, of course, the Russians walked through. They didn't liberate anything, because by the time the Russians got to Bucharest, we had already taken prisoner fifty-thousand German troops, from the top general to the last soldier. We cleaned it up ourselves, except for two pockets somewhere around the oil fields. The Russians didn't fire a shot.

"And I must say, I don't like to blow one's own trumpet, as they say, but this did shorten the war by quite a bit. The whole southeast fell immediately." It's undisputed that losing the flow of Romania's oil was a critical blow to the Nazi war machine.

But the young king's hopes that Romania would resume an independent constitutional monarchy were naïve. Even before the war was over, the Soviets started calling the shots in Romania.

"The sixth of March 1945 was the worst," the king told us. "That's when Vyshinksy came." Andrey Vyshinsky was deputy foreign minister of the USSR. He rushed to Bucharest after Romanian Prime Minister Nicolae Rădescu, citing the Allies' declarations of liberty at the Yalta Conference, had scheduled elections in Romania.

"Vyshinsky insisted that Groza [Petru Groza, a Communist sympathizer] be named prime minister. And I said, 'You can't do that, because constitutionally, I've got to consult,' and so on. That's when he banged his fist on the table, walked out, and slammed the door so hard he cracked it."

Red Army tanks surrounded the palace where Michael was living. Soviet soldiers disarmed Romanian troops and occupied telephone and broadcast centers. Without Western support, the king yielded. Rădescu lashed out at Communist leaders as "hyenas" and fled to the British mission.

It was the beginning of a heartbreak that would extend more than forty years, despite attempts to persuade the West to confront Communism head-on in Romania.

"Politically speaking, we were very disappointed," the king told us in another burst of understatement, "because the American military and civilian mission especially—and the English, also—saw exactly what was happening. I had contacts with them all throughout that time. I know very well that they saw all these telegrams I sent to Washington and London on what was going on, practically begging Washington and London to do something. And then not much came of it."

The disappointment was especially bitter because, although Michael was born and bred in Romania, he had royal relations all over Europe, including England. In November 1947, his cousin, the future Queen Elizabeth, married another cousin, Phillip of Greece. King Michael attended the wedding in London—and many of the Communists back home expected he'd stay in the West.

King Michael of Romania in the late 1940s

But the handsome young king surprised them on two counts. At the wedding festivities, he met a beautiful young royal, Princess Anne of Bourbon-Palma, and proposed to her a week later. But he didn't stay in the West. To the chagrin of Romania's government, he returned home.

Michael had been back only a few weeks, and was spending the Christmas holidays at the royal hunting lodge up the mountainside from Peleş Castle, when Prime Minister Groza sent word for him to come to Bucharest to discuss "family issues." Michael thought it must have something to do with his impending marriage.

As it turned out, the embassy residence was not much more than a mile south of the Elisabeta Palace, the royal villa where Michael received Prime Minister Groza on December 30, 1947. Groza brought with him, unannounced, the secretary-general of the Romanian Communist party, Gheorghe Gheorghiu-Dej. As Michael told the story, Gheorghiu-Dej lectured him and handed him a piece of paper—an abdication letter for the young king to sign. Michael thanked him courteously and said he would go into his office to read it. Next door, in his office, he found the phone lines cut, his guards replaced by Soviet police, and threats against him escalating. Groza told him that if he refused to abdicate, scores of students who had demonstrated for the monarchy a few weeks earlier would be executed.

"I could not accept that responsibility," the king told us at lunch. He signed the abdication letter. Decades later, at the U.S. ambassador's residence, the king mimicked how Groza had ended the meeting: "He took my hand and placed it over the pocket of his dark blazer." Michael felt, outlined in Groza's pocket, the cold barrel of a handgun. Groza turned to Queen Helen, Michael's mother, and said, "This is to make sure I won't end up like Antonescu."

As he left Romania, Michael and his mother were allowed to take nothing but their clothes from Peleş, plus four automobiles—the Jeep the Americans had given him after the coup in 1944, and three General Motors cars he had just bought for use at the palace. The cars were packed on two railroad wagons for the trip to Switzerland.

When Michael arrived in Western Europe on January 3, 1948, he had just turned twenty-six.

Ex-KING STILL LOOKING FOR WORK

"FIRST, WE HAD TO collect our thoughts, because the abdication had been a bad shock," the king told us. The ever-neutral Swiss were very keen that he not use their country as a base to speak out against those who had taken power in Romania. They even wanted him to fill out his residency papers as "Michael Hohenzollern," the Austrian name of his forebears. He held out for a year, insisting that he was Romanian and should be registered as "Michael of Romania." On that, he prevailed. But Villa Serena at Versoix, near Geneva, was never a place from which he could speak out.

In those early months of 1948, he recalled, "The first place I could open my mouth was London—that was the first place I could get a press conference and make an official declaration of what had happened, and how, and so on."

From London, Michael went to America. He spoke to the Overseas Press Association in New York, visited Romanian expatriates in Detroit and Cleveland, and met with President Harry Truman at the White House. Michael remembers that as a brief meeting, perhaps "ten minutes, a quarter hour—you can't say very much in that amount of time. I thanked him very much for having given me the Legion of Merit. He just said that he hoped that Romania would be free again soon."

We asked the king if he met with any other heads of government besides Truman during the ensuing decades of Communism. "The queen, of course," he said, referring to his cousin, Queen Elizabeth. Then a long pause. "Others? No."

The deposed king could not spend all his time drumming up support for Romania. His wedding was just six months away. He was unemployed, with few assets. He had to figure out a way to make a living.

"It was a terrible handicap, because I wasn't brought up for that sort of thing. So I had to learn anew, to learn from zero. The only job that wasn't too difficult for me was flying, because I had already become a pilot in Romania. And that was one of my passions—flying."

Ever since he was a tot, Michael of Romania had had a passion for airplanes, motorcycles, and automobiles—in fact, anything with an engine. Apparently, as a teenager, he used to ride his Jeep up and down the stairs of Peleş Castle, and drove himself at breakneck speeds on Bucharest's grandest avenue.

When we asked the king why Romanians, including himself, still like America despite being ignored after World War II, he points to America's technological prowess in cars and planes. So, in the mid-1950s, it was a stroke of good luck when someone introduced him to William Lear, of Learjet fame. For years, Michael had read about Lear in aviation magazines, and the entrepreneur was intrigued to learn that the transplanted king knew, and loved to fly, airplanes. They hatched a plan for Michael to become a test pilot and sales rep for the Lear, Inc. operation then starting up in Switzerland. Lear took Michael to Santa Monica, California to get advanced instrument training.

The king chuckled, remembering some of his conversations in America—for example, the mechanic in Santa Monica who asked him, "What does it feel like to work for a living?"

"So, I just said, 'Look here, I've been working for my living for I don't know how many years.' The guy just couldn't get it in his head, you know."

And then there was the commercial flight he took with Lear, when the stewardess asked him who he was. "I said to her, 'I'm King Michael of Romania.' She looked strangely at me and said, 'Come off it!' I was sitting with Lear himself, and he finally told her it was so."

The happy connection with Lear, Inc. lasted just two years before the operation shut down in Switzerland and moved back to the United States.

"I had to find something else," the king told us. "So some of the technicians formed an electronics and plastics company. That went on for five or six years, until the competition was such that we couldn't keep going."

Business was not Michael's forte. And, by 1964, he had five daughters to support.

"We were getting into difficulties," he reflected. "So my uncle,

King Paul of Greece, who likes to keep the family together as much as possible, tried to find something for us. He got the idea that I should become a broker on the New York Stock Exchange."

The idea was that he would become a rainmaker, a networker, and a source of European connections for the Wall Street brokerage Droulia and Company. Michael dutifully spent a few months in New York, studying to get his broker's license, then returned to his quiet life in Versoix. Talking to rich people about their money was not something he found interesting. He's more animated describing what he called "the sideline of selling second-hand airplanes," which often involved flying a plane to a customer or a customer to a plane.

Indeed, in the book his family published in honor of Michael's eightieth birthday in 2001, only six paragraphs are devoted to the five decades of his exile. And one of those paragraphs exposes his true obsession: "King Michael had always had a great passion for cars and especially for military Jeeps built in the first years of World War II. Since 1956, when he came to Switzerland, His Majesty has entirely rebuilt or renovated nine original cars, Fords, or Willies. Some of them have been exhibited at automobile museums or taken part in rallies."

The BBC and Voice of America, each year at Christmas, broadcast a message from King Michael into Romania. And to the West, he kept trying to spread the word about tens of thousands of Romanians dying in prison or labor camps. To us, he expressed frustration that the Western press paid little attention until the 1970s, when Ceauşescu "started ruining the villages and pulling down the churches. That's when they started to wake up, after we'd been saying it for I don't know how long."

When the Revolution did come, forty-two years after he was forced out of Romania, it caught the king by surprise. Within months, he tried to return to Romania. But its new leaders would not allow him entry.

"Four times I was put out," he told us, and then added for emphasis: "Three times since 1990."

Three of his daughters were allowed in, and got their first glimpse of Romania within weeks of the Revolution. They brought supplies of food, toys, clothes, diapers, medicines, and syringes to help the children in Ceaușescu's orphanages. But when the king himself tried to enter for Easter 1990, he told us, the new leaders "wouldn't have it. I actually got into Bucharest, but then was stopped on the road and put out.

"In 1992, they more or less accepted my return until they saw the crowds that came out for me. And then they got cold feet—too much for them—and put me out.

"I tried again in '94—I was invited to come by another group in Romania to talk about the twenty-third of August [the date of the World War II coup]. When I arrived in Bucharest, they wouldn't even let me into the terminal building at the airport. I got down the plane's steps, but they wouldn't let us go any farther onto the tarmac."

As the king recounted it, his visit fell prey to a government ruse. The government insisted that he arrive on a Friday, but, as it well knew, it granted no visas on Fridays. The attempt to trick him seemed to annoy the king as much as the refusal to let him enter.

"While we were waiting in that little bus, [an official] came back and said, 'Look, while you're waiting, we invite you very politely to get in that airplane next door here and have a cup of coffee.' Now, that airplane over there had its engines running! I said, 'No. At least I'll go back on the same plane!' I mean, really—can't you be truthful with me?"

The king shrugged, mimicking the answer he got from the captain in charge that day.

It wasn't until 1997—a half-century after his exile—that King Michael was given back his Romanian passport. He traveled throughout Western Europe, making the case for Romania to be included in NATO. A few years later, he won back some of the Hohenzollern properties expropriated by the Communists, including use of the Elisabeta Palace where he had been forced to abdicate.

As the king saw it, the years of Communism had snuffed out a spark in the people he grew up with: "Because of the special oppression we suffered, the people have lost their sense of initiative; they've lost their way of thinking." He describes visiting a village with a bridge that needed a small repair. When he was young, he said, the villagers would have just pulled out their tools and fixed it. Now, he said, the people wait for someone from a government ministry.

"It takes a lot of time for them to wake up," the king said. Sheilah thought he was referring to the national anthem, whose words include, "Wake up, Romania!" But if so, the king didn't belabor the point. "One old man in one of the villages, just after 1992, said, 'Wake up? We've woken up, but we are incapable of *standing* up!'"

TRANSYLVANIA

CHAPTER 7
INSIDE TRANSYLVANIA

THE DRACULA WHO DREW BLOOD, THE DRACULA WHO DRINKS BLOOD

Vlad Ţepeş, also known as Dracula

TO AMERICANS, TRANSYLVANIA MEANS just one thing: Dracula. Never mind the centuries of epic struggle between opposing empires over this strategic territory.

Never mind that the clash of cultures here has evolved into some of the most workable ethnic cooperation in Europe.

Never mind that the customs of its villages and elegant cities stretch back to a time before Columbus thought of sailing west.

Never mind that Transylvania's landscape is not shrouded in

gloomy moss and bats, but beautiful hillsides dotted with plump sheep and curvaceous haystacks.

Never mind all that: Let's talk vampires. The trouble is, Dracula is an import. There is very little Romanian about the Dracula character who so excites Americans.

Yes, of course, the roots of the Dracula legend go back to Vlad Țepeș, the fifteenth-century ruler in southern Romania famous for impaling his enemies on pikes.

Impaling is gory, but it is not revivifying corpses, shunning the light, and sucking the blood of victims. It is not vampires. Looking back from the twenty-first century, it's not at all obvious that the world would someday come to identify vampires with Romania.

It probably never would have happened had the beleaguered Vlad still been around to defend his name. Apparently, it was his name that got him into this fix.

Before we go into that, though, a few words about the Transylvanian town where he was born, Sighișoara (Schäsbrich to the Saxons, Segesvárto to the Hungarians).

If Vlad were to come back from the grave today, he might well recognize Sighișoara. When he was born in 1431, Saxon settlers had been there more than two hundred years. A millennium earlier, the spot had been a Roman fort, and by the fifteenth century, it was a free town, bustling with trade and controlled by craft guilds. Each of them—the shoemakers, the tailors, the tinsmiths, the butchers, the tanners, the rope-makers, etc.—was required to finance construction of a fortified tower and defend it during attacks; nine of the towers still stand.

Sighișoara is one of the best-preserved medieval towns in Europe, with a bewitching silhouette of battlements and spires. The reinforced three-story building where Vlad was probably born, inside the Citadel, is still there, now housing the Citadel Restaurant. It's a stone's throw from the massive clock tower punctuating the fort's east wall. The tower was built a century before Vlad's birth, although the oak figurines that dance out of little doors to announce each new hour arrived a few centuries later. Most of the other buildings behind the citadel's dense walls date from the seventeenth and eighteenth centuries, after the great fire of 1676 that swept through the citadel and the lower town. The fortified church of St. Nicholas, the so-called Church on the Hill, may still have been under construction when young Vlad was a boy.

His father (also named Vlad) was the illegitimate son of an autocrat known to Romanian schoolchildren as "Mircea the Old." Mircea put together an empire that stretched across Wallachia and southern Transylvania, from near today's border with Serbia in the West all the way to the Black Sea. Mircea sired one legitimate son and a brood of illegitimate heirs who squabbled for power after his death in 1418.

The older Vlad was one of the bastards. In 1431, he was living in Sighişoara, guarding the border and plotting how to dislodge his half-brother from the throne, when he received and welcomed a summons from the Holy Roman Emperor to be inducted into the Order of the Dragon, or, in Latin, *Societatis Draconistrarum*. Members of the Order pledged to fight for the Cross of Christ and to do battle with its enemies—heretics, Hussites, and the infidel Turks.

If you're the bastard son of the guy who ruled over a vast stretch of land, and if you're deeply enmeshed in a sibling rivalry aimed at getting the crown yourself, joining the Order of the Dragon is a great networking opportunity—a terrific way to strike fear in your enemies while building alliances with other Central European princes.

Vlad Senior was so pleased with his new fraternity that he redesigned his coat of arms to show off the figure of a dragon—jaws open, paws out, wings spread, tail coiling around the head. At that time, a dragon had a white-hat, good-guy image. The idea was not that that members of the Order would *become* devils, but that they would figuratively *slay* the Dragon of Evil, Satan, as St. George does in all those icons and paintings. To drive the point home, Vlad called himself Dracul, the Romanian word for dragon (from the Latin, *draco*).

From our vantage point nearly six hundred years later, it's hard to see that "Hi, my name is Dracul" would be a winning public-relations strategy. Even in the fifteenth century, it had mixed success. Vlad

Dracul eventually did gain power and held it for about five years before he was assassinated in 1447. One of the deals he had to cut along the way was to send his two younger sons to Anatolia, Turkey, as hostages of the Sultan. The young Vlad was about eleven years old and his brother Radu only seven when they were sent off. As far as we know, the two were not harmed physically, but who can tell the psychological scars? The younger boy, known as Radu the Handsome, reportedly fought off sexual advances by the Sultan's own son until, at some point, he stopped fighting. Meanwhile, big brother Vlad was taking notes on how the Turks used terror to control their enemies.

Two years into their captivity, their father and older brother cooperated with the Christians, fighting against the Turks at the Bulgarian port of Varna. It was not a smart move. The battle turned out catastrophically for the Christians, and going back on his word to the Sultan put Vlad Senior's hostage sons at even greater risk. Apparently, he did it quite consciously—he wrote the Saxon fathers of the Transylvanian city Braşov, to prove his loyalty to their cause, "Please understand that I have allowed my children to be butchered for the sake of Christian peace."

As it turned out, his children were not butchered. But it's easy to see how such experiences could warp a kid's concept of trust.

Mysterious Origins of the Legend

Did young Vlad grow up to be a sadistic torturer because he never bonded with his father? Maybe so. But that still didn't make him a vampire. *That* connection was forged nearly half a millennium later.

Before then, after Vlad Dracul was killed by Romanian noblemen, his son inherited his sobriquet with the diminutive ending "a" to indicate "son of the dragon." The son proceeded to give "Dracula" a really bad name. In part, this reflects the truism that history is kind to those who write it. Much of what we know about the punishments Vlad Dracula meted out—the impalings, the disembowelings, the flayings of flesh, the roastings, the boilings-alive—we learn from the accounts of his enemies. German chroniclers wrote vivid descriptions of how Vlad Dracula dealt with enemies who were German, or allies of Germans.

Back from Turkey, Vlad Dracula spent the rest of his brief life in a constant struggle for power, fighting with brothers, noblemen, Turks, Germans, and Hungarians. He held power for six years, then spent twice that length of time under house arrest by the Hungarians. In 1475, after his brother Radu died of syphilis, the Hungarian king made Dracula an offer he couldn't refuse: convert from Orthodoxy to Catholicism and reassume the throne, or die in prison. Vlad Dracula was not yet forty-five years old. He did not hesitate to grab freedom.

Yet he was dead in less than a year. The circumstances are not clear. Was he mistaken for a Turk and killed by his own men? Was he ambushed by a rival and killed by a hired assassin? Tradition holds that monks of the monastery he supported on Snagov Island, about twenty miles north of Bucharest, found his mangled, headless body and buried it near the altar in their church. Some chroniclers report Dracula's head was preserved in honey and sent to the Sultan in Constantinople, where it was displayed as a trophy.

To use a cliché, the tomb of Dracula is shrouded in mystery. In 1931, five hundred years after Vlad Dracula's birth, two Romanian scholars were commissioned to excavate the tomb at Snagov. One was the archeologist Dinu Rosetti, and the other the genealogist George D. Florescu, who traced his family back to the wife of Dracula's brother, Radu the Handsome. What they found in the grave at the foot of the altar, the spot presumed to be the Impaler's sepulcher, was shocking: no casket, no human remains—just a huge grave-pit with a few animal bones, some ceramics, and other items dating back to the Iron Age. But there's more to the story.

Sheilah learned about the excavation from George Florescu's nephew, the historian Radu R. Florescu, Sr., famous as Dracula's biographer. He described his uncle as a brilliant Victorian eccentric, who usually wore nineteenth-century clothes—"his way of showing he still believed in the past." He had studied engineering and then medicine before dropping out of school and teaching himself how to write history, including a chronicle of Bucharest.

"He knew every church, every street, every old boyar house," Professor Florescu said. "I did a lot of touring with him when I was researching Dracula."

Young Radu Florescu was not yet a schoolboy in the summer of 1931 when George Florescu and Dinu Rosetti stared into the empty grave near the altar. He told of how his uncle and Rosetti persevered, turning to another grave, oddly placed at the right side of the church entrance. What they found when the stone was moved was even more startling, Professor Florescu said. Inside there was a casket, holding a skeleton, partly covered in the tatters of what had once been a sumptuous silk brocade. The sleeves of the garment had originally been crimson, the color of the dragon cloak.

As soon as it was exposed to the air, "the carcass disintegrated," Radu Florescu recounted. "All that was left was a ring on one finger, and a chain with some kind of dragon."

Still, he said, his uncle and Rosetti did not believe they had found the remains of Vlad the Impaler. The skeleton in this tomb had not been decapitated, and every Romanian knew the legend of the Sultan's humiliating display of Vlad Ţepeş's skull.

What his uncle didn't know about, Professor Florescu told Sheilah, is the grisly finding turned up in recent years by his colleague, Matei Cazacu of the French National Center for Scientific Research: "The Turks did not behead the remains—it was the *skin* they took off, so the skull remains. What was exposed at Constantinople was the skin."

So, it may be that, after forty-five years of violent life, Vlad Dracula did find a more or less peaceful resting place in the monastery at Snagov.

None of this would have been connected with vampires if the Irish novelist Bram Stoker had not stumbled upon a history book in the public library in Whitby, the English seaside resort where he was writing a novel in the summer of 1890. Stoker's notes indicate he originally created a villain named Count Wampyr from Styria, in Austria. But during a visit to the library, he read in William Wilkinson's *An Account of the Principalities of Wallachia and Moldavia* an erroneous footnote: "Dracula in the Wallachian language means Devil. The Wallachians . . . at the time, as they are at present, used to give this as a surname to any person who rendered himself conspicuous either by courage, cruel actions, or cunning."

It was intriguing enough to nudge the novelist to rename his villain Count Dracula.

But why transplant him to Transylvania? Why not Wallachia, if that's where Dracula is such a frequent handle? The answer may lie in another monograph that fell into Stoker's hands—a rather condescending catalogue of superstitions of Transylvanian peasants. It was written not by one of said peasants, but by the Scottish wife of a Polish-born Hungarian cavalry officer stationed in this outpost of the Austro-Hungarian Empire. Her description of rustic conviction in vampires apparently was enough for Stoker to switch the count's home from Austria to Transylvania, though he had never set eyes on the Carpathian Alps. He may also have reacted to early criticism that his original plan for *The Undead* seemed to borrow heavily from Irish writer Joseph Sheridan LeFanu's 1871 vampire novel *Carmilla*, about an enigmatic countess who turns out to be a vampire.

Did Stoker consciously model his protagonist on the historical Ţepeş? No one has explored the question more fully than Radu Florescu and his fellow professor Raymond T. McNally. But unearthing the connection was not Florescu's original plan.

Radu's father Radu Alexandru (brother of George) was a Romanian diplomat in European capitals between the wars. He was labeled an "enemy alien" when he broke with the fascist leaders of pre-war Romania. No longer welcome in his own country, his son Radu studied at Oxford, Texas, and Indiana universities, before accepting a teaching job at Boston College. His first chance to get back to his native land was a quarter-century later, in 1967, as a Fulbright scholar.

He remembers that time as a brief interlude when Ceauşescu was popular for resisting Soviet domination. "This was the only time when, had there been a free election in Romania, Ceauşescu might have won," Florescu noted. He told the Fulbright Commission he would use his year in Romania to study the foreign policy of Alexandru Ioan Cuza, the nineteenth-century prince who united two parts of Romania—a suitably scholarly subject.

Then his colleague from Boston College, the late Raymond McNally, wrote with questions about research he was doing on Stoker's novel—questions like, "Can you travel from Cluj to Bistriţa?" and "Is there a Borgo Pass?" Florescu grew more intrigued. "Dracula was big in the world," he told Sheilah. "But [in the 1960s], it never crossed Romania. No one knew about it. In fact, I had never read Bram Stoker's novel."

He began to see Dracula as an interesting research project. But it wasn't simple.

"I had to explain to the Fulbright people that I was switching from Cuza to Dracula, from the nineteenth century to the fifteenth century," Florescu said, grimacing at the academic headache. "Finally they gave permission, which generated a problem for the Romanians. They didn't know who Dracula was." And to the extent they did know, they did not find it an agreeable topic, he said.

The book he and McNally published in 1972, *In Search of Dracula: A True History of Dracula and Vampire Legends*, became a huge success. It introduced Vlad Ţepeş to millions of vampire fans who knew nothing of the Romanian prince, and it made the case that Stoker, for years, had collected information about the life and times of the historical Vlad Ţepeş before planting his count at the Borgo Pass. There is a Prundu Bârgăului in northeastern Transylvania, and it's as gorgeous as Stoker described it without ever having seen it.

The success of the book, and its several updates, was a mixed blessing for Professor Florescu. "This did me a lot of harm in the eyes of those who knew me," he recalled wistfully. "They asked, 'How come you have degenerated into a vampire researcher?' It was difficult for me at the time. I lost a lot of friends."

DRACULA AS GEORGE WASHINGTON

As FLORESCU AND MCNALLY point out, the German and Turkish judgment that the historical Dracula was a gruesome psychopath is just one way to interpret the facts. A late fifteenth-century Russian diplomat posted to Moldavia, Transylvania, and Hungary, Fedor Kuritsyn, reached a very different conclusion—that Vlad Ţepeş was cruel but just. Kuritsyn collected tales about the recently deceased prince, in part from interviews of Dracula's widow, sons, and Stephen the Great of Moldavia, his cousin and ally. The report he wrote, *The Story of Prince Dracula*, was not published during his lifetime. Instead, it was filed like a diplomatic dispatch, Florescu and McNally write, "for the exclusive benefit of Grand Duke Ivan III and his successors, to enrich the political education of the Russian head of state, much in the manner of Machiavelli's *Prince*. From this viewpoint, Dracula, far from being an irrational killer, was an effective ruler, who threatened torture and death to advance the principles of justice and good government."

Niccolo Machiavelli was still a teenager. He would not write his book of political counsel until 1513.

A far different legend of Prince Dracula comes from Romanian peasants, passed down through oral folklore—Romanians didn't have a written language until generations after Dracula's death. In this view, Vlad the Impaler is a hero, almost a George Washington-like figure.

Tales have come down through the centuries of the Impaler rewarding loyalty with bequests of land and wielding his tough brand of justice to maintain order in his realm. In a land that has seen so much marauding and war, there's great admiration for the deterrent value of impalement. The conventional wisdom is that crime was not much of a problem during Vlad Ţepeş's day. Romanians see him as a despot, but he's *their* despot—and something of a Robin Hood to boot, because he took on the lesser lords who were his rivals.

In the 1994 update of *In Search of Dracula*, McNally wrote, "The official Communist party historians portrayed him as a national hero and played down or rationalized his cruelties. None exhibited that hero-worshipping attitude more than the late dictator Nicolae Ceauşescu, who according to some authorities shared many character traits with Dracula."

Florescu and McNally note that there have been Romanian princes who were more distinguished, and many who ruled longer, but none remembered more reverently by the people.

The great nineteenth-century Romanian poet Mihai Eminescu, agonizing over the state of Romanian politics and diplomacy in his historical ballad "The Third Letter," called to Vlad Ţepeş to save the Romanian nation from what he saw as its venal leaders: "Where are you, Lord Ţepeş, to get control of them and split them into two gangs, the fools and the rascals?"

When Traian Băsescu was running for president in 2004, he likened his plans for attacking corruption with the methods Vlad Ţepeş used to punish illegalities. Băsescu won the vote.

It might be easier for Westerners to embrace the Vlad Ţepeş honored by Romanians if there was more than one contemporaneous portrait of the Wallachian prince. That one visual image we have depicts him with bug eyes, an impressively bushy mustache, and wavy dark locks cascading below his shoulder, crowned by a tight, bejeweled, velvet cap. The net effect is something between cartoonish and menacing.

It is definitely *not* the image Westerners have from, say, Béla Lugosi's 1931 silver-screen portrayal of Bram Stoker's count. (Lugosi, incidentally, was born to Hungarian parents on land that's now in western Romania, and took his stage name from that town, Lugoj.)

Neither the Dracula books nor the movies were permitted in Ceauşescu's Romania; Stoker's novel was not published in a Romanian translation until two years after the fall of Communism. These days, ever interested in drawing closer to the West for psychological as well as economic reasons, Romanians are somewhat more willing to embrace the Dracula known to the West. If Westerners fancy the celluloid versions of Dracula, and want to believe that Vlad Ţepeş is his prototype, some Romanians engagingly flesh out the details.

So they're glad to show you that monastery on Snagov Island, about an hour from Bucharest, where Vlad Țepeș is said to be buried. They're eager for you to visit Sighișoara, Vlad's birthplace in Transylvania. In fact, a few years ago, there was a flurry of activity to build a Dracula theme park near the medieval city. Lack of funds delayed the project until environmentalists and preservationists were finally able to drive a stake through it.

You can buy some decent Romanian red wine with Vlad Țepeș's picture on the label. You can also find a truly tacky blood-red "Draculina," alcohol content a staggeringly high seventeen percent, with a label that displays a shapely young woman, bodice asunder, about to be ravished by a vampire. In a similarly cheesy vein, tourists can find various T-shirts emblazoned with a gaunt face and blood-dripping fangs.

At the Dracula Club Restaurant in Bucharest, the legend (taking the form of actor Petre Moraru) comes face to face with guests like former Maryland State Senator Arthur Dorman.

For a slightly higher level of cultural engagement, we sometimes suggested that our houseguests visit the Dracula Club Restaurant in downtown Bucharest. It has a pretty good Transylvanian menu, but the real draw is the cheerfully spooky actor who wanders room to room frightening diners in several languages. They love it.

He is Petre Moraru, a veteran stage performer. He begins his evening's work emerging from a stand-up coffin enveloped in artificial mist, wearing a long black cape with scarlet lining and a white silk scarf. His hair is gray, swept back from his aristocratic features. He holds a lit candelabra as he moves among the diners, commenting ominously on the beauty of the ladies' necks or the rich color of the meat on plates.

"We're beginning to find Dracula interesting as well as lucrative," Moraru told an interviewer. "Why fight it?"

VISITING THE HOLY LAND . . . OF UNITARIANS

ON A TRIP TO the Apuseni Mountains in southwestern Transylvania, Jim visited a hunting lodge. Sixty percent of the brown bears in Europe live in Romania, and hunting in Romania is a big deal. When Jim arrived in 1998, the Italian ambassador to Romania was known as a "hunter-diplomat."

Jim is not a hunter, but was curious to visit a lodge and talk with the Romsilva rangers who ran one.

The lodge he visited looked comfortable—not luxurious, but not threadbare or rundown, either. This was a profit center for Romsilva, the state company which owned the Romanian forests. Romanian and foreign hunters were not poor.

But it wasn't hunters, Italian or otherwise, whom he found there. It was Unitarians from the United States. He was only mildly surprised. By now, he was used to running into American Unitarians in Transylvania—on mountaintops, in hotel lobbies, on sidewalks.

They were there because the American Unitarian Church has one of the two most impressive partnerships with Romanians, the other being the relationship between the Alabama National Guard and the Romanian military.

The Alabama connection is of more recent vintage. After 1989, the Pentagon decided to promote citizen armies in Eastern Europe by pairing up State Guard units with armed forces in the East—Maryland with Estonia, Alabama with Romania, etc. The result was quite amazing. Not only did it fulfill its military purpose, but it also built valuable cultural ties. It put Alabama on the map for Romanians and Romania on the map for Alabamans.

The bonds between Unitarians reach back for half a millennium. All over Transylvania, but mostly in small villages, American Unitarian congregations have partnered with Romanian Unitarian churches. Visits are reciprocated. Material help flows. And most important, personal friendships grow.

Unitarianism was founded in Transylvania in the sixteenth century. It's older than Methodism and older than the Baptist denomination, which was also founded in Eastern Europe and has strong, centuries-old roots in Romania. Today, more than eighty thousand Hungarians in Transylvania worship in Unitarian churches. Some villages are entirely Unitarian. In Cluj, the largest church is Unitarian, and the city hosts a major Unitarian university and seminary. Among Unitarianism's most famous adherents was the composer Béla Bartók.

Peter Raible, a retired Unitarian minister from Seattle, explained the ties between American and Romanian Unitarians this way: "I live in a land where nine out of every ten Unitarians did not grow up Unitarian. Some tend to think that Unitarianism began last Tuesday, when they walked in the door. Knowing about Transylvania gives them a heritage. I say to them, 'Transylvania is our holy land.'"

To American Unitarians, something else about their roots in Transylvania makes them feel at home—the cry of religious freedom.

Unitarianism and other Eastern European branches produced by the Reformation were more radical than branches founded by Martin Luther or John Calvin. They championed not only alternatives to Roman Catholicism, but freedom for every person of every faith to find God in his or her own way. In twenty-first-century America—and Romania—that's the law. In the sixteenth century, in what was then Hungary, that was a radical idea.

Reverend Bruce Clear of Indianapolis's All Souls Unitarian Church tells the story of one of the church's early leaders, Francis David

(David Ferenc in Hungarian) of Cluj (Kolozsvár), which is recorded in a painting that hangs in Unitarian churches throughout Romania.

"He began life as a Catholic, but started his ministry as the head of the Lutheran churches of Hungary. Later, he headed the Calvinist churches of Transylvania. As he took over the church in Kolozsvár, his theology became increasingly Unitarian, and over the course of his ministry there, virtually the entire town converted to Unitarianism. He eventually became the head of all Unitarian churches in Transylvania. Through the influence of Francis David, King John Sigismund of Transylvania became a Unitarian—the only Unitarian king in history.

"In January of 1568, King John called together representatives of various religions to a debate in the city of Turda. The Catholics, the Lutherans, the Calvinists, and the Unitarians all showed up. Francis David spoke for the Unitarians, and was known widely as among the most eloquent speakers in the land.

"David, to be sure, was the clear winner. Such debates were not unusual in Reformation Europe. The pattern was, of course, that the winners would receive special favors and privilege, and the losers would lose favor, perhaps be outlawed or banished from the kingdom.

"What David, as reward for his victory, requested was only this: complete religious freedom for all religions throughout Transylvania. King John was persuaded by David, granted his request, and issued the following proclamation on January 6, 1568:

> "The preacher should everywhere preach the gospel, according to his own belief, and the community might accept it or not. Nobody should compel it, as this would not ease anybody's soul, but the community should have the right to keep such a preacher whose teaching it likes. None of the religious authorities, or others, is allowed to do any harm to the preacher; no one should be hurt for his religion . . . Nobody is allowed to threaten anybody with prison or with expelling him from his place of teaching."

Among Transylvanian Unitarians, January 6 is now a special religious holiday.

"So here we find the first declaration of complete religious freedom in Western history," said Clear. "It is the legacy of our Unitarian heritage, coming directly from Transylvania."

If you grew up Catholic, as we did in the United States, who knew that Transylvania was the Holy Land for Unitarians?

THAT ROMANIAN WORK ETHIC

ON ONE OF OUR visits to Braşov, we traveled by train, a trip of about two hours from Bucharest. The day was cold and snowy. One of the news stories about our visit reported that we had come by train—apparently unusual for a government official—and that Jim had worn "cute boots." They were pretty good-looking rubbers, but there may have been some kind of translation problem that converted them to "cute."

In any case, one of the U.S. companies we had heard about in Braşov was Cambric, an engineering firm that did work for American farm machinery manufacturers. It's a small company based in Salt Lake City, Utah.

We arrived at the nondescript building and walked up the stairs to the Cambric offices. Inside were dozens and dozens of young Romanian engineers at computer terminals, working on engineering designs for farm machinery. They were doing their work over the internet, collaborating with Cambric engineers in the United States who had direct contact with their customers.

At that time, Cambric contracted with U.S. companies like International Harvester and John Deere to transform the old two-dimensional blueprints of their products into three-dimensional computer-based designs. The old blueprints were on desks, and the new ones were on the computer screens—in many more colors than blue.

We walked from one room to the next. Jim stopped to ask several of the young men to talk about what they were doing. We got the big picture, but the details—driven by state-of-the-art CAD software—about finite element analysis, 3D parametric modeling, and digital assembly creation went immediately over our non-technical heads.

So Jim decided to take another tack in his effort to make conversation. "Let's not talk tech. Let's talk about relationships. What's the most difficult part of working with your American colleagues?" he asked a thin, dark-haired young man. He expected him to say it was the language or the seven-hour time difference.

"Truthfully," he replied, "it's that the Americans take off the weekends. Because we're operating seven days a week, they get behind us."

So much for the question of whether Romanians, raised in a Communist system without incentives to work, can compete with the good old American work ethic. Evidently, they can.

Within several years, Cambric's office in Braşov had grown to nearly two hundred engineers, and its clients were increasingly looking for company help on more complicated projects than converting old blueprints. It had also opened offices in Germany and Luxembourg to serve the Western Europe market.

"HOW MANY ATTACK HELICOPTERS WOULD YOU LIKE?"

WHEN THE PRESIDENT OF Israel was asked about Romania's proposed $1.8 billion purchase of one hundred U.S. attack helicopters, he reportedly mused aloud, "And who are they to protect Romania from?"

It was a good question, and one that neither the United States nor Romanian governments wanted to ask.

In 1997, Dallas-based Bell Helicopter had signed a letter of intent with the Romanian government to sell them the helicopters and, in exchange, to buy the IAR Ghimbav aircraft factory in Braşov.

If the Romanian government had guaranteed the loan to finance the project, it would have been a very big deal.

At that time, Romania's entire GDP, the total measure of all goods and services produced in the economy, was only about thirty-three billion dollars. This one deal would have comprised five percent of the whole economy. It would have been, by far, the biggest foreign sale to the Romanian government. And it would have been a significant U.S. investment in Romania, though not the biggest.

More importantly, some, but not all, top Romanian officials thought the deal could help secure U.S. support for Romania becoming a member of NATO. Their view was that U.S. defense contractors were powerful lobbyists in Washington, and that if a big U.S. company owned a significant facility in Romania, the United States would want to protect it.

None of this stopped the project from being controversial in Romania, the United States, and elsewhere.

The local representative of the IMF, John Hill, was particularly incensed that Romania would take on such a huge debt.

Economists in both countries believed the deal to be totally useless, unaffordable, and therefore unlikely ever to happen. The Romanian finance minister, economist Daniel Dăianu, repeatedly refused to sign off on the loan guarantee simply because he thought it a waste of taxpayers' money.

Romanians, whose heating was periodically cut off during the winter, understandably questioned the priorities of those who supported the deal.

And almost everybody in the U.S. government who focused on the deal thought it was simply embarrassing for both countries.

Yet the company and its local and Israeli partners lobbied hard for it. U.S. government officials were afraid to look as if they weren't supporting a U.S. company. And Romanian officials were afraid to sign the deal, and afraid to kill it. So, month after month, they delayed a final decision.

Then, in the fall of 1998, Prime Minister Radu Vasile, on his first visit to the United States, went to Washington, and Jim traveled with him. On Vasile's D.C. schedule was a meeting with Deputy Treasury Secretary Larry Summers.

Most of the talk between the two was about the Romanian economy and the pending IMF agreement. Then, out of the blue, Vasile raised the Bell Helicopter deal.

"What do you think about it?" he asked Summers. Jim knew very well what Summers thought, but didn't know how he'd respond.

Summers slipped Jim a note: "Should I go for it?" Jim scribbled "yes" and passed the note back.

Summers couched his answer in official U.S. verbiage: "Getting an IMF agreement is key, and that means not taking on more debt than you can afford. Reforming the military is important, and buying new weapons is, of course, appropriate when you can afford them. It's your decision what, and when to buy weapons. And, of course, if you do decide to buy helicopters, we hope you'll buy American."

Vasile seemed pleased with the response, and the meeting ended soon after.

Several days later, on returning to Bucharest, he was greeted by the normal clutch of reporters. Asked if the Bell helicopter deal was discussed in Washington, Vasile replied:

"The issue came up . . . It is certainly a subject that worries the U.S. administration, considering the financial problems with the balance of payments . . . which may be reason to make us believe that such a contract may be postponed."

And with that, the wind went out of the project's sails. The next time the letter of intent came up for renewal, the government let it die. Economic experts Larry Summers and Radu Vasile evidently spoke the same language.

How Romanian monks saved a civilization

Orthodox monasteries are important in Romania, not only in a historical sense, but in a religious and cultural way as well. Old monasteries are preserved and new ones built. Like historic sites in the United States, monasteries get public funding.

Romanians were always inviting us to visit their favorite monasteries. Several times, we visited monasteries with public officials. Each time, the visit's clear focus, at least from the priests' point of view, was to pitch the finance minister, the prime minister, or whichever official was there, for additional public money. It was just like Jim's invited visits to LARS, the center for the homeless in Laurel, or to the College Park Airport Museum, both in his legislative district in Maryland. Our hosts, according to the implicit pitch, were serving the people, and thus were most deserving of the public's support.

Prime Minister Vasile kept inviting us to visit a monastery with him, so one weekend, we did. Late Saturday morning, he and Jim left our house with an entourage of security, Vasile at the wheel of an SUV and Jim in the front seat next to him. (Sheilah had stayed behind to wait for Ambassador Dick Schifter, President Clinton's brilliant and relentless seventy-five-year-old special representative for Balkan integration, who was arriving that afternoon; the two would follow later. Born in Vienna and a leader in the American Jewish community, Dick had a charming and effective way of getting everyone—from junior foreign service officers to prime ministers—to make his agenda their agenda. We cheerfully signed on.)

Vasile and Jim took off for the Sâmbăta de Sus Monastery. It's in the foothills of the Făgăraş Mountains, which separate Transylvania from southern Romania. It's about an hour's drive along the plain, then up through the mountains until you get to the other side. Vasile, like most Romanians, drove very fast. He had security in front of him and behind him, which made it easier.

This was during a period when he was quite strong politically, though under attack from all directions. Jim and Vasile spent part of the drive in a long talk about a coalition between some of the union leaders and Romanian business oligarchs whose roots were in the Securitate. They were not happy with his government's moves to open up the economy.

Sâmbăta de Sus (literally, "Upper Saturday") is not a big town. It looks as if it was built in the 1960s or '70s by developers who didn't want to spend excessive amounts of money on architects or building materials. Passing through the city center, Vasile and Jim turned left and headed out of town via a long, tree-lined driveway, a bucolic scene that contrasted sharply with the city itself. The monastery came into view, its brilliant white towers surmounting the sturdy walls. Like most Romanian monasteries, it was designed to be a fort, with a big gate in front and turrets around the outside corners.

The core of this monastery was built in the seventeenth century, but most of the complex was relatively new. Under Communism, the government had discouraged Romanians from going to church. But unlike Stalin and the Soviets, the Romanian government did not try to destroy the Orthodox Church, and it didn't close the monasteries, although it nationalized the monasteries' lands. Before Communism, the monasteries had owned millions of acres of farmland and forest. Quite a bit of what became state farms under Communism had once been church-owned farms, some owned by the dioceses, some by the monasteries. They were major economic assets of the Church. Monasteries were largely self-sufficient, raising their own food.

After Communism fell in 1989, the succeeding new governments invested in the monasteries as part of their effort to strengthen their relationship with the Church. The Orthodox Church was coming back. It was popular with the people, who identified it with Romanian nationalism. This particular monastery was built as part of that process.

Vasile and Jim drove though the gate and were met by the head of the monastery. He was probably thirty-five or forty years old, with a long beard. Large and jolly, he welcomed us with a nice smile and led us on a tour of his monastery. It had been built with a traditional design. Like every priest everywhere in the world, he was eager to show off his chapels, and like every Romanian priest, he was also eager to show off the icons they had and the icons they made.

Then it was off to lunch in a beautiful second-floor dining room with a table that would have easily accommodated a dozen people. The group was small—just Vasile, Jim, the head of the monastery, and another priest. It was a normal Romanian lunch, lasting about three hours.

The visit took place just before Easter, and the two priests supposedly were fasting for Lent. The Orthodox fast, at least in theory, is much more rigorous than that of Roman Catholics in America, in that it's not just a couple of days a week. From Ash Wednesday until Easter, the Orthodox don't eat meat, but that, to them, does not preclude dining on fish. So these monks had more fish dishes—hors d'oeuvres, soups, and filets—than Jim had ever seen. And then there were the vegetable dishes. It was all delicious—fresh and tasty.

By the end of lunch, Sheilah and Dick Schifter had arrived from Bucharest. Jim, Vasile, and the head of the monastery greeted them and took them on the tour that Jim and Valise had completed three hours earlier. By then, of course, it was almost time for dinner. We had drinks on the porch facing the mountains, sipping their homemade țuică. The day had been warm, but we were in the mountains, so by early evening, the breeze was cool. And then dinner came. It consisted of more fish and more vegetables, and it didn't involve much fasting.

That night, we slept in their guest rooms—nothing fancy, but not severe, either. It was more like Motel 6 with hardwood floors than something in which Saint Francis of Assisi would have been found.

Sunday started with a big meal, during which we watched the monk who had dined with us Saturday in the backyard of the monastery, facing the mountains, playing a couple other monks in a pickup rugby match.

When Jim told the head of the monastery how much he liked the mountain trout he'd eaten at the last three meals, the priest suggested we visit the aquaculture ponds in the mountains nearby. Right next to them was a small new hotel, evidently built by one of the companies in town. In Romania, a lot of firms, particularly the old state companies, own all kinds of unrelated businesses, such as hotels and restaurants. This one was three stories tall and wooden, with probably twenty rooms and a café downstairs. When we entered, everybody recognized the prime minister. We sat in that café while he talked to the customers, just as an American politician would when stopping at McDonald's.

By mid-afternoon, it was time to head back to Bucharest. This time, Schifter was in the front passenger seat of Vasile's SUV. We were in the back. Again, Vasile drove like a Romanian. Along what are usually two-lane roads, he was propelling us smack-dab down the middle, as government security convoys regularly do in Romania. The police want to force other drivers to pull to the curb on either side. This would be understandable from a security point of view, if there really were a security issue, but in fact, there isn't, and the maneuver drives ordinary Romanians crazy, because of both the inconvenience and the sense that it's really more about the officials' self-importance than about security.

When we reached Braşov, Jim asked Vasile why there was an ambulance in our convoy. We hadn't had one earlier in the trip. As we moved from *judeţ* to *judeţ* (county to county) with a security guard entourage, the local police would pick us up and then hand us off to the police in the next *judeţ*. The security detail changes. Why, in Braşov, had we picked up an ambulance?

After Jim's question, Vasile slowed down rapidly. The security guards in front of him kept going and then, all of sudden, figured out they had lost the prime minister and backed up. The security guys came over and conferred with him in Romanian.

We asked him what they had said. At first, he told us the ambulance was there because he had two American ambassadors with him. We didn't buy that, and he laughed. They had told him, "You're the prime minister, and we want to be sure that if anything happens, we can rush you to the hospital."

Nice gesture. When we left Braşov, we lost the ambulance. Apparently, Braşov was the only county concerned about getting Vasile to the hospital in a hurry.

Years later, we asked Vasile why he had invited us to Sâmbăta. His answer was sweeping: "I consider these monasteries and their culture to be the single most original and valid value of Romanian culture."

Reading the surprise on Sheilah's face, he began to apologize for his English. "No," she said, "your English is clear, but why do you feel that way?" Vasile, a convert to Catholicism, said it went deeper than the institution of any church, Orthodox or Catholic. It was more akin to the argument that Irish monks saved civilization.

"The Romanian culture had many opportunities to disappear," Vasile explained. "These monasteries were the keepers of Romania's history and existence."

Vasile, ever the professor of economic history, explained his view: The history of a country is not measured by statistics or politics, or even the sum of the course of individual lives, but its shared culture. For Romanians, even those who are not religious, a visit to a monastery, he asserted, is a source of peace and inspiration.

"That's why I said they are the keepers of Romanian life in culture, dreams, and hopes."

"That function of being the keeper, the guardian, the transmitter," Sheilah asked. "You think that continues today?"

"Yes," Vasile answered, "it continues." That's why he wanted us to taste a bit of it.

THIS JUST IN: HUNGARIANS AT PEACE IN ROMANIA

MOST PEOPLE IN THE United States have no idea that almost a million and a half Hungarians live in Romania. They know about ethnic minorities in Iraq, Spain, Ireland, Bosnia, and Sudan, but not in Romania. There's a simple reason: In Romania, the large Hungarian minority lives in peace.

That doesn't mean there are no conflicts, and it doesn't mean they don't have a long, sometimes violent history. It's simply that today, because Romanians and Hungarians work hard at living together in peace, and because history has dealt them a little good luck, they manage their conflicts democratically.

As always in competing ethnic histories, especially those involving land, there is debate about who got to Transylvania first, the Hungarians or the Romanians. The Romanian case is that they were there with the Romans more than seventeen hundred years ago.

Hungarians argue they've been in Transylvania for one thousand years, and that the Romanians moved there from south of the mountains sometime during the past five hundred years. Intensifying the

Hungarian claim is the fact that much of Hungarian culture and history is centered in Transylvania rather than in present-day Hungary.

In any case, no one disputes that Hungary governed Transylvania until 1918. But to say "governed" understates what life was like for Hungarians and Romanians. In a world in which a person was officially labeled Hungarian, Romanian, German, or Jewish on his or her identity papers, which ethnic group controlled the government was more than a matter of politics. Across Transylvania, Hungarians were the top dogs. They, and German and Jewish minorities, lived in the cities. Romanians lived overwhelmingly in the villages. For those visiting a Transylvanian city, even today, echoes of that history are alive in the statues of Hungarian nobility erected in city squares, in the public high school buildings converted from nineteenth-century Hungarian preparatory schools, and in the location of Romanian churches outside of city walls.

In 1918, the world of Transylvanian Hungarians and Romanians was turned upside down. Hungary had backed the losers in World War I, Romania had backed the winners, and the border of Hungary moved miles northeast. Transylvania was now part of Romania, where it remains today.

Between the World Wars, the Romanian government worked to integrate Transylvania into Romania and to lift up the lot of Romanian residents. New schools where the Romanian language was taught, jobs in public service, and other forms of what we might call "affirmative action" were used to make the region a cultural as well as political part of Romania. For local Romanians, it was a historic opportunity. For many Hungarians, it was the collapse of their way of life.

Romanians feared, not unrealistically, that some Hungarian leaders would not accept the borders of 1918 as permanent. Europeans were familiar with borders changing with the shifting tides of military victories and defeats. And, in fact, during World War II, with the support of the Germans, Hungary took control of northern Transylvania from 1940 to 1945.

During the Communist period after World War II, the Romanian government periodically made efforts to strengthen Romanian domination of Transylvania, again through education, but also by encouraging Romanians from Moldavia to move west across the mountains for jobs in the new industries Ceauşescu was building.

The result was that, by 1989, Romanians were a large majority in Transylvania. Today, most Hungarians live in cities with Romanian majorities. Their homes are in the same apartment blocks as their Romanian neighbors, not in Hungarian neighborhoods. They probably watch Hungarian television and read Hungarian newspapers, but they speak Romanian as fluently as Hungarian. A smaller number of Hungarians live in their own villages.

And then there are the several hundred thousand who live in two counties, Harghita and Covasna, where Hungarians make up the majority.

Harghita and Covasna are in the center of Romania, hundreds of miles from the Hungarian border. In these counties, known as Szeklerland, you'll find the only Hungarians who speak little or no Romanian. And you'll find Romanians who know what it's like to live as a minority.

Jim started his tour of the Szeklerland in Târgu Mureş, a city almost evenly split between Hungarians and Romanians. Before Communism, it was more heavily Hungarian, and served as the unofficial capital of the Hungarian majorities in the country. After 1989's Revolution, it was also the scene of major conflicts between Hungarians and Romanians.

Traveling with him in the van from Târgu Mureş were two of the embassy's Hungarian staffers, Emőd Farkas and Toni Niculescu. Amazingly, when Jim first got to Romania, he found that, while the embassy had an office in Cluj in the center of Transylvania, it had only one Hungarian staff member, an able IT expert in Bucharest. But on the political staff, the economic staff, and the USAID staff, there were no Hungarians. He made it a priority to fix that. By the end of his first year, he hired Emőd and Toni, both experienced young professionals committed to improving ethnic relations in Romania.

East of Târgu Mureş, the landscape changes. Almost imperceptibly, it has less the feel of Eastern Europe and more the feel of New England. Partly, that's due to the Catholic and Protestant church spires that dominate these small, neat towns. Part of it is because of the lack of industrialization, which resulted from Ceauşescu's effort to isolate these communities.

On his first day in Harghita, in addition to visiting several Hungarian communities, Jim and embassy staffers visited the one majority-Romanian town and met its mayor. They also visited a Romanian Orthodox monastery nearby. The cultural contrast could not have been more dramatic. Coming from the understated Hungarian community into the Romanian church, Jim felt an immediate change. The incense, the singing, the exuberant hospitality—all made him feel as if he was back in Bucharest.

They sat down to talk with the head of the monastery and the mayor. Jim asked the mayor what it was like to be a Romanian in Harghita. The mayor said that, oddly, while there were issues, there was no serious conflict. Later, Jim learned that Hungarian leaders in the area resented the expansion of the Romanian monastery.

One evening, Jim and the staffers stayed at a modern high-rise hotel in the mountains of Covasna. It had a beautiful view of the mountains and a clientele made up largely of Israelis of Romanian origin who loved the clear mountain air. That night, they had dinner with the chairman of Covasna's county council, a young heavyset man who was clearly an activist.

Jim asked him what it was like for Hungarians in Covasna. The council chairman cited no examples of violence or outright repression, but he focused on issues that sounded remarkably like ones from ethnic minorities in the United States. Hungarians were free to carry on their businesses, but there were hardly any Hungarians in the local police forces, and hardly any in important state institutions. He felt there were elements in Romania that were trying to repress the reinvigoration of Hungarian culture in Covasna and in Harghita.

In Bucharest, it was easy to find Hungarians who felt that the

Romanian government was being unfair to their people in Transylvania. And it was easy to find Romanians who felt that when Hungarians were the top dogs, as to some extent they are in Harghita and Covasna, Romanians could be the victims. But in those counties, it was hard to find anything more than the kind of ethnic tension you would find in most multiethnic cities in the United States.

THIS COUNTRY HAS CHANGED

IN EVERY ROMANIAN *județ*, you can find American citizens, most of whom grew up in Romania, putting their money where their roots are.

In Harghita, we ate lunch at Pearl of Szentegyháza, a beautiful wood restaurant just outside Odorheiu Secuiesc (Székelyudvarhely). The owner is Gábor Radi. He was born in Harghita, but served in the U.S. Army and graduated from North Dakota State University in 1989. Right after the Revolution, he came back to Romania and started making small investments. He moved back full-time in 1994, and within a few years owned several stores, a meat-processing company, and a fish farm, in addition to the restaurant.

Joining us at lunch was Márta Károlyi. She grew up in Odorheiu Secuiesc and defected to the United States in 1981 with her husband Béla Károlyi, the famous gymnastics coach. They've coached Nadia Comăneci and Mary Lou Retton, and run a school for young gymnasts near Houston, Texas. In Odorheiu Secuiesc, they and childhood friends have invested in several local businesses, including Digital 3 TV, a private Hungarian-language station.

One uninvited guest showed up at the lunch—the owner of Chicago's Little Bucharest restaurant. A Serbian, he had been trying for years to get Jim to come to his restaurant's annual Romanian festival in Chicago. When Jim visited Chicago, he hadn't been able to make it or even talk with him by phone. So when the restaurant owner was in Romania and heard Jim was coming into town, he showed up at lunch to give his pitch. It showed a lot of entrepreneurial zeal. Unfortunately, we weren't able to go to his festival while Jim was ambassador. We still want to.

As we arrived at Pearl of Szentegyháza, we hopped out of the embassy van and passed a couple eating lunch at an outdoor table. Sorin Gogeanu, the United States Information Agency (USIA) press guy with us for the trip, overheard their comments.

"Isn't that the U.S. ambassador?" the wife asked as we arrived and exited our van.

"Yeah, I think it is. But if it were him, wouldn't there be a big motorcade of security cars, too?" her husband replied.

"I don't know."

Halfway through lunch, when Sorin stepped outside for a smoke, the couple was still pondering whether or not the U.S. ambassador would visit Odorheiu Secuiesc without a security motorcade.

Finally, the wife said, "I think it was him."

"If the U.S. ambassador really travels around Romania in a van without security, things have really changed in this country," her husband concluded.

They were right. We were safer there than driving the Capital Beltway around Washington, D.C.

The fact was that most foreign ambassadors did not travel with a lot of security. Exceptions, understandably, were the Israeli and Turkish ambassadors.

The Turkish ambassador was not paranoid. In 1999 his government arrested the leader of the Kurdish PKK opposition party. The same year, while we were in Romania, a murder in Bucharest was attributed to the PKK. The story was that someone associated with a Turkish restaurant a few blocks south of our embassy, and one where Jim dined several times, was murdered in a shootout. Allegedly, the PKK was attempting to collect money from Kurds in Bucharest, and the victim hadn't paid his share.

The American businesspeople we met that day at lunch were interesting and committed. But they were only two of the twenty-eight Americans who had invested in Harghita, and the approximately twenty-five hundred Americans who had invested across Romania.

People were often incredulous when Jim told them that, according to U.S. government statistics, American investment here grew forty percent in 1998, putting our citizens among the top three outside investors in Romania (after the Netherlands and Germany). Except for a few high-profile consumer-product companies like McDonald's and Coca-Cola, most American investors are almost invisible. Perhaps it's because so many trace their roots here and, unlike us, have perfect local language skills.

The Americans working in small Romanian businesses or on humanitarian projects are not naïve or complacent about Romania's difficulties. Almost all have tales about corruption, complaints about bureaucracy, and disappointments with U.S. visa decisions concerning their Romanian colleagues. Born or naturalized, these red-blooded Americans were not shy about complaining to the U.S. ambassador—or anyone else, for that matter. But also as Americans, they seem to believe in their bones that problems can be overcome and that the future will be better than the past. For Romanians at that time, in the third year of a deep recession and only ten years after the fall of Communism, we couldn't think of a more valuable U.S. export than that—confidence in the future.

WHO WOULDN'T WANT A GERMAN TO BE YOUR MAYOR?

"THEY'RE WELL-ORGANIZED. They make things work."

That's what Sibiu Romanians told us when we asked why the city, historically German but now overwhelmingly Romanian, had elected Klaus Johannis, an ethnic German and candidate of the micro-minority German Democratic Forum, as mayor.

Johannis is a tall, cheerful, English-speaking man, with a strong resemblance to Arnold Schwarzenegger. His wife, Carmen, is a German-speaking Romanian who teaches high school English. After serving as superintendent of schools for Sibiu and thereby gaining much notoriety, Klaus won direct election as mayor with the support of a center-right coalition.

The lesson is universal—not all ethnic stereotypes are negative. So much for the impossibility of moving beyond ethnic struggles that last one thousand years.

COMING FOR ORPHANS, STAYING FOR FAMILIES

A STRANGER TO DOWNTOWN Sibiu in December might have been surprised to see two tall men in slightly seedy red robes cinched at the waist, fake white beards tied around their chins, and jingle bells in their hands, begging passersby to drop some money into a copper pot. And, oh yes, hovering in the background were a few reporters and photographers.

Jim and Mayor Klaus Johannis working as Santas in Sibiu, raising money for the poor

But no one familiar with Sibiu would have been surprised to learn that the Santa Claus doppelgangers were none other than the mayor and the U.S. ambassador, both drafted to raise money for Sister Mary Rose Christy and her nonprofit group.

Sister Mary Rose Christy is a force of nature. She's very good at making her agenda your agenda—and her agenda, crystallized over more than a decade in post-Communist Romania, is to bring out the best in Romanian families and help them cope with the worst.

It all started about five months after the Revolution. She was in Arizona, a Sister of Mercy with degrees in nursing and social work and a master's in political science, on sabbatical from her activities as a social worker. A CNN report about Romania's orphanages came onto the television screen with scenes so horrific she started yelling at the set. "I'm going there to help," she recalled telling herself. "I'm a nurse, and even if I wasn't, I know I can take better care of children than that!"

For Romanians, it's sometimes difficult to understand the frenzy about Romanian "orphans" which swept the American media that spring. Human interest and genuine altruism trumped politics. The Romania of Ceauşescu, Dracula, and Nadia Comăneci was transformed, in millions of Americans' minds, into the Romania of children suffering in Dickensian orphanages. ABC's 20/20's episode on the subject won some of its highest ratings, and American TV came back to the subject again and again. The good news was that it moved many Americans, like Sister Mary Rose, to devote years of their lives to helping those children. But it is also understandable why many Romanians felt, correctly, that it painted a narrow and misleading picture of their country and its people. Yes, there were thousands of Romanian children who suffered needlessly in institutions, as there were in other countries. But no, that was not the typical experience of Romanian children, who in fact generally benefit from stronger family ties and support than do many in the United States.

In May 1990, Sister Mary Rose started raising money and securing supplies, and linked her efforts with those of the San Francisco Rotary and retired British actress Angela Mason. (Networking is another of Sister Mary Rose's strong points.) Thirteen months later, with the blessings of her religious order, she was in Sibiu. She plunged into work at Râul Vadului, the home for handicapped kids and adults south of Sibiu, and worked four years at the orphanage.

As she began caring for the children, she could see they were dehydrated, anemic, and vitamin-deficient, so she began to prowl the open markets to see what produce was available. Then she spotted a van and persuaded its owner to shop with her each day so she could get the healthy food back to the kitchen of Râul Vadului.

All the while, she was watching the situation with the questioning eyes of a social worker and a political science student. Why were conditions so bad in the orphanages? To her, it seemed that too many Romanians had grown so accustomed to chaos and inhumane interactions, they didn't expect anything better.

And why were there so many kids in the orphanages to begin with? Most of them had living parents. Certainly, Romania's then-devastated economy was part of the problem. But Sister Mary Rose concluded that the reasons ran deeper—a profound lack of self-esteem, individually and collectively, that weakens families and opens the door to dishonesty and corruption.

After a few years, Sister Mary Rose decided that fixing problems at the orphanages was a less direct way to help children than strengthening families so they wouldn't shed their children to begin with. She founded the nonprofit Romanian American Association for the Promotion of Health, Education, and Human Services. (Alas, the name is no more mellifluous in Romanian, with the acronym ARAPAMESU.)

At first, she encountered the same dysfunctional behavior she had seen at the orphanage: staff and volunteers who nodded and agreed with her plans and directives, but then did nothing, or what they had intended to do all along.

"I had to put my foot down and say, 'Please stop treating me like a Communist boss.'"

Sister Mary Rose is back at her convent in California now, and Romanian staff and volunteers are steering ARAPAMESU. It tries to show poor families what they can do, and encourages them to do it. It's what Lyndon Johnson's antipoverty program called "empowerment." ARAPAMESU provides job training, and also some job creation by helping clients barter skills they learn—skills like carpentry. It organizes community events—a spring carnival, a protect-the-environment day, and, of course, the Christmas Action, including street fund-raising. There's daycare, a summer camp, and an apprenticeship program for school dropouts. There are sports tournaments and short-term distributions of food, furniture, and clothes, as well as of eyeglasses and medicines.

In its first ten years, ARAPAMESU estimates it assisted twenty-five hundred families, diverted thousands of children from orphanages, and positioned thousands to work in the booming Sibiu economy.

The results have come in part from Sister Mary Rose's fearlessness about asking those with power or money to use it on behalf of her families, and her energy in conscripting volunteers and staff. In large part, the results come from the response of Romanians themselves.

"A little bit of hard rain, and a lot of sunshine, and the people begin to respond. They blossom," Sister Mary Rose said. "When you give people the feeling they can do something themselves, they do it!"

BRAM STOKER CAME AND THE GERMANS LEFT

BISTRIȚA IS NOT ON the average foreigner's itinerary for Romania. There's no airport. It's not on a road to Bucharest or to Hungary.

But it's an interesting place.

For one thing, it's in Bram Stoker's *Dracula*. The hero, Jonathan Harker, stopped there to eat on the eve of St. George's Day on his way to meet Count Dracula. The Golden Krone Inn where he dined was converted from fiction to fact by the local tourist agency in the 1980s. East of town is the newer Hotel Castle Dracula, a product of post-Communist capitalism.

Bistrița was also one of the seven Saxon German cities built in the twelfth century to defend Christendom from the Turks. The others are Sibiu, Brașov, Cluj, Mediaș, Sebeș, and Sighișoara. Together, they are the Siebenbürgen, or "seven boroughs."

The downtown square of Bistrița is dominated—in fact overwhelmed—by the Biserica Evanghelică, a Lutheran church built in Gothic style during the fifteenth and sixteenth centuries by the Saxon Germans. Its 246-foot spire is said to be the tallest in Romania.

Germans dominated the city until the end of World War II. In 1940, the German and Hungarian armies occupied northern Transylvania, including Bistriţa. The local German Saxon population welcomed them. Only a little over twenty years earlier, Bistriţa had been part of the Austro-Hungarian empire. To many, the occupation was liberation.

But when the tide turned and the German army retreated in 1944, most of the local ethnic German population felt threatened, and left with the troops. The result was that, while monuments to German culture like the Evangelical Church remain, few Germans live in Bistriţa today. Farther south in Transylvania, where the German Army did not occupy Braşov, Sibiu, or Mediaş, the Saxon Germans stayed throughout the postwar period, but in Bistriţa and the rest of northern Transylvania, Germans whose families had lived in Transylvania for hundreds of years left in a few months. In a town of eighty thousand people, today no more than a few dozen are Germans.

Bistriţa is seventy miles northeast of Cluj. Jim visited with Nick Chakos of International Orthodox Christian Charities (IOCC), the U.S.-based international aid arm of the Orthodox churches. During the war in Kosovo, we had feared that the hundreds of thousands of Albanian refugees that Milošević was pushing into Macedonia might need a haven in neighboring countries, including Romania. We talked to the United Nations Commission on Refugees and various American aid organizations, mostly Protestant, that had experience with refugees.

"Aren't there any Orthodox charitable groups we can involve in this effort?" Jim asked. After all, this was Romania, eighty-five percent Orthodox. And because the Serbs are Orthodox, it wouldn't be bad if we were encouraging Orthodox aid to the Albanian Muslims.

One of the embassy's young Foreign Service officers, Tom Underwood, quickly found out there was such an organization—International Orthodox Christian Charities. It was active around the region, just not yet in Romania. And it was based in Baltimore, Maryland. Jim was embarrassed he'd never heard of it. He called Peter Marudas, top staffer for U.S. Senator Paul Sarbanes from Maryland. Marudas seems to know every Greek and every Orthodox cleric in America. Peter gave IOCC rave reviews, and introduced Jim to its executive director, Constantine Triantafilou.

As it turned out, the war ended before we had to face an onslaught of refugees into Romania. But IOCC had now decided to start operating in Romania. Particularly exciting was that, in Orthodox countries, IOCC naturally partners with the local Orthodox church. Thus, an American charitable group would be working with the Romanian Orthodox Church, the most popular and ubiquitous institution in the country. That clearly had practical and political benefits for U.S. efforts in Romania. Our smart USAID director, Denny Robertson, started thinking about how to help IOCC.

In 1999, there were floods in eastern Romania. Each U.S. ambassador has a small amount of money to help with natural disasters. Denny suggested we use it for emergency food supplies to flooded villages, and ask IOCC to organize the distribution through local Orthodox churches. It was an inspired idea. The church had local storage and disbursement facilities everywhere we needed it. Within a few days, the Patriarch and Jim were at a loading dock. The Patriarch was blessing. Jim was hauling. Jim then took a day to help distribute the food in several villages. An IOCC staffer who had worked on relief projects around the world told me it was one of the best organized he'd ever seen, which was not that surprising. The Orthodox have been on this case for over one thousand years.

When IOCC decided to get involved in Romania, they must have gone to central casting, because they definitely sent the perfect guy. Nick Chakos looks like a choir boy. With enormous brown eyes and dark curly hair, he is short, cheerful, and upright in demeanor. Most importantly, he projects a well-scrubbed innocence that's hard for anyone to resist.

He quickly ingratiated himself with all the right people at the Patriarchy. It didn't hurt that he himself grew up the son of a Greek Orthodox priest in the United States. It also helped that he was extraordinarily competent. He had worked for several international relief organizations, so he understood a lot of the logistics, he understood the church politics, and he threw himself into making it all work.

Come to think of it, Nick was as good at ingratiating himself with the bureaucrats at USAID, the source of IOCC's funding in Romania, as he was at bonding with the Patriarch's staff. Apparently, both enjoy having their hands kissed. Figure out one hierarchy, you've figured out them all.

We came to Bistrița to promote an after-school center for kids, sponsored by the local Orthodox church with support from IOCC. The plan was for Jim and the local bishop to help whitewash the walls of the center, preparing it for the children.

Quickly, Jim concluded that the bishop had never run for office in the United States. While Jim reached for the paint rollers, the bishop held back, not clear exactly what was expected. He was cheerful enough—and pleased with the project—but not really interested in doing the paint job himself.

COMING TO AIUD . . . TO PRISON

AS YOU HEAD NORTH from Albă Iulia, the road follows the river Mureș past farms and old vineyards. Wine has been made in this region for centuries. In about half an hour, you spot the tower of a fortress more than seven hundred years old. This is Aiud—Nagyenyed in Hungarian, Straßburg am Mieresch in German. The stories of the Romanians, Magyars, and Saxons are intertwined here.

Aiud is also the site of one of the most famous Romanian political prisons of the Communist era. For six of Ion Diaconescu's seventeen years in prison, it was his residence, too.

"To Aiud were taken the former leaders, the ones that had been ministers and party leaders. We were young back then," he recalled. Diaconescu was a thirty-year-old leader of the youth wing of the PNȚCD when he was arrested.

"In 1944, the Russian troops came to Romania, but the Communist regime wasn't crowned until 1947. That's when we were put in prison," he explains. "The ones in prison for political reasons stayed there for different periods of times. Some for a year, or just a couple of months, others for five, ten, fifteen years. There were approximately two hundred thousand people in prison. The rest of the people got scared.

"Where the Senate [was], where the Communist Party headquarters was before 1989, back then it was the Ministry of Internal Affairs building. They had a prison right there in the basement. That was my first prison." That building, today just across the Piaţa from the Hilton Athenee Palace, was the site where Ceauşescu gave his final disastrous speech on December 22, 1989, and then flew off in a helicopter.

"But that wasn't the worst prison. And neither was Aiud," Diaconescu emphasized. "The worst was Râmnicu Sărat. The worst! Because of the total isolation imposed on prisoners. There was just one prisoner in every cell. In no other prison until then was there this rule, to stay by yourself for years in your cell.

"Nonetheless, Corneliu Coposu and I kept in touch using codes. We had different alphabets, but the most used one was the Morse Code. We would knock on the wall. The guard would listen, so it became dangerous and prohibited after a while. Then we came up with an invention. We were taken outside to a yard, one at a time, for some fresh air, in sessions lasting twenty to thirty minutes. Every cell window faced that yard. A security guy who didn't know Morse Code supervised us there. Here's the invention: We coughed in Morse Code, because coughing wasn't prohibited. In general, the prisoners were sick, so it was almost natural to cough. To say one letter, you had to cough quite a few times in a row. So, in one walk, we could express one idea, consisting of maybe ten to twenty words, like somebody died or something happened.

"When I was done with this twenty-minute walk, I was exhausted from all the coughing. I stayed in that prison in Râmnicu Sărat for six years. In six years, you have time to cough your ideas out."

"Were you and others physically tortured?" Sheilah asked.

"It was like a lottery," Diaconescu said. "I was beaten before and after Stalin died. But you could have stayed there for years and not get beaten, or you'd get beaten three days in a row. We were beaten when they wanted us to declare whatever they wished us to declare."

Diaconescu had grown up in the PNȚCD. His father was an Orthodox priest whose cousin was married to Ion Mihalache, who founded the Peasant Party in old Romania before the unification of Transylvania into Romania. Diaconescu grew up in Boteşti in Argeş, a mountainous area about seventy-five miles northwest of Bucharest.

"Mihalache was a teacher," he recounts. "He came from a poor family. Peasants back then lived in unfavorable conditions. They didn't have enough land. Mihalache came back from the battlefield of World War I a hero with a medal, and he established this party after the war. The Peasant Party was very successful and it based itself on teachers and priests. The common peasant didn't have a political education. In a village, the only leaders were the priests and the teachers. In 1926, after the unification of Romania, the Peasant Party and the National Party from Transylvania merged, forming the PNȚCD.

"My father was one of the founders of the Peasant Party. He never had an important position in the party. He was just a member. But he went to prison, too. He stayed in prison for two years and they took everything from him—his house, his properties, and his church. I had uncles in prison, too. In general, the Communists would put an entire family in prison."

His home-based roots were in the PNȚCD, but his activism came in college.

"If you asked me when I was seven what kind of political party I supported, I would have said the Peasant Party. But I wasn't active," he recalls. "When I became a college student in 1936, I was impressed in a bad way that the college students had been won over by the fascist movements. In Romania, there was a large fascist movement called the Iron Guard, which had lots of fans among college students.

"When I became a student at Politehnica Bucharest, I could see the pressure from the extreme-right organizations, which tried to enlist everybody in their parties. The democratic parties wouldn't do such a thing. Our parties were thinking that if you're in school, you should think about school and not politics. But this fascist movement's founder was a college student, and that's why this tradition that they have—to dominate the universities—existed."

Seeing all this as he started college galvanized Diaconescu to become politically active.

We asked why the Iron Guard and the fascists were attractive to college students in Romania in the 1930s.

"First of all, it was in fashion in Europe—in Germany and Italy especially—so that influenced us," he answered. "Secondly, there were social problems. In Romania, as in all the other countries, the high social class was wealthy, but there weren't too many of them, and there was a huge mass of poor people."

That opened the door for Communism—populism from the left— and also for a populist reaction from the right.

"The Iron Guard was connected to the Orthodox Church, and that's how the believers were drawn to their party. They were anti-Communist, but they wanted everything to be done the 'extreme-right' way. This movement didn't win over the whole church, but there were lots of priests who adopted the 'extreme-right' party.

"Part of it was an anti-Semitism movement. In Romania back then, there were around one million Jews. They generally would have much more than the common Romanian peasant would. And that was one reason for people to adopt the 'extreme-right' movement. The Mussolini and Hitler 'fashion' and all the other reasons I mentioned created a powerful extreme-right party.

"Back then, I knew this movement was wrong from all points of view. I was explaining to my colleagues that putting aside internal considerations, you can't be anti-Semitic. My leading argument was, 'You, with this extreme-right policy, want to align Romania to Germany and Italy.' At that time, internationally speaking, Hitler's theme was the revision of the Treaty of Versailles, and the Western powers of England and France wanted to maintain the existing order. The U.S. was neutral but still supportive.

"I was trying to convince my friends that aligning ourselves with Germany was against Romanian interests. Romania became unified after the Treaty of Versailles. That was my ultimate argument. I would ask, 'Hey, do you want Transylvania to be part of Romania?' and they would say, 'Yes.' I would shoot back at them, 'So why would you want to align yourself to Hitler, if Hitler doesn't want that?' When Hitler had the chance to conquer Transylvania in 1941, he immediately took advantage of it. That's why, in '36, I created the Peasant Party student organization at the Politehnica."

Diaconescu was not yet twenty years old.

After Romania split with Germany in 1944, the pre-war parties—the PNŢCD and the PNL—came back to life. In Diaconescu's party, Mihalache became vice president, and Iuliu Maniu president. Corneliu Coposu, who, with Diaconescu, would lead the party back to power after 1989, was Maniu's secretary. Diaconescu himself was one of seven youth leaders of the party.

Seven decades later, still erect and vigorous, Diaconescu reflected what Romanians expected from the West, especially the United States, after World War II.

"In 1944, the resistance against Russians was the main theme of our party. Stalin came to our country, and he never left. The Russians felt that the eastern part of Europe had to be theirs. Stalin promised the Americans all sorts of things regarding the eastern part of Europe, but never kept his promises. In all those international conferences, at Yalta and so on, the Americans said that human rights would be respected. We knew that the Russians didn't respect any of those rights. We knew it from our own history, our own former relations with Russia. But we also knew that they had their own fears—and if the West forced them, they would honor those rights!

"At that time, Russia got all its weapons from the United States and the Western countries. Russia was in poor shape in '44 and '45 . . . and even worse after the Americans dropped the bomb. Just two bombs, and the Allies' problems with Japan were solved. So the United States had great power without having made too many sacrifices of men. With one or two threatened bombings, they could have made Stalin keep his word in Eastern Europe.

"That's how our leaders and all the Romanian people saw it: We were the ones making righteous requests. The Russians had made a commitment and had to respect it. The Americans, the English people, the French people promised they'd help us. We thought that the United States wouldn't leave Russia alone until the Russians respected their earlier commitments and withdrew. If not, Russia could become so powerful that they would be able to make their own atomic bomb.

"The majority of Romanians lost hope when the Russians got their own atomic bomb in 1951. I was in prison in Baia Sprie. Until then, we were always thinking, *Why weren't the Russians bombed in order to settle them down once and for all?* When our leaders were arrested in 1947, we believed that the problem would be solved in one year."

His memories helped us understand better what Romanians are thinking when they greet Americans with, "We've been waiting for you for forty years." We still don't understand why they smile when they say it.

For three years, Diaconescu did hard labor in the lead and copper mines of western Romania. As the years in prison dragged on though the 1950s and into the early 1960s, reality set in—but hope never died.

"Everybody knew Russia's weaknesses. So even when the Russians got their atomic bomb, people in jail would say, 'A miserable Russian bomb is no match for the Americans' weapons.' We didn't lose faith, even if hope weakened among those of us in jail.

"But what was our alternative? To escape from jail and tell people they were wrong? When you suffer for an idea, and you invest a lot of emotions in one idea, to give in after all that time is to admit your failure. It's hard to give up an idea that you committed yourself to a long time ago. You go on.

"The Americans' strategy didn't consider an open war with the Russians. The Americans were sure that Communism would collapse under its own burdens. And that's exactly what finally happened. But it lasted for forty years. Communism collapsed without any American bomb. Communism collapsed as a result of its own faults. But this took forty years, which was a very long time for us. For the Americans, it wasn't that long, but for the countries under Communism, it was terror."

In 1964, in response to U.S. pressure and the Romanian government's desire to loosen its ties to Russia, Diaconescu was one of thousands of political prisoners who were released. He was forty-seven, and had spent more than one-third of his life behind bars. He found work in Bucharest as an engineer for a small elevator company, and stayed until he retired.

"They released us from prison but didn't give us any political freedom," he said. "They continued to exert all kinds of pressure. In 1944, '45, '46, people were waiting, thinking Communism would be over soon. By 1964, after twenty years of Communism, it was thought that nothing would be changed, and most people didn't have the courage to make things change. Society's reaction was much weaker than before.

"We were investigated, threatened, and supervised. Some of us were in prison for half a year to a year just to scare everybody. We couldn't form an organization because all our movements were supervised by the Securitate. Every house had microphones in it. We were watched everywhere we went. At our workplaces, we would have God knows how many informers. Our houses were searched all the time. We were 'free,' but we had no freedom."

But he and his political allies did not lose contact with each other.

"We wanted to stay in touch, as many of us as possible, but we needed a non-political reason to do so," he said. "We would gather at a birthday party, an anniversary, a baptism, a requiem, so we could have an honest answer to 'Why were you there?' when you were called in for questioning."

Diaconescu told us he never seriously considered leaving Romania to avoid arrest.

"First, it wasn't that easy to leave the country. The Communist system makes it really tough to get out of the country; everything is under their control," he remembers. "Second, I had nothing to do abroad. If you go, you need to justify your existence. I said to myself, 'If this lasts for one year, I'm better off here!' If it were for a little while, I would have gone abroad. But if somebody had told me that, if I go abroad, I wouldn't be able to come back to Romania for forty years, I would have stayed here. You need some sort of confidence that you can survive elsewhere in the world. I was too connected—my roots here were too deep to be able to that."

After another quarter-century of Communism came Gorbachev, the fall of the Berlin Wall, and Ceauşescu's December 22 speech at the site of Diaconescu's "first prison."

"I was in Piaţa Unirii and I saw the people marching in," he said, recalling Bucharest residents filing into the rally that Ceauşescu had called to counter the rebellion begun in Timişoara. "And those people looked so upset, they looked like they were going to a funeral. They were taken to the Piaţa Revoluţiei, and I saw them on TV from then on. Ceauşescu began his speech with his usual nonsense, but then he started to say that over in Timişoara, enemies were plotting. Suddenly, the TV broadcast got cut and people said, 'Something must have happened.' I'm not clear what did happen, not even today. Because of the explosion, people broke free from their assigned positions, the agitation started, and somebody started screaming, 'Freedom! Down with Ceauşescu!' That was the start of the Revolution.

"That night, I listened to Radio Free Europe and Voice of America to learn what was going on. The next morning, I walked—there was no public transportation—towards the center of town. Coposu was living near Piaţa Unirii. On my way to the center of the city, I saw an empty tram with a sign that read, 'Down with Ceauşescu! Down with the tyrant!' Tears were running down my cheeks. I'd been waiting for this for fifty years.

"So, we started to gather. The younger ones went to the streets. We, the older ones—we went, too. On the twenty-third, we wrote our first manifesto, which was broadcast on Europa Liberă. We started to reorganize ourselves and to think how to revitalize our party."

It was clearly a historic turning point, but one of the continuing debates in Romania is whether it was really a revolution or just a coup d'état. John Florescu, son of Dracula biographer Radu Florescu Sr. and a sophisticated student of all things Romanian, reports that in the spring of 2009, when human rights champion Kerry Kennedy spoke in Romania about "the glories of '89 at press conferences, people reacted with reassured indifference—as if to say, 'Yeah, but not really.' To Romanians," Florescu continued, "December 1989 is not the Boston Tea Party or the storming of the Bastille or Budapest in 1956—nor will it be written that way in Romanian history."

Florescu is surely right that many Romanians doubt that it was the people in the streets who pushed Ceauşescu from power, rather than the Securitate or even the Russians. Our own view is that, like most dramatic political changes, leaders and followers both played a role, as did outside powers. After all, would our forebears have won the American Revolution without French military support? Does that diminish the sincerity of Sam Adams or Thomas Jefferson? Or make the break with Britain and the creation of American democracy less revolutionary?

John Florescu told us that Mikhail Gorbachev told him years later of his conclusion that Ceauşescu "had to go, and I had put the apparatus of the state in that direction." Was Gorbachev revealing the inside story of a coup d'état, or claiming credit for somebody else's revolution? It's hard to know.

Either way, December 1989 marked the end of one political regime in Romania and the beginning of a dramatically different direction. Men like Diaconescu had the perspective that comes with age.

"Since getting out of prison," Diaconescu told us, "it has been our goal to assure the survival and continuation of the party. In people's consciousness, the true opponents of Communists were the Peasants. This history helped us a lot. This was our strength. But we had weaknesses, too. One weakness was that we were a party of old people—all the leaders were old. The people accepted us, but the public wanted someone young. Even I, when I was young, thought the same: 'If you're old, stay home!'"

But his party was successful. They won seats in the first free parliamentary elections in Romania since Communism. And in 1996, a coalition led by Diaconescu's party won the presidency and control of parliament. Diaconescu himself, at eighty, became chairman of the Chamber of Deputies.

Diaconescu regrets that his center-right coalition didn't accomplish more during its four years in power.

"But we did something that's very important: We won the ideological battle. Now, Iliescu and all the former Communists are convinced that our way, about which we talked in '89, was the right way. In '89, they didn't say anything about returning properties to their pre-Communism owners, nor did they say anything about privatizing state companies. They said that would be selling our country to foreigners.

"Now, everybody, even Vadim Tudor [the nationalist head of the Party of Greater Romania], is talking about privatization, and about Europe, NATO, and the Americans. What we said before, now everybody agrees on. So we won, ideologically speaking. We have this strength, and we'll go on, the young ones in our party, and the old ones, because we are young in our hearts. The ones in our party have a history. We went to prison because of our beliefs, but the other party came in with new and changed beliefs. Our strength is that we stuck to our beliefs over the years."

STAYING IN AIUD . . . FOR EUROPE

THE WALL SURROUNDING AIUD'S ancient fortress is punctuated by nine towers. In the Middle Ages, each was maintained and defended by one of the guilds, such as the tanners or the weavers. Around the wall, there are elegant small homes that date "only" to the seventeenth century, and newer ones that are little more than a hundred years old. It wasn't the fortress that drew Sheilah to Aiud, but the next building—the old college building. Caroline Carver spent a year teaching as a Fulbright professor at this, one of the oldest Hungarian high schools in Transylvania. Bethlen Gábor College was founded as the Academy of

Philosophy and Theology in 1622.

For centuries, it carried the torch of Hungarian education in Transylvania. Its nine hundred students (from primary grades through high school) are drawn from around the region, and its graduates include many of the region's leaders, scientists, and artists. It's also an important teachers' school, similar to what used to be called "a normal school" in the United States. Its graduates can be certified to teach in any primary school or kindergarten in Romania, and in some foreign countries, without university degrees. Still, most (about sixty percent) of Bethlen Gábor's graduates go on to college.

Caroline's fellow teachers told Sheilah that until the Communists nationalized the college and its lands, Bethlen Gábor was one of the richest schools in Eastern Europe. It had thousands of acres of forests, farmland, and vineyards, as well as houses, other buildings, and its own printing press. In the old days, professors invited to teach at Bethlen Gábor were compensated with use of a two-story home, servants, animals for food, and wood for winter heat, as well as a stipend. Caroline's accommodations were nowhere near as grand, but she did have a nice apartment and solicitous neighbors who worried if the landlord was late turning on the heat.

The assortment of buildings the school occupies now includes the three hundred-year-old dormitory, two hundred-year-old classrooms, and a science lab that's nearly one hundred years old. The school is fighting in court to get back some of the lands confiscated by the Communist regime. The government pays the salaries of the staff and the utilities used in the nineteenth-century building the school now occupies, but it doesn't pay for the pupils' books.

Bethlen Gábor College is an important Hungarian institution in a city with a deep Hungarian history and a population that today is less than one-fifth Hungarian. How does that work? Pretty well, according to Caroline's students, colleagues, and neighbors.

Sheilah spoke with Judit Katona a few weeks before she was to graduate from Bethlen Gábor. Judit had attended only Hungarian schools, but said neighborhoods in Aiud are not segregated ethnically.

"We get along with them very well," Judit said. "They are very friendly and they accept us. I have to say I have many Romanian friends. When I was little, I went to a Hungarian kindergarten, and I didn't know Romanian at all; we spoke Hungarian in our family, and I didn't know how to speak with neighborhood playmates. They taught me, and it was great. I learned by playing."

Judit seemed to feel more at home in Aiud, with Romanian and Transylvanian neighbors, than she might in Hungary.

"I have to say that Hungarians don't like us—they do not consider Transylvanians like me to truly be Hungarian, and this fact makes us not like them so much," she said. "This isn't so with everybody in Hungary—there are many who don't feel like this. Still, I don't think many people on either side want to see Transylvania and Hungary reunited."

At dinner that night with Caroline's friend Ildiko and her family, Sheilah raised the question again: "I was told Hungary still grieves for the loss of Transylvania," she said.

Ildiko jumped in. "Yes, but they can't take just the physical beauty. They have to take the people, too—and we've changed since 1918."

Her sister-in-law Kati added, "The assimilation worked."

"Only unreasonable people," their mother Eva said, "would think it possible to be reunited."

To be sure, the adults agreed that there are tensions between Romanians and Hungarians—tensions sometimes stoked by political interests. We discussed the 1990 anti-Hungarian rampage in Târgu Mureş, in which the writer András Sütő, a graduate of Bethlen Gábor, was beaten so badly he was blinded. But the consensus at dinner a decade later was that relations were good between the Hungarians and Romanians, who live as next-door neighbors and work side by side.

Caroline and her husband, Vic Fingerhut, a political science professor at the University of Mary Washington in Virginia, came to the same conclusion about the younger generation in Aiud. Vic made several visits during Caroline's year in Aiud, and in her classes led a series of discussions on democracy.

Vic not only teaches political science, but he's a veteran pollster. He asked these Hungarian-speaking middle school and high school students a series of questions about their personal day-to-day inter-actions with Romanians of the same age. Some of these kids lived in Aiud, some commuted from smaller towns in Transylvania, and some lived at the boarding school.

The overwhelming majority of the students told Vic they had friends who were primarily Romanian. They didn't have stories of inter-ethnic conflict to share. And when Vic probed deeper, asking whether they had Romanian-language friends they considered "close," real friends with whom they could talk about personal matters, Vic was surprised that well over half responded that they did—surprised, because these were kids with a strong sense of cultural identity. They were attending a special Hungarian-language school. But he picked up no sense of ethnic conflict or social or personal isolation.

Almost half indicated they would "go out" with Romanians, and about one-third said it would be "no problem" for them to marry a Romanian.

Vic, ever the pollster, noted that he got these responses from a relatively small sample—slightly more than one hundred students. And Caroline observed that Hungarian-language kids usually "hang out" with Hungarian speakers, and Romanian-speaking kids tended to hang out with Romanian speakers. But that may say less about their attitudes than about the fact that they attended different schools in dif-ferent parts of town.

Perhaps a more telling illustration stemmed from Vic's self-appointed mission to introduce baseball to Transylvania. On one trip from the United States, he brought a trunkful of bats, balls, and gloves. It took no effort at all to get students from the Romanian-language and Hungarian-language high schools in Aiud to learn to play the great American pastime—with each other.

There was another striking result from Vic's polling of Caroline's students. When he asked the seniors how many intended to leave

Romania to find work, all of them said they would. "One hundred percent said they'd leave," Caroline mused. "They don't want to leave, but they feel they have to."

Finding work was the main focus of the seniors Sheilah spoke with in Aiud. Issues of economics seemed to weigh on them more than issues of ethnicity. Aiud's unemployment was about four times the national average, and its population was dwindling. Some of the operations that provided jobs during Ceaușescu's industrialization had scaled down—the cement factory and the metallurgical industry both employ just a fraction of the thousands who used to work there.

The Aiud prison, which dates back to the Hapsburg Empire and held political prisoners like Diaconescu during the Communist regime, is still there, one of the biggest prisons in Romania. It raises its own produce and makes many of its own tools, but employs just a few hundred guards and other workers.

Judit was unusual in being optimistic about finding work in Transylvania. From her, Sheilah heard the same opinion as from some of Caroline's Romanian neighbors: "Why all the political fighting over whether to create an autonomous Hungarian university?" She noted that several universities in Transylvania have Hungarian sections in which students can study any subject—not just language and culture, but engineering or math or business—in Hungarian.

In any case, Judit was planning to attend a Romanian university, because she intended to stay in Romania. Six years later, studying for her master's degree in Holland, she said she was glad she had earned her undergraduate degree at a Romanian college.

"It helped me a lot to integrate, and made me much more confident in my interactions with Romanian people," she said. Knowing she could express herself clearly in the Romanian language "really eliminated some feelings of being a bit 'discriminated-against' as a Hungarian. I guess most of that was just in my head, but still, it was there. Now it's gone. I really think that if you speak the language [Romanian] well, no one really cares when they hire you if you are a Hungarian ethnic or not, except for the fanatics, who are present in both groups, Romanian and Hungarian. But I totally ignore them."

For good measure, Judit added that discussing the possibility of returning Transylvania to Hungary "is just a waste of time and resources—and very soon of my taxes, too! It doesn't make sense, especially since we are in the EU."

BREAKING UP (STATE PROPERTY) IS HARD TO DO

WHEN WE FIRST HEARD about churches fighting to get back property seized by the Communists, it was hard to visualize the other side of the argument—allowing the government to keep it.

After Jim's trip through Szeklerland, it was a lot easier for him to understand why there were two sides to the argument.

In Miercurea Ciuc (Csikszerada in Hungarian), where the residents are overwhelmingly Hungarian, Health Minister Gábor Hajdú, a representative of the Hungarian UDMR Party, which was part of the government, was anxious for Jim to hear directly from the local Roman Catholic bishop. Jim was happy to meet him. He had visited several Hungarian schools that the community was trying to get back, but had no experience with church property involved in restitution cases.

Jim and the minister arrived in town and went directly to the bishop's office. He was a gracious host, but wanted to get right down to business. They sat at a square table with the minister and Toni Niculescu of Jim's staff.

The bishop explained that the diocese had its church, but it wanted to get back a large nearby building that it had built before the war. The bishop had filed all the papers and made all the appropriate claims, he said, but was not making any progress.

"Why don't we go look at the building?" Jim said. He was curious, and ready to stretch his legs.

The bishop led them across the street. It's a big building, maybe three stories with several wings. And it seemed full of people.

"I'd like to go inside, if we can," Jim said.

The bishop reminded him that he didn't control the building, which is why we were there.

"I understand," said Jim, "but let's introduce ourselves and see if we can take a short look around."

When they entered the front door, Jim saw several women in white lab coats. Toni explained who Jim was and that he just wanted to look around briefly. It didn't seem to be a problem.

The place had an institutional, medical feel. Jim was getting the drift, and didn't see the need to go door to door throughout the building.

As they walked back to the bishop's office, Jim asked, "Exactly what do they do in the building now?"

"It's a lung-disease hospital," the bishop said.

"What would happen to the hospital and the patients if you got the building back?" Jim asked.

The bishop didn't know. The government would have to figure that out.

"Well, if you get it back, what will you use it for?" Jim asked.

He didn't know that, either. But he wanted it back.

By 2009, the Church had received the legal title to the building. The Health Ministry would be allowed to use it until 2010. The local government just needed to find a new place for the hospital.

TEACHING AT MARYLAND, LIVING IN TIMIŞOARA

DON LANGENBERG, THEN-CHANCELLOR OF the University System of Maryland, stayed with us for a few days when he came to Romania for a conference in Sibiu with other college presidents.

One evening, we were joined by Rich Bartholomew, our savvy and entrepreneurial U.S. Treasury budget advisor, who was helping the Romanians figure out how to improve the financing of higher education. During the conversation, Langenberg bragged about how fast the University of Maryland University College (UMUC) online program was growing.

At that time, forty thousand seats, or actually computer screens, were filled with UMUC students taking classes online instead of in classrooms. And the number was growing by fifty percent a year.

But the university had a big problem, one that could constrain its growth. One of its two major categories of course offerings was technology. At that time, the United States was in the middle of its dot-com boom, which resulted in a shortage of computer science professors, particularly of the adjunct types the UMUC relies on—those people who work in the industry and teach part-time. During the dot-com boom, their time was being sucked up by their day jobs. Even full-time professors were leaving academia for IT companies.

Rich and Jim looked at each other, knowing they were thinking the same thing. *Wouldn't it be interesting if we could get Romanian professors signed up to teach?*

Langenberg was immediately interested. He said he would talk about it with Jerry Heeger, the president of University College. Then, the next time Jim was back in the United States, he met with Langenberg, Vice-Chancellor for Academic Affairs Chuck Middleton, and a member of Heeger's top staff. The operating folks were a bit skeptical. They didn't know much about Romania or the high quality of its IT academics. One of the understandable questions raised was, "Do they speak English?" But the direction from the top was clear.

Rich identified two computer science professors, one from the polytechnic in Timişoara, one from Cluj. He raised money from a Romanian computer company to send them to UMUC's training course at its headquarters in Adelphi, Maryland for three weeks in the summer of 2000. (Why online teaching can't be taught online was never clear to us.)

By the end of their first week in Adelphi, the University College people were convinced. They realized the Romanians' English-language skills were more than adequate and that their computer-teaching skills were superb. The Romanian professors returned home and, that fall, began teaching as the newest members of the UMUC faculty.

By that time, University College, still desperate for teachers, was asking them if they had Romanian colleagues who would also like to work for UMUC. So Rich got on the case. In late 2000, a university representative came to Bucharest, met with thirty Romanian computer science professors, and recruited more than a dozen for Maryland's online program.

By 2008, dozens of Romanians were UMUC faculty members. Romania is the home of more UMUC faculty than any country except the United States and South Korea.

This partnership helps UMUC meet its demand for professors without accelerating a brain drain from Romania. Because the University pays the Romanian professors the same salary it pays American professors, it is not undercutting the wages of the Americans, but the Romanian professors can substantially increase their incomes without leaving their universities in Romania for jobs in industry or outside Romania. They teach their regular classes of Romanian students in Cluj, Timişoara, and Bucharest, and then teach one or two other courses that are very highly paid by Romanian standards. As Don Langenberg said when we first talked about it, online teaching makes as much sense as online learning, so there's no reason why Romanians can't be teaching Maryland students and other students around the world.

LAST TIME WE DIDN'T GO TO CLUJ

MAYOR GHEORGHE FUNAR OF Cluj was a piece of work.

He was one of the two best-known anti-Hungarian politicians in Romania. He was the mayor of one of the major cities in Transylvania. And he'd earned a reputation as a good mayor, much the same way the first and second Mayor Daleys of Chicago made their city work well.

All three of these factors came into play near the end of Jim's term.

More than a year before, the embassy had put together a small effort to reduce bureaucratic hurdles for small businesses in Romania.

IRIS, a nonprofit think tank and consulting firm based at the University of Maryland, had developed a package of deregulation ideas for local governments. It was called *simplu şi rapid*, meaning that the reforms would make it "simple and fast" for Romanians to open businesses in these towns.

"Why don't we offer the package to all the cities?" Jim suggested to them. For those that adopted the package of reforms first, he'd go to the city, recognizing the city fathers as leaders in helping small business. It would create competition and reward initiative.

Jim figured that a lot of cities would be interested if the U.S. embassy recognized them as pro-small business. But if none were, why waste money trying to push water uphill? If a lot were interested, that would be great.

It turned out lots of cities *were* interested—more than eighty at the start.

By the time we approached the deadline for determining which cities had met all five goals—and thus would be recognized—four cities had made the grade.

Timişoara was a somewhat predictable winner because it's a prosperous city in the west controlled by a center-right mayor. Iaşi was another major city with a hard-driving, Western-oriented mayor. The biggest surprise was Giurgiu, a smaller city on the Danube governed by a leftist coalition that included the nationalist party of Vadim Tudor.

And finally, there was Cluj, Mayor Funar's town—not a big surprise given the city's reputation for good government. But given Funar's anti-Hungarian stance, it was a diplomatically dicey place for the U.S. ambassador to stand up and praise the mayor.

Jim was not looking forward to Cluj's participation at an awards ceremony, but a lot of government officials and businesspeople there had worked hard on this, and the city deserved the recognition it had been promised.

So he made plans to go to each of the winning cities and do a big media event with the mayor and business leaders.

We set a date for Cluj. And then Mayor Funar got cute.

He and his allies in the Party of Greater Romania (PRM) were in the middle of one of their periodic rants against Hungarian-language education. They planned a rally in Cluj. And they scheduled it for the same day—and place—as our *simplu şi rapid* event.

To this day, Jim's not sure what the mayor was looking to accomplish—Jim walking away from the anti-Hungarian rally, thousands of xenophobes cheering for small business, or what?

Jim decided to skip his own event and send the plaque in the mail. But he also decided to make it clear why he wasn't showing up.

So the morning of the scheduled event, he called Funar to tell him that, because of his effort to use the anti-language event to detract from the small business one, he wouldn't be coming.

Then he did press interviews in Bucharest explaining why he wasn't going to Cluj, and flew off to Iaşi to present its *simplu şi rapid* award.

The next day, the media trumpeted stories about his change of plans.

"Rosapepe does not come to Cluj" read one banner headline.

It's the only time he's gotten headlines for not showing up.

WALLACHIA

CHAPTER 8
DEEP IN THE HEART OF ROMANIA

WHY AMERICAN FLYERS KNOW PLOIEŞTI

IF YOU ASK MOST Americans in Romania what you shouldn't miss on a visit, they generally say the painted monasteries of Bucovina, or the fortified Saxon churches of Transylvania, or the Palace of the Parliament in Bucharest. These are all interesting places.

But when Jim answers that question, he adds the Petroleum Museum in Ploieşti. It's not big. It's not elegant. But it is fascinating.

Ploieşti is the heart of the Romanian oil industry. As you drive north from Bucharest toward the mountains, oil derricks begin appearing on the horizon. Texans and Oklahomans feel right at home.

The museum tells two related stories, both of relevance to Americans. The obvious one is the history of the Romanian oil industry— how oil was discovered there two years before it was found in the United States and how, by World War II, Romania was the biggest oil producer in Europe and one of the largest in the world. The museum showcases technology designed in Romania and America.

Baby boom-era American kids like us grew up thinking that oil was discovered in Titusville, Pennsylvania. But in fact, Romanians were revolutionizing the energy industry in the late nineteenth and early twentieth century, at the same time John D. Rockefeller was. Perhaps globalization of disruptive technologies was not the invention of our generation. Romanians had already become world-class competitors when Jim's great-grandfather contracted to make barrels for western Pennsylvania oil producers and insisted on cash rather than stock—he wasn't sure the oil business would really take off and pay off.

Some Americans aren't as ignorant as we were of Romania's oil heritage. They are the veterans of World War II who served in Europe and know that Ploieşti's oil fields fueled Germany's blitzkriegs. Armies run on their stomachs, but tanks run on oil. Hitler understood, as keenly as Churchill and Roosevelt, that the Ploieşti oil fields and refineries were a strategic battleground of World War II.

That's why Hitler wooed and dominated, but did not invade, Romania as long as the oil flowed his way. And that's why, in 1944, the Allies bombed and bombed and bombed Ploieşti.

To an American, what's extraordinary in the Petroleum Museum is that, in addition to telling the industry's history, it tells the story of the American attack on the city. And it displays the letters from American servicemen, shot down in bombing raids, thanking their Romanian captors for protecting them from the Nazis.

"The Romanians treat us good," Lieutenant Sears wrote to Barbara Sears back home. "We get the same food that their troops get . . . we can get almost anything we want. This morning we had fresh eggs for breakfast, and the bread they have is the best I have ever eaten. It's sort of dark bread, wheat, and it's really swell. Maybe I can bring a loaf home with me but guess it would be very old by the time I get there."

"The Romanians took us in, almost as welcome guests, giving us immediate medical attention, packets of cigarettes, coffee, food," wrote Lieutenant John J. Rhodes. "And to top it all off, beer! Imagine such treatment for foreigners who had just devastated their country!"

It's an amazing story. For Americans who can't imagine a time or a place where victims of American military power saw that power as a good thing, we have one suggestion: Visit the Petroleum Museum in Ploieşti.

DOWN IN THE MINES

IT'S A BEAUTIFUL DRIVE south from Sibiu through the mountains into the Jiu Valley, just as it is from Braşov heading south to Bucharest. But the road from Sibiu takes you to a very different place. Economically, the Jiu Valley is the West Virginia of Romania. It's synonymous with coal mining. To many in post-Communist Romania, it's also a symbol of fears about anti-democratic extremism.

During the Communist period, Ceauşescu pushed rapid industrialization. He also pushed development of domestic energy sources. He built electricity plants on a massive scale, and all were dependent on coal.

Sheilah and Jim emerging from the mines in Petroşani, the West Virginia of Romania

Romania's coal industry goes back centuries. But under the Communists, it was expanded to the point where hundreds of thousands of workers were added to the payrolls. They developed the Jiu Valley in a way it had never been developed before.

Like mine workers elsewhere in the world, Romanians in the Jiu Valley were a cohesive and politically strong force. During the Communist period, some of the major labor revolts against the government took place in Jiu Valley. In response, Ceauşescu gave coal miners higher wages than those received by most industrial workers.

The miners also played a big political role. In the months after the revolution in 1989, the conservative elements of the post-Communist government used miners from the Jiu Valley to intimidate anti-government forces in Bucharest. Several times during the spring of 1990, miners were brought by train from the Jiu Valley to disrupt demonstrations against the government. It's not too strong a statement to say that the political division in post-Communist Romania between the party of Ion Iliescu and the opposition parties grew out of disputes involving the miners of the Jiu Valley when they came to Bucharest in the spring of 1990.

The miners were also used by the party's conservative elements to drive Petre Roman from the prime minister's chair in September of 1991. It's said that he resigned because he knew that miners were coming to physically drive him from power.

Immediately after the 1996 election, and continuing into the late nineties, shrinking the mining industry was a top priority for the World Bank and the IMF in their efforts to reduce subsidies to the Romanian economy and open it up to market forces. It was also a priority of the center-right government to reduce the political power of their opponents.

There is no good analogy in contemporary American politics. But for baby boomers old enough to remember the early seventies in the United States, the Jiu Valley miners are the symbolic equivalent of the construction workers in New York who opposed anti-war demonstrations.

Thus, when we decided to visit the Jiu Valley mines in 2000, our visit had a political as well as economic context.

Jim wanted to visit the Jiu Valley to learn about its economic hardship, which was severe, as well as to better understand the culture of Romanian miners. We went to a hospital where the doctors reported that a very high number of their cases were related to mine injuries, an experience not that dissimilar to hospitals in mining areas all around the world.

But we also wanted to meet with union leaders and to visit the mines ourselves.

It took Jim's staff a good bit of effort to schedule a visit to the mines. The management and the union were somewhat resistant, and a little skeptical, of having the U.S. ambassador actually go down into the mines.

But they agreed and, on a bright June day, we arrived in Mine

Number 2 in Lupin. We met the mine managers, who took us into changing rooms to get out of our street clothes and into miners' gear: blue uniforms, special heavy socks, boots, and, of course, hard hats with lights. Then we walked to the entrance of the mine.

We got on a small elevator that could hold no more than three or four people and began the long descent underground. After a few minutes, we got off and walked down some corridors to another elevator that took us still lower. We exited the elevator and boarded a small train to travel along a mine shaft into an area where mining was active.

As we got up from the train, everything was pitch black—black walls, a black floor made up of coal hacked from the walls, and several miners covered with black coal dust.

Walking through that tunnel, seeing men below the earth's surface with pick-axes in small caverns, the danger of coal mining, in Romania or anywhere, became very real. We walked toward the wall of coal as the miners chipped away, and Jim almost fell over a bed of coal fragments.

We stayed not more than a half hour, and then returned to the surface. Coming out of the elevator on our arrival at the surface and seeing the sunshine and people above ground, we felt an enormous sense of relief and understood a little better why miners all around the world have to be as tough as they are to do what they do.

WHY THEY STAYED UNDER COMMUNISM

WEST OF GALAȚI, A few miles from Buzău, lie the few acres of family property which Dan Floru won back after 1989. Dan was never a fan of the Communists. His father was a diplomat in the years before Communism.

"My father was a commercial counselor in Vienna," Dan recalled. "The Germans created a puppet government with some Romanian fascists, and my father was asked to join them. He said, 'No, I'm faithful to my country and the king.' So the whole family was arrested, including me and my brother, who was one month old.

On the porch of the Florus' traditional home in Cărpinştea—
Sheilah, Julia, Jim, Julia and Dan's daughter Ioana, and Dan

"We were put in German camps in Bavaria for eight or nine months. In the last weeks, the German guards were not applying much pressure. I have a photo of my mother on a snow slope, and beneath it, my father wrote, 'The pioneer comes back with food.' She spoke good German, and would go to houses there with some things of value—rings, watches, even a camera—and trade them for potatoes. It was interesting. Finally, we were rescued by a Polish brigade of the U.S. Army."

The family returned to Romania. By the time Dan was ready to go to college, the Communists had been in power for almost a decade. Because diplomats were neither workers nor farmers, Dan had difficulty getting into college in the 1950s.

"I finished high school in 1956. It was immediately after the Hungarian Revolution," he told us in the living room of his traditional two-story home. "So the Communists, among them Iliescu, who was very influential as the president of the association of young Communists, instituted a quota for the sons of intellectuals. This quota limited us to ten percent of all the places in the university. We had a written and oral examination. I ended up with a seven and ten. The last ones accepted had scores of seven and fifteen. So I failed to get in.

"I worked as a plumber for about seven or eight months. Then I got a letter from the Ministry of Foreign Trade, which wanted to create specialists in foreign trade who knew foreign languages. They went to the Polytechnic Institute and took the dossiers of those with the best scores who hadn't been admitted. So I was asked by the Ministry of Trade to try to become a trade person. In the beginning, I didn't want that, but then I talked to my father, who told me, 'Look, I was a trade professional. Why don't you try? If you don't like it, maybe you can go back to the Polytechnic Institute.'"

Dan spoke good French. He earned a degree from the Faculty of Foreign Trade at the Academy of Economic Studies (ASE), and then went to work in the Trade Ministry.

"By 1963, I had worked in several different foreign trade organizations. I never went higher than department chief because of my dossier"—that is, his family background. "At one point, they told me if I wanted to keep my position, I should join the Communist Party. I was told this again when I was in line to be promoted to deputy department chief. Without joining, it was not possible. So I joined, but it was not out of conviction. Frankly, probably ninety-five percent of the members of the Communist Party were pure opportunists. I'm sorry and sad to say that, but that's the truth.

"In the mid-seventies, when I was working in the foreign trade division of the Ministry of Industry, my brother defected [to Germany]. So they kindly told me to leave. I ended up at the Bucharest Metro System."

Sheilah wanted to know, "Why didn't you defect when your brother did?"

"Because I'm a stupid, romantic guy," Dan answered. "I had many opportunities to leave, and I might have come back now in a totally different position, as an American citizen."

"I don't know if you know," his wife Julia interjected, "but Dan has an aunt in New York who wanted him to come there."

Dan explained, "She asked me to stay there, but I was stupid enough to come back to Romania." He laughed.

"She wanted us in 1982," Julia continued. "She had a cosmetic company and wanted me, as a chemist, to help her. *Okay*, we thought, *we'll go*. But our parents and our aunt—we couldn't go without thinking about what would happen with them. We couldn't. We lived in Romania for forty years with our parents and aunts. We were the only young people able to do something for all our family"

Dan chimed in, "We had responsibilities. Believe it or not, after my brother defected, I had to take care of the burial of at least eight or nine relatives. They were all very old. We were the only able people."

"During this period, I cooked and carried food to three old families—my uncle, another aunt, and Dan's aunt," Julia added. "Really, we couldn't leave them. We just couldn't."

A DAUGHTER'S CHOICE TO LEAVE AFTER COMMUNISM

WHEN DAN FLORU CALLS himself a romantic, he's talking about more than his duty to family.

"We're talking 1970," Dan explained. "I believed Romania might go another way. I might have used the knowledge I got from the Wharton Business School [where he had studied in the 1960s with permission from the Communist government] to improve things here. I thought my duty was here. Stupid."

But even then, family was a strong tie to Romania.

"I thought my family would be punished, even persecuted, if I defected," Dan said. "But that didn't keep my brother from making a different decision."

He didn't tell Dan he was leaving, although Julia picked up a hint from his wife.

"This is the grudge I have against him," Dan said.

But his brother wasn't the only defection. In 1984, Dan and Julia accompanied a friend to the train for a trip to Germany. As the train pulled out, the friend announced quite loudly, "Bye-bye, we won't be returning."

"We couldn't believe it," Julia said. "We said, 'Oh my God! What will happen?'"

"We will be arrested now," Dan said. "Crazy guy. Crazy guy."

They were not arrested. When the Revolution came in 1989, Dan was working at the Bucharest Metro agency as chief of the design workshop for trams.

"A month later, someone called. He knew me from the 1980s and repeatedly tried to bring me back into foreign trade, but to no avail because of my dossier. But then he found me a job with the Ministry [of Trade]. I started working with them in May 1990. At that moment, they knew the people they needed but hadn't been able to get before '89 because of their dossiers. So immediately after the Revolution, they could."

He was general manager of the American division for the next two and a half years before he left to work for the U.S. Commerce Department in the embassy in Bucharest.

Their daughter, Ioana, an engineer, now works in France.

"It's her choice," said Julia. "My choice is to stay here. Her choice is to work in France."

"Now there is freedom to travel," Dan said. "She might stay three or four years there, then come home. Things are totally different. It's no longer a lifelong choice."

ROMANIA 2.0

A FEW MILES FROM Buzău was a half-built hydroelectric plant that Harza Engineering, the largest U.S. designer of hydroelectric plants, wanted to finish and run. The company had come to Romania to build hydro projects. It soon discovered that Romania has great hydro engineers as well as software developers.

Kevin Candee, the Harza executive supervising the project, quickly developed a plan to put Romanian hydro engineers to work on Harza projects elsewhere in the world. They would do design work in Romania, and then he would send them to Nepal, Latin America, and other places to work on similar projects.

In 1999, they had a big IT project they wanted to do at company headquarters in Chicago. Kevin had a couple of IT guys in his office in Bucharest who were world-class. He wanted to send them to Chicago to work with Harza's IT staff there.

So far, so good.

Then, one day, he called Jim's office for an urgent meeting. Rose Stafiej—Jim's smart, hardworking secretary who came to Romania with him right after graduating from Johns Hopkins University—juggled the schedule to accommodate him.

Kevin was upset. The consulate had turned down visas for his Romanian IT specialists to work in Chicago for several weeks.

"First, I had to convince the Harza managers in Chicago, who don't know how good Romanian skills are, that I want my guys to come," Kevin said, "so it was a tough sell to begin with. But they agree to give them a chance, we schedule the work, and book the flights. Then their visas get turned down!"

Kevin is not a screamer. But his whole body exuded exasperation. "Why is my government doing this to me?"

"Good question," Jim said. "I'll call Steve Pattison." Steve was the consul general responsible for the visa decisions in the embassy—and, much to the benefit of American taxpayers, a born problem-solver.

It turned out that, even though Harza was the biggest U.S. hydro-electric firm and one of the international leaders in the field, no one in the consulate had ever heard of them. They seemed to doubt it was a real company and worried that the visa-seeking IT guys were lying about why they wanted to go to the United States.

Once we filled in the factual blanks—they're a major U.S. firm, we're working with them closely here in Romania, and they're going to do real work—the visas were approved.

It's fair to ask why the consulate didn't look them up on the internet or ask someone about them in the embassy's commercial section, or why Kevin didn't ask Jim to introduce Harza to the consulate *before* they applied for visas. The answer to the first question is that consulates basically work on a complaint basis. If someone gets a visa, they don't complain. If someone who is rejected complains, then they can deal with it. That's what happened with Harza.

The answer to the second is that Harza didn't ask for an introduction because they assumed people who work for the U.S. government would know who they are—or at least ask. It turned out to be an unreasonable assumption. Experiences like this make too many American companies believe the U.S. government is neither competent nor sympathetic.

It was not an isolated incident.

During the dot-com boom in the United States in the late 1990s, there was tremendous U.S. demand for Romanians with IT skills. American companies were opening software-development operations in Romania and partnering with Romanian software companies.

The result? Many Romanian companies needed to send their IT people to the United States. Sometimes, as with Harza, it was to work with U.S. firms on joint projects. Other times, it was for the Romanians to get trained in U.S. customer needs, or in how the American parent company operated—in other words, to pick up business culture as well as proprietary expertise.

But this was not the world in which consular officers, most of them recent political science and international relations graduates, lived. The dot-com boom in America was foreign news to them, and they were chained to their interview windows, unable to visit U.S. software and engineering firms in Braşov and Iaşi as Jim could do.

So, time after time, the consulate would reject temporary business travel visas for Romanian IT professionals because they'd never heard of the company and assumed the application was a fraud. Why *would* they have heard of every Romanian company doing business with U.S. partners?

Once we figured out the problem, we could see how to solve it. We needed to tell businesses they ought to contact the consulate ahead of time, introduce themselves, and prove to the consulate that they were real businesses.

We found a wonderful lawyer named Linda Dodd-Major, who

worked for the Immigration and Naturalization Service (INS) doing business liaison. It turned out our problem was a problem around the world for American companies. The INS hired Linda to help businesses figure out the system. She had a particular interest in Romania because she had worked here in the early nineties for the American Bar Association's legal consulting program. We arranged for the Embassy's Trade and Development Group to sponsor a daylong seminar on business visas. The room was packed with several hundred people, primarily from the software industry, who came to learn how to make a presentation that would maximize the chances of getting their people going back and forth between Romania and the United States.

FAST FOOD AND FAST DEALS

As OUR VAN PULLED INTO Piteşti late one afternoon, Jim was starving. We hadn't had lunch, and it would be another hour or more before we got back to Bucharest.

Jim loved Romanian food, particularly meat, soups, and salads.

But there are times when convenience trumps cuisine. And Piteşti, like most major cities in Romania, had a McDonald's.

In one way, they were a reminder of home—the golden arches, the clean toilets, the red and white colors. But for Americans who, to put it diplomatically, have gotten used to a wide range of service quality in McDonald's restaurants in the United States, stopping at a McDonald's in Romania is sheer joy. The young people behind the counter are unfailingly eager, cheerful, and quick. The reason is clear. Given the economic situation in Romania, these are much better jobs than they are in the United States.

But also, many of the employees took pride in working for an American company with high standards. Working at McDonald's didn't mean you were a NATO member, but you were part of American culture.

We ordered Big Macs, crispy chicken, regular Cokes, and a Sprite. (The one big drawback of Romanian McDonald's was that they didn't offer diet soft drinks. Now they do.) Just as we were getting ready to pile back into the van, Jim's cell phone rang.

Mayors throughout Romania wanted a McDonald's in their town. Jim stopped at every one he could to meet the young Romanians who put customers first.

It was Dr. Emanuel Zervoudakis, or Dr. Z, as we called him—the top Romania guy at the International Monetary Fund. Jim had been trying to reach him for a couple of days, so he wasn't going to let this opportunity pass.

The IMF has a well-earned reputation for promoting conservative fiscal policies—and for trying to micromanage the countries they lend to. In Romania, while we were there, they were focused like a laser on cleaning up the country's plundered, state-owned banks. And they were right to do so.

But most of their staff was in Washington, away from the action. The IMF, which had more influence over Romanian taxes, budgets, interest rates, and privatization than anyone outside Romania—and all but a few people *in* Romania—had only one professional staffer on the ground. Everyone else blew in and out of town for a few days or a few weeks at a time. In contrast, the World Bank has substantial staff in Romania, headed when we were there by an insightful and adept Pakistani economist, Ziad Alahdad. Our U.S. Treasury advisors to the Finance Ministry, who lived full-time in Bucharest, shared the frustration of Romanians every time a new IMF delegation would show up to go over the country's books. They'd have to educate a new group of young Washington, D.C. economists on the same issues they'd covered with the last group six months before.

Likewise, some of the IMF theories hatched in Washington didn't even work in theory, let alone in practice. Nobel Prize-winner Dr. Joseph Stiglitz, who headed President Clinton's Council of Economic Advisors and was the World Bank's chief economist, called one of their initiatives in Romania a "particularly mystifying example."

In the wake of the Russian devaluation and collapse in the summer of 1998, the market for Romanian debt nosedived for no more rational reason than, as Jim jokes with bankers and government leaders, the names of both countries start with the letter R.

In his book *Globalization and Its Discontents*, Stiglitz explains that, after criticisms of its bailouts in the Asian financial crisis of 1997, the IMF decided the next year to test its "bail in" strategy on "powerless countries like Ecuador and Romania, too weak to resist the IMF." To qualify for IMF loans under "bail in," Romania would have to get loans first from private lenders. It was mystifying to the Romanians, to Dr. Stiglitz, and to us because, if the country could have gotten private loans on reasonable terms, it would not have turned to the IMF.

"The creditors suddenly had enormous leverage," Stiglitz noted. "A twenty-eight-year-old man in the Bucharest branch of an international private bank, by making a loan of a few million dollars, had the power to decide whether or not the IMF, the World Bank, and EU would provide Romania with more than a billion dollars." For most of the year, Romania resisted the IMF's scheme. Finally, the IMF relented.

"Less competent or more corrupt governments might have been tempted, but Romania did not accept the offer," Stiglitz wrote.

The issue Dr. Z was calling about that day in Piteşti was Banca

Agricolă, the state-owned agricultural bank that had been bankrupted by insider deals no more creative than those that destroyed the American savings and loan industry in the mid-1980s through the early 1990s. Romanians are very smart, but Jim saw little evidence that their crooked bankers had shown innovative flair. They lent bank funds to their friends, who didn't pay back the loans.

Dr. Z wanted to close Banca Agricolă. The only problem? The Romanian government didn't want to—not because it didn't see the problems, but because closing banks was hard politically. Obviously, it would not go down well with the bank's ordinary, honest depositors and customers, or bank employees. It would also look like another government failure. The Romanian government's view would not surprise Americans who watched in 2008 and 2009 as the U.S. government bailed out its major banks rather than close them.

Under IMF pressure, the Romanian government might *promise* to close the bank, but "promise" and "do" aren't synonyms, even in English.

Jim had phoned Dr. Z to convince him he should give the government the option of selling the bank. Either way, the taxpayers would have to cover the losses, but a sale would be much more palatable to the Romanians. The price fetched would not be high, but the bank did have valuable assets—deposits, customers, and one of the largest branch networks in the country—even if most of its loans had to be written off.

When he reached Jim at the Piteşti McDonald's, Dr. Z was skeptical but open-minded.

"You have nothing to lose by giving them the option," Jim argued, "particularly if I'm right, that they're not going to close it anyway. Insist that the government put it in receivership, so more money isn't stolen, and give us a chance to find a high-quality buyer."

Jim doesn't know what persuaded him, but Dr. Z said yes. "See what you can do and keep me posted," he said.

"Hot dog!" Jim said, immediately realizing he'd uttered a term that could be regarded as slightly subversive in a McDonald's parking lot. We climbed into the van and headed back to Bucharest.

Now there was the small problem of finding a buyer.

There were no obvious American prospects. The only U.S. bank on the ground was Citibank, but this was not their kind of deal—the bank in question was too retail-oriented, too small, with too many problems. We had just worked with GE Capital to privatize BancPost, the postal savings bank, but GE Capital was not looking for new Romanian acquisitions.

Then, at a dinner for the board of the Romanian American Enterprise Fund (RAEF) in the garden of a restaurant in Piaţa Lahovari in downtown Bucharest, Jim began to hatch an idea. Why not the RAEF itself? The fund is capitalized by the U.S. government to stimulate private enterprise. It had acquired a smaller private bank—Banca Românească—in 1998. Banca Agricolă would be too big for the Fund alone, but it could find a partner, a European bank or a bigger investment fund.

Dan Dăianu—former finance minister, leading economist, occasional TV sports commentator, and a RAEF advisor—liked the idea, as did Horia Manda and John Klipper, RAEF's top officers.

We had the lead investor. Now all we needed was a co-investor.

Obvious candidates seemed to be European agricultural banks. As always, USAID's entrepreneurial, well-networked local agriculture advisor Lawrence Johnson knew exactly how to proceed. Rabo, in the Netherlands, would be the best, he said, and in France, Crédit Agricole. The Agricultural Bank of Greece (ABG) might be the most interested. We hit the phones.

We had an interesting meeting with the Greeks, whose representative thought his bank would be a perfect partner. The official explained that ABG was very experienced in building its portfolio of loans over several years and, when many of them went bad, most successful in getting the government to cover the losses. We thanked him for his interest and wished him good luck.

The RAEF team then found an investment fund based in London that was buying broken banks in the Balkans. We had exactly what they were looking for. And their majority investor was the Wisconsin State Investment Board. This could be a win-win for Romanians, Americans, and the IMF.

They quickly put together a partnership with RAEF, and we proceeded to introduce the new suitor to the Romanian government. And then everything ground to a halt.

The Romanian central bank, finance ministry, and the IMF economists seemed to experience a simultaneous mind-meld. They agreed with Jim that the bank should be sold, but they wanted RAEF's partner to be a bank—"a strategic investor," in financial parlance—instead of private equity investors. They had at least two good reasons: A bank, particularly if it were large, could put its own staff on the ground to overhaul BA, and it could provide more capital if needed.

But Jim had been through this same issue in 1996 while on the board of the Albanian American Enterprise Fund, the sister investment fund to RAEF. When the Albanian Enterprise Fund wanted a foreign bank to partner with them, none was interested, so the Fund built its own staff—and the American Bank of Albania became an enormous success.

Jim thought they were being more than a little rigid. Starting with his chat with Dr. Z in the parking lot of the Piteşti McDonald's, Jim had created the opportunity for a sale, found the lead investor, and thus discovered a way to get the bank off the government's books—a win for Romania, a win for the IMF, and a win for U.S. investors.

The standoff went on for months. And then a white knight appeared. Raiffeisen is an Austrian bank focused on building its business in Central and Eastern Europe—the old Austrian empire, in effect—and it already had banking operations in Romania. Seeing the deadlock and the opportunity, they approached RAEF about taking over the position of the London-based investment fund.

A new deal was quickly struck, though not without ruffling feathers in London, and the Romanian government and the IMF signed on. A few months after we left Romania, Raiffeisen and RAEF took over Banca Agricolă. It was later renamed Raiffeisen, and was making a variety of loans: mortgages, consumer loans, and small business loans.

MOTHER-IN-LAW OF THE YEAR

"IMPROBABLE" IS THE ADJECTIVE that often comes to mind when we remember our times in Romania. As in, "Can you believe we really did that?"

"Improbable" is a good description of our appearance on a TV variety show called *Marina's Arc* (*Arca Marinei*). The show's title was a play on the name of its effervescent host, Marina Almăşan, and its nautical theme. The idea was that Marina and her sidekick, Sinbad, were navigating the world looking for traditional or peculiar customs and events. Sinbad was actor Eugen Cristea, who dressed in a French sailor's blue and white striped shirt, showcasing his impressive musculature. (By contrast, the stuffed-toy version of Sinbad, which they give to guests, is puffy and cuddly, with a white hat, blue hair, long skinny arms, and a huge red nose. We still have the one they gave us.)

The episode for which they invited us was mostly devoted to the person they'd designated "Mother-in-Law of the Year." Doamna Paraschivoiu, a charming white-haired lady who looked to be in her seventies, had been chosen in a national contest begun on earlier episodes. We were never clear what the criteria had been, or even why Arca Marinei wanted to name anyone mother-in-law of the year. Doamna Paraschivoiu was energetic, feisty, and outspoken—all qualities we had encountered in other women of a certain age in Romania.

The episode was to be broadcast live, on the main national television channel, from the courtyard of the mother-in-law's home, capitalizing on the rural charm of the village of Bărbăteşti. The show's producers wanted us to make a conspicuous entrance, and neither they nor we had any desire for us to show up in a shiny black American car. So, it was arranged that we would ride in the back of a horse-drawn cart, the kind you still see on Romania's rural roads carrying produce to market. As planned, when we rounded a corner into camera shot, Marina, in mock surprise, exclaimed something like, "Oh, look who's dropping in—the ambassador and his wife!" at which point we dismounted and walked toward the home.

Jim dancing with "The Mother-in-Law of the Year" — on national television

Out came the mother-in-law of the year, greeting us at her front gate with the traditional Romanian welcome offering—a magnificently-braided golden loaf of bread and a little glass dish of salt. Camera rolling live, she told us in Romanian how much she loves Bill Clinton. Someone nearby translated for us, *sotto voce*. Doamna Paraschivoiu asked Jim to relay to President Clinton what a big fan she was, which, of course, Jim promised to do, though we're not sure whether diplomatic channels could convey the full dimensions of her message.

Together we went into the courtyard, where more live cameras were positioned. We settled in on some wooden benches in the courtyard. The mother-in-law of the year has a fairly large house, which may have been a factor in choosing her. We were dressed in casual clothes, Marina and Sinbad were in sailor attire, and Doamna Paraschivoiu was wearing the heavily embroidered blouse and skirt typical of that region. Just another typical summer Sunday afternoon at her house. Even in Romania, the scene was somewhat improbable.

Conversation continued. Marina interviewed the mother-in-law of the year and her husband (as far as we could tell, he had not automatically been designated father-in-law of the year), as well as their family and other guests, including a pop star who performed a song. More conversation, more music. A children's group played wooden flutes (and quite well). The ambassador gamely took a turn on the flute, producing more noise than tune.

Traditional foods were served. More conversation. Traditional dancing. We joined in, not very gracefully. This was a two-hour live show. It went on and on.

The producers had asked us in advance for some casual snapshots of ourselves. Not knowing what to expect, Sheilah had supplied mostly photos of previous vacations, including some that involved boats. But the picture that had caught their attention was the one of our unprepossessing home in College Park, Maryland, with its black shutters, steep shingled roof, and white picket fence surrounding a yard with a flowering dogwood.

They showed the photo full-screen as Marina asked Jim, "Did your father-in-law give it to you?" In Romania, that's not an improbable question—it would be very typical for a bride's father to give the groom a house as the daughter's dowry. But we were in our thirties when we married—in fact, Jim already owned the College Park house—and Sheilah was taken aback by the idea that the house might have been a present from her dad. She felt she needed to set the record straight, and started to explain how mortgage financing works in America: "No, no, we bought it—well, actually, we're in the process of buying it, because, see, the way it works is, we pay a little every month . . ." Marina, who speaks and understands English perfectly, stared at Sheilah with a blank expression, and Jim whispered to her to give it up—she was not going to be able to explain the U.S. mortgage system on this live Romanian variety show.

So the conversation moved on to Marina asking Jim, "Well, how do the peasants spend their time in College Park?" Again, not an improbable question in Romania. After several years in the country,

Jim knew a peasant in Romania means a farmer—the word doesn't carry the notion of abject poverty that Americans attach to it. So he described some typical College Park activities.

Eventually, with everyone in the courtyard holding hands and singing heartily, the show wrapped. Marina's bubbling energy, Sinbad's cheerful rapport, and the multiple talents of the other guests had kept it moving, even when our stumbles threatened to stall it.

As the lights dimmed and the cameras went dark, the music played on. The crew who worked on the show and the local notables who had come to take part and watch were gearing up for a huge shindig. More food was rolled out. It's quite possible that wine and țuică appeared. We stayed for a little while, and when we finally drove away, it seemed that the crowd at the mother-in-law of the year's house would be partying far into the evening. In Romania, that's not at all improbable.

How Romania shrank state firms . . . without layoffs

At first glance, one of the great mysteries of the Romanian economy after 1989 is how the huge, overstaffed state companies were right-sized without causing extraordinary and politically volatile levels of unemployment. We asked Mugur Isărescu, the long-serving governor of Romania's Central Bank and key architect of its twenty-year transition from Communism, how Romania did it. His answer: early retirement on a massive scale.

"The number of registered workers decreased from eight million to four million from '89 to 2000. They were cut in half," said Isărescu, who served as prime minister in 2000. These were the workers who paid into the state retirement fund—the equivalent of our Social Security and private pension systems. Unregistered workers, including farmers, whose numbers grew as laid-off industrial workers returned to their families' small plots, do not pay into the state retirement fund.

"Outrageous. The number of pensioners has increased from 2.8 million persons to 6 million persons," Isărescu continued. "The main reason was the fact that all governments except mine not only accepted early retirement, but stimulated it. It was done particularly before all elections, '92, '96, 2000. I had not only refused to do that, but I was totally hostile to it. The governing coalition and the opposition joined hands and started to use popular slogans: 'Look, these are people, Mr. PM. You don't have mercy!'"

"What exactly are you saying?" Sheilah asked. "That they were using pensions as unemployment benefits?"

"Exactly! This was preferred, so we decided to set the average retirement at below fifty years of age. They started with the Securitate Officers, which was necessary in '91. There was also pressure from the U.S. and Western countries. After that, they moved to army personnel. There were a lot of reasons for doing this. Then they moved to factories."

"But why?" Jim asked. "They felt they couldn't just kick people out of the factories? Why would they think it's more advantageous to put people into the pension system than to keep them in the factories?"

"It was political," said Isărescu. "Because, for external purposes and for domestic ones, too, we had to prove we had restructured these sectors. Before '89, the Communist system worked on the basis of fixed prices. Ceauşescu liked to build the largest machine-tool factories in the world, and he succeeded. And it appeared to be visionary, because everything was subsidized. A lot of what I call 'big white elephants' in the corporate sector were thus developed, particularly in the seventies and the eighties.

"After '89, when prices, particularly for energy, were liberalized, these factories appeared, in a clear mirror, to be totally inefficient. So the pressure was there not only for external reasons.

"The solution which was found was our pension funds. The pension funds here are not exactly what you are used to in the U.S. They are paid for through the contributions of working persons. This was the system. The working labor force was paying for the pensioners. At first, it was OK. But then the system started to run deficits. So they increased the contributions. The contribution was increased from fifteen percent in '90 to forty-five percent ten years later."

Nearly half the paycheck of a Romanian worker was going to pay the pensions of other workers.

"In a way, it was another illusion," said Isărescu. "It was not exactly paid by the employee. It was paid by the owners of the factories, as part of their business plan, as a percentage of total wages."

This rang a bell with us. Romanians, unlike Americans, always quote their salaries as net of taxes. (After 1989, governments of both the right and the left created several other payroll tax funds.) Isărescu found this strategy outrageous, and it certainly was not sustainable. But for a country making a rapid transition from communist to capitalist economics without substantial outside help, it worked. Romania avoided the economic and political crises that befell other nations and emerged in less than two decades as the tiger of the Balkans.

THE BISHOP OF FINANCE

MUGUR ISĂRESCU STRIKES US as the kind of guy who, if he wore blue jeans, would have a sharp crease running down their front. But we can't imagine him in blue jeans. From his prematurely silver hair to his polished wing tips, he seems very buttoned-up, very formal—trim and fit, but not sporty. While Bucharest Mayor Băsescu seems perpetually rumpled, Isărescu seems always organized, and always neatly pressed, with never a hair out of place. He dresses, talks, and comes across as a technocrat.

In addition, his English pronunciation is very good, which tends to impress American listeners even more than his excellent comprehension. Westerners feel immediate confidence in him.

He grew up in Râmnicu Vâlcea in southern Romania. "My mother wasn't rich," he told us in his neatly arranged office paneled with polished wood. "She came from a middle-class background of small landowners. My mother's father was a priest. My father was a middle-class peasant."

Jim asked what it meant to be a middle-class peasant. How much land? How many properties?

"It was supposed to be around twenty-four hectars; the rich ones were supposed to have more," said Isărescu. "My grandfather on my mother's side had only sixteen hectars, but he had houses and he was also a wine trader. My father was a teacher. In those times, people were going to school only until seventh grade; only the rich children were going to high school. My father went to a special school for teachers, but he didn't have access to the university. Soon after he graduated from this school, he worked as a teacher, and after that as an officer in the Royal Army. He fought both on the Eastern and Western fronts during World War II."

"He had a lot of influence on me. During my childhood, he used to tell me stories about his time in the war, about the Red Army, about the American Army. After the war, as you know, what was good about the Communist system was the fact that they opened the gates of education to everybody. The first pro-Communist government was Petru Groza's. He took everybody who graduated from the normal schools and gave them access to universities and, after the fifties, attendance was free of charge. From 1946 to 1950, my father was able to attend and graduate from the Academy of Economic Studies.

"He was a banker in a small city for seventeen years. Then he worked as a chief accountant. We lived in Drăgăşani, near the two villages my mother and my father came from."

Mugur Isărescu remembers counting bank notes as a small boy when he visited his dad at the office. When it came time for him to go to college in 1967, the admissions process was different than it had been for his father.

"Up to '61, irrespective of your scores, they looked at your file. For instance, if you came from a rich family, you were not accepted. For me, getting into the university was based only on the scores. After that, many entered using their relations and their connections."

Soon after graduation, Isărescu went to work for the World Economy Institute, a government-funded research and think tank, known for close connections to the security services.

During his years at university and the Institute, he built relationships with men who would join him in leading post-Communist Romania, just as Harvard graduates populate President Barack Obama's administration in the United States.

Isărescu is a classic central-bank economist in that he's politically dexterous. Mastery of domestic politics is an indispensable skill for a central banker. Isărescu may know how to play the game as well as anyone, as evidenced by the fact that he is one of the longest-serving central bank governors in the world—from 1990 to today.

His tenure at the bank was nominally interrupted by an episode that gives further witness to his domestic political skills: The president of the country, Constantinescu, asked him to become prime minister, and when Constantinescu decided not to run for reelection, he supported Isărescu to be his successor. Isărescu failed to close that deal with the voters—domestic political skills do not guarantee external political skills—but after his electoral defeat, he smoothly negotiated his way back to heading the central bank.

Central Bank Governor Mugur Isărescu (far right), a frequent visitor to Ţigăneşti Monastery near Bucharest, brought his counselor Lucian Croitoru and Jim to dinner with the nuns.

Partly because he is so low-key, and therefore doesn't seem to be looking out first for his own interests, Isărescu has a way of building trust in the people he deals with. As a banker, his true constituencies are international institutions like the IMF and the financial markets. He makes good use of those connections.

Because he seems so thoroughly Western to Westerners, it surprised us a bit to see his close professional connection to the Orthodox Church. The central bank makes significant donations to the church—very much in the tradition of the temporal rulers of centuries ago whose images you see in the frescoes inside the big churches they funded. The bank has paid for the refurbishing of several old churches.

Not long before we left Romania, Isărescu invited us to Sunday dinner at a monastery near Bucharest. The nuns provided an extraordinary meal, with course after course. There was a point to all this hospitality: The monastery had been a weekend retreat for the bank, and hence a handy source of extra income for the good sisters. But that bank use was being cut back. Would the Americans be interested in using the spot for R&R? We passed the word along.

CENTRAL BANKER SHOPTALK WITH ALAN GREENSPAN

IN 2000, JIM ACCOMPANIED Isărescu, then prime minister, to a meeting in Washington with Alan Greenspan, then chairman of the U.S. Federal Reserve Board. As fellow central bank governors of long tenure, they were old friends. Greenspan teased Isărescu about how lucky it was that he, as an economist, was playing a big role in designing the economic system of his country, just like Viktor Yushchenko, the former Ukrainian central bank governor and then Ukraine's prime minister. That opportunity was long gone in the United States, Greenspan said. Jim thought he sounded a bit envious.

They talked about inflation in Romania, which was much more severe than in other Central and Eastern European countries at the time. Unlike Poland, which had liberalized most prices in 1992 and 1993, Romania had kept price controls until the late 1990s. Raising prices meant inflation. Inflation meant depreciation of the currency. The leu dropped dramatically as price controls were lifted, and that fed inflation. Every market economy faces such challenges. But Romania, which still had a big state sector, had other problems.

"In a practical sense, the money supply is not very clear here," Isărescu said. "We have Romanian lei, dollars, euros, and deutschemarks, plus surrogates of money which are called 'arrears.' That means that when a company is not paying its bills from suppliers, particularly for energy, or to the state in taxes, it actually is creating something like money. I don't have control of the total money supply. I have control only over the leu."

With the "big white elephants" creating Romanian money by paying workers and small suppliers in lei while running up huge debts to the government and the state-owned energy company, classic tools of monetary policy were not very effective.

"Our monetary policy was killing the good companies in the private sector," Isărescu said, "and the big white elephants are laughing at us. The good companies are paying the price. Not Sidex!" Sidex, a huge steel company, was at that time still owned by the state. "[The companies] accumulated debts, and cried, with workers in the streets—a monstrous coalition between management and the trade unions."

He said this problem of inflation, caused by the "arrears" of state companies, was probably bigger in Romania than in any other post-Communist country other than Russia.

"Why is that?" Jim asked.

"Because of three things. Historically, Ceauşescu was the last Stalinist. He would visit Moscow only for short periods to discover what Stalin was stressing economically—heavy machinery, steel, energy." Ceauşescu would copy it, and Communist Romania ended up with seven oil refineries, six steel mills, and twelve heavy-machinery plants—and no place to sell much of the output. "Somebody had to find markets for all the heavy machinery we produced," said Isărescu. "In 1985, the market for such big machines all over the world was around two or three pieces. Romania's potential for production was twenty."

"The second reason is that sometimes, in the history of a nation, fortune can become misfortune. In our case, the situation was clear— the illusion of Romania having oil caused the Communist system to overdevelop energy-intensive businesses."

"And that's another analogy to Russia," Jim said.

"Yes," Isărescu said. "But they *had* energy."

Romania has oil, natural gas, and coal, but not in nearly in the same quantities as Russia.

The third factor Isărescu cited was colossal government projects.

"You know, building the canal between the Black Sea and the Danube was extremely expensive," Isărescu said. "It was more expensive than the Palace of the People. And it also cost to maintain it. Ceaușescu continued to build totally inefficient factories, and turbo-power electric plants based on very low-calorie coal."

"To what extent was there a debate about these things—this over-development, this energy-intensive development?" Jim asked.

There was a debate, Isărescu said, though it was secret—and those who opposed the big developments (allied with the Iliescu faction of the Communist Party) were dismissed from government. At the same time, he noted wryly, Ceaușescu was ahead of his time in worrying about energy conservation.

"But the only ones he asked to conserve energy were the people. For us, it was all about energy-saving! In our institutes, we were switching off and on the lights just to save energy. It was incredible! How we lived in the eighties—madness! *Madness!* And on the other side, the huge factories" continued to guzzle energy.

After dismissing much of his government, Ceaușescu defaulted on Romania's foreign debt for two months.

"That's why I have been so eager not to default—because he defaulted. He made the decision to continue the industrialization with the monsters and to pay back, up to the last cent, our foreign debt."

That made a huge difference when Communism fell across Central and Eastern Europe. The West helped Poland's economy, for example, by forgiving half of its foreign debt. By that time, Romania had no foreign debt to forgive—Ceauşescu had paid it all off by turning out the lights and exporting the food of his people.

"Was there a point, up until December 23, 1989, when you thought the Communist system was going to fall apart?" Sheilah asked.

"Each month I had to present a report on the world economy," Isărescu said, explaining his job at the Institute. "So, day by day, I learned about the economy in the West. I also traveled there. The Marxist economy was taught to me in school, so it was simple for me to make a comparison. Something was not working. The economy was supposed to be centrally-planned, but that was nothing but an illusion. When somebody was in a high position, they acted according to their own wishes. So I was not astonished about the collapse."

ARE FOREIGN CHILDREN A NATIONAL SECURITY PRIORITY?

WE LEARNED RATHER EARLY in our stay that one of the few things most Americans "know" about Romania is that, under Ceauşescu, tens of thousands of abandoned children were warehoused in "orphanages." Whenever we'd meet Americans who hadn't been to Romania themselves, one of their first questions would be, "How are the orphans doing?"

Anywhere we went in Romania, we'd find Americans who, in one way or another, were trying to help these kids. Some were trying to improve the state institutions; others were running group homes that allowed children to leave the institutions. Some of these helping Americans had been in Romania since 1990, working full-time to aid the cause of "orphans." Others were visiting for a few weeks, providing dental treatment or better housing.

Early one summer, we visited Târgovişte with U.S. Senator Mary Landrieu of Louisiana and her husband Frank Snelling. Mary loves kids and dogs, so she definitely had come to the right place. She's a social worker by training, the mother of two adopted children, and obsessed with helping kids who need homes. Frank repeatedly joked about his apprehension that she'd bring some more kids home with them.

During one long weekend, she visited more Romanian orphanages and group homes than anyone we'd ever heard of. She insisted on getting up early on Sunday morning to visit two more in Bucharest, and then made sure we helped her make a personal donation to one of them.

In Târgovişte, we met Ileana Grosu, a middle-aged woman from Houston, Texas. Through two nonprofits, Los Niños and Hope World-wide, she was living at Shelter for Mother and Child, helping teenage girls overcome the crises in their lives before deciding whether or not to give up their babies.

We found Americans like her all across Romania. An amazing number were the individuals who heard the cries of abandoned children in the early 1990s, came to help, and stayed. In 1990, Marolen Mullinax was an independent insurance agent in Texas. She saw a story about Romanian orphanages on ABC's *Prime Time Live*, came to Romania and, in 1991, created Casa Speranţa (House of Hope) for AIDS babies in Constanţa.

When we visited Suceava one time, we found Elyse Zuckerman, a social worker from Chicago. In 1991, she read a *New York Times* story about the plight of abandoned children and came to Romania. Together with Nancy Wellhousen, she created Bridges, a nonprofit organization supported by friends in the United States. They work with handicapped kids at the hospital-home in Sasca Mică, a small community in Suceava.

Over mineral water, Elyse poured out her heart to us—the problems the children face, the resistance to change she'd encountered among too many Romanian bureaucrats, and the failure of one of her Romanian associates to qualify for a visa to the United States.

Soon after the Revolution, the U.S. government, through USAID, started investing millions of dollars in efforts to improve the lot of these children. They trained social workers, helped fund NGOs (non-government organizations), and worked with the Romanian government to promote family reunification and local adoption.

So Jim didn't think he was doing anything controversial when, in laying out the embassy's priorities for the next year, he identified child welfare as one of our top ones, along with helping to reform the Romanian military and improve the economy. How wrong he was!

In one of the U.S. government's periodic reviews of embassy activities, an official looked over Jim's annual priority list ("Mission Program Plan," in government jargon). He had a variety of small concerns—and one big one.

"Why did you insist on making Romanian child welfare one of the embassy's six priorities?" he said. "What does that have to do with American strategic interests?"

It was hard to know where to begin.

Jim pointed out that USAID's involvement predated his arrival in Romania by quite a lot, so, while he appreciated the personal credit the fellow was giving him, he didn't think he'd earned it.

Jim talked about the deep and broad interest of ordinary Americans in helping Romania's abandoned children. If Americans care about it, shouldn't their embassy care, too?

And he made an argument that seemed obvious to him then, but is even more compelling post-9/11. "It's very much in U.S. national interests," he said, "to help people in other countries solve their problems so that, when America needs help, they'll help us. That seems like Politics 101." The skeptical reviewer was not impressed or persuaded. He shook his head and moved down the list.

TAKING AN AMERICAN TO LUNCH

ROMANIANS AND AMERICANS HAVE a lot in common—a fierce individualism, widespread religious faith, and a well-earned skepticism of both Western Europe and Russia. But one thing they don't share is a concept of time.

For example, during Jim's first year in Romania, he visited the nation's preeminent fruit and vegetable research institute. He'd been mildly interested in agricultural research for the past decade or so, because the legislative district he represents in Maryland includes the Beltsville Agricultural Research Center, the USDA's largest research hub.

Romania has some outstanding agricultural specialists, and they were anxious to show off their work. After an hour's tour of fields and labs, we retired to lunch at about 1 p.m. The table was full of options—tomatoes, cheese, cucumbers, and certain unidentifiable delicacies that, as usual, Jim didn't have the courage to try.

Jim chatted amiably with the institute's director and researchers about their crops. Time passed. Wine was offered. Water glasses were refilled. The time approached 2:30 p.m.

Some fish appeared— fried, succulent, and totally delicious. The conversation started to lag. For whatever reason—boredom, courtesy, or something else—Jim's hosts weren't taking the conversational lead. Whenever Jim stopped asking questions, the table fell silent.

Now it was 3:30 p.m. More food arrived—roast pork and fried chicken cutlets. After taking a couple of bites, Jim maneuvered himself to the side of Tony Pavel, the Romanian USDA employee who had organized the trip. Tony, who had worked for the embassy for twenty-five years, knew more about Romanian agriculture than everyone else who works for the United States government combined. He is as deferential as he is knowledgeable.

"Tony," Jim whispered, "how long will this go on? Can you speed it up?" Tony sounded genuinely interested in solving Jim's problem. "Let me talk to them," he said.

Time passed. It was now past 4 p.m. Jim decided to take a risk. He thanked his hosts and suggested they should wrap up. They answered they were honored by his visit, and he couldn't leave yet—he hadn't sampled their fruits.

Good point. We were now three hours into the lunch and hadn't tasted their pride and joy. Jim looked directly at Tony. Tony, concerned that Jim was concerned, nonetheless resigned himself to the situation.

Out came the fruit—apples, grapes, strawberries. They really were quite good. Three hours earlier, they would have been a treat. By now, it was about 5 p.m. Most of the researchers were chatting with each other. Jim had run out of questions about biotechnology. The sun was sinking. And nobody was acting as if lunch might be coming to an end.

Jim gave up. He got up, walked over to Tony, and said, quietly, "We have to leave."

Tony nodded, understanding if not agreeing. Jim told his hosts what an experience it had been (true), how impressive their work was (true), and how much he'd enjoyed their hospitality (a bit of a stretch). They responded with expressions of regret about how little time they'd been able to spend together, and how they were looking forward to his next visit. Jim shook every hand and bolted for the car.

MARAMUREŞ

CHAPTER 9
IN THE MOUNTAINS OF MARAMUREŞ

CAN JELLY DONUTS KILL?

FOR AS LONG AS I remember
I was a bit of a drinker
Of much wine and plum brandy,
And with it enjoyed a lady.
Just as I was doing fine,
Death arrived to end my life.
It seemed all so unexpected,
One morning as I lay in bed!
Lived 59 years, died 1983.

Săpânţa is a village about two hours north of Baia Mare, one of the two major cities in Maramureş. Although it's far up in the mountains, Săpânţa is quite a tourist attraction, for one reason alone: the witty inscriptions on the headstones in the village cemetery behind the Orthodox church.

The Merry Cemetery, as it's called, was developed in the 1930s by a local carver, Stan Ion Pătraş, who was in charge of making the oak grave-markers. Inspired by the tales he heard from family and friends at wakes, which often went on for several days, Pătraş started inscribing epitaphs on the tombstones, along with carved images of the deceased in life. One tombstone shows a woman working at her loom. Another shows a barber cutting hair. Over there is a farmer milking a cow, there a shepherd tending sheep, and here a villager appreciating a bottle of brandy. The grave-markers are brightly painted, with many decorative details outlined in a brilliant, cheerful blue. The poems are written in first person, and reflect a Dacian philosophy that doesn't fear death.

Come all together
I'll give you plum brandy.
Drink this glass
To forget your sorrows.
I'll give you brandy from the barrel.
Instead of one, you'll see double.
When I was alive,
I used to make strong palinca.
I left all this
When I was 54.

We first visited Săpânţa at the end of a three-day trip, at the invitation of Decebal Traian Remeş, the country's finance minister, who hails from Maramureş. It was our last stop before going to the airport in Baia Mare. There was one flight each day to Bucharest, and we were supposed to be on it—a real defined external deadline we had to meet.

The folks in Săpânţa know how to put on a show. They met us a little way out of town and, to make our entrance, put us in a carriage drawn by horses whose ears were bedecked with the red tassels typical of Maramureş.

Entering town, you can tell it's a tourist mecca, albeit a small one. People are selling souvenirs at little tables along the street. We were met by Father Luţai, the priest who took us on a tour of the Merry Cemetery, translating and explaining the gravestone verses.

Here we rest for the hereafter
Turda George and my missus.
As long as we lived on earth
We used to plant fine trees.
My old lady spun the yarn.
I plucked apples by the basketful
From the orchard under the rock
To eat 'em all together.

But we didn't eat too many
For the collective took 'em all.
I lived 56 years 1941
My old lady 61 years 1945.

Father Luțai talked about how he wanted to have the annual international meeting of cemeteries come to Săpânța sometime soon. Everyone in Romania has a plan, and in this age of globalization, it generally has an international angle.

Credit: Emanuel Tânjală

Crosses on grave sites at the Merry Cemetery in Săpânța

After the tour, Father Luțai invited us to lunch at his house, across from the cemetery. When the schedule for the trip was initially put together, we had said that we couldn't lunch with him because we had to allow two hours for the drive to the airport. When Father Luțai again invited him, this time orally and on the spot, Jim again aid, "No, thank you so much, but we can't do that. We won't have time."

Of course, Father Luțai insisted and insisted and insisted, and finally said, "My wife has prepared all this food for you. Please come." So Jim said we would walk over to his house. When we got to the courtyard beside the house, there was a lot of food—and a lot of people.

Immediately, Father Luțai started giving us wooden gifts, woven gifts, and virtually anything that wasn't nailed down. We particularly remember huge blankets or carpets. Jim wasn't sure what they were other than large swaths of woven wool. They filled Jim's arms so high he couldn't see over them.

Then Father Luțai said we needed to sit down, because his family had put so much energy into making the food. We knew that the biggest mistake we could make was sitting down. If we did, we'd be spending another truly delightful day in Maramureş, but we'd miss our plane back, with meetings unattended and duties untended in the capital. So our goal was to stay on our feet, regardless of what they handed us, whether edible or inedible.

After ten or fifteen minutes, Jim said, "Thank you so much. This has been wonderful, but we have to leave." We started walking back to the van. The priest and various family members and neighbors briefly followed, then disappeared. We climbed into our van.

Suddenly, someone said, "Wait, wait, the priest wants to say goodbye." Jim told the driver, "Okay, he's coming, I've got to say goodbye again." We were sitting on the seat behind the driver, across from the open van door. We could see Father Luțai jogging toward the van. Jim leaned forward to shake his hand and thank him once again for his over-the-top hospitality.

Out of the blue, bags of jelly donuts came flying into the van through the open door. These are what Romanians call papanaş, a popular pastry with sweetened fruit, served with cream on top. They are delicious, but to the American palate, they are still jelly donuts.

For a moment, Romanian hospitality seemed to have turned violent. There were a lot of bags and a lot of papanaş, and they don't feel like cream puffs when they're coming at you. But once we figured out what was going on, we relaxed and broke into laughter. It was typical Romanian hospitality, just more so—over the top and into the air. We said, "Thank you, thank you, thank you," closed the van door, and headed off down the mountain at breakneck speed to catch our plane, which we managed to do.

THE CABBAGE CURE FOR FRACTURED JOINTS

UNDETERRED BY THE ATTACK of the flying jelly donuts, Sheilah returned to Maramureş in October 2000. The visit was Dr. Vasile Bodnar's idea. Dr. Bodnar is an interesting man with a smile that could eviscerate the Cheshire cat's. He's an obstetrician, a Seventh-Day Adventist, and a relentless promoter of his home region. He can pack more energetic good cheer into a few words than anybody—and he is not a man of few words. As soon as Sheilah answered her mobile phone, Jim, across the room, could hear Dr. Bodnar's joyous greeting: "I called to tell you that you miss us!" And he was right.

Dr. Bodnar, who radiates ideas and attracts friends with equal energy, was organizing a third millennial celebration in Sighet, the town on the border with Ukraine where he lives and practices. He invited Sheilah, the wife of the French ambassador, the chargé of the German embassy, his wife, and Prince Sturdza. The Sturdza family had helped shape Romanian history for generations, so his presence would link the event to an age before the Communists abolished the monarchy in 1947. A Romanian prince is a Romanian prince, even if he was then living in Switzerland. If you're going to have a celebration, it never hurts to invite some sparklies.

The group was to gather in Baia Mare, the county seat of Maramureş, to take in the Chestnut Festival before heading north to Sighet. Sheilah had an early flight from Bucharest. Racing to leave the residence, she tripped down the second-floor staircase and landed knees first. It didn't hurt too much, and she could still walk, so she managed to catch her plane. As she was flying, both her ankles began swelling. By the time she arrived in Baia Mare, her ankles were the size of cantaloupes, and the nerves had come out of shock to announce *throbbing pain*. She could hardly walk.

Dr. Bodnar met her at the airport in his normal and vigorous good humor. He was very happy about everything. She was in a lot of pain. He exuded equal parts good cheer and attentive sympathy. Being a doctor, he had some aspirin with him and gave it to her.

The Chestnut Festival was in full swing, with a parade, folkloric dancers, high school bands, and much more. Dr. Bodnar never dropped a smile as he guided his diplomatic guests to various points of interest and kept an eye on Sheilah's halting movements. At one point, he suggested she skip her duties in the reviewing stand with the other diplomats and instead head to the county hospital to have her ankles x-rayed. Good idea. Predictably, with Dr. Bodnar's connections at the hospital and Sheilah's celebrityhood, there was no wait. Doctors at the hospital concluded nothing was broken. Good news! The group drove north over the mountains to the town of Sighet.

But the smart hotel Dr. Bodnar had booked had a half-flight of steps into the lobby, and no elevator. With her swollen ankles, Sheilah couldn't manage those few steps twice a day, even with the aid of the ancient wooden crutches Dr. Bodnar had conjured up. Without a second thought, he drove her twenty minutes up to Săpânţa, his family's hometown, to stay with his mother on her farm.

Doamna Bodnar is slender, erect, silver-haired, and elegant in a homespun, kerchiefed Maramureş way. She cuts a graceful figure in the knee-length pleated skirts and full cotton blouses that make some Maramureş women look like fireplugs. And she is as serene as her son is outgoing.

Neither she nor anyone in her farm household spoke English, but they managed to communicate on Sheilah's meager Romanian and impromptu gestures.

The doctor's mother mothered Sheilah with traditional medicines of Romanian folklore—ice, various creams and salves, and, most memorably, cabbage leaves wrapped around her ankles to draw the swelling out.

Sheilah could not imagine a place like this at home. There are not many other spots in Europe, either, where the hospitality would be so immediate, the care so tender, and the technique so ancient.

Sheilah, on crutches, and Dr. Vasile Bodnar.
He and his mother introduced Sheilah to the cabbage cure.

When Sheilah got back to Bucharest, the embassy nurse-practitioner sent her to the head of x-rays at one of the city's Western-style clinics. She compared those x-rays with the ones taken in Baia Mare, and concluded from the Baia Mare set that there was a tiny fracture in the bone on one side.

The doctors in Baia Mare evidently hadn't seen it. It wasn't all that clear. But they had actually taken a better picture than the new Western-style x-ray machine in Bucharest.

So one ankle was sprained and the other was slightly broken. It took about six weeks on crutches before Sheilah was back to normal.

"CHRIST IS RISEN! TRULY, HE IS RISEN!"

EASTER IS CELEBRATED MUCH more intensely by the Orthodox than by most Western Christians. It's as big a deal as Christmas is in the

West. (Not that the Orthodox give short shrift to Christmas. Romania's repertoire of Christmas carols is breathtaking.)

Nothing approaches the fervor of Orthodox Easter festivities. This is the feast of God's victory over death and His assurance to His faithful that they will share in that triumph. For anyone who believes that, or wants to believe it, it's a promise of deliverance from generations of hard times and disappointments. It's a great joy—and a good reason to party. Easter traditions like colored eggs, functioning as symbols of fertility and life, are not just for kids in Romania. Church liturgies honoring the paschal lamb are followed by family feasts of spring lamb. And Romanian cooks set store by using *all* of the lamb—entrails, brain, you name it. Each stars in its own Easter recipe, or two or three.

So many Romanians share a common faith, of greater or lesser fervor, that it spills beyond church and family during Easter. Villagers, and even some city folk, greet each other on the street on Easter and during the following weeks with "Hristos a înviat!" ("Christ is risen!"), to which the reply is "Adevărat, a înviat!" ("Truly, He is risen!").

We first experienced the exuberance of a Romanian Easter on Holy Saturday, when, at about 10 p.m., we walked the few blocks north from our residence toward the replica of the Arch of Triumph that dominates the boulevard. Even before we turned off to the left and could see the Orthodox church, we heard the buzz. The church, inside and out, was brightly lit against the dark, and several hundred people—maybe a thousand—were standing outside. There were people of all ages, but predominantly young, most of them smartly dressed, some paired up on what seemed to be a date. This was not the typical covey of gray-haired *bunicas* dressed in black who are the bulwark of daily congregations in city churches. This was a mainstream, urban, yuppie flock in a high-rent district of Bucharest. It was clearly cool to take part in the Easter Vigil.

On the church steps, several priests in embroidered vestments said prayers and sang, their voices floating by loudspeaker to every corner of the church. The crowd sang short responses. Both priests and congregants frequently made the sign of the cross. Then the priests started to move around the church. There was such a throng that people couldn't really follow—they sort of milled around, made room for the priests to pass, and sang. The air was crisp but not cold, and everyone seemed pleased to be there. After a few hours, with no evidence the service was building to a climax, some congregants drifted away. Eventually, we headed for home, too, with plans to join the much simpler Roman Catholic service in the nearby French church in the morning. Behind us, hundreds of worshipers still echoed the priests' harmonies in the night.

By contrast, Sheilah spent the next Easter far from urban trends in the warm sociability of the Bodnar family in Maramureş. Dr. Bodnar and his wife, Toni, expressed nothing but delight when Sheilah said she wanted to show two visiting Americans some of the delights of Maramureş. The reply came quickly: "Come! Stay with us! We are waiting for you! *Vă aşteptăm!*" Dr. Bodnar planned a tour of Easter services that began Saturday afternoon in his own spare Seventh-Day Adventist meeting house, and continued through the region, and through history.

Covered with thousands of delicate shingles and topped by spires that stretch toward heaven, Maramureş churches are incomparable. The architecture is so iconic that, when Romania was spotlighted at the Smithsonian Institution's 1999 Folklife Festival, the curators insisted on moving a real Maramureş wooden church to the Mall in Washington, D.C. The idea came from Dr. Eliot Sorel, a Romanian-American psychiatrist. Part of what made it so exciting was that the embassy was able to issue visas for Romanian woodworkers to come to Washington to reassemble the church. (This was before 9/11 triggered a crackdown on visa policies.) We were told that was the first time a church had been erected on the National Mall, in sight of the Capitol. After the festival, the church was disassembled and transported to Chicago, and is now the home of a Greek Catholic congregation there.

So these wooden churches are bewitching enough in themselves. To encounter them on Easter Eve, as believers were gathering for the great feast of the year, was indescribable.

A wooden church from Maramureş was the first church ever on the National Mall in Washington, D.C. It was brought in pieces from Romania and reassembled for the 1999 Smithsonian Institution Folklife Festival.

The daylight already was starting to lengthen in the northern spring, so we had sunlight as we set out on our pilgrimage. We visited one of the oldest churches in the region, the Uniate (or Greek) Catholic Church in Surdeşti, built in 1766, with a graceful needle spire that reaches 175 feet into the sky. After a visit to several other churches, our pilgrimage ended at the Easter Vigil of Bârsana, a new monastery for Orthodox nuns, built since the Revolution. The formidable young mother superior, Filofteia Oltean, oversaw the construction, pacing it to match contributions as they came in. She used the region's traditional building techniques—hand-hewn planks and no nails. And she built a spire even taller than the one at Surdeşti.

It was nearing dark and the air was crisp when we reached Bârsana. Hundreds of people of all ages were milling around the new church, holding small tapers. Several priests led the service from the doorway of the church. Most of the worshippers were too far away to see the priests. It didn't matter. The songs of the priests were amplified both electronically and by the congregants' singing. The rising music and the candlelight around us, the trees on the nearby hillsides, the soaring oaken spire reaching to the stars in the dark skies—all seemed to underscore the hope of resurrection.

REMEMBERING THE HOLOCAUST . . . AT ELIE WIESEL'S HOME

VISITORS TO MARAMUREŞ COUNTY usually describe the area as untouched by the twentieth century, let alone the twenty-first. Outsiders are charmed by the stocky, sometimes toothless, peasant women in short black pleated skirts and chunky woolen sweaters; the soaring spires of churches made of thousands of wooden shingles; the village where young women in search of a husband hang their brightly enameled pots and pans on the trees to signal a rich dowry; the tasseled horses pulling rustic carts; and the traditional singing and dancing.

Indeed, Maramureş is its own world, mostly because of the mountains. It's where the Communists took the longest to gain control after 1947. There are farm areas here that were *never* collectivized.

But, in fact, the twentieth century did not pass over Maramureş. The two most brutal movements of the age, Fascism and Communism, touched down here like tornadoes. Invading dictatorships came one after another. The ghosts of those encounters still haunt the timeless simplicity of the place, and whisper in plain buildings that stand today as museums to the past and to the people who shared this landscape.

You see the traces of this history in Sighet, the former capital of Maramureş. A town of about forty thousand people on Romania's northern border, it's situated just across the Tisa River from Ukraine. During Communist years, when Ukraine was part of the Soviet Union, that proximity gave the prison in Sighet special importance.

But before that, Sighet was the birthplace of Elie Wiesel, who survived Hitler's Holocaust and was awarded the Nobel Prize for the witness he bore.

"Sighet is a small town, but it will be looked for by tourists because of its cultural heritage, the geography of the region, and also the Jewish monuments bound to this place," explained Mihai Dăncuş, a local historian.

During our first visit to Sighet, our host pointed out the Wiesel home, but warned us not to linger long on the street outside, so as not to intrude on the privacy of the family living there. Within two years, the situation had changed, as Sheilah learned when she went to report a story for PBS's *Frontline/World*.

In the spring of 1944, more Jews than Gentiles lived in Maramureş, a remote part of Romania then under Hungarian control. Some of the families had lived there for two hundred years. Most had come in the late nineteenth and early twentieth centuries, fleeing the pogroms of Russia. Some worked the farms, and some lived in villages and towns, working as traders and craftsmen. There were synagogues in most villages, and in the regional capital, Sighet, Jews worshiped at the elaborate synagogue on Nagykoz Street.

Dăncuş, director of Sighet's Ethnographic Museum and its newest addition, the Museum of Jewish Culture in Maramureş, has labored for three decades to uncover his town's complicated history. A vigorous man of sixty with penetrating eyes, he grew up in a nearby village, the son and grandson of Greek Catholic priests. Dăncuş says that between the World Wars, relations were warm between the Jewish and Gentile communities, and their children played with one another: "They were together; they were very good friends, the poor with the poor and the rich with the rich. It was a normal life."

According to Dăncuş, one Jewish trader was especially popular with Romanian peasants from surrounding villages. The first Monday of each month was market day, and peasants needed to arrive the night before to have their produce in place. Shlomo Wiesel allowed them to park their horse-drawn carts in the yard of his house at the corner of the Street of Snakes and Dragoş Vodă Street.

In the late 1930s, reports of anti-Semitic attacks in eastern Romania seemed distant here in the north. After the Vienna Diktat of August

1940 made Maramureş County part of Nazi-occupied Hungary, Jews began to be barred from some jobs and their children were declared *persona non grata* in local schools. In March 1944 came the order from Hungarian authorities that all Jews in the area were to wear a yellow cloth star on the left side of their coats.

A few weeks later, early on Easter morning, Father Grigore Dăncuş, from the Greek Catholic parish in Botiza, a village near Sighet, watched as police went door to door in the Jewish neighborhood.

"They evacuated every Jew and sealed their homes," the priest wrote in an orderly script packed tight onto the narrow lines of a cloth-bound ledger. The historian Mihai Dăncuş, only a toddler when his father wrote these words, discovered the journal more than five decades later.

"Their fortune, furniture, cows—all of it was given to be used and cared for by the Christians . . . All the Jews were boarded at the synagogue, to which they were permitted to take only linens, bed sheets, two pairs of undergarments, and food for fourteen days."

Three days later, the deportations started.

"At the Vişeul de Jos train station," the priest wrote, "special German wagons were waiting for them, which did not have windows, except a single opening in the ceiling for air. Into these wagons they were loaded, and then the wagons were closed and sealed. From here they went to Sighet, and up to now, no one knows anything about what happened to them."

Fifteen-thousand five-hundred Jews were deported from Sighet. One of the Jewish families deported were the Wiesels of Dragoş Vodă Street, including their fifteen-year-old son Elie. Elie's mother Sara and younger sister Tipuca were killed at Auschwitz in Poland. The father Shlomo and his son Elie were sent in 1945 to the Buchenwald death camp in Germany, where Shlomo died. Elie Wiesel survived, and went on to write about his experiences, becoming a voice for all Holocaust victims. In 1986, he was awarded the Nobel Peace Prize.

In July 2002, Wiesel's simple birthplace was dedicated as a memorial to his family and a museum of Jewish culture. Wiesel, his wife, son, and older sister, Hilda, along with Romanian President Ion Iliescu, were greeted at the dedication by five thousand cheering residents. To the jubilant vibration of fiddles and voices, they were offered bread and plum brandy, the traditional gifts of welcome.

Credit: Mihai Dăncuş

Holocaust survivor and Nobel Peace Prize winner Elie Wiesel in Sighet, signing the book of honor in July 2002, when his boyhood home was opened as a memorial of Jewish culture

"It was an extraordinary moment," Dăncuş says of Wiesel's visit.

Wiesel had returned to his hometown twice before, but said he wasn't prepared for the flood of emotions on this occasion, or for the bittersweet memories of those he loved who were no longer there. Of the 12,500 Jews deported from Sighet with him in 1944, only 2,000 returned after the war. Of them, most died, or left Romania during the forty years of Communism.

On the steps of the town hall, Wiesel told the crowd that he had come without bitterness, and that he held none of them responsible for what had happened to his family and friends. Still, he urged the residents of Sighet to remember, and to ask their parents and grandparents about the past.

"Ask them what happened when Sighet, which used to have a vibrant Jewish community, all of a sudden became empty of Jews," Wiesel said. "Ask them if they shed a tear, if they cried, if they slept well. And then, you children, when you grow up, tell your children that you have seen a Jew in Sighet telling his story."

If Wiesel's words stung the Sighet citizens who had turned out to greet him, they didn't show it. Mayor Eugenia Godja, one of the officials who welcomed Wiesel, said everyone understands he bears a great sorrow.

"He speaks like a man who has suffered enormously," she said. "He, his three sisters, and his parents were taken and deported. He holds on to that image of the desperate child, because he follows his dad, his mom, and one sister, and they die in the concentration camp. His dad dies one month before the general release in April '45, and he's by himself not knowing anything about the other two sisters [who survived]. So, it's clear that in his mind as a child, the suffering was enormous."

For Sighet's historian, Mihai Dăncuș, opening the new museum was a professional and personal victory. His cluttered office at the Ethnographic Museum holds stacks of documents—requests, rejections, and more requests to city, county, and national authorities, with signatures, stamps, and seals the evidence of his multi-year efforts to get government support.

Why did Dăncuș push so hard and so long?

"I'll tell you why: Because in Maramureș alone, forty thousand Jews in 1944 disappeared from history," he said, his voice rising. "All deported! As a historian, as an educated person, I know we will be condemned by history if we don't speak this truth."

And Dăncuș knows the feeling of being an underdog: After the

Communists took power at the end of World War II, Greek Catholics were persecuted. His grandfather, a founder of the Liberal political party as well as a priest, was jailed. Mihai Dăncuş himself was expelled from high school, along with the daughter of a rabbi.

So he persevered in bringing the museum to life. In 2000, a prime minister under the previous president found funds to repair the Wiesel house, and a year later, Iliescu's government came up with money to create the museum. In a country where the median income is the equivalent of $125 a month, spending $75,000 for a museum caused a stir. But any debate, Dăncuş said, was over the cost, never over whether the cultural contributions of Jews should be highlighted.

Pressed to respond to the unspoken challenge of Wiesel's remarks—whether the Gentile citizens of Sighet had been indifferent to the sufferings of their Jewish neighbors—both Dăncuş and Mayor Godja said, no, the people could not have done more.

"The Romanians couldn't do anything because we were under the Hungarian regime here," said Mayor Godja. "It can't be said that the Romanians did not help them. In villages around us, Jews were hidden by Romanians—in garrets, in cellars, in the woods."

Even Hari Markus, head of the community of about one hundred Jews who now live in Sighet, agreed that a family caught hiding a Jew would have been shot on the spot. Like many of the Jews around him, Markus came from someplace else—in his case, Moldova. He is an engineer by training, retired from running a large clothing factory.

If dedicating the new museum brought mixed emotions to Wiesel and stirred up old memories for Christians in the town, it seemed an unalloyed pleasure to the Romanian whom Wiesel calls his friend, former president Ion Iliescu.

Certainly, this homage to Sighet's famous son, now an American citizen and the only Romanian-born person to be honored with the Nobel Peace Prize, fit into a larger strategy for the former president. In part, Iliescu may have been trying to respond to Westerners who say that unless Romania acknowledges its role in the Holocaust, it should not expect to be welcome among Western Europeans. But in part, Iliescu, a former Communist himself, may have come to Sighet to acknowledge the complexity of Romania's past.

THE MEMORIAL TO ARRESTED THOUGHTS

TO UNDERSTAND WHY ROMANIANS tend to see themselves as victims, not perpetrators, of the great tragedies that swept across their territory, you need walk just four blocks from the plain house where Elie Wiesel grew up, to the severe yellow building that was the Sighet prison, its hard lines unbroken by trees or flowers.

Sighet is where the Communists held political prisoners during the early years of the regime. From here, prisoners could be hustled inside the Soviet Union in an hour, should even a hint of an invasion materialize.

It was not only ordinary Romanians who spent the late 1940s and '50s scanning the skies, expecting the Americans to come. Communist leaders in Romania, like some American anti-Communist leaders, were obsessed with the idea of a liberation movement originating from outside Romania. So while the regime sent many leaders of the pre-war republic to hard-labor camps in the south of the country, the intellectuals whom it feared most were incarcerated in Sighet prison, built in the last years of the nineteenth century.

Between 1948 and 1952, about 180 members of Romania's pre-war academic and government elite were rounded up and imprisoned here. Most prisoners spent seventeen or eighteen years in these cramped cells, and fifty-two of them died from the cold or bad food, or from torture. The dead included Iuliu Maniu, president of the PNȚCD, condemned in a spectacular show trial for "fascist activities"; PNL leaders Constantin and Gheorghe Brătianu; and academics.

These were the prisoners the Communists most did not want to escape, and whose ideas they wanted to snuff out. These were the opinion leaders—the politicians who believed in democracy, the academicians with credibility to challenge collectivization, the religious leaders who could speak of faith. The inmates included four former prime ministers and seven bishops of the Roman and Greek Catholic churches. Because of its distinguished inmates, this came to be known as the Ministers' Prison.

One prisoner who did not die here, who was young when he was first incarcerated and still young when he was allowed out, was Ioan Istvan. He was a law student who had spoken out against Communism. In the late 1940s, this was an unforgivable crime.

"It was 1948, on the twenty-fifth of September. I was in Cell 82, by myself, starving and stressed by all the interrogations, which were still not over. Though faced with all these problems, I realized it was my eighteenth birthday," he told us when we visited the prison.

"I was celebrating my eighteenth birthday alone in this cell. I walked over to the window, which was high up on the wall. There was one pipe here below the window, low to the floor, a little lower than the one here today. By putting my foot on the pipe, I could haul myself up just enough to peer out and see the mountains. And I prayed: 'Help me, God, one day to look back at the prison from the mountain.'

"Just then, a guard came and looked through the peephole in the cell door. He saw me looking out the window. It was not allowed. Not that he thought I was trying to escape—we just were not allowed to look out to freedom. The guard put me in the Black Cell [solitary confinement]. For twenty-four hours, I was pounding on the door, demanding, 'Why do you keep me here? Let me out.' And they called back, 'Stop the ruckus. If you knock again, we're going to tie you down.' I said, 'Where are you gonna tie me? How?' I didn't know . . .

"I did this . . ." He reenacted his discovery in the pitch dark cell by shuffling sideways, one foot scraping the floor to meet the other, until his left foot encountered a metal ring embedded in the stone floor in the center of the tiny cell.

"Then I realized what they could do with this ring. I didn't pound on the door anymore. Only one guard had seen me. He could have just closed his eyes and walked away. No one else would have known. Instead, he took me to the Black Cell. I thought he was a bad person.

"But on the next Easter Day, that same guard who I thought had no soul was on duty while we were eating breakfast. When he walked out, he left the door ajar. He didn't close it with the key. He said, 'I'm not going to lock the door. But, please, don't go out in the hallway.'

"And because the door was not locked, we could breathe the freedom. We could sense it. Just because the door was not locked, we had the feeling that we were free—and we could feel that it was Easter.

"Even though it's been fifty-one years, I never forgot it. I realized that in his heart, he was human—at least a little."

Istvan was released after about three years' imprisonment.

"When I got out, I was very sick. It took me about two months to get a bit stronger—strong enough to go to the mountains with my friends. I didn't tell them why I wanted to go. We arrived at the top of the mountain a little before lunchtime. The sun was shining directly at the mountain, and directly in my eyes . . . so I couldn't see anything when I looked back toward Sighet. So I chatted with my group all afternoon, trying to distract them, not telling them why we were lingering. Finally, it was near sunset.

"Then I saw the sun shift position, and I had a chance to catch an angle on the prison. I thanked God, because he had answered my prayers."

When Sheilah met him, Istvan was director of what the prison had become. After the 1989 Revolution, it was transformed into the Museum of Arrested Thoughts and Center for the International Study of Totalitarianism. It offers seminars and research focused on the importance of remembering, and of memory as a tool of justice. The Communist prison memorial stands as an indictment of a cruel system.

By contrast, the little museum dedicated by Wiesel and Iliescu offers itself as a celebration of the contributions Jews made to the life of Maramureş County. But it too speaks of memory's importance. Both museums were inspired by the drive to bear witness, so those who died will not be forgotten.

"If you don't know your past, you can't face the present," Dăncuş said. "You can't count on anything from the future, except maybe worse things to come."

LESSONS AFTER THE REVOLUTION

EVEN BY ROMANIAN STANDARDS, Maramureş is a poor region. Today, thousands of Maramureş men leave to work in Western Europe and send money back to their families. Before 1989, it was one of the places top graduates of Romania's best universities were sent to teach in the schools of workers and peasants—the Romanian equivalent of America's inner-city schools.

One friend of ours was sent *to* Maramureş. Born and raised in Bucharest, this city girl had been admitted to, and graduated from, the Faculty of Languages at the University of Bucharest, neither of which is easy. Like all college graduates during the Communist years, she didn't need to worry about a job after graduation. The government told her where she'd be working. Because she had excelled at Ukrainian, as well as English and French, she was assigned to a school in Maramureş.

Like many border regions, Maramureş is home to ethnic minorities who are majorities across the border. Thus, many of Romania's one hundred thousand-plus Ukrainians live in this region. Others live in Banat, which borders Serbia and Hungary, while some are in the Danube Delta. More than one hundred Ukrainian villages dot the Romanian countryside.

Our visit to the Ukrainian high school in Sighet, Taras Shevchenko, which offers a whole curriculum in Ukrainian, was memorable for one very undiplomatic reason. The principal looked and acted like Peter Sellers. He practically jumped from room to room, showing us his students and his school. He was so proud of them. In one class, they sang for us while he conducted.

Thousands of students in more than sixty schools study Ukrainian as a native language, along with Romanian, and four state universities offer Ukrainian language and literature.

Our friend started teaching there only a year before the fall of Communism. From the fall semester of 1989 to the spring semester of 1990, the world of her school was turned upside-down. The Romanian and Ukrainian languages didn't change. But schools and the labor market for teachers did.

Within a year, she was back in Bucharest, looking for a job in the new market economy, where she has since excelled working for foreign companies. At the same time, the Maramureş students who, under Communism, had the best language instructors in the country are now working in Italy and Spain, learning some new languages.

EARMARKS FOR GOD'S WORK . . . AND HIS WORKERS

ON OUR FIRST TRIP to Maramureş, our host was Finance Minister Decebal Traian Remeş. He looks as if he should run the Public Works Department in Chicago. He drinks like an Irishman—or a Romanian. Unlike Dan Dăianu, who preceded him as finance minister, Remeş is not an intellectual, not a child of apparatchiks, not a TV sports commentator, not an economist in the Western sense, and not a speaker of English—at all. In the capital, he did not move in the circles that tend to be known, much less frequented, by Western diplomats. The day Remeş was appointed to the cabinet, Jim's embassy staff felt compelled to write something about him in a cable to Washington, but they didn't know him. The focus, based on hearsay, was on Remeş's Pat Moynihan-like love of fermented plums. Not very complimentary and, it turned out, not accurate.

As events proved, the IMF, the World Bank, the EU, and the U.S. Treasury never had a better soul mate than Remeş. He believed in privatization. He would make tough budget cuts. He wasn't terribly concerned about the next elections. And he didn't survive them.

Remeş had invited us to visit with him, in his home region, no doubt with some political motivation, and Jim was pleased to accept. As some Boston pol once said, "If you won't help your friends, whom will you help?"

Whenever we traveled around the country, we invited along U.S. government staffers who could help us—and who could benefit from the trip. Phyllis Hodgkins, an ex-IRS official who was U.S. tax advisor to the Finance Ministry, joined us. A southerner with a keen sense of politics, both American and Romanian, she had a great relationship with Remeş and was a wonderful traveling companion.

We touched all the usual bases, from radio interview shows to multi-course dinners with local officials, shots of țuică, and exuberant dancing. Remeș's beautiful wife Steliana liked to dance, and held us spellbound with her singing.

The most interesting part of the trip was a dinner at a monastery. The food was plentiful and delicious, the monks hospitable, and the location beautiful—up a mountain in the woods. The monks were cheerful enough with Phyllis and us, but Remeș was clearly the target of their interest. Why? Because the Romanian government subsidizes recognized churches, including, most importantly, the Romanian Orthodox Church.

Halfway through the dinner, we realized the good monks were lobbying the finance minister for what we'd call in Maryland a "local bond bill," or what *The Washington Post* would call a "Congressional earmark"—government money for a monastery building. As a Maryland state senator, Jim sponsors bills for local nonprofits focused on youth sports, on senior citizen centers, and on museums. In Romania, which doesn't share the American vision of separation of church and state, "bond bills" for monasteries make perfect sense. Tip O'Neill said all politics is local—and Decebal Traian Remeș couldn't have agreed more. He expressed sincere sympathy, made no promises, and offered a toast. Who says democracy hasn't taken root in Romania?

WHAT THE COMMUNISTS DID WELL

THE NEXT DAY, ON the way down the mountain in our van, Jim talked with the chairman of the Maramureș County Council, Radu Petrescu. Unlike Remeș, who was a member of the PNL, Petrescu belonged to the PD-L, a center-right party then headed by Petre Roman, who was president of the Senate and had become prime minister shortly after the Revolution.

As we careened around a hairpin turn, Jim asked why Petrescu was a Democrat and not a Liberal.

"My parents were peasants," he said. "The only reason I could go to college was that the government helped. They wanted the children of peasants to get ahead." He gives the Communists credit for that.

The Romanian PD-L is the party of the children of the Communist era, not that of the ideologues or the secret police. These are people in their forties and early fifties who personally benefited from the opening of opportunity to the children of peasants and workers, but they also abhorred totalitarianism. They rejected Communism, but had not embraced anti-Communism.

In contrast, the PNL to which Remeș belongs is what the Romanians call a traditional party. Founded in the nineteenth century, it was liberal in the American Democratic Party sense of favoring a strong central government and opening opportunity to the lower economic classes. But it was crushed by the Communists, its leaders killed and imprisoned, and after 1989 emerged as a party of the right.

Several of the other parties in the center-right coalition that included the PD-L were great champions of "restitution"—returning its previous owners' property seized by the Communists. To the American ear, that sounded only fair.

But to this county politician and his allies in the PD-L, restitution wasn't a burning issue. The cooperative farms had been broken up, and land returned to its original owners, in the early nineties. They didn't see a need to do more. People like him weren't going to get anything back, because they hadn't had much to start with. He was more focused on building a capitalist future than recapturing a capitalist past that had left out people like him.

In Romania, as is the case around the world, politics is really about sociology, not ideology. The PD-L's adherents were the Romanian equivalent of the children of America's GI Bill and Social Security. They were the soul mates of Bill Clinton and Tony Blair—the "third way."

"We want to integrate with the West," Petrescu told Jim. "We want to be in NATO and the EU. We want democracy like you have, and prosperity.

"But we don't want to go back to the way things were before. Only the wealthy and the big landowners could live well, and people like my family couldn't get ahead."

His answer would have warmed Ted Kennedy's heart.

BUCOVINA and MOLDAVIA

Chapter 10
It's Moldavia, not Moldova

How well does your priest sing?

The singing priests of Huşi—in the wine cellar

In Romania, you get used to hearing musical priests. Singing and chanting by clergy is much more prevalent than in most churches in America. So we weren't surprised when we visited the monastery at Huşi, a small town in northeast Romania near the Moldovan border.

We were greeted by the bishop, a Burl Ives look-alike. In a country of warm hospitality, he was a super-patriot. A multi-course meal was laid out on tables between the chapel and other buildings. Monks and nuns were everywhere.

After a tour of the chapel, which was brighter and more modern than most we had seen, the bishop insisted we visit the monastery's wine cellar. We descended the stairs into a dark and cool room, surrounded by barrels and bottles. Just as we walked in, the cellar filled with the voices of monks singing as an *a cappella* choir.

It was like walking into your storage basement to be greeted by three barbershop quartets—sporting black cassocks and long beards. It wasn't bad. In fact, it was wonderful. They had great voices and the acoustics of the wine cellar worked.

After a glass of wine, the bishop suggested we return above ground. We exited the exquisite sounds of the singing monks.

Now it was time to visit the bishop's offices. On the second floor, he led us to a small museum celebrating the monastery and its history. As we walked in, he introduced us to a young monk. Jim reached out to shake his hand, but the monk burst into song. This was not like walking into a room and finding a choir. This was more like we had been cast in an off-Broadway musical, but hadn't been told.

In a country of singing priests, the monks at Huşi were in a class by themselves.

Here today, tomorrow in Focşani

One night during his first summer in Romania, Jim got a seven o'clock call at home from Costin Borc, the prime minister's thirty-something chief of staff. He wanted to know if Jim could come see Prime Minister Vasile the next morning to talk about a couple of things. "Of course," said Jim, "but where?" Well, Costin said, the prime minister is up in the mountains north of Bacău for a few days of R&R. That's where they'd meet. Jim told Costin he wasn't sure if he could get there that fast. *Nici o problemă*, Costin said. He'd check into transportation and get back to him.

About an hour later, he called back. "It's all set," he said. "Just go to the Băneasa airport and get on the 7:15 a.m. plane to Cluj. I'll meet you at the Bacău airport."

The next morning, Jim went to the airport and boarded the plane to Cluj. Like most of the 1970s-era TAROM planes that fly domestic flights, it had thirty-two seats, two on each side of the aisle, with a minimum of leg room separating the rows. The bulkhead seats on the left had lots of foot room, and the ones on the right shared a generous space with two seats that faced the back of the plane.

As always, Jim, who's six-foot-three, bolted to the front of the plane to try to capture one of these seats. By then, he had flown so frequently in Romania that the flight attendants often seemed to be saving one of those seats for him. Given his long legs, it was one of the job's few perks that meant anything to him.

He settled into his bulkhead seat, stretched his legs, and started skimming the Romanian papers. After takeoff, the flight attendant started down the aisle with offers of mineral water, orange drinks, and small cheese sandwiches.

After about forty minutes, she announced in Romanian that they were approaching Bacău. Made sense to Jim—that's where he was going. After the plane landed, he stood up to retrieve his briefcase. He expected to have to wait for other passengers to scoop up their things and depart. But as he looked down the aisle, no one stood. For a minute, he worried that he had misunderstood the announcement and they weren't in Bacău. Then, catching the expressions of his fellow passengers, it dawned on him that the plane was indeed in Bacău— and all the other passengers wanted to be in Cluj, two hundred miles to the west.

Jim hurried off the plane to a hearty welcome from Costin. "So, does this flight normally stop in Bacău on its way to Cluj?" Jim asked as soon as he was in the car.

"No," Costin replied. "That's what I had to arrange last night between our two calls."

They drove up into the mountains to a resort at Slănic Moldova. Vasile was staying at a multi-story hotel on the side of a mountain. They found him quickly, and Vasile took Jim off to a patio for a private talk. Mostly, it was about privatizations and potential American investors. He wanted to move forward and asked Jim what he could do to encourage U.S. companies to come to Romania. Jim wanted to know which privatizations were really open to U.S. investors and which weren't. He wanted to be able to give U.S. companies useful guidance to help them win deals and save their time and money chasing impossible targets.

Jim had to get back to Bucharest by 7 p.m. for an event at the residence. The Cluj fight was not circling back to Bacău to pick him up, so Costin, along with his wife Monica and young son, planned to drive Jim back.

Costin and his family had recently returned from Madison, Wisconsin, where he had completed his Ph.D. in economics. As they raced along the two-lane road from Bacău, Costin and Monica regaled Jim with their personal stories and their views of Romania.

They were predictably anti-Communist. Costin was a close relative of Corneliu Coposu, the man who had led the resurrection of the PNȚCD in 1990 and who had crafted the coalition that elected Constantinescu and the current government in the 1996 elections.

Like most effective politicians around the world, Costin had strong views but a personality that won him friends and allowed him to work with antagonists. For example, he told Jim that Viorel Hrebenciuc, a top leader of Iliescu's party, was one of the best people to work with in the Parliament—even though before 1989, Hrebenciuc had been a Communist leader in Bacău and always a top target of critics of Iliescu's party. But Costin said Hrebenciuc knew what he was doing, kept his promises, and got things done.

Monica was also a delightful traveling companion. But as a scientist, not a practicing politician, she felt much less motivation to find the good in those on the other side of the political fence. Listening to her opine on the former Communist leaders was like watching *The Daily Show with Jon Stewart*. From her, Jim could understand the fervor with which most young, urban, educated Romanians mistrusted Iliescu and his allies and voted for the center-right parties.

After about an hour, they reached Focșani, a city of about one hundred thousand people, the county seat of Vrancea County. From the zooming car, it looked just like another dusty crossroads in rich farmland, situated as it was between the East Carpathian Mountains and the Prut River, which forms the border with Moldova. But the region is well-known for its wine. Vineyards cover over thirty-five thousand hectares of the county.

Perhaps it's this abundance of wine, and the mental fog that can be induced from it, that backs up the Romanian version of the English idiom, "Here today, gone tomorrow." In Romanian, you say, "Today here, tomorrow in Focşani."

Madame de Rothschild is said to have claimed, "Winemaking is easy, once you learn how. It's just the first two hundred years that are difficult." The Romanians have been making wine since at least the 1400s. So they've made the cut.

A few years ago, *Foreign Policy* magazine commissioned an article on the world wine business. The authors pegged Romania as the eleventh-largest wine producer in the world, just behind Chile. (France and Italy remain far in the lead, despite competition from the United States, Spain, and Australia.) But unlike most of their larger competitors, Romanians share the distinction, with Germans and Argentineans, of consuming more wine than they produce. We can and do buy Romanian wine a few blocks from our home in Maryland, but Romanians keep most of it for themselves.

STEEL CITY, ROMANIA

GALAŢI IS ROMANIA'S SEVENTH-LARGEST city, a major port on the Danube as it flows to the Black Sea.

A Greek-American friend of ours, Aris Melissaratos, was born there. When Jim was in the Maryland House of Delegates, Aris was the top local executive for Westinghouse. He retired, but came out of retirement to head enterprise development for the State of Maryland and later for Johns Hopkins University.

We didn't know until we came back home that he had been born in Galaţi. His family was part of the substantial Greek community in Galaţi before Communism. Greek traders were a major part of the local economy for centuries. When the Communists came to power, Aris's family left Galaţi, first for Greece and then for the United States.

Today, a small Greek community remains focused around a huge church that reflects the years before Aris and his family left.

Galați is first and foremost a steel town. The giant Sidex Works, now part of ArcelorMittal, the world's largest steel company, employed forty-six thousand workers at its height in the late 1980s. Three hundred kilometers of railroad tracks run inside the plant, and its docks on the Danube enable it to ship its products all around the world. The main road into downtown is lined sculptures of human forms—made of steel.

When we were there, Sidex was still government-owned, with profits siphoned off to trading companies—or "leeches," as they were called in Romania. The management had all kinds of arguments for why privatization hadn't taken place.

As he did at other visits to big companies, Jim asked to meet privately with the union leadership. They showed much more enthusiasm about privatizing Sidex, and laid out to Jim their ideas on how more early retirements and the return of workers from rural areas north of Galați could cut the payroll to something closer to an efficient number. Like union leaders at some, but not all, other state-owned companies Jim met with, they wanted to fire their owners—the government—and get honest, forward-looking private leadership.

Heh, heh, heh

The Romanian Orthodox bishop in Galați wanted us to see everything in his world: the cathedral, the returned building he was turning into a church-run orphanage, and his private chapel several floors up in the rectory.

The bishop had invited us to stay for lunch, but we were starting to run behind schedule, so, as Jim followed him down the stairs, he said, "I don't think we can stay for lunch. We need to leave in about ten minutes."

Jim couldn't see his face, but he heard, and will never forget, the bishop's entire response:

"Heh, heh, heh." The tone suggested he wasn't totally on board with our planned time of departure.

We stayed for lunch.

THE AMERICANS HAVE COME TO A JULY 4 PICNIC NEAR YOU!

ONE YEAR, WE WENT to Bacău for the Fourth of July.

During our last year on the job in Romania, we crisscrossed the country to participate in July 4 events organized by American citizens and companies in as many towns as we could. In Bacău, there was a concert on the river island in the middle of the city where families came to soak up the rays. The mayor, a controversial figure who drew shouts of "thief, thief" when he appeared on the bandstand, arranged for a group of MIGs to fly overhead. Two Romanian paratroopers jumped out, one waving a small American flag, the other a small Romanian flag. It was quite amazing.

When we first arrived in Bucharest, we discovered that the embassy already had begun planning for the Fourth of July celebration months later at the ambassador's residence. The general model, at U.S. embassies around the world, is to invite a couple hundred of the embassy staff's "contacts"—other diplomats, government officials, major businesspeople, and reporters and editors. Jim heard pretty quickly that a lot of Americans were unhappy that they had not been invited in prior years. The story was that several longtime American residents of Romania, including a septuagenarian nun, would show up every year uninvited and talk their way in.

"Why can't we invite all the Americans who live in Romania?" Jim asked. The garden of the residence where the party would be held is two acres, so there was more than enough room. And, to many Americans living abroad, celebrating our Independence Day meant a lot more than it did to the Romanians with whom we interacted regularly.

Jim had one other idea for the July 4 party. Invitations to other countries' national day celebrations always said, "Business or national attire." That meant a suit for men, unless you represented a country with distinctive formal dress, as for the Indians, or tribal robes for Arabs and Africans.

Jim said, "Why don't we make our celebration casual?" Of course, he always wore a suit to other countries' events, but this was an American event. No American in the United States wears a suit on the Fourth of July. And it was going to be extremely hot. Who would complain about dressing cool? We kidded about whether "national attire" for Americans on the Fourth of July meant shorts and a polo shirt.

When July 4 finally came, the event was memorable.

Quite a number of the other ambassadors evidently didn't believe we were serious about "casual" dress. The Japanese ambassador looked particularly sharp—and hot—in his black suit. Teoctist, the Romanian Orthodox Patriarch, showed up in full regalia—a very impressive and warm-looking white cassock with a cross and gold chain on his chest.

The Israeli ambassador had no such confusion. He congratulated us for going casual. He said he was considering it for his national day, because men in the Israeli government never wear ties.

For the first time, we met Princess Lia, a San Franciscan and former wife of the late U.S. mega-lawyer Melvin Belli. She was now married to Prince Paul, a pretender to the Romanian throne. We weren't sure whether she was there as a Romanian "contact" or as one of the American citizens Jim had suggested inviting.

Guests repeatedly congratulated us on our national day, as if we had personally played a role in writing the Declaration of Independence. One charming Romanian woman congratulated Sheilah on the U.S. Independence Day, and also expressed her condolences to the wife of the British ambassador about the loss of Hong Kong to China.

Some Romanian guests felt the urge to bring us presents, including, as always, some beautiful icons and paintings. Why one guest felt the need to push through the crowd on the residence's patio to present Jim with a toaster (in its box) never became clear.

The celebration itself was a success. The total crowd was about a thousand people, probably half of them Americans. Americans who had never been invited in the past but came that year seemed thrilled. Even those who were invited but didn't come mentioned it over the next two years as we met them around the country.

The response from the Americans was so positive that we decided to throw a winter holiday party at the Residence each year for any Americans who wanted to come. The turnout was smaller than for the July 4 party, in part because many Americans go home to the United States for Christmas, but one of the benefits was that we met dozens of Americans from around Romania, learned what they were doing, and heard their perspectives on the country.

In planning the July 4 activities, we learned that the party at the ambassador's residence was not the only, or even the biggest, communications opportunity created by our national independence day. For several years, the American Chamber of Commerce had sponsored Independence Day fireworks in Herăstrău Park in northern Bucharest. Tens of thousands of Romanians came every year to watch what was claimed to be the largest July 4 fireworks display outside the United States. As it turned out, the Romanian press covered both the fireworks and, to some extent, the party at the residence.

What a great public diplomacy opportunity! National TV gave the U.S. ambassador the chance to explain directly to Romanians what democracy means to Americans. Jim made sure he did as many TV and radio interviews as possible for the early evening news shows and later in the park that night with the fireworks in the background.

So July 4 was an enormous opportunity to communicate with Romanians. We kept hearing from Romanians that they were disappointed that there weren't more Americans in the country. Remember, they'd been waiting for us for decades. We knew that, in fact, thousands of Americans *were* in Romania—teaching, working, and helping solve social problems. They were all over the country. But they weren't visible to most Romanians.

Why couldn't we use the intense media interest in July 4 to draw attention to the good things Americans were doing in Romania? We came up with an idea. The next year, we'd ask interested Americans—businesses, church workers, Peace Corps volunteers, Romanian-Americans who had returned home—to host July 4 parties in their own towns in Romania. They'd invite the other Americans in town, the local notables, and the local media. We'd produce a short video with profiles of Americans doing great things throughout Romania. Carmen Petroya, a Romanian staffer at USIA, immediately grasped the power of the idea and took responsibility for organizing it.

Thousands of Americans and Romanians gathered at July 4 celebrations the U.S. Embassy and local Americans hosted around Romania.

When we market-tested the idea with some local Americans, they were enthusiastic. They figured out quickly that it wouldn't hurt their relations with local Romanians if they invited them to a party. They asked two more things: Could we come to their event, and could we get them American flags, tapes of patriotic music, bunting, and other decorations?

The second request was easy. The first was more challenging. It would be difficult for us to be in several towns on the same day. But we promised to include a short message from Jim in the videotape and have someone from the embassy attend each event. We had more than enough volunteers for the six cities where there were events. What American doesn't like a July 4 party? Kristin Panerali, who had worked in the White House before becoming Jim's results-oriented special assistant, went up to Bacău to represent the embassy at that event. The organizers there provided her security—big muscular guys in black outfits. They had a big concert. She was the star for a day in Bacău.

The Ogilvy & Mather office in Bucharest volunteered to produce the video. They suggested the title: *The Americans Have Come.*

The original idea was that the video would be played at the local parties, the way a campaign video would be played at a house party. It turned out that there was a lot of media demand for the video. All four national TV networks played all or part of it, and it was picked up by some local stations as well.

Based on the first year's success, it was clear we could scale up our July 4 effort. So, the next year, we ended up with events in fourteen towns around Romania. This time, we scheduled them around the weekend before the Fourth of July, on staggered days, because most places wanted both of us to be with them if we could make it. We ended up going to ten cities and towns, thanks to Stan Platt, a Brit who ran an emergency medical service. He volunteered the use of his six-seat airplane, as long as there were no medical emergencies. There weren't. He piloted, and the embassy's naval attaché volunteered to be co-pilot. We flew and drove over the long weekend, from Friday through Monday.

Two of the cities we flew into didn't have airports. In Galați, we landed in a field just yards away from a cow, who paused her grass-chewing just long enough to look us over with enormous, skeptical brown eyes, as if to ask, "What is your airplane doing in my pasture?" The Galatians had held their major celebration before we got there—a big fireworks display and concert the night before. Having missed that, all we attended was an indoor reception with the powers-that-be.

In Brașov, we landed in a field behind the IAR Ghimbav helicopter factory, which had been the focus of so much controversy with Bell Helicopter. Brașov had wonderful ethnic dancers and singers as part of the celebration.

In Râmnicu Vâlcea, we went to a reception organized by NCH, the biggest U.S portfolio investor which had put $200 million in Romania. Because they have investments in all kinds of businesses across the country, we just asked them where they'd like to host a party. In Râmnicu Vâlcea, they owned a bakery and retail stores. The celebration of America's revolution took place in a decidedly un-revolutionary guesthouse with a crowd of local big shots. It was the most formal event we attended all weekend. They were dressed up, but we weren't.

In Sibiu, the American community organized a sports competition and a walk. We hiked alongside all kinds of people, including Mayor Johannis.

That year, six thousand people attended the event at our residence. We put up a huge TV screen to show that year's videotape, *Sharing Values: Americans in Romania*. That Fourth of July in Bucharest was the hottest in fifty years. Everyone was perspiring.

That night, Antena Unu, one of the major privately-owned TV channels, sponsored live coverage of the fireworks in Herăstrău Park and a concert to go along with them. It was a delightful evening—the weather had cooled off—and tens of thousands of Romanians enjoyed a festive time in the park.

There is nothing that compares with celebrating the Fourth of July with a bunch of people who have lived through fascism and Communism, and are now paying attention as if the declaration of *your* democracy holds some special meaning for the development of *their* democracy.

Why do they celebrate? Maybe half the reason is that Romanians love to party. And they know how to do it. Add Latin gusto to Levantine melancholy, and you get a special understanding of the art of the party.

In addition, a special regard for American culture is tied up tightly with democracy. For Romanians who lived during the isolating years of Communism, the United States was a kind of dream, and celebrating the dream publicly was more than they could imagine. The mayor of Bacău, one of the cities that put on a huge Fourth of July celebration, told us, "From the time I was a little child, until my father died when I was twenty-six years old, when you said USA or the United States of America, you were saying democracy, truth, prosperity."

HEAVENLY MONASTERIES, DOWN TO EARTH

THE PAINTED MONASTERIES OF northeastern Romania are remarkable—these churches have been standing in Bucovina more than half a millennium, exposing their colorful frescoes to summer sun and winter snow in testimony to God's grace.

They are all that. But the first time Sheilah visited one of them, she was impressed with the connection between the remarkable and the everyday, down-to-earth aspects of life at the monastery.

On a clear, cold early spring day, she visited Voroneţ, 20 miles west of Suceava. Voroneţ is sometimes called the "Sistine Chapel of the East" because of its magnificent frescoes. It was built at blistering speed—less than four months—in 1488 by Stephen the Great to give thanks for a victory over the Turks.

Voroneţ blue, an intense shade made from lapis lazuli, is known to artists around the world. Sheilah stood staring at the west wall, wondering why, if medieval artists could make such vivid pigments last outdoors for centuries, Sherwin-Williams can't make a house paint that holds its shade for twenty years.

Pushing her mind past that conundrum, she began to recognize some of the faces in the Last Judgment laid out before her. Several of the angels looked very much like the Romanian women she'd seen at breakfast at the hotel in Suceava. One of the saints resembled a taxi driver she'd noticed on the street. Then she looked more intently at the figures of the damned, roiling in hot coals at the Lord's feet. Here she didn't recognize features, but she did notice that many of the condemned were wearing Turkish turbans, a clue that Stephen the Great's Moldavian artist knew who he regarded as the bad guys. Also writhing among the tormented was a character wearing a Catholic bishop's mitre.

As Sheilah was absorbing this very site-specific interpretation of the biblical story, one of the monastery's young nuns came to her side and struck up a conversation in English. Sister Gabriela Platon was slender and erect, with serene brown eyes. She looked as if, just that morning, she might have stepped to earth from the ranks of angels praising God at the Lord's right hand. The faith she expressed was not only simple, it was practical and matter-of-fact. Describing the saints depicted on her church's wall, she told Sheilah, "They are taking our petitions to God. That is their job."

Voroneţ was closed as an Orthodox monastery in 1785 under the Catholic Hapsburg Empire—perhaps they didn't appreciate that image of the accursed pope—and only resumed life as a working monastery in 1991, after the Communist era.

On Sheilah's next visit, the stocky, gray-haired woman who leads the community, Mother Superior Irina Pântescu, invited her in for a visit. They toured the stable, which housed several cows, one new calf, and an enormous sow suckling seven tiny pink piglets. Then, at 11 a.m., Mother Irina poured glasses of home-fermented ţuica, and discussed her plans to build a wooden guesthouse so more pilgrims could spend a few days tasting the heavenly faith and homely lifestyle of Voroneţ.

ART AS RELIGION *AND* AS HISTORY

ON JIM'S THIRD VISIT to Bacău, he finally got a chance to see some of the city. He visited two American-owned machine tool companies and meat stores owned by one of the bigger agricultural combines. There, one of its shareholders, Viorel Hrebenciuc, the shrewd political strategist of the PSD, insisted Jim join them in visiting the new Roman Catholic church. Hrebenciuc said he had fought for the state funding of the church and was pleased to show off the result.

That night, we visited the country home of George Enescu, the late, great Romanian composer. It's about an hour from Bacău, up toward the mountains. We went there to visit Andrei Pleşu.

It was dark by the time we reached the town of Teşcani. Inside the big, comfortable house, we found a collection of other visitors, all drawn, as we were, to the memorable conversation of Andrei Pleşu and his wife Catrinel.

Pleşu had just wrapped up two years as Romania's foreign minister, and had returned to his first love, academia. He had resumed running the college he had founded, New Europe College, where he again surrounded himself with students and academics. The house in Teşcani served as an offshoot of the college, a retreat for seminars and discussion. Hard as it was to believe, as we lolled on the vintage overstuffed chairs with a generous array of food on the sideboard, this was also the site of Pleşu's exile in 1989.

The story of that banishment—and how an art historian who specializes in angels was drawn into the world of politics—says a lot about what led to Romania's Revolution and what has followed.

At one level, Andrei Pleşu doesn't seem to be taking any of it too seriously. He communicates a cheerful but thoughtful skepticism about government, about public discourse, and about life in general. There's something like a twinkle in his eye even when his words are discouraging.

But at another level, Pleşu takes it all very seriously. He is always working at what he understands is his special contribution—to be verbally memorable. He's not just competent, not merely intelligent, but superlatively unforgettable. He doesn't count on achieving that result without effort. He works at figuring out how to boil his message down to one point, and then how to convey it in a way that is understandable, unusual, and indelible.

We watched him prepare for a meeting with U.S. Secretary of State Madeleine Albright in Washington, D.C. Romania had failed to be invited into the first round of NATO expansion, at a time when lust to join the Atlantic alliance was so intense in Romania that Pleşu called it "our national neurosis." Facts, figures, and policy positions couldn't begin to capture that intensity for Albright.

He also faced the challenge that Albright knew and cared a lot about the region. The daughter of a pre-war Czechoslovak diplomat, she championed the Clinton administration's successful effort to bring Yugoslavia into the circle of democratic Europe. Early in 1998, a year before the war in Kosovo broke out, a fellow NATO ambassador in Bucharest asked Jim if he thought the U.S. was serious about stopping ethnic cleansing there. Jim paused briefly and answered, "Yes. Don't forget: Madeleine Albright is secretary of state now."

Pleşu couldn't bluff his way through his first meeting with her. How could he make a lasting impression in a short meeting?

A few days before the meeting, Pleşu was lounging on the deck of a small sailboat on the Potomac River near Washington, D.C. He is a stout man with a beard, reminiscent of Peter Ustinov, and conveys that same sense of appreciating the finer things in life. The sail was meant as a respite after his travel, but Pleşu spent it working. He was testing out what he would say to Albright.

He knew a secretary of state might meet with several foreign ministers in a day. What could the chief envoy of a relatively small, poor country say that would stand out? He knew her schedule would be packed, and most of her visitors would try to overstay their allotted few minutes. So it would be both appreciated and unusual if he was brief, and gave some of his time back to her schedule. Beyond that act of charity, what would even be remembered at the end of the day?

He settled on sharing with her his sense of history. When the time came, he walked into Secretary Albright's office with no notes and told her, with airy detachment, "We have a problem with time. We've had a bad experience with the past. The past fifty years have been a mess. We have a bad experience with the present, and unfortunately, we have a bad experience with the future, because we have always been told we must sacrifice ourselves for two or three generations, so our great-grandsons will have a happy life. And this future, of course, never comes. So we Romanians have a sense of not belonging. We're not in the East any longer, and we're not yet in the West. But we are used to biding our time." So, he concluded, "When you are ready, call us. We will be waiting."

There it is again—that Romanian refrain. "We are waiting for you."

It was on that same trip to Washington that Pleşu, who had previously served as culture minister and who had studied and taught art history, declined an offer to tour the National Gallery of Art. His staff had spotted a two-hour opening on his schedule, and thought the gallery would be a treat for him. But Pleşu told them that making such an abbreviated visit to such a great museum would be "an occasion of melancholy." (Museum visits are generally an occasion of melancholy for Jim, also, but not because they're too brief.)

DUCKING BEHIND THE ANGELS

PLEŞU WAS BORN IN 1948, as the Communists were consolidating their power in Romania. His family moved around a lot as Andrei was growing up. His father, a surgeon, was not allowed to practice in big cities because he was said to have a "bad origin"—before Communism, Andrei's grandfather had owned mills and engaged in commerce in the Danube region. It was considered to be "logically inappropriate."

"I was an immensely bored, brilliant schoolboy," Pleşu recalled when we asked him about his early days. Despite his bourgeois background, he was admitted to college and studied art history.

"From the very beginning, I was very curious about religious matters—that is, philosophy of religion, history of religion. But these were difficult subjects. I had to do it discreetly and for my own pleasure. Otherwise, I was acting as an art historian and an art critic."

Studying angels in art sidestepped the confrontation he could have expected if he had tried to study religion and philosophy in a system where, as he once wrote, "the only tolerated expression of faith was atheistic propaganda."

An excellent student, he was expected to join the Communist Party, so he did, in 1968. After a three-year fight for a passport, he was able to accept a scholarship to study in Germany in 1975. (His German, we are told by others who speak the language, is even more elegant than his English, which is graceful and polished.)

When his scholarship in Germany was over, he returned to Romania and taught on the Fine Arts faculty at the University of Bucharest. Then came 1982, when he and two hundred others attended an innocuous-sounding seminar at the Institute of Psychology.

"A guy came and spoke about a spiritual technique from India teaching us how to breathe, how to listen, and so on," said Pleşu. "It was transcendental meditation. And after one year, the Securitate decided it was a very dangerous activity—a sort of espionage thing. Why?

"Because at the end of the conference, a guy said, 'I will give each of you a mantra.' A mantra is a special, personalized word or saying that you have to repeat in order to get relaxed. This is an old tradition in India. But you also have to declare that you will not give your mantra to others, because knowing it is not good for them. Each mantra is good only for the person who gets it. And this commitment to not give your mantra to others was considered sort of the same thing as keeping a state secret, and, thus, a danger. Because if you agree to keep a secret, that means you have some commitment to some international organization.

"Looking back, I think it was simply a way for the Securitate to demonstrate that they were very useful and vigilant. So they made a lot of fuss about it, and then the Party people took very serious measures. All the people [who attended the meeting] were expelled from their working positions. The Institute of Psychology was destroyed and my wife, who had never accompanied me except to this single conference, was expelled, too."

Pleşu, thirty-four at the time, had been a lecturer in the Faculty for Fine Arts at the University of Bucharest, and his wife Catrinel had been a researcher in literature. They had two young children.

"And suddenly, we had no jobs and no prospects. We were offered jobs as unqualified workers in some factories—my wife was given a job in a factory making socks, and me a job in a glass factory. We refused."

We heard a slightly different view of the transcendental meditation episode from Mircea Toma, a founder of *Caṭavencu*, the satirical journal. It's hard to believe now, reading the irreverent publication he started, but Toma worked as a low-level psychologist in the Ministry of Defense for fifteen years during Communism. Toma himself didn't attend the 1982 seminar.

"I was invited, but I was too lazy to go," he told us. "It started to rain or something."

But he said he wouldn't have been afraid to, because he understood the lecturer had come to Romania with Elena Ceauşescu's blessing. Only later did the Securitate discover that some of those being pulled into the transcendental meditation movement were colonels, policemen, and others involved in guarding Ceauşescu.

"It was officially assumed that this was an attack on Ceauşescu," Toma told us. "And attendees were punished. The Institute of Psychology was closed.

"We had a guy, a doctor who had a Ph.D. from Germany, cleaning laundry. [Another] was a specialist in putting electrodes in a very small spot at the rear of the brain, and he had written some books on this subject. [Now] he had to make buttonholes . . . He was paid based on the number of holes he was making per month. So everybody was telling him, 'Come on, come on, come on. Just make holes faster, faster, faster.' [But he said:] 'No, I can't.'"

Toma said most of the exiled workers were "rehabilitated" after about three years.

Pleşu's career path was more complicated. Not only was he barred from working as an academic during the mid-1980s, but he also was not allowed to publish or sign articles. Hearing of the constraints, the same German foundation that had given him a scholarship eight years earlier offered him another one—but he could not get a passport to take advantage of it.

"Then a scandal arose about me in free Europe," Pleşu recalled. "Suddenly, a Securitate officer comes to me and says, 'If you want to leave, why didn't you tell us? Tomorrow you will have a passport.

Don't you want to have your son with you, too?' I shut my mouth for some months until September, when I still didn't have the passport, and in the end, he said, 'Look, we will give you the passport, but you will not come back because we have given the passport to you. You will not die because of that.' It was a hint—and then when I did come back, they were rather irritated. I came back after one year, and I sent my child back in September to start school."

Pleşu told us he never considered staying abroad.

"No, never . . . To put it bluntly, this was my country, too. And if they stayed, I thought I should stay, too," he told us. "Also, I am very connected to language, to speaking, to writing in Romanian. I see myself as Romanian even when I am using other languages. In '82, because my situation was very bad, there were all sorts of proposals coming to me. For instance, Radio Free Europe offered me a position. I turned it down. Then the Voice of America and the University in Germany did the same, and I again refused. It was a sort of obstinacy that I should still come back to Romania."

He took a job shuffling papers at the Union of Fine Artists. After a few years, he was rehired to the faculty, at the lowest level. Then, early in 1988, he and his outspoken friend Mircea Dinescu got into trouble for having discussions with foreigners and not filing reports about them with the Securitate. They were placed under house arrest, and at first not allowed to see each other.

After a time, they were allowed to walk together around a lake, with the same two or three Securitate officers tailing them. After quite a few tours of the lake, Pleşu recalled, one of the followers said, essentially, "If you're just going to walk around and around and around, we'll wait here while you do it. Just don't leave the track."

On one outing, as Pleşu remembers it, Dinescu stuck his head in a food shop, asked the clerk for some tomatoes, and was told there weren't any. "Dinescu said, 'I'm a poet. I have to eat something,'" Pleşu remembers. "'Being a poet requires courage.' And then the store guy said, 'If you are a poet, you should be courageous. Not all poets are.'" Pleşu said Dinescu answered, "But I am." And then, the shopkeeper disappeared and came back with five kilos of tomatoes. When Dinescu left the store with his eleven pounds of tomatoes, Pleşu said, one of the Securitate officers on his tail asked, "'Could you help me get two kilos?' So Dinescu went back into the shop and said, 'Look, this is the guy following me. He's a nice guy. Give him two kilos.' And they both left with tomatoes."

A WEED IN THE GARDEN OF SOCIALISM

PLEŞU KEPT TAKING RISKS. Unwittingly, he played a part in the case of a former Securitate officer who first turned diplomat, then turned dissident. His name was Dumitru Mazilu. A friend asked Pleşu to pass a small package to an American Foreign Service officer (FSO) whom Pleşu had met in Paris three years earlier. The FSO, Michael Palmley, was by then stationed in Bucharest.

"Irresponsibly, I said, 'yes, give it to me.' I didn't even ask what it was," Pleşu said. "Michael came to my place. I gave him the package, and Michael opened it. It was a videocassette showing people following Mazilu, and doing all sorts of other things. Michael said, 'She gave that to you to give to me? It is much too dangerous. You shouldn't have accepted it. It's not worth doing that.' And from that moment on, he didn't speak to me—he wrote me notes in my house and burned them immediately after. [But Palmley] took the cassette—and Mazilu was again in the ministry."

A few months later, after the Securitate stationed a watch at Pleşu's door, Palmley sent a message asking whether Pleşu jogged. The rotund Pleşu reenacted his mock horror. "Never, and I never *will* jog!" he said. But Palmley replied, according to Pleşu, "'Still, at least do it once, and I will join you in the streets somewhere so we can talk a little bit.' It was the only time I had jogged in my life, and it worked! The people did not follow me."

Pleşu continued to thwart the government's efforts to keep him from talking to foreigners. We asked him why.

"I was rather bored, and I felt in a way that because nobody is talking to those people, you should come and talk with them if they ask. The British ambassador and the Dutch ambassador were very nice people, so we got to be friends . . . The most active, a very tough guy from Amsterdam, came to my place by bicycle and quarreled with the officers stationed there.

"So, I protested. I wrote a letter to the minister of education. I said, 'I am free to choose my friends. I have no state secrets.'"

In response, the minister of education, whom Pleşu described as the one who had falsified Elena Ceauşescu's academic diplomas, and was therefore politically untouchable himself, called Pleşu in for a little chat. He was responsible for the ideological purity of all professors. He warned Pleşu that if he didn't stop seeing foreigners, he would face huge problems. And then, Pleşu said, the minister offered an analogy. In a garden, he said, you have flowers and other good things, but you also have weeds. There is the same thing in the garden of socialism."

"I see," Jim said. "You were a weed in the garden of socialism."

Judging by Pleşu's bearded smile, the description delighted him.

Eventually, the Securitate had had enough. They cut off Pleşu's walks with his beloved fellow reprobate Dinescu. One day, an officer, who was not part of their regular detail, pulled them apart in the street and shouted that they would never see each other again. Not long after, the government ordered Pleşu to take the post of musicologist at a small museum in Bacău, in the poorest part of Romania. He made a counterproposal: If they wanted to isolate him, why not put him in the Enescu house in Teşcani, twenty miles west of Bacău? At least there, he figured, he would have a library and someone to cook for him. The Securitate, anxious to stop staking out the Pleşu home in Bucharest, agreed.

Pleşu's exile in Teşcani, where we visited him, began in May 1989. No one knew a revolution was brewing. Catrinel, back in Bucharest with the kids, would occasionally phone him, but the calls were tapped.

"They thought we were giving each other secret messages," Pleşu told us. "Which was wrong. When they imagined something was suspect, they would immediately close the conversation . . . For instance, in order to get a salary there, I had to have my birth certificate. I didn't have it with me. So I told my wife, 'Catrinel, will you please send it to me from that stack of documents?' *Bop.* They immediately thought, if he is asking for documents, this must be something very serious."

As a result, on December 21, 1989, when Catrinel really *did* have news for Andrei that the Securitate might have wanted to block, she tried to convey it in code—and he missed it completely. She wanted to communicate that the protests against the government had spread from Timişoara to Bucharest.

"She said, 'Everybody's got a cold here.'" With raised eyebrows, Pleşu repeated his answer: "Really? Why don't you have aspirin? Everybody should have aspirin. Is it so serious? Is it an epidemic?" Catrinel tried another tack: "The weather is bad." Andrei: "Hmmm. It is not so good here, either."

Later that day, listening to the radio, Pleşu realized something was up. He told us it was common to listen to Radio Free Europe, even though the Securitate could use that against you if they caught you doing it. He said he knew of a customer in a store who questioned the power of a radio he was considering buying in 1980. The sales clerk immediately tuned in Radio Free Europe to prove its capability. "That was typical, at least for Romanian Communists, and for Communists in general," Pleşu said. "It was a mixture of tragedy and ridiculousness."

Pleşu decided he wanted to be part of the Revolution, so he'd defy the Securitate and hustle back to Bucharest. No train was available, but he persuaded someone with a car that *he* wanted to see the Revolution, too. They arrived in Bucharest at 11 a.m., December 22.

"It was already rather bad. Fighting. Shooting . . . I was very confused. Scared. I was sure of nothing," Pleşu told us.

Things moved fast. Three days later, the Ceauşescus were executed. A few days after, as a new government was being formed, Pleşu was nominated by Silviu Brucan, a liberal in the Communist regime, to be minister of culture.

When Pleşu had been in his new office but two or three days, who should show up but one of the Securitate officers who had dealt with him in the 1980s? He had once told Pleşu, "You'll have time enough to think that what we're doing is right and what you're doing is wrong." Now the shoe was on the other foot.

"Mr. Minister, I'm ready to serve" is how Pleşu remembers the agent's offer. "I suppose we have to fight any counterrevolutionary activities."

"I don't think we need that," Pleşu said.

FIGHTING PRE-REVOLUTIONARY BATTLES

PLEŞU SAW DISTURBING EVIDENCE that certain things hadn't changed. In the spring of 1990, Dinescu said he'd heard rumors that the secret police were still eavesdropping on cabinet ministers, only now they were sending reports to the prime minister instead of to Ceauşescu.

"I called Virgil Măgureanu, head of the domestic secret police, and asked him if the rumors were true. He said, 'Possibly yes, because a lot of Securitate officers left with a lot of equipment, and might eavesdrop for blackmail.' I went with Dinescu to see [President] Iliescu and asked him in a very direct way if anyone was listening to our calls. Iliescu asked why, and Dinescu pretended that when he talked on the telephone, he heard the same funny noises as he heard before the Revolution. The idea that the president couldn't be sure about such a thing was amazing."

Perhaps the clearest testimony came from one of Pleşu's old Securitate handlers.

"When I was a minister in 1990, an officer came to me and said, 'You might remember me. I was in Teşcani.' He had come as an officer, on a mission to check on me. He said to me, 'You made a very good impression on me and that's why I'm risking my position by telling you something—we know that reports are being sent to the prime minister.' [Prime Minister Petre] Roman later confirmed that he had received such reports. In 1990, the leaders were very confused."

In the midst of that confusion, Securitate officers were not the only characters from Pleşu's past who popped up again. The former minister of education, Aurelian Bondrea, the one who had called Pleşu "a weed in the garden of socialism," had reinvented himself as an educator in the private sector.

"When I was minister of culture in 1990, there was a team of American experts," Pleşu said. "I was told they decided not to give [aid] money to the ministry of education because the government which I was part of was supposed to be full of Communists."

Instead, they told Pleşu, the aid would be channeled "to an independent initiator of private education"—none other than Bondrea. The decision rankled Pleşu, because the minister of education at that time, Mihai Sora, was, in his view, "an old philosopher who studied in Paris and had a wonderful doctorate there. He had had no right to be a professor [in Romania] before 1989 because of Bondrea. And now, Sora was the king of Communism and Bondrea was the good guy. It was the atmosphere then."

Less than a year after he joined the government, Pleşu had had enough. On Christmas Day 1990, he quit, outraged that King Michael had been stopped on the road on his first attempted visit to Romania since the Communists had forced him to abdicate forty-three years earlier.

"He came out of the plane, he left the airport, and he wanted to go to Curtea de Argeş, where the tombs of his forefathers are—and he was stopped on the way and brought back," Pleşu said. "I resigned, not as a monarchist, but because I could see that the government was not consulted and this was a decision implicating the whole government. I was trying to call Petre Roman to ask for some explanation, but he was not to be found. I called the Ministry of Youth and said, 'Andrei Pleşu speaking, I would like to talk to the minister,' and the officer said, 'How do I know you are Andrei Pleşu?' So I resigned."

But he didn't stay resigned. Măgureanu, head of the secret police—and therefore one of the officials Pleşu assumed was responsible for preventing the king's visit—called to congratulate him on his resignation. None of it made any sense to Pleşu.

"I had the feeling that any resignation was a weapon in a scenario I didn't control," Pleşu said, so he resumed his work as minister. Eventually, Pleşu did leave the government, and returned happily to academia, working with the college that preoccupies him in Teşcani. In 1998, after the forces of the right defeated Iliescu's party, Pleşu was named foreign minister—a post for which he had precious little training.

He told us some of the best advice he then received came from George Schultz, who had been U.S. President Ronald Reagan's secretary of state.

"The conversation with him is one of the best experiences I had during that period. He seemed to me very clever, very warm-hearted, open. I remember I told him, 'You are a very experienced foreign minister. I am a very inexperienced one. Give me some advice.'

"Immediately, as if this was already prepared, Schultz said, 'I have three pieces of advice to give you. First of all, don't accept invitations in the evenings. They kill you. Go only if it's an important dinner invitation—from a president or someone else of high importance. Otherwise, never go out of the house in the evenings.

"'Secondly, never read all the files you are given. You will get more information, more quickly, if you simply invite your experts for lunch. Have a talk with them over lunch and you will know enough to do the job.

"'And, thirdly, at least once a week, shut the door of your office, think a little bit, and ask yourself why the hell you are doing your job.'"

Pleşu was still laughing when Jim asked him, "Did you do it? Did you follow all three pieces of advice?"

"I couldn't. I accepted more invitations in the evening than I wanted. I also had a complex about not being professionally trained in foreign relations, so I read all the files. But the third thing I did *more* than once a week!"

MENNONITES IN MOLDAVIA

DURING ONE OF OUR last trips to Moldavia, in northeastern Romania, we visited an orphanage outside of Suceava Judeţ run by Mennonites from Ohio. We drove up to what looked like an Ohio Mennonite farm community. The men had full beards and the women wore beautiful organza bonnets—cloth caps that tie beneath their chins.

Jim and Sheilah visited homes for needy children throughout Romania.

The children were dressed the same way. Girls wore frilly skirts of mid-calf length. The boys wore white shirts with suspenders. Their pants had buttons as well as zippers.

In the immediate aftermath of Ceauşescu's overthrow, the media, particularly the Western media, discovered the atrocious conditions in Romania's overcrowded orphanages. Flashed across television screens in Western Europe as well as the United States was footage of undernourished, often handicapped, children living in nineteenth-century conditions. The response was almost immediate. Sympathetic Westerners—social workers, nuns, church people, and just plain folks—got on the few planes to Bucharest to figure out how they could help. Many of the Americans we met in Romania, particularly in the outlying areas, had come for the first time in 1990 or 1991 to help the orphans.

Romania's orphanages were poor because the country was poor and the children, like all Romanians, lacked political power. The orphanages were large because Ceauşescu had banned abortion and promoted child-bearing in an attempt to strengthen Romania by growing its population. But by driving down living standards at the same time, his policies grew an underclass of poor families who could not support their children. Most of the children in the state institutions were not, in fact, orphans in the sense Americans use the term—children with no living parents.

According to Nicholas Chakos, head of the International Orthodox Christian Charities office in Bucharest, child abandonment in Romania was largely the result of economic hardship and the perceived inability of families to care for their children. Only a small fraction of abandoned children are orphans—eighty-four percent have at least one living parent, and sixty percent have two.

Like many European countries, Romania did not have a welfare system in which the state gave cash to single parents to help them raise their children. The normal way poor parents helped a new child whom they could not support was to take him or her to the state orphanage. In many cases, they would take back the children when their financial circumstances improved. It's not a stretch to say that the system former U.S. House Speaker Newt Gingrich proposed in the 1990s as an alternative to our Aid to Families with Dependent Children had been tried in Romania.

By the time we got there, ten years after Ceauşescu, the foreign and Romanian response to the abandoned children had become institutionalized, mostly in the good sense. The single volunteers of 1990 had morphed into full-scale charities, like the Mennonites. Foreign adoptions had grown, including five thousand a year to the United States alone, making Romania at that time one of America's top five sources of foreign adoptions. The Romanian government, with support from UNICEF, the World Bank, and USAID, was promoting group homes, foster parenting, and domestic adoption to reduce the number of children in the orphanages.

It was quite a culture shock to find this neat little Mennonite farming community deposited in the rolling hills of Suceava. The kids worked on the farm and lived in well-maintained dormitories. As they showed us around, we saw presentations on each of the children—exactly the kind of information Americans are used to seeing from charitable groups they support. They invited us to the dining room, where they offered cake and homemade ice cream, and the children sang a song based on the gospel story of the crucifixion and resurrection. It was a song with many, many verses.

When we finally told them we needed to go, they didn't toss jelly donuts at us, as had the priest in Săpânța, but we could tell they were not pleased.

ROMA IN ROMANIA

ON THE SAME TRIP, we stopped in to visit with Roma leaders in Suceava. The trip was put together by an NGO that works with the Roma community. We met in a meeting hall that probably could have held sixty or seventy people. Only fifteen to twenty were present.

Jim introduced himself and asked people to tell us their concerns. Fairly quickly, the group fell into disputes among themselves. One young woman talked entirely about her desire to go to the United States. Another started arguing that others in the Roma community wouldn't give her, or people like her, a chance to express their views. It was a very different conversation than we were used to having with ethnic Romanians, or with any other Romanians, for that matter.

Roma are a Rorschach test for foreigners—and for Romanians. Opinions about them say more about us than about them. There's no question that most people in Romania, of whatever ethnic background, hold the Roma in low regard. A public opinion survey the embassy sponsored showed that while twenty percent of Romanians have negative views of Jewish people and forty percent have negative views of Hungarians, ninety percent view Roma negatively. On this point, Hungarians in Romania do not disagree with their ethnic

Romanian neighbors.

In Western Europe, the Roma image is largely of petty thieves and itinerants. In America, it's more of exotic itinerants, as appear in the French opera *Carmen*. Today, in parts of Western Europe, Roma and Romania fuse—into a single negative image.

Romania has one of the largest Roma populations in the world—perhaps one million. In 2007, 45 percent of Roma who were polled told the Soros Foundation they considered themselves assimilated, or "Romaniacized Roma," while less than a quarter said, "I am just gypsy." Most of the rest identified themselves with some of the traditional occupations of Roma—woodworkers, bucket-makers, bear-trainers, brick-makers. That doesn't mean they have jobs training bears or making buckets, but that's what they call the traditional family business, and that's how they see themselves. The thousands of Roma women who sell flowers in tiny shops and sidewalk kiosks, catering to Romanians' passion for blooms, did not show up in the Soros survey.

While their history is unclear, Roma are thought to have come originally from northwestern India, perhaps as long as one thousand years ago. Through the centuries, they've kept their unique language and culture intact. Contrary to Western images, they are not primarily itinerants. In fact, until the 1860s in Romania, they were like serfs or slaves tied to the land. Their emancipation paralleled the emancipation of America's African slaves.

When Sheilah interviewed Costel Bercuş, head of the Roma non-profit advocacy group Romani CRISS (Romani Center for Social Intervention and Studies), a few years ago, he complained that the prejudices of the slavery period were "burned into the brains" of every Romanian. Things were better for the Roma during Communism, he said. True, assimilation was forced on the Roma, Bercuş said, but the same structures were also forced on the Romanian majority. Everyone had to work, every young person had to go to school, everyone had health coverage. Roma started to have an equal status.

In Bercuş' view, the lot of the Roma deteriorated after 1989. "When the Communist era ended and the centralized economy became decentralized, the Roma encountered more difficulties in finding jobs, because this new type of economy was competitive, and focused a lot on the skills of the workers," he said. Even in this century, he added, "the houses that belong to Roma families are still at the edge of the village. Most Roma are not qualified for any job, so the only jobs they can get are in agriculture or other jobs that don't require special skills."

The Roma's itinerancy—the constant moving that outsiders see and distrust—Bercuş contended is mostly Roma searching for seasonal work. Bercuş tied the Romas' post-1989 financial stress to social stress: "The prejudice that had been quiet showed itself. The conflict between the majority and the minority started to be more intense after the Revolution."

So, while some Roma have assimilated into Romanian society, most have remained outside it. Roma are four times as likely to live in poverty as other Romanians. Half the Roma polled by Soros said they had either never attended school (23 percent) or attended only primary school (27 percent).

Their status today in Romania is analogous to that of African-Americans in the Mississippi delta of the 1920s. Theoretically, they have legal equality. But because of their self-isolation, as well as discrimination and stereotyping, they are fundamentally outside mainstream society. Their neighborhoods on the outskirts of cities usually have no paved roads. Many of their children drop out of school or end up in state orphanages because their families are so poor.

Most Romanians see them as less honest, less intelligent, and less hardworking than themselves. Americans and some Western Europeans, particularly liberal ones, rebel against these stereotypes.

The head of the Peace Corps contingent in Romania told us that several Roma tried to filch some money from him on a bus. (He was trying so hard not to stereotype them as he described ladies dressed in colorful, full skirts.) When he felt a hand in his pocket, he told us, he inserted his own hand, pulled back on the fingers he found, and caused a great deal of pain to the would-be pickpocket. When the bus stopped and the Roma hopped off, he tried to give chase. That's when one of the ladies threw her blouse over her head, exposing what was underneath. He told us he faced a split-second decision whether to grab what he saw in front of him or to let the woman go. She got away, and he laughed at himself as he told the story.

POLES IN THE UNMELTED POT

IN THE NINETEENTH CENTURY, Chicago wasn't the only place Poles went for opportunity—or for freedom from the draft. Bucovina, including what is now Suceava and Botoşani in Romania, was a place where Poles, as well as Germans, Jews, Czechs, and others, could live outside the reach of serfdom.

Today, there are about four thousand Poles living in Romania. As an officially recognized minority, they have a member representing them in the Romanian parliament. Eighteen recognized minority groups are guaranteed at least one seat in the lower house of the Romanian Parliament—from Albanians and Serbs to Italians and Tartars.

The Polish member of Parliament once invited Jim to visit his community. Most of the Romanian Poles live in Suceava, in the nation's far northeast, bordering Ukraine. Many are integrated into the rest of the population, but three villages are exclusively Polish.

In addition to a school, the Polish community has a cultural center. It's filled with memorabilia of their forebears.

Poles settled in Suceava in the early nineteenth century, when Bucovina was the westernmost region of the Austrian Empire. It's said that many were attracted from elsewhere by the fact that serfdom was not enforced there, and that the Austrian army, whose mandatory service terms lasted fourteen years, did not draft young men from the region.

This was the century when the Poles did not have their own state. After Poland adopted the Western world's second written constitution in 1791, Russia, Prussia, and Austria chopped the country up. Southern Poland and Bucovina remained part of Austria until 1918, when the Polish state was reconstituted (it had been one of Woodrow

Wilson's fourteen points) and Bucovina became part of Romania. For the next twenty years, Romania and Poland shared a border.

THIS YEAR IN IAŞI

IAŞI WAS ONCE A city of synagogues.

It was also the heart of anti-Semitism in Romania.

While Jewish people had lived in Romania for centuries, the anti-Semitic policies of nineteenth century Russia drove thousands of Jews into Romania, and the Jewish population of Romania rose correspondingly. America's first diplomatic representative in Romania saw his mission as largely focused on the plight of Romanian Jews. Iaşi was the capital of Jewish Romania.

When Jim first went to the city in January 1999, the weather was cold and the Jewish congregation he visited was small. No more than a dozen older men were gathered for prayer. But the sense of history and the sense of loss were overwhelming. On the second floor was a museum filled with photos of Iaşi's Jewish past. So many synagogues. So many believers. And so much tragedy. In the museum was a photo of Jim's predecessor, Alfred Moses, a great friend of Romania and a great champion of the Jewish people in Romania and around the world.

Toward the end of that same day, Jim went to take a look at the new Roman Catholic church under construction in the city. The priest who greeted him talked about the Catholic community in town and the plans for the church.

Just as they were wrapping up, he took Jim's hand and said, in English, "Mr. Ambassador, may I ask you a favor?" That sort of question was usually a tip-off that he, the church, a student, or a friend was having problems getting a visa to visit the United States.

"Of course," Jim replied. "How can we help you?"

"Please take a message to President Clinton," the priest said. This was starting to sound like it might be a *big* visa problem.

"Yes," Jim said, with a little less enthusiasm.

"Please thank him, for us, for all he is doing to bring peace to the

Middle East," he said. And that was it.

"I'd be pleased to. Thank you."

This was the month of the president's impeachment trial in the U.S. Senate. NATO's bombing of Serbia was on the horizon, Romania was in a deep recession, and the most important thing a Roman Catholic priest in the far northeast of Romania wanted to tell Clinton's ambassador was, "Thank you for working for peace in the Middle East."

Talk about America's "soft power."

DOBROGEA

CHAPTER 11

THE BLUE DANUBE AND THE BLACK SEA

J.R. AND SOUTHFORK RANCH ON THE ROAD TO CONSTANȚA

DRIVING FROM BUCHAREST TO Constanța takes about three hours. On the route, the diverse history of Romania becomes clear. On one trip, we talked with Romanian Tartars, an Asiatic people like those in the Tartary of Robert Kaplan's book. Their ancestors came to Romania centuries ago. Of course, like other officially recognized ethnic groups in Romania, they have their own representative in parliament.

We passed a big house off the road on the left. It looked like Southfork, the ranch house in the TV series *Dallas*, because it was built by a Romanian wheeler-dealer in the 1990s to look like Southfork. This was not exactly a part of American culture we were anxious to share, but it turned out to be one of the more influential. Several Romanians told us they learned English by watching *Dallas* and other American television shows, and "Dallas" and "J.R." were household words in Romania.

While we were there, Princess Lia, the interesting San Franciscan married to Prince Paul, pretender to the Romanian throne (he and his half-uncle King Michael are not close), brought actor Larry Hagman, the J.R. of *Dallas* fame, to Romania.

Hagman told an interviewer later that as soon as he got off the plane, "Somebody rushed up to me with tears in his eyes saying, 'J.R., you saved our country!'" Hagman said he was told the Ceaușescu regime aired *Dallas* to show how corrupt America was, but Romanians saw all the glamour and asked, "Why don't we have that?" He relished the idea that J.R. Ewing helped lay the groundwork for the Romanian Revolution of 1989.

Romanian fascination with J.R. didn't end in 1989. A year later, Centrade Saatchi & Saatchi, the local affiliate of the global advertising firm, brought *Dallas* back to Romanian TV, two reruns a week.

"It was a monster success," recalled John Florescu. He and his brothers Radu Jr. and Nick own the Saatchi affiliate in Bucharest. Raised in Boston by their Dracula-scholar father and French mother, they went to Romania soon after the Revolution, and over the years have become pillars of local business and the American community.

"When Romanian TV (RTV) tried to raise the rates, we threatened to cease delivery of the tapes," John said. "The RTV boss said he would take the series off the air. Which he did—for one night. It was suicide." Florescu said viewer outrage ran so high, flooding the RTV switchboard and government officials with phone calls, that the RTV boss tendered his resignation. Peace was restored when RTV backed down and J.R. kept his date with viewers the next week.

Hagman had been in Romania only a few days when Lukoil, then Russia's second-largest oil company, and the recent acquirer of a Romanian refinery, found him and offered him a deal he evidently couldn't refuse.

How would J.R. like to be Lukoil's poster boy for its retail marketing in Romania?

Within weeks, huge billboards of J.R. in his Texas Stetson sprang up around the country, urging Romanians to fill up their Dacias at a Lukoil pump. Given Romania's and America's tortured history with Russia, it was globalization at its weirdest.

BUILDING THE CANAL

AS YOU GET CLOSER to Constanța, you cross the Danube Canal. It's this part of the infrastructure that makes the port of Constanța the second-biggest in Europe. By using the canal rather than cruising all the way down to the Danube delta, barges save days of travel.

The construction of the canal was also part of the infrastructure of Communist terror. It was begun by Gheorghiu-Dej in 1949 with political slave labor. The digging was suspended in 1953, but Ceaușescu restarted it more than twenty years later. It went on for nearly another decade before the canal was opened.

One of those who built the canal was Mircea Ionescu-Quintus, a lawyer who, by the time we were in Romania, was eighty years old, chairman of the PNL, and president of the Romanian Senate.

"Because I was a member of the National Liberal Party, I was arrested twice, once in 1952, and once in 1954," he explained to us one day in his Senate office. Before the Communists came to power in 1947, he had been president of the National Liberal Party in Prahova County, just north of Bucharest. His party, whose roots go back to the founding of Romania in the mid-nineteenth century, was one of two major democratic parties that had governed in the years before World War II. Its top leaders were imprisoned when the Communists took power.

"During those three years, when I was arrested, I worked at the canal," Ionescu-Quintus said.

What was it like?

"Terrible," he said. "Less terrible for me because I was only thirty or so. But thousands of older people died there because they were forced to dig ten or twelve hours a day. I persevered because I was young, but a great many men did not survive.

"We were working either during the day or during the night. In the morning, from seven 'til the evening, we were digging. And we put what we were digging in special wagons. We had to dig eight kilometers a day. Working the night shift was terrible. We went to work when the day-workers returned. During the ten or twelve hours of working, we had half an hour when we were given some sort of food. We had to eat then and also attend to any other necessities.

"Civilians recorded what we did and, fortunately, they wrote down higher quantities than we managed to achieve. They were humane. Still, the effort killed thousands of people."

At the end of three years, Ionescu-Quintus was released, along with all the other survivors, because work on the canal was completed. His son had been born while he was imprisoned.

"I saw my son for the first time when he was three years old," he said. "He had talked of his father, but his father was nowhere to be seen. So my wife showed him a picture of me, and she said, 'This is your father.' And many years after I came back, my son continued to call me 'the father in the picture.'"

Once, he was interrogated, but not arrested.

"The officer told me, 'You had very important political positions,'" Ionescu-Quintus told us. "I was only thirty-five years old then. And I said, 'No, I did not have any political positions.' 'You are lying,' he said. 'What political positions?' [I said]. So, he said, 'You were the vice president of the chamber of deputies in 1920.' I was only three years old then. I was being mistaken for my father. I said, 'That's impossible. I wasn't even a pupil then.' The officer talked to the other person and they said, 'Oh yes, okay, we were talking about your father.' So that was the interrogation. Nothing else was asked and he set me free."

We asked if he had thought Communism would remain ascendant in Romania for the rest of his life.

"Yes," Ionescu-Quintus replied. "That's why, in 1979, I accepted it when my only son left Romania for Germany. He is in Germany now. If I'd had any hope that the Communist regime would end, I wouldn't have let him go. Knowing well all the sufferings we went through, I let him go to begin a new life. I didn't believe he would survive the Communist regime."

Ionescu-Quintus was arrested again in 1956.

"They said I'd reestablished the liberal organization in Prahova Judeţ," he said.

Was it true?

"No, it wasn't. I would have been proud of that, if it had been true, but no, it was not true. When the ex-president of the party was buried, about ten years after any political activity had ceased, old members of the party had dinner after the funeral and they said, his place should be taken by Ionescu-Quintus because he's young. Someone present told me what he had said. I was not there."

He was held in jail while they tried to convict him in court.

"The trial took some while. It was the toughest period for me," Ionescu-Quintus said. "From six in the morning, when they woke us, 'til ten in the evening, we were not allowed to sit. We had to stand.

Only when they let us eat could we sit, on the edge of the bed. In a few months, I lost twenty kilos. The doctor came to see me. Because he saw that I'd lost so much weight, he allowed me to lie down two hours every day. So I was lying down for two hours, but the guard forgot to check. I took more than two hours every day lying down. I think that saved me, because otherwise I could not get through this. The interrogations were done only during the night. But in the cell they always kept a light on. It was never dark. You had to sleep with your head out of the blanket. I slept with a handkerchief on my eyes, so as not to see the light all the time. Even now, whenever I rest, day or night, I use a handkerchief to cover my eyes."

The interrogations were to get him to admit that he was organizing the PNL.

"But I kept saying, 'I was not there. I don't know what they talked about. I was not present.' But the trial went on with the prosecutor asking every witness if I was there or not. They had to listen to all the witnesses that were present. They waited, hoping at least one of them would say that yes, I was present. But there was nobody saying that because nobody saw me there. So, finally, they gave up." He was released.

After that, he was never again arrested, no doubt in part because he began to secretly collaborate with the Securitate.

"Three times, the Securitate tried to recruit me. And every time I said no. But they needed a personality in their area. Starting from '57 to '89, at least once a month, I was questioned or cross-examined," he said.

"I was called about whether I knew this person or that person. What kind of man is he? 'He's a very nice man.' 'But if he goes outside Romania, do you think he'll come back?' And I said, 'Yes, I think he'll come back because he has a family here.' Or they asked me if I knew Liberal Party colleagues who came back to ask me to restart party activity.

"Most of the time, I said a lot of untrue things because I didn't want to cause trouble to the persons they were asking me about."

When did he come to believe that Communism might someday end?

"I didn't believe it until the helicopter took Ceauşescu off the roof of the Communist Party headquarters."

They call it Romania for a reason

When you arrive in Constanţa, the second biggest city in Romania, you know you're in a port town dating back to Roman times. Partly, it's the name, which came over a millennium ago from Constantia, the sister of Constantine the Great, the man who converted the Romans to Christianity.

You won't be in Constanţa long before you find out that Ovid, the great Roman poet, was there, too. His statue, in Piaţa Ovidiu, faces the history museum in the downtown area.

When Ovid was there, from 8 to 17 A.D., the town wasn't called Constanţa. It was Tomis, founded as a Greek colony hundreds of years before as a base for trading with the Dacians. The Romans seized it in 29 B.C. Ovid had not come to town to trade. For reasons that remain unclear, he was banished there by Caesar Augustus, much as Andrei Pleşu, almost two thousand years later, was banished by Ceauşescu to Bacău. And like Pleşu and other writers through the ages, he didn't let an unplanned move interrupt his vocation. In fact, critics in later centuries said Ovid did some of his best writing in Tomis.

American high school students know Ovid best as the master of the elegiac couplet. With Virgil and Horace, he's one of the big three of Latin poetry. He died in Tomis in 17 A.D., never having returned to Rome.

In many ways, Constanţa is a classic port town—international, beautiful, and corrupt. For centuries, sailors and traders have dominated it. There's a nineteenth-century casino, a multi-modal transportation hub, a clutch of ethnic minorities, and several mosques, which are a reminder of the reach of the Turkish empire. There are terminals for oil, grain, and manufactured goods. There's a beautiful beach—and polluted water.

From Pikesville to Constanţa

ONE OF THE TRADERS Constanţa attracted between the World Wars was Leon Vlodinger, a Jew born in 1890. By the late 1930s, he had built a successful fruit-import business as well as a splendid four-story Italianate house for his family on a high bluff overlooking the beach.

Then came the rise of the Nazis and the fascists. The Romanian government, allied with Nazi Germany and awash in homegrown anti-Semites, started taking property away from Jewish families. Just after the Vlodingers moved into their new home, it was seized from them and became the stage for the twentieth-century parade of powers in southeast Europe, first as regional headquarters for the German Wehrmacht, then as housing for officers of the invading Soviet Army, then as a civil center for the new Romanian Communist government, and finally as a vacation spot for the Securitate.

Leon Vlodinger survived the war, but never again set foot in the home he loved. He moved to Bucharest, worked quietly as an accountant, and eventually emigrated to Israel, where he died at age seventy-four. His daughter, Jackie Waldman, recalled that her father didn't talk much about the war years, but spoke often about the house. "It was almost like another child for him, a baby he made and lost," she said.

The Romanian government still controlled the twenty-four-room mansion in 2000. That summer, a delegation of U.S. senators and congressmen—including the new House majority leader, Steny Hoyer—visited Bucharest for the annual meeting of the Organization for Security and Cooperation in Europe (OSCE) parliamentary assembly. The OSCE includes governments from Western Europe, North America, and the former Soviet bloc. Contrary to the stereotypes of congressional junkets, nearly all the delegation members were urgently trying to pack in, atop their OSCE schedule, meetings and visits to learn more about Romania.

In the group were then-U.S. Congressman, now-U.S. Senator Ben Cardin and his wife Myrna, both friends from Maryland. Ben's grandparents were U.S. immigrants from Lithuania.

The Cardins joined a group to visit the Great Synagogue near Piaţa

Unirii in Bucharest. Built in 1850, it had survived both World Wars and the Communist era. After services, the Jewish community laid out a sumptuous meal around an L-shaped table.

Halfway through the meal, Ben handed Jim a letter.

"I'm going to give this to President Constantinescu tomorrow," he said. "I'd like you to look at it and see if you can help."

It told the story of Leon Vlodinger's house in Constanţa.

Cardin became involved because Jackie Waldman, Vlodinger's only heir, was a constituent of his in Pikesville, Maryland. In the mid-1990s, she had begun the process of getting the house back. She had won at each stage of the legal process, but the Romanian government appealed each court decision in her favor.

Jim told Ben he'd look into it.

A few days later, Jim realized he'd be going to Constanţa in about a week to participate in a U.S. military exercise. It seemed like a great opportunity to learn about the case.

He called Waldman. She told him a bit about the house and gave him the name of her lawyer.

Together with Dan Lungu, the knowledgeable and deeply pro-American embassy economist who had organized this trip, Jim met the lawyer in front of the house on the bluff overlooking the beach. Just as Waldman had told him, it was a magnificent building, with Moorish columns framing a high balcony.

The lawyer told us that the house was well-known in Constanţa as a vacation spot for middle-ranking officers of the security services. Before 1989, that would have been the Securitate. Now it was their successors, the Romanian Intelligence Service (SRI).

While we were standing on the sidewalk admiring the house and the view, a door opened on an upper floor and a shirtless man, probably in his thirties, walked out onto the balcony. He looked like a spy on vacation.

The lawyer thought he'd be successful in the next rounds of the court case, as he had been thus far, but he wasn't surprised the government was fighting Waldman every step of the way. It was a nice place.

Who would want to move out until they had to?

What could Jim do to help?

The case was already on appeal to Romania's highest court, and the lawyer doubted the government would drop the case now. Jim could ask the mayor or the prefect, but he wasn't optimistic.

But once Waldman won the appeal, the government could agree immediately to begin the process of turning over ownership of the house instead of further delaying the execution of the decision.

To Jim, it sounded reasonable.

He put it on his list of topics to discuss with Dudu Ionescu, the young minister of the Interior. He was one of the few young leaders of the PNȚCD.

Jim told him the story and asked if Ionescu could direct his lawyers to drop the appeal. If he wouldn't drop the appeal, would he at least turn over the house promptly if Waldman won at the next court level?

The minister turned to his staffer and asked, in Romanian, about the situation. She explained that Jim's facts were right.

Without betraying his opinion, he said he understood what Jim was asking for and would look into the situation.

For weeks, we heard nothing, and the Interior Ministry proceeded with its appeal.

Finally, the court heard the appeal, the judges ruled for Waldman, and the Interior Ministry agreed to abide by its ruling.

Over the next several months, the Waldmans and their lawyers worked out the details of the return. In January 2001, Jim joined them in Constanța when they regained possession of the house.

Jackie had never been in it. She was born after her parents moved to Bucharest. Accompanied by her husband and children, Jim, and the entire local Constanța press corps, she unlocked the door, went inside, and broke into tears.

The Interior Ministry had done a decent job of cleaning up the house. The rooms, spacious with high ceilings, looked like those of any large, upscale townhouse from the first part of the twentieth century. On the fourth floor was a wide terrace with a spectacular view of the Constanța beach below.

In the years since, the Waldmans have visited every year and restored the house. Their son moved there full-time and married a Romanian. They're living in the house their grandfather was thrown out of seven decades and two regimes ago.

CIAO, ROMANIA

OF ALL THE GIFTS we received in Romania, few are more memorable than the memento presented to us in Greci. It's a village in the Dobrogea region, inland from Constanța, dominated, at least historically, by stonemasons. Actually, we were given two gifts. Each was about six inches across, and each was a large, heavy granite ball. No inscription, no painting—just the real thing.

Credit: Emanuel Tânjală

Greci, the center of Romania's Italian community, specialized in stone work, and gave Sheilah and Jim a special gift—granite balls.

Our visit to Greci was memorable for another, more important reason. It's a village of descendents of Italians who immigrated to Romania in the nineteenth century. As we walked down the main street with the mayor and later talked with the hundreds of towns-people who packed the local auditorium, we came to a conclusion: This was the immigrant history every American learns as a child, but turned upside-down.

In the late nineteenth century, Jim's great-great-uncle, Giacomo Rosapepe, and his brothers left the mountain town of Contursi, south of Naples, to come to America. Thousands of Romanians, particularly from Transylvania, then still controlled by the Austro-Hungarian Empire, left for America, too. Their grandchildren and great-grandchildren can be found in Chicago, Detroit, and Cleveland.

In those same years, when Italians and Transylvanians were struggling, the new sovereign nation of Romania was booming. Together with Ukraine, its farmland was the breadbasket of Europe. Its oil industry was developing. Romania was one of the economic tigers of late nineteenth-century Europe.

Like all economic booms, Romania's attracted immigrants—some to work in lower-paid jobs, some to exploit entrepreneurial opportunities, and some to put their special skills to work.

In the mid-nineteenth century, the Italians came first to the ports of Galaţi and Brăila, on the Danube River, and to Constanţa on the Black Sea to work in the nearby granite quarries. After the turn of the century, the wave of immigration continued from Northern Italian regions like Friuli and Veneto. They, and their children and grandchildren, stayed.

"Italians arrived in the territory of present-day Romania as early as 1850," explained Modesto Gino Ferrarini, a Romanian of obvious Italian heritage, to Radio Romania. "Their trades were less frequently encountered here: mosaic layers, and bridge-, road-, tunnel-, and viaduct-builders. Because they were highly skilled in their trade, they could easily find work. They got along very well with Romanians, whom they said were cheerful, enjoyed hearty meals and drinking, and, most importantly, spoke a language very close to theirs."

Unlike Hungarians, Germans, and Jews, few Italians left Romania when they could.

"We are more Romanian than Italian. It cannot be otherwise," Ferrarini said. "This is the place you have lived all your life, you know everyone around, and you got to know their customs. You could ask me why Italians from Romania did not leave for Italy. They did not leave because they are fond of Romania."

Today, fewer than ten thousand Romanians trace their heritage to Italy. Nonetheless, as one of the officially recognized ethnic minorities, they, like the Tartars, are guaranteed at least one seat in the Chamber of Deputies.

THE TURKS WHO STAYED

THE SAME IS TRUE for the Turks. We visited a village south of Constanța and far off the main roads. It's close to Bulgaria, where almost seven percent of the population is Turkish. In political terms, the Turkish minority in Bulgaria is much like the Hungarian community in Romania—too small to be a threat to national stability, but big enough to be a real political factor, and crafty enough to stay allied with the governing party for most of the past decade, even as control has shifted between left and right.

In Romania, however, the Turkish population is small. Many live in Turkish villages in southern Dobrogea.

Even by the standards of Romanian villages, the people of this region put on for us an extraordinary show. The melodies and dance moves of the young people and the fezzes the men wore, made it clear we weren't in ethnic Romania anymore. The costumes of bright, almost neon hues were very different from the intricate embroideries typical in Romanian villages.

The Turkish member of parliament was more than pleased to bring us here, for all the right political reasons. His villages get few American or diplomatic visitors. Our appearance was a statement in itself. His communities were obviously on the "other side of the railroad tracks" when it came to investment in basic public facilities, so having the representative of the world's main superpower see the places and the people he represented couldn't hurt. But mostly, he and his constituents seemed proud of their culture and happy to show it off.

IF IT'S TUESDAY, WE MUST BE IN ISTANBUL

ON JIM'S FIRST TRIP to Constanţa, his guide was the embassy's so-called "mil-to-mil" guy (military liaison to the Romanian military) whom Americans, at least, called the "mayor of Constanţa." He was an American Babbitt, in the good sense—glib, friendly, and sincere. He knew and liked everyone in Constanţa. He was Jim's kind of military diplomat. Unfortunately, the Pentagon was wedded to one-year tours for mil-to-mil officers. America's loss.

A few months later, Jim went back to Constanţa—from Istanbul.

The U.S. government organized a conference in Istanbul for U.S. companies interested in oil and other business in the Black Sea region. Jim attended, along with Bill Crawford, the embassy's commercial officer. We arranged for several dozen company representatives to fly to Constanţa for a day to view the port and see first-hand the opportunities in Romania.

Traian Băsescu, who was transportation minister then and is now president of Romania, lined up transportation for the U.S. business executives on the state airline, TAROM.

Băsescu is a working-class visionary—in the Al Smith, not Franklin Roosevelt, mold. A ship captain before 1989, he hails from Constanţa and believes that average Romanians can be world-class competitors. And he's right.

Most Romanian political leaders are intellectuals who built their pre-1989 careers in Bucharest. During his years out of favor with Ceauşescu, Ion Iliescu ran a publishing house. Petre Roman taught electrical engineering. Theodor Stolojan was an economist. Adrian Năstase was a law professor. And, of course, Emil Constantinescu was a lawyer, geologist, and rector of the University of Bucharest.

Băsescu is different—very different. He was born near Constanţa, graduated from the Naval Institute there, and joined the merchant marines. For six years in the 1980s, he captained Romania's biggest oil tanker. In the final years of the Communist regime, he headed the state shipping company's office in Antwerp.

But biography is far from the only way he stands out. To most Romanians, it's the way he talks. *Limbă de lemn*, or "language of wood"—that's what Romanians call the oratorical style of most of their leaders. Part of it probably stems from the age of totalitarianism, a time when direct talk could put you in jail. Part of it is just Romania—everyone speaks more formally, and at greater length, than do most Americans, in politics and other endeavors.

When Jim wrote short statements for Romanian radio or television, his language teacher Vivi Palade always reminded him that his English version could be only half as long as the time allotted. It would take someone, twice as long to say the same thing in Romanian.

But even in Romanian, Băsescu has a gift and penchant for speaking directly and clearly.

Jim and Băsescu first met when Jim invited him to lunch at the residence. The embassy had been working with some U.S. companies that wanted to rehab railway cars owned by the Romanian state railroads. Dan Floru, the embassy's transportation expert, had suggested a meal, rather than a meeting in Jim's office, because he thought it would be "a nice gesture." It was—but one we never repeated.

Băsescu and Jim had a perfectly good discussion—and, of course, given the skills of the embassy chef, Mihai, a great lunch. But it was clear that, just as Jim thought he was doing Băsescu a favor by taking two and a half hours out of the middle of his day to meet with him, Băsescu thought he was doing Jim the favor. They quickly concluded that they were both results-oriented, not process-fixated. They met many times over the subsequent years—in Băsescu's office mostly—talking about what Băsescu needed from Jim, and what Jim needed from him.

That "let's get to the point" style endears him to foreigners as well as to Romanians. He was the World Bank's favorite minister simply because he hired competent people and made things happen. Of course, not all foreigners adapted easily to his style. The night before the end of the Kosovo war, Băsescu patiently listened to a European ambassador read his talking points about stopping Milošević from shipping oil up the Danube—*after* Băsescu had laid out the plan to get it done.

Romanian President Traian Băsescu, underlining his commitment to the "West" with his choice of headwear

He's also a tough and crafty political infighter. In 2000, when his party was heading for a train wreck in the fall elections, he grabbed the nomination for mayor of Bucharest and won the June election for a four-year term. The result? He had one of the county's three highest-profile jobs—even when his party lost in the fall.

Within days, he went to work on two of his major campaign promises—catch and remove abandoned dogs, and close the illegal kiosks that crowded Bucharest's sidewalks, which were thriving, in part, because they weren't collecting the required taxes on their liquor sales.

The next spring, he elbowed aside longtime PD-L leader Petre Roman and took the party chairmanship for himself. In 2004, he was re-elected mayor over then-Foreign Minister Mircea Geoană, winning a majority in the first round of voting. Then, in the fall, when his coalition's candidate for president, Theodor Stolojan, withdrew, Băsescu dove into the presidential race. Coming from way behind, he forced Prime Minister Adrian Năstase into a runoff and eventually defeated him by several percentage points.

Then things got interesting. In the parliamentary elections, the PSD won more seats than Băsescu's coalition. Many expected what the French call "cohabitation"—a president from one party and a prime minister and governing coalition from its opposition. Băsescu was not interested in that. First, he nailed down the support of the UDMR Hungarian Party, which wanted to go with the winner. Within days, the tiny Humanist Party, created by the local businessman who owns one of the TV channels, and which had run and won its seats in a coalition with the PSD, switched sides and provided Băsescu just enough votes to put his team in charge.

In 2008, Băsescu's party led the parliamentary elections, formed a coalition with the PSD, now led by Mircea Geoană, an able diplomat and a determined politician. Emil Boc, who four years earlier had defeated anti-Hungarian nationalist Gheorghe Funar for mayor of Cluj, was made prime minister.

All that electoral drama lay ahead when Băsescu as transportation minister met with the American business visitors in Constanţa as part of the Istanbul conference. Băsescu charmed them mostly with candor and humor, but they were not naïve about the challenges of investing in Romania. Jim returned with them to Istanbul that night on a TAROM plane.

When they arrived, it was dark and Jim was tired. He expected to move quickly through border patrol and customs, along with the U.S. businessmen, and arrive at his hotel. But when he presented his diplomatic passport, he was asked: "Do you have a visa?"

What?

"Why do I need a visa?" Jim asked. "I flew in this morning. I'm just coming back from a day trip to Romania."

"Diplomats need visas," the Turkish border official said. Then, trying to be helpful, he asked, "Do you have a regular passport?"

Jim did have a regular tourist passport, but it was back in his briefcase at his hotel in Istanbul. He knew from a previous visit with Sheilah that tourists could buy visas at the airport, but it turned out you needed a regular passport to do that.

"I don't have it with me," Jim said.

Jim had entered the land of Catch-22. Emerging from it proved challenging, and an education on the Turkish culture that has played such a role in shaping Romania's.

"So what can I do?" Jim asked.

"You need to show me a tourist passport," the border official replied evenly. So much for ambassadorial—and American—privilege.

But, of course, there *was* a solution. This was southern Europe, the Balkans, the Mediterranean—not Norway. A member of Jim's delegation, right behind him in line, was a Turkish businessman. He spoke perfect English—and Turkish. Understanding Jim's problem—and understanding Turkey—he said something to the border officer.

It could have been, "Don't be an idiot. This is a U.S. ambassador. Figure out a way to let him in." Or it could have been, "Do me a favor—I'll make it worth your while." Or it could have been, "This blockhead is American. He didn't take the trouble to learn the rules. But you're a good man. Please give him a break."

Since Jim has no Turkish language skills, he has no idea what the businessman said. But, whatever it was, it worked. The border guard said, "Give me your diplomatic passport. I'll hold it while you go downtown to get your tourist passport."

Yes! There is a God! His name might be Allah, but at that time of night, Jim was willing to be flexible. He went to his hotel, retrieved his tourist passport, returned to the airport, and entered Turkey legally.

WOMEN'S HEALTH, LOCAL POLITICS

ONE FALL DAY, SHEILAH was invited to take part in a women's health event in Brăila organized by the U.S. Agency for International Development. The event, she was told, was designed to give women information about family planning and other available services.

Sounded great. She promised to come, but then her mother became ill, and she had to cancel. "No problem," came the word from Brăila. "We'll reschedule for a date when Mrs. Ambassador can attend." At the time, Sheilah was touched by the sweet gesture. Only later did she wonder why the Mayor of Brăila would cancel an event involving hundreds of women on three days' notice, just because the wife of an ambassador couldn't come (though, true, the ambassador's country was supplying some of the funds for the event).

How little she understood then about the way things work in Romania, let alone in Brăila!

Brăila sits on the left bank of the Danube River about fifteen miles south of Galaţi. The Siret River runs between them, creating a "twin cities" relationship reminiscent of Minneapolis and St. Paul. Together, they make up the second biggest metropolitan area in Romania. As port towns, they have been cosmopolitan and commercial for centuries. Located in the center of the Danube watershed, which feeds the fertile grain-basket of Ukraine and Romania, Brăila was the heart of grain-trading a century ago. Back then, the world price of wheat was set by trades for on the Brăila exchange, not on the London market.

As Sheilah left Bucharest early on a foggy November Saturday for the rescheduled Brăila event, she pictured something like a community fair, with booths where women could get information on health issues important to themselves and their families. She didn't quite envision what she, given her poor Romanian language skills, would add to the event, but she was game.

She was a bit late getting underway, so her driver ignored the fog as they zipped past the flat farmland that stretches east toward the Danube. (Let's be frank—they were speeding.) As they hurtled across the line into Brăila County, they saw a police car by the side of the road. It pulled into the lane behind them, lights flashing. Inside their USAID minivan, they debated among themselves: Were they being busted or escorted? They decided to assume the best and treat it as a police escort until forced to conclude otherwise. A few minutes later, they got the answer they were hoping for—the police car pulled ahead of them, lights still flashing, and led the way.

So they zoomed the remaining few kilometers into the city of Brăila, with other motorists careening to the shoulder to let them pass. It was exactly the kind of entrance Romanians had come to expect when VIPs come to town—exactly the kind of escort the Brăila mayor would have provided to some member of the national nomenclature during Communist times. Sheilah was embarrassed, not just because of the escort, but because, even with the speeding escort, she was late.

At the edge of town waited Mayor Anton Lungu. A pacific smile gripped his round face as he waved away her apologies and presented her an enormous bouquet of flowers.

Sheilah and her merry band from USAID headed to the center of town, to a beautiful nineteenth-century Beaux-Arts theater. There, they received another greeting, this time by a children's choir arrayed on the decrepit stairs. Their angelic voices poured out lyrics specially written for the occasion, exhorting women to "choose health."

By now they were well past the advertised start time for the event. Sheilah assumed they'd hustle into the theater, but Mayor Lungu was in charge, and he had something else in mind: Mrs. Ambassador should first view every work of art—oils, acrylics, watercolors, and collages—entered in the local art competition. And of course, if she expressed interest in one or two, they should be given to her.

Eventually, Mayor Lungu thought it was time to invite Sheilah into the theater. The wine-colored velvet curtains were threadbare in spots, and the molded plaster decorations had lost some of their gilt, but the interior still suggested the elegance of nearly a century earlier, when Brăila's economy was thriving, when it was a main port in this rich breadbasket of Eastern Europe.

As in many of Romania's impressive public buildings, the light bulbs in this theater were too few and too weak to cut the gloom. A few minutes later, when Sheilah's eyes finally adjusted, she could see that the shadowy theater was more than half-filled with women waiting for the program to start. How long had they been waiting?

On stage, various dignitaries and experts already were seated. Sheilah took her seat near the end of a very long table. Mayor Lungu began speaking, then turned the microphone over to a sturdy, bearded Orthodox priest. Sheilah smiled and tried to look devout during his invocation, which lasted several minutes. Only later was it explained to her that his prayer went from beseeching God's blessings on us to denouncing birth control and asserting that women's highest calling was to bear as many children as possible. They all said "amen." Nothing altered Mayor Lungu's tranquil smile as he turned the microphone over to Randal Thompson, head of USAID's office of social strategies. She is a caring, adept champion of women's reproductive health, and delivered, in Romanian, a very different message.

Then Sheilah heard her name and stood up, translator at her side. She had prepared just a sentence or two in Romanian, including her stock apology for not being able to express herself better. She switched to English and, through the translator, thanked the mayor for rescheduling this meeting until she could be part of it, and added a few more sentences about how her mother would have been proud of them for taking care of themselves. She declared that, unless women are healthy, their families cannot be. They applauded, as they had every other speaker, and she sat down.

Much as the theater didn't have enough light, it also didn't have enough heat. It was chilly. Sheilah was ready to move on to the next phase of the event, whatever was scheduled. But first, there were more speakers. A relatively long greeting from the city health director. A fairly technical report from a university medical expert. After each speaker, polite applause. Sheilah told herself these speeches were dry and boring to her only because she couldn't understand the language—they must be more interesting in Romanian. But the few faces she could see in the dim audience did not seem interested. They just seemed resigned.

Unbelievably, nearly an hour had ticked by in the cold theater. Sheilah had long since told her translator to relax, that she'd pick up on her own whatever she could understand of these detailed presentations, when she heard her name fall from the lips of Mayor Lungu. He was still smiling. Fearing another round of speeches, she whispered desperately to her interpreter, "What's happening?"

As it turned out, they had finally arrived at the point in the proceedings which had drawn these women to this dark, cold theater. The mayor, with Sheilah at his side, was about to distribute bags of used clothes for their families.

Sheilah did not know then that these women all had big families. In fact, it turned out that's how they were chosen—by the number of children they were raising. All she could surmise at the time was that they were fairly poor, and had not spent all Saturday morning in a cold theater because they found the speeches so gripping. They had, in effect, been held hostage by the promise of handouts. She was mortified to have been part of it. Now that Mayor Lungu had reached his objective, though, it did not seem the right moment to remove herself from the action.

Three or four beefy aides to the mayor were pulling large plastic trash sacks from behind the worn velvet curtains. Dozens of mothers wearily mounted the stage, and the mayor, his team, and Sheilah did their dance. One of the aides would pick out a sack and hand it to the mayor. His smile never changing, he would hand it to Sheilah. Sheilah would smile brightly and pass it on to a mother with some cheerful, if rudimentary, admonition—she mostly alternated between *Noroc* ("Good luck") and *Sănătate* ("Good health!"). They looked at her blankly and mumbled thanks. She suspected she could have conveyed her wishes in Urdu with about the same impact.

Doling out the mayor's beneficence took a lot less time than the speeches that preceded it. The mothers lugged their sacks of clothes out of the theater. Mayor Lungu led the American group and local dignitaries to a large sightseeing boat, where a lovely multi-course lunch was waiting. Mayor Lungu didn't speak English, and Sheilah didn't speak much Romanian, but as they cruised the Danube, he smiled at her across the tiny U.S. and Romanian flags in the center-piece. He seemed very satisfied with how the women's health event had unfolded.

FROM COMMUNIST BOSS TO "MAYOR FRIENDLY"

FEW OLDER ROMANIAN POLITICIANS from the Communist era have made a successful transition to democratic politics. Some have gone into business, and others have retired. Brăila's Mayor Lungu was an exception. To meet him was to understand why.

During his stint as ambassador, Jim visited every major city in Romania, and before each visit, a Romanian staffer from the embassy would do an advance trip, figuring out where Jim would go and who he would meet with. The mayor's office would be contacted, and generally a staffer there would make suggestions and help with con-tacts. The energetic embassy staffer who organized Jim's first visit to Brăila told him later that Mayor Lungu personally accompanied him to scope out each stop on his visit. It was no accident.

Lungu looked just like an old-time American political boss—heavy, cheerful, and eager to please. We began our rounds to local cultural sites, businesses, and community centers. At each one, the hosts would present Sheilah with a huge arrangement of flowers, a traditional welcome. And each time, a man whom she did not yet know would scoop them out of her hands, graciously offering to store them in the van while we talked with the local notables. About halfway through the day, Sheilah asked Jim who the congenial man was. "That's the mayor!" Jim whispered back. His approach was so understated and helpful, it was easy to doubt he was the city's top dog.

But he was a tough politician when necessary. He had to be to survive as Communist party boss in Brăila before 1989 and as elected mayor afterwards. He stayed in office until he was seventy-three, and died three years later. Some of his critics in the city certainly testify to his toughness, to brutal behavior and outbursts of anger, but in the post-Communism era, his "I'm here to serve" style would be recognized by most American voters.

What would not be recognizable to the American eye would be the aggressive gift-giving.

As we ended our tour of Brăila, the mayor went back to his car and returned with several huge boxes for us. Jim said to him, "Thank you very much, but we really can't take these." (In addition to ethical considerations, our van was already bursting with flowers.)

"No, no," he said, "you absolutely have to take these."

"No, no, no, we can't take these," Jim repeated.

They almost got into a shoving match, Jim trying to push boxes back while the Mayor was thrusting them at us. Sensing this was not the best way to end the visit, the ever-attentive mayor cheerfully retreated, and we drove off with a van full of flowers.

HER HIGHNESS

ON OUR LAST VISIT to Brăila, which was part of a longer trip around Dobrogea, we stopped by the County Chamber of Industry and Commerce to meet with local American and Romanian businesspeople. Not many Americans were doing business there at the time, but lots of Romanian companies hoped to do business with American companies. Thirty or forty people, almost all Romanian, squeezed with us into the table in the Chamber's conference room.

The Chamber president did not speak English, so he welcomed "Domnul Ambasador şi Înălţimea sa." His young interpreter looked at us intently and said, "As president of the Brăila Chamber of Commerce, I'm very happy to welcome to our office Mr. Ambassador and . . ."

She took a long pause. She seemed to be searching for the right English word to convey his meaning.

"And her highness," she finally concluded.

Sheilah smiled and shot Jim a look that warned, "Don't laugh!"

CRIŞANA and BANAT

CHAPTER 12
BACK IN EUROPE

WHY ARE ROMANIAN GYMNASTS SO GOOD?

IF YOU WANT TO understand why so many world-class gymnasts are Romanian, go to Deva, a city of about seventy thousand on the Mureş River. That's where you'll find Cetate Deva, Romania's national training school for gymnasts, the school which Nadia Comăneci and the rest of Romania's Olympic champions attended.

Comăneci is one of the few Romanians known worldwide. Sometimes it's hard for Americans to understand how large the Olympics loom in other cultures. It's one of the few ways that smaller countries can beat bigger countries on the world stage.

Comăneci is popular and active in Romania, too, even though she and her husband Bart Conners now live in Oklahoma, where they run a gymnastics school. She travels between the United States and Romania often. She stays involved with the Olympics, and as a board member of the Special Olympics, founded by Eunice Shriver for handicapped children, pushed to launch their activities in Romania.

Girls as young as ten compete to attend Cetate Deva. The gyms look like any you would see in the United States—blond wood floors, high ceilings, balance beams, parallel bars—and they're filled with small Romanian girls working very hard. The secret to Romanians' success in gymnastics? They practice a lot.

Just months after we visited, these gymnasts went on to win medals at the Summer Olympics in Sydney, Australia. Romanians earned the three highest scores, and the corresponding medals, in the Individual All-Around category. And the Romanian team came in first, ahead of Russia and China, winning the gold medal for the first time since 1984.

Dark-haired sixteen-year-old Andreea Răducan, who earned an individual gold medal, was a true star. Born in Bârlad in Moldavia, she started gymnastics when she was four years old and came to Cetate Deva ten years later. At the Olympics, she weighed in at ninety pounds. The last Romanian who had won the gold medal for all-around performance was Comăneci in 1976.

The reaction in Romania was understandably enthusiastic—America loves to see its teams win, too. But for smaller countries, particularly one like Romania which rarely gets worldwide television recognition for the world-class accomplishments of its people, Olympic wins are a very big deal.

A few days later, though, the International Olympic Committee (IOC) announced it was taking back Răducan's gold medal because the team doctor had given her Nurofen, an over-the-counter cold medicine, the night before the competition. She had tested positive for pseudoephedrine, and so had her teammate, Simona Amânar. But because Răducan is so small, the amount in her body was over the legal limit, while that in Amânar's was under.

Romanians, and millions of other Olympics fans, were outraged. The IOC itself said the medicine had given her no competitive advantage. "We consider it an accident," said the drug czar, Prince Alexandre de Merode of Belgium. "The medication was prescribed by the team doctor. [Răducan] is not directly responsible. But we have rules and we have to apply the rules."

With Răducan disqualified, the silver and bronze medal-winners who would move up, Romanians Amânar and Maria Olaru, initially wanted to decline their upgraded medals. Romanians saw the IOC decision as outrageously unfair, and others agreed. When the head of the IOC, Francois Carrard, said, "We have to be tough and blind to emotions and feelings," Elliot Harris of *The Chicago Sun-Times* wrote, "Blind is one thing. Dumb is another."

The decision was appealed, to no avail. Amânar and Olaru were convinced to take their medals. Răducan returned to Romania to a heroine's welcome. Amânar gave her the gold medal, saying, "I didn't win it. It was won by Andreea and belongs to Andreea." Prime Minister Isărescu won unanimous backing in Parliament for a special appropriation to give Răducan the financial reward she had earned with her performance, but denied her by the IOC.

In the end, the Romanians—the sixteen-year-old gymnast, her teammates, the political leaders—rallied together and took the high road. The IOC, one of those ubiquitous institutions of globalization, didn't make the best case for the "rule of law" as the touchstone of twenty-first-century sports.

STUDYING IN AMERICA, RETURNING TO ROMANIA

DANIEL TIRITEU GREW UP in Timişoara, where the 1989 Revolution began. He's smart and energetic, and almost got sucked into a brain drain he didn't want to be part of.

Many bright young Romanians look for jobs abroad, but some who have studied abroad want to invest their lives and education in the country of their birth. Still, Jim kept hearing that those in the latter group were having trouble making the connections that could get them hired. To help them, with the support of USAID and the non-profit International Research and Exchanges Board (IREX), he set up a program called Return to Romania to link people studying at U.S. schools with potential employers in Romania.

Dan Tiriteu was one of those students. He sat down with Sheilah at his office in Timişoara to tell her his story.

"In '89, I was already in my first year in computer engineering at the Politehnica in Timişoara," he recalled. "I was pleased with the education I was getting.

"I don't know how it is today, but at that time, the only way to get in was to do well on really tough entrance exams. It was a state university. You also had to work really hard during high school. But what you did in school was not enough. You had to have a private tutor, and you had to study a lot on your own. There were limited seats and a lot of candidates for those seats."

Within months of starting at the Politehnica, he was offered a scholarship to study in the United States.

"The opportunity came to me through my church, the First Baptist

Church of Timişoara. My pastor had traveled to the United States. One of his goals was to get some scholarships for Romanian students so they could go abroad for their education and then come back to our country. The Revolution was in December. In April, we already had twenty-three scholarships.

"When the opportunity arose, I at first didn't consider it. I had worked too hard to get to the Politehnica. As I said, it was the result of years of intense study, like ten hours of math per day. It had been really difficult, and I did not want to give it up.

"At the same time, I was also working, doing electronics maintenance at a plant here in Timişoara. One day during lunch break, I went to one of my workmates, who was also an IT student but in his last year. I told him about my opportunity to study in the United States. If *he* had that opportunity, he said, he would go now, even though he was a senior. That was mainly because of the lack of practical education here. There was a lot of theory, but we had very poor labs, and few opportunities to see how things really work. That really made me think. I called my pastor and accepted the last available scholarship."

In August 1990, Daniel went off to Tennessee Temple University, a Baptist school in Chattanooga, Tennessee.

"I started my degree in computer information systems. My English was very poor. The only English I'd practiced was with some Americans who came to our church. Tennessee Temple took special care of us. Some American students helped us with our homework. They had some English classes just for Romanians. The system there was very different from here. I didn't know anything about credits or GPA.

"During my second year, I realized the curriculum wasn't exactly what I'd thought. In Romania, I was pursuing more of an engineering degree. In Tennessee, I was taking a lot of business classes. But I really started to like them. When I was in Romanian high school before '89, anything related to business was economics embedded with Communism, and I hated it. Here, I really loved economics. I started enjoying the business classes. So I decided to focus more on business. I decided to continue my education, to go on to a master's degree program.

With the degree I was getting, I had to go for a master's in computers. But deciding to go more for business classes required me to go for an MBA.

"About once every two years, I could come back home to visit. During the summer, we could work and get paid. This way, I was able to save some money during the summer and go home for a couple of months.

"In 1997, I completed my master's. Both my degrees—bachelor's and master's—were with honor. I then had two options: either come home right away or get a visa and start to work in the U.S. I was looking for a job. I still had two months to legally stay in the U.S. I found Stuart, a company manufacturing some electronic components, where I got a job as a training coordinator. I got a work visa for three years. My intention was to stay for just one year. Then I extended that to two years, and in 1999 I came back home."

Sheilah pressed him about why he came back, when so many young Romanians want to leave and stay away.

"From the beginning, the purpose of the scholarship was to train people like me abroad, who would then go back to Romania to help the country," Dan explained. "I took that seriously. For me, it was a promise. At one point, I was hesitant, because I liked a girl in the U.S., but [I was only hesitant] for a very short time."

When he finally did come home, he had a wife and two daughters—and no job.

"I started looking. I read an announcement in the newspaper that Continental, the German tire company, was starting a plant in Timişoara. I wanted to do production and operations management. When I went to see them, I told them I would like to work in production as a manager. They said I'd first have to be an engineer before becoming a manager. That was my first shock."

He was also surprised by the resistance he felt for having studied abroad.

"People were suspicious. 'Why did you come back?' It was not normal—many people wanted to leave Romania for good.

"Then, in December 1999, my mother-in-law heard on radio about the Return to Romania program."

Dan contacted Jim, and the project staff contacted three companies and sent out Dan's résumé. Three months later, he signed on with Alcatel.

"At that time, Alcatel had no human resources department, so I started building up its recruitment efforts. The company was expanding, so for the next year and a half, that's what we focused on. We hired about 150 after I came here. I like it. I would not go back to production management. I've been very involved with people, which is something I like. I give them hope they'll find a job. It's one of the reasons I came back here—to help others."

Sheilah asked whether Dan would be comfortable in the United States.

"Yes, it's like my second home. We have friends there. I lived there for nine years."

Since 9/11, getting the chance to study in the United States has become more difficult. But even before, it was complicated and unpredictable. Not only must a student be accepted by a U.S. college and have the money for tuition and other expenses, but a student from a country like Romania, which doesn't have a "visa waiver," must convince a U.S. visa officer that he or she will return home after she graduates. In our last year in Romania, one visa officer decided to reject virtually all student visas. In just a few weeks, colleges across America started calling Jim to protest.

What is going on? Jim asked Steve Pattison, the consul general, and Susan Johnson, Jim's deputy. Susan, a career foreign service officer with the mindset of an entrepreneur, dug into the issue. One consular officer, she discovered, had heard that many foreign students like America so much they want to stay after they graduate. So he decided that Romanian students who said they intended to return home weren't telling the truth.

"What 18-year-old Romanian—or American—knows what they will do when they graduate?" Susan asked. "How can we tell them not to study in the U.S. because we know their intentions better than they do?"

Steve—and Jim—agreed, and the student-visa window opened again.

Eugenia Isvan went to Washington, D.C. in 1998 to work and to earn a master's degree in business administration at Johns Hopkins University. She had graduated from a science and physics high school and the Politehnica in Bucharest, specializing in machine construction and robotics.

"After I graduated in 1995, I started to work as a sales representative for a computer company here in Bucharest. They sold software. Then I worked as a web developer, a webmaster, and a database administrator."

She came back to Romania within months of earning her MBA in December 2001.

"I saw my parents only twice in two and a half years, so I needed to return home. I liked living in the U.S., but for me it was too far from home. I need my parents, my family, and my friends, to be very honest. I missed my family and my boyfriend. This distance—it's like our enemy sometimes.

"But I like the order and the way American companies work. If you have an idea, you can implement it. You can get the advice of other people. The network works. But here, it is not like that. This is my impression. Nothing is better now than it was in Romania in 1998," she said in 2002. "Actually, I think it's worse. In three years [away], I was expecting to find another way of thinking from the people—maybe changes in the schools and political stuff, political issues. I would like leaders and people to focus their ideas more—not be so ambiguous."

Eugenia was just starting her job search back in Romania, touching base with investment companies, financial consulting companies, and banks, but she was exploring other ideas, too.

"Actually, I have a dream. I would like to open a Romanian subsidiary for the Oster Company. It's a Sunbeam subsidiary. We don't have their products here. But I contacted them and they said, 'Yeah, we can sell you our products, but you have to take care of the importing, transportation, and other problems.'"

What kind of products was she talking about?

"They are selling animal clippers, to cut the hair—dog clippers, sheep clippers. I have a very good friend who's a veterinarian. It's her idea, actually. She's working in this field and she knows there is a market."

"Sheep clippers? I never thought of that," Sheilah said. "There are a lot of sheep to be clipped in Romania."

TRANSPLANTING A DREAM

JIM'S GRANDFATHER, ATTILIO ROSAPEPE, grew up in Contursi, a small mountain town in southern Italy. He went to medical school in Naples, met and married Riva, and moved to America in 1914 with their infant son, Joe (Jim's father). For the next forty years, as he practiced medicine in Youngstown, Ohio, Attilio dreamed of returning to Contursi to open a modern hospital. He was never able to realize his dream. But in the small town of Beiuş in Transylvania, Dr. Peter Lucaciu is living out Jim's grandfather's dream.

We visited his clinic and listened to his story.

The Lucaciu family had emigrated to the United States in the dark days before Ceauşescu's fall, settling in Chicago. But as his wife Ana told us, Peter is a "dreamer," and his dream was set in Beiuş.

A month after the Revolution, with the support of an ecumenical group of American medical missionaries, he came back to Romania for a visit. They built a clinic that within a decade was serving two thousand local patients, and many more in nearby villages. The Romanian staff of twelve was augmented by dozens of American medical specialists who volunteer their time—some give weeks, some give years. When we visited the clinic, our guide was Dr. Belinda Castor from Bedford, New Hampshire. She had been working in Beiuş for two years.

Peter Lucaciu's story spoke to us not because it was unique. On the contrary, it demonstrated something we saw everywhere we traveled in Romania: Americans—some with roots there, some without—investing their time and their spirits in forging the country's future.

BUILDING A BETTER ROMANIA

DURING THE SAME VISIT to Beiuş, we joined in Habitat for Humanity's first build in Romania.

Early in Jim's tenure, an American involved with Romania's Habitat for Humanity came to make the pitch—that they were building up Romania's effort and wanted Jim's support. Adrian Ciorna, Habitat's dynamic young in-country coordinator, was a true believer in the cause. What impressed us most about Habitat for Humanity—what surprised us as compared to other non-government organizations—was how extremely well-organized they were. They had a model. They had a game plan. They knew what they wanted out of the embassy. It was limited and specific. They wanted Jim's name, but they also wanted us to attend their first housing build, a quick build, up in Beiuş in the summer of '99. So, of course, we did it.

With our niece Samantha, we stayed overnight at a little motel attached to a gas station outside of Beiuş, an hour southeast of Oradea. For these builds, Habitat for Humanity brings in teams from several countries. There were Americans and Irish in this group, along with several staff people. They use every possible promotional angle, giving everyone involved credit, particularly the companies which donate the building materials. The groups that come from other countries have a great sense of solidarity and pride in what they're doing. And the local Habitat office selects a limited number of working-class families to help build the houses.

Each house was built for a specific family, who helped in the building. There's nothing anonymous about Habitat for Humanity.

Habitat does a lot of preparation. Boards are cut, holes drilled, screws and nails counted out, in advance. Then they have a large number of people in a very short time actually finish putting up the houses. It takes just a few days to go from basic slab to walls, roof, doors, windows—a home.

They had a reception the night before in Beiuş to raise money from local sponsors. One local company was particularly prominent—European Drinks, which produced and distributed a Romanian soft drink branded "American Cola." It was Coca-Cola's chief competitor in the country. The American company felt—with good evidence—that European Drinks was competing unfairly in many ways. On this worksite, European Drinks was generating maximum PR value. Seemingly everywhere were European Drinks hats, labels, and drinks, which made things slightly awkward for the U.S. ambassador.

The next day, we went to the build. The prefect, the political chief of the county, came along with us. Lucian Silaghi was a young PNŢCD member who had come out of the Forestry School at Braşov, was not from Oradea, and was deeply involved in fighting corruption in the county. The mayor of Beiuş also joined in. We spent half a day hauling boards, drilling holes, and slapping up wallboard.

The next time we came, we painted walls.

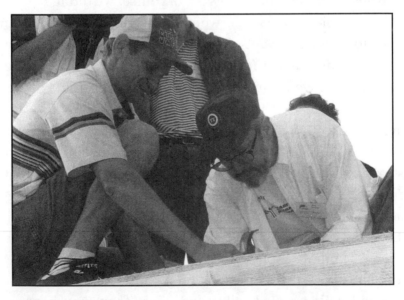

Jim and Beiuş community leaders building new houses for working families during the annual "build" organized by Habitat for Humanity

The key thing was that there was a tremendous amount of media coverage. Habitat for Humanity goes out of its way to get media. Getting the U.S. ambassador there was helpful to that, but they were getting a lot of media anyway.

Because our visit had made national television and maybe national newspapers, in the weeks that followed, many people mentioned it to us. Most of those who mentioned our visit were critical of Romanian politicians for not doing "that kind of thing." They didn't mean photo ops. They didn't see what we had done as a photo op—they saw it as Sheilah and Jim out there working for poor people. Romanians hadn't seen enough of that to be cynical or complacent about it. It made an impact. But the Romanian politicians or other ambassadors didn't seem to do it very often. To us, it was an easy way to help, so the reaction was surprising.

The public criticism that Romanian politicians weren't doing enough wasn't fair—after all, the prefect and the mayor were out there with us, hauling boards and putting up drywall. But for national television, we overshadowed them, so the confusion was understandable. We hope they got attention in the local press, which would be more important to them.

Over the subsequent years, we heard a lot about our brief visit to the Habitat build. It sent a very powerful message about people helping people and about Americans helping Romanians. It was not about the orphanages or the other things foreigners tended to be more visibly involved in, which are outside the experience of most Romanians. It was a mainstream charitable activity, helping working-class Romanians obtain decent houses—easier for people to identify with because, particularly then, many people had housing problems in Romania.

MAKING UP IS HARD TO DO, TOO: RECONCILIATION IN ARAD

TO US, IT SOMETIMES seemed that Romanians put more energy into arguing over the past than into planning for the future. That thought crossed Sheilah's mind in Arad, a city in western Romania northwest of Timişoara, when she was introduced to the Plaza of Reconciliation.

In Arad, the nineteenth-century Hungarian "statue of liberty"
shares the Plaza of Reconciliation with the 2004 monument
to Romanian freedom fighters of 1848.

Here's a version of the history at issue in Arad, as told to Sheilah:
The Austrian Empire routed the Ottoman Turks at the end of the seventeenth century, though not until after the Turks had burnt Arad to

the ground. To minimize Hungarian power in the depopulated area, the Austrian Hapsburgs settled other ethnic groups here, including Romanians, Serbs, Slovaks, and Swabians. When the spirit of revolution swept Europe in 1848, the Hungarians in Arad rose up against the Hapsburg establishment, and Romanians sided with Austria against the Hungarians. It seems to illustrate the precept that "the enemy of my enemy is my friend." When Austria put down the rebellion the following spring, the Hapsburg army hanged thirteen of the Hungarian generals in a showy execution near the citadel that still dominates Arad's skyline today. Years later, as Hungary gained more clout in the Empire, a monument to the generals was erected near the spot.

Fast-forward to the twentieth century. After World War I, Arad was part of the area transferred from the Austro-Hungarian Empire to Romania. The Romanian government moved the monument to a less conspicuous place near the military academy.

After World War II and forty-five years of Communism, Romania was holding elections in the last decade of the twentieth century, and the votes of ethnic Hungarians were a significant factor in the election that ousted Romania's first elected president, Ion Iliescu.

In 2000, Iliescu, running for his second term as president, met with ethnic Hungarian leaders in Romania. He heard their plea that the monument to the generals they call "the martyrs of Arad" be restored to the town's main square, and offered a compromise: a new plaza to be constructed expressly for this monument.

Sheilah heard all this history from her friend Ovidiu Martin, a young Romanian family man with a huge heart who works with handicapped kids and poor people in Arad. Full of the abundant spirit of Romanian hospitality, Ovidiu gave Sheilah a tour on a beautiful spring day.

Ovidiu also told Sheilah that the Romanian majority in Arad received candidate Iliescu's promise to pull the Austrian generals out of storage "like a hot coal"—that is, the decision was searingly unpopular. It would fall to Arad's mayor, Doru Popa, of the same Social Democrat Party as President Iliescu, to get the monument moved, and it would become a hot topic on the national news in both Hungary and Romania.

Here's how Ovidiu recounted the saga: In 2002, two years after Iliescu's election, the monument was moved in sections to a Hungarian church, where it was lovingly cleaned by Arad's Hungarian residents, who were expecting the sections to be reassembled soon. But the future plaza was still a flea market, and work on transforming it stalled; some signatures were missing on authorization forms. The interior minister came to inspect, and found no visible progress. Time dragged on, and the national controversy simmered. Someone suggested a national referendum on repositioning the monument. Instead, the Romanian parliament appropriated the equivalent of three hundred thousand dollars to build a *Romanian* monument to share the plaza with the Hungarian generals. It was to be dedicated to the "Heroes of the 1848 Revolution"—the Romanians, mostly on the Austrian side, who fought, died, or were exiled.

By now, three years had passed since President Iliescu made his promise, and Hungarian leaders were giving television interviews complaining that the PSD was going back on its word. Tempers were short.

Finally, the date for dedicating the monument to the Hungarian generals was set for March 15, 2004. The presidents and the prime ministers of both Hungary and Romania were invited. Busloads of dignitaries from the majority-Hungarian counties of Covasna and Harghita were expected. A Hungarian brass band was rehearsing.

But the Romanian monument was nowhere near ready. Romanian officials discovered that the ground was frozen solid—much too hard, they pointed out, to dig the foundation for the massive Magyar monument. "No problem," came the word from Budapest—"we'll send a bulldozer." On the newly dug groundwork, the pieces of the monument were fixed in place beneath a classic female figure clad in fine chain mail, and proffering a wreath. The bas-reliefs of the thirteen slain generals were mounted around the base. There were no excuses left.

On March 13, with two days to go, Romanian President Iliescu sent word that he wouldn't be able to attend the ceremony. The next day, Romanian Prime Minister Adrian Năstase also sent his regrets.

March 15 dawned cold. The highest-ranking Romanian on hand to greet the president and prime minister of Hungary was Mayor Popa. The Hungarian brass band drowned out only some of the shouts of the Romanians who gathered in protest: "Shame, shame! You made heroes of people who killed our grandfathers! You sold us out! You betrayed us!" The Hungarian band played louder. The armor-clad maiden held out her stone wreath.

By summer, Hungarian-language guidebooks included a picture of the refurbished monument for summer visitors to Arad. But the Romanian monument was still not ready. Finally, just in time for the elections in November 2004, in which Iliescu's party again lost its grip on Romania's presidency, the monument to the heroes of the 1848 Revolution was completed.

Today, it sits across the large piazza from the classic Hungarian monument, an arch of golden sandstone, through which straggle a motley group depicted in bronze. Some wear top hats. Most are gaunt, in the style of Picasso's vision of Don Quixote. Above the arch, in Romanian, is the declaration: "We are the people of Freedom. For this we revolted. For this we gave our blood. And we are resolved to give our blood to the last Romanian."

The rightmost figure of the group, Sheilah was told, is that of Avram Iancu, the Transylvanian lawyer who organized thousands of peasants to fight the Hungarians in 1848. On the left is writer Nicolae Bălcescu, a leader of the 1848 rebellion in southern Romania. And back in the second row, the middle figure is casting a sidewise glance at the Hungarian generals across the park, as if to ask, "Who invited *them*?"

BAPTISTS IN THE BALKANS, REBUILDING THE SOCIAL MINISTRY

WHEN SHEILAH FIRST MET Ovidiu Martin, she felt as if she knew him already, and she realized later that might be because he looks so much like Buddy Hackett—not that Ovidiu, an occasional practical joker, is a slapstick comedian. Ovi's face, though chubby like the rest of him, is not big enough to contain his persistent smile. It radiates from him, and attaches itself to anyone he's talking to.

Ovidiu is an unabashedly committed Baptist in a place where that has often been hard to be. He told Sheilah there have been what he calls "neo-Protestants" in Arad since the turn of the twentieth century, and now about ten percent of Arad's residents are Protestant—double or triple their national percentage throughout Romania, but still small. Ovidiu's grandfather, on his mother's side, converted from Orthodoxy.

His grandfather was considered a fanatic and a traitor, Ovidiu told Sheilah, because "at that time, to be Romanian was to be Orthodox. It was part of the tradition." That changed when the Communists took over after World War II.

"Because I declared myself a Christian, I was oppressed," Ovidiu said. He remembers that when he was fourteen, in the 1980s, the secretary for youth in the local Communist party called him and a Jewish boy to stand up in front of the group. "Look at them," Ovidiu recalls the official saying. "They believe in God. They're crazy. Don't have anything to do with them."

"Were you scared?" Sheilah asked.

"Not really," he said. "They were always trying to scare us." But his public confession of faith did cause complications. Like other boys of eighteen, he had to enter the Army. "Because I said I was a Christian, the officer told me, 'You'll have a bad time in the Army.'" Ovidiu said the best assignments, like security and military police, were closed to him, so he expected to spend his stint in the military as many others did—performing back-breaking manual labor in unsafe conditions, without enough food.

Ovi was the second-youngest of six brothers whose father had died when he was twelve. His mother worked in a chicken factory, which was a difficult job, but one that gave her a way to help Ovi with the Army. She had access to a precious commodity—eggs! She managed to bribe a colonel to assign Ovidiu to a relatively safe unit—the fire company in Braşov County, about as far from his home as the drive from New York to Washington, D.C. He served there for sixteen months, and was even promoted to corporal. Then the colonel looked more carefully at Ovidiu's file and saw the note about his faith. Ovidiu remembers that he was on the chow line when the officer called him out.

"What kind of sect are you? A fanatic one?" is how Ovi recalls the question. "Because I seemed normal, he was surprised. They didn't allow me to carry a gun for a while, because they thought I was a danger . . . It didn't make any difference what you were—Baptist or Pentecostal or Greek Catholic or Orthodox," Ovidiu said—all religion was suspect in those years. Still, he asserted, "I know members of the Communist Party who went to church on Christmas and Easter."

Ovi himself is definitely not a Christmas-and-Easter-only kind of believer. His cheerful confidence in Jesus Christ is part of every day and every conversation. After the Army, he worked as a driver for Arad's mayor, a job that put him in a position to see how the political system works and how deals are done. Most Romanians have an instinctive appreciation for the value of connections; Ovidiu's understanding seems especially acute.

So he was an ideal contact when an American nonprofit group called Romanian Christian Enterprises (RCE) started looking for a way to help children with special needs. RCE had come to Romania two years after the 1989 Revolution with the idea of helping Romanian small businesses build a post-Communism society. But the small loans didn't work out, and the needs of Romania's children, especially children in orphanages and children with handicaps, were immediate and pressing. RCE started what Ovi calls "the caring project," visiting and finding resources for kids in hospitals and orphanages. His wife Doina was working for Americans a few days a week, and Ovi, whose day job was still on the staff of the mayor, started volunteering with RCE. "My part was to resolve all the American things, for all the missionaries that come," he said, "including handling coordination with the mayor."

In 1993, one of RCE's social workers found a small boy abandoned in the children's wing of the public hospital. His name was Darius. He had a direct gaze and a winning smile, and he had cerebral palsy. He had trouble thinking and trouble walking.

"Doina got involved personally with this boy," Ovi recalled. In those days, in the state-run hospitals, "if you had special needs, you didn't receive special treatment. She tried to take care of him. She would visit him, and take him outside, [bring] special food like bananas—he likes bananas. She would cook for him. With her dedication was born an idea, or maybe a plan: Let's build a house for Darius."

As Ovi and his colleagues look back, they didn't realize how big a challenge they were setting for themselves, even though, to them, it was a new idea: that a religious group could raise money, hire people, and put them to work full-time caring for kids with physical problems. Ovi's skills in working the system were put to good use. For RCE, he looked for the right plot of land, negotiated its acquisition price, applied for the right zoning and other government approvals, and oversaw the construction.

Darius moved to the new house in 2000 with a half-dozen other children with different handicaps. Their new home was called Darius House (*Casa Darius*).

In 2004, next to the group home, RCE opened a school for handicapped children called Sunshine School (*Şcoala Rază de Soare*). By its second year, it had three dozen students in five classes.

Along with the group home and the school, RCE had a dream shared by many in Romania—that children in orphanages should have real families. In Arad, RCE received the necessary training to be licensed to arrange adoptions, and took a very focused, local approach. "We are looking for Christian families who want to dedicate their lives to, and invest their lives with, children, and are ready to adopt many children," Ovi said. Part of his job was to visit churches and talk to pastors to find such families.

Because RCE was not trying to place children with American or non-Romanian European families, it was not caught up in the controversy over international adoptions. But still, as Ovi recalls, they were in some sense competing with organizations arranging adoptions as a business.

"They're looking to make some profit," he said. As he describes it, not only does RCE not build a profit into its fees, but it won't pay the gratuities that are common to grease the wheels of Romanian business.

"We will not accept anything. And we will not give a bribe or tip to anyone. If it's not possible, we'll stop the process and give back the license. You understand, we want to be a testimony for that, and we pray for that, that we won't be touched or corrupt." As Ovidiu spoke in 2003, six families were about to adopt.

Sheilah's introduction to Ovidiu and RCE started with an American connection. A longtime friend from our hometown of College Park, Maryland e-mailed us that some of her fellow teachers were about to pay another visit to Arad. They trekked back and forth between Maryland and Romania fairly regularly.

It turned out that teachers at the James E. Duckworth School in Beltsville, Maryland, a public school for children with special needs, had heard about *Casa Darius* through a local church and formed a partnership. On their own time, teachers, therapists, and psychologists came several times a year, filling their airline luggage allotment with toys and equipment for the Romanian kids. On each trip, they would spend a week or more with the Romanian staff, devising lesson plans, suggesting techniques, evaluating the kids, and generally sharing their expertise.

Sheilah wanted to meet them, the Americans *and* the Romanians. It took a bit of planning—Arad is essentially across the country from Bucharest, and you don't just zip over for an afternoon. It was going to be a two-day trip, even by plane. But Sheilah figured she could probably sleep on someone's couch, so the plane fare would be her major expense.

Once the Romanians at Darius House learned that Mrs. Ambassador was coming, however, nothing would do but that she stay at the villa that the dictator Nicolae Ceauşescu used when *he* visited Arad. She resisted, mostly because she preferred to given RCE the $130 she would pay for the sumptuous overnight experience, but the more she resisted, the more they insisted.

It made for a schizophrenic introduction to Arad. Ovi scooped Sheilah up at the airport and took her first to Darius House, where she met the kids, some of the Romanian staff, and some of the Maryland teachers, and saw how they interacted—lots of energy, lots of laughter, a shared meal with lots of good food.

When it was time to go to the Ceauşescu villa that evening, Sheilah felt like a royal exile.

The stucco mansion had been built in 1925, a time of Romania's economic surge, by Baron Neumann, a wealthy liquor magnate who owned about forty properties in Arad. His title of "baron" stemmed from the days of the Austro-Hungarian Empire. After World War II, the Communists moved quickly to nationalize his house—Baron Neumann escaped—and turned it into a facility for party officials. After the Revolution, others could pay to stay there.

Inside, when the unsmiling caretaker let Sheilah in with an enormous key, there was more brocade than she remembers ever seeing in a private dwelling. Her suite included a dining salon with walls covered in elegant gray, black, and brown brocade. The wood cabinets for the fancy porcelain were carved with exotic creatures.

The next room was lined in gold brocade, with a floral carpet loomed especially for it. White-carved French doors led to a red salon, which was dominated by a round table of inlaid wood under a Rococo ceiling festooned with cherubs and gilt chains. Sheilah was told this had been a protocol chamber for high-level meetings, and the table made expressly for Ceauşescu's negotiations with the president of Hungary.

The décor of the bedrooms was equally ornate. The bed seemed wide but short. Sheilah thought that was appropriate for Ceauşescu, who was fairly squat, but she also thought it might have been an optical illusion—everything, including the gilded replicas of Louis XVI furniture, was dwarfed in this space. You could have had a party for seventy-five people in just this suite, and she was rattling around in it alone—but only until morning, when the sun spilled its cheerful light over Arad and Sheilah rejoined the joyful teachers and kids at RCE.

FIVE FAITHS IN FIVE HOURS

ONE OF THE JOYS of post-Communist Romania is the rebirth of religious celebration following more than four decades of repression.

In a few short hours in Oradea, a city of two hundred thousand near the Hungarian border, we saw the faces of the rebirth.

In the downtown square, the Orthodox church is a solid, but not dominating, presence. Inside, it's gloomy. Dark icons hang in gilded frames. Several icons stand near the altar. At midday, a clutch of elderly believers murmur prayers.

The next stop is the synagogue. It is much lighter, and though dusty and rundown, still elegant and historic. As elsewhere in Romania, the Jewish population in Oradea today is tiny—probably a few hundred people. The synagogue was built for a thriving community, so the facility is not filled now. But its majesty is still apparent.

The Roman Catholic cathedral in town is itself a statement. The Catholics here are Hungarian, and Hungarians used to rule Oradea. The church's baroque design and stately bell towers would be familiar to Catholics in any American or European city. With statues of saints, images of the Blessed Mother, and a vaulted ceiling, this pre-Vatican II church is lighter than the Orthodox church, but darker than the synagogue.

But there's more. Near the church is a beautiful baroque museum, with 365 windows. It used to be the palace of the Roman Catholic bishop, but was nationalized in 1945, and in the 1950s, it housed Greek Communists who had fled after losing the civil war there (when Stalin conceded Greece to the West and Churchill conceded Romania to the Soviets). The palace was returned to the Roman Catholic church in 2003, and today it's a museum of history, ethnographic art, and natural sciences, and features fossils of dinosaurs and birds from nearby bauxite mines.

When we visited, the Baptist church in Oradea seemed brand new—white walls, with no icons, paintings, or statues. Sunlight streamed through the large windows. A school was attached, and a business school had just been built in the suburbs. A group of young people was playing bells. If the pastor and congregants hadn't been speaking Romanian, we might have thought we were in suburban Dallas, Texas.

There is also a Greek Catholic cathedral dating to 1806, but the Greek Catholics we visited worshipped in a makeshift basement space. Even half underground, it admits more light than the Orthodox church. The energetic priest welcomed us in, apologized for his limited English, and said he'd be going to America in a few weeks to become more proficient in the language.

"Oh," said Jim, "where are you going?"

"Las Vegas," he replied.

ROMANIA's NEIGHBORHOOD

CHAPTER 13
LIVING IN THE BALKANS,
IN THE SHADOW OF THE KREMLIN

WOULD NATO BOMB TRANSYLVANIA?

NATO's BOMBING OF YUGOSLAVIA started on a Friday in late March 1999. Jim had scheduled a press conference on another subject for the following Monday. Knowing that reporters would ask about the war, he mulled over some of the possible questions ahead of time and read the background material.

On Monday, the auditorium of American Center, the USIA building where he held press conferences, was full of print, radio, and TV journalists. After his opening comments and a few questions he and his team had expected, a young reporter near the front raised her hand to be recognized.

"If NATO is bombing Yugoslavia to promote autonomy for Kosovo within Yugoslavia, isn't that a precedent for NATO attacking Romania to promote autonomy for Hungarians in Transylvania?" she asked.

Tough question! And not one he'd planned for.

"Well," Jim said slowly, stalling for time so his brain could consider all the possible ways he could answer this query wrong and complicate the war effort.

Finally, words came out of his mouth.

"It's a very different situation," he said. "There had been autonomy for Kosovo decades ago. Milošević took away that autonomy. That is a very different situation from Hungarians in Romania."

Mercifully, no one asked a follow-up question. But looking out at the reporters, Jim sensed they weren't satisfied with the answer.

Why hadn't he or others thought of this question before the press conference? From a Romanian perspective, it was a perfectly reasonable thing to ask.

The next time Jim was asked, he gave more or less the same response, and got just about the same lukewarm reaction, or worse.

The issue was not going to go away.

Finally, after rolling this question around in his head for a few days, practicing Thomas Edison's dictum about perspiration and inspiration, Jim came up with a new answer.

At his next press conference, he was asked, "Will NATO bomb Romania?"

"I reject your premise," he replied. "What's going on in Yugoslavia is not a precedent for what should happen in Romania. What's happening in Romania is a precedent for what should happen in Yugoslavia. Romania is a democracy, where Hungarians can participate in the political process. They have freedom of speech, they have the ability to participate in society, and they're treated with respect. So I would say that Romania's ethnic relations are the model for Yugoslavia and not the reverse. We're saying that Albanians should be able to expect the same in Yugoslavia."

Bingo!

That made more sense to Romanians—and frankly, to Jim, too.

The media coverage was overwhelmingly positive.

A few weeks later, Deputy Secretary of State Strobe Talbott came to Bucharest to thank the Romanians for their support of NATO's action. The embassy planned another press conference in the American Center. Before he went on, Jim and Talbott talked backstage. Steve Strain, embassy public affairs officer, was running down for Talbott the kinds of questions that might come up. One of them was our old favorite. Immediately, one of Talbott's staff guys broke in, giving him the answer about "history" and "autonomy" that Jim had proved to be a flop. Jim cut him off and said, "No, I've tried that—it's not persuasive here. Here's how to answer that question." He laid out the answer. Talbott understood immediately.

As Talbott's luck would have it, the question did not come up at his press conference. But Jim Swigert, a top State Department official for Southeast Europe who was traveling with Talbott, heard all this.

When he got back to Washington, speechwriters for President Clinton were trying to explain what the U.S. was doing in Kosovo.

In April 1999, Clinton spoke in San Francisco and repeated Jim's answer about Romania and Yugoslavia. "Who is going to define the future of this part of the world?" the president asked. "Who will provide the model for how the people who have emerged from Communism resolve their own legitimate problems? Will it be Mr. Milošević, with his propaganda machine and paramilitary thugs, who tell people to leave their country, their history, and their land behind, or die? Or will it be a nation like Romania, which is building democracy and respecting the rights of its ethnic minorities?"

The next day, the headlines in Romania were more than favorable.

Romanians live in a tough neighborhood—the Balkans—and they know it. Culturally, Romania may be a Latin island in a sea of Slavs (with Hungarians as a neighboring island), but in terms of national security, no country is an island. Fearing invasion is not a paranoid thought. Romanians themselves sum it up this way: Over the centuries, we have had only two good neighbors—Serbia and the Black Sea. That puts Hungary, Russia, Ukraine, Bulgaria, Turkey, and, with a small geographic stretch, Austria and Germany in the other category.

This also meant that the war in Kosovo, which to Americans seemed like a simple morality play, was to Romanians part of the eternal jostling for land and power among the region's ethnic groups, complicated by the intervention of big powers from outside the region.

KOSOVO: THE WAR NEXT-DOOR

EARLY IN THE KOSOVO War, General Wesley Clark, who was running the military campaign as NATO's supreme allied commander, decided he wanted to be able to overwhelm Yugoslavian anti-aircraft units by flying sorties from the east as well as from the west. Up to that point, NATO bombers had flown in only over the Adriatic, after departing the Aviano airbase in Italy.

To enter Yugoslav airspace from the east, however, required the permission of its eastern neighbors—Hungary, Romania, and Bulgaria. So the United States and NATO allies asked their governments for permission, and these countries' leaders had to ask their parliaments for approval.

President Constantinescu and his center-right colleagues in the Romanian government supported our request. The opposition, led by former president Iliescu, did not.

The Constantinescu group had the votes in parliament, but feared (correctly, as it turned out) the electoral impact of the opposition from Iliescu's center-left party, so the president's staff called Jim and asked him to lobby Iliescu to support, or at least not strongly oppose, the NATO request when it came before parliament. Jim quickly agreed.

Iliescu and Ioan Paşcu, his chief defense adviser and close party ally, met Jim in the headquarters of Iliescu's party, the PSD. It is a beautiful nineteenth-century mansion right on Kiseleff Boulevard, across from the U.S. ambassador's residence. Like many Bucharest mansions, it faces sideways, so when you walk up the driveway, the entrance is to your left. Jim walked up a couple of steps and was met by one of Iliescu's aides, who escorted him up the half-flight of stairs.

They entered the large lobby, which always seemed to have too little furniture. That day, as on others, several men were sitting on a small couch, doing nothing in particular. They could have been staff, or they could have been party functionaries waiting for a meeting. It was never clear, at least to Jim.

The ceilings are high and all the rooms huge. To the right are three rooms—one where the party leadership would meet, with a conference table that seats at least twenty-five; one for Iliescu's assistants; and one for the party leader himself.

Iliescu's office always seemed dark. There was a big window behind his desk, but it was dwarfed by the room's huge dimensions and the lack of big, bright lights.

On the left was a modern black couch with a coffee table and two relatively comfortable chairs. That's where Jim had his first meeting with Iliescu in early 1998. Jim's first impression was of a tightly wound, rigid ex-Communist. It was the same impression other Americans had on first meeting Iliescu. But it was not the right impression.

When Jim entered his office this day, Iliescu greeted him warmly, as he always did, with one of the biggest smiles on the Eurasian continent.

That ever-present smile, his trademark, is regularly caricatured by Romanian cartoonists. His face, framed by thinning, straight gray hair, seemed broader than it is because of the perpetual smile stretching across it. He's relatively short and compact, and seemed younger than his sixty-nine years.

We always thought he had an advantage over some other Romanian politicians we met, because he seemed to be having a good time and they didn't. He's a natural politician. We don't tend to think of natural politicians springing out of the Communist system, but some did.

But just because he's a natural pol doesn't mean he's not a polarizing figure. He is. Public opinion polls showed Romanians either very pro- or very anti-Iliescu—high negatives, high positives. After all, he was leading the brand new democracy in 1990 when demonstrators in Bucharest's University Square were beaten by coal miners whom Iliescu and his allies had encouraged to come.

To buttress their argument that Soviet thinking has shaped his mind, his critics from the right like to emphasize that Iliescu graduated from Moscow State University. His degree was in fluid mechanics, but that didn't deter him from getting active in politics when he returned to Romania. He headed the youth wing of the Communist Party, and he was part of Ceauşescu's entourage on the famous trip to North Korea in 1971, the journey that opened Ceauşescu's eyes to the benefits of a personality cult.

As Iliescu tells it, he was the one who dared tell Ceauşescu that Romania should not follow that path. Not long after, he was stripped of his party position and banished, assigned to run a technical publishing house in Bucharest. This was definitely not the political fast track, but it did give him a chance to indulge his interest in technical and environmental studies; he is proud of having published the environmental work of Lester Brown in Romanian in the 1970s.

Despite his falling-out with Ceauşescu, Iliescu didn't drop out of politics entirely. One Western observer who spent time in Romania in the mid-1980s told us Iliescu was seen as the logical next leader in Romania, long before anyone envisioned how or when a change in power might come about. When it did come, in the chaos that surrounded the 1989 Revolution, Iliescu indeed emerged quickly as Romania's leader.

He was seen then as a stabilizing figure. The word is that at the end of 1989, when Communist governments were collapsing all over Eastern Europe, Romania's military leaders said Iliescu had to be involved or they wouldn't go along with a change in power.

Romanian President Ion Iliescu, flanked by Jim and Sheilah

Within the first months of the new democracy in 1990, Romania's intellectual elite grew disillusioned with Iliescu and criticized many of his moves, especially his apparent alliance with the miners who came to Bucharest to break up protests against the new government. Andrei Pleşu, who held posts in governments under both Iliescu and Constantinescu, remarked years later that if the intellectuals had embraced Iliescu instead of breaking with him so quickly, Iliescu's first term as president might have been more in tune with their goals than it turned out to be.

Many in politics find Iliescu approachable and likeable. He is a sincere ideological social democrat who, at the same time, is a practical politician.

In fact, other politicians—even Constantinescu, who defeated him and then was defeated *by* him in campaigns for the presidency—seemed to like him personally. They see him as someone you can talk to, and work with—a serious politician who wants to find a way to work things out.

Mircea Toma, the editor of *Academia Caţavencu* and the Jon Stewart of Romanian journalism, sums Iliescu up this way:

"He grew. He grew. He changed. He received a lesson of democracy in those years. The best thing he did during his first six years of staying in power was to lose power via a democratic mechanism.

"He contributed. And we contributed because he remained alive, which made him the first Romanian president to remain alive after losing the job. We only had two."

On this particular day, after greeting Iliescu, Jim said hello to Paşcu and gratefully accepted his offer of a glass of mineral water. Then they settled at the conference table, Iliescu at the end, Paşcu on his left, Jim to his right.

Jim knew that Iliescu had been publicly critical of NATO's action, but didn't really know how he'd react to a U.S. request to support overfly rights. Jim opened with a straightforward pitch on the merits.

"It will shorten the war," he said. "And that's good for everybody, including the Serbs and the Romanians."

Iliescu answered with his view of U.S. interests.

"Friends need to be frank with each other," he began. "And as a friend of the U.S., I must say you are making a mistake in Yugoslavia.

These kinds of political disputes, between the Serbs and Albanians, can't be settled by force. That simply doesn't work in this zone. We know the Serbs. They are very tough. They will not back down."

Jim found it hard to argue that he knew the Serbs better than Iliescu did, but he couldn't concede the point.

"We're not going to back down, either," Jim said.

They continued like this for another ten or fifteen minutes, until Iliescu finally convinced Jim he wasn't going to change his mind. Time to go to Plan B.

One thing Jim understood from his eleven years in the Maryland legislature was that you didn't need your colleagues to *agree* with you—you just needed them to *vote* with you.

"OK," Jim said, "we'll agree to disagree about whether or not NATO's action is a good idea.

"Whether or not the U.S. is right, Americans are going to remember who was with us—and who wasn't—when we needed help in ending the war. People in the administration and in the congress will remember whether or not Romania supported us on this. And, particularly if the PSD comes back to power next year, as you hope, we'll remember whether or not the PSD helped us."

Jim hoped it didn't sound too much like a threat. He knew that, over the years, Iliescu had stared down many guys tougher than he. But he believed what he said. American policymakers, and Western European ones, too, would remember what Iliescu and his party did on this vote.

Iliescu didn't respond immediately. Breaking the awkward silence, Paşcu jumped in.

"What if we abstained?" he asked.

On numerous levels, Jim was relieved to hear the comment—he didn't have to break the silence and risk negotiating with himself, they hadn't stood up and invited him to leave, and Paşcu had opened the door to a compromise.

"That's a lot better than voting against it," Jim said, trying to move the ball forward without losing control of it.

He turned to Iliescu, who looked less than thrilled. If Paşcu and Iliescu had planned a good cop-bad cop routine, they were performing it exquisitely.

"Abstaining would be very difficult," Iliescu said with a frown. "Our parliamentarians are very much against the war."

Jim was sure his second statement was true. Most Romanians *were* against the war.

Iliescu's party activists were mostly former Communists who had strong historical ties to their Yugoslavian counterparts, even if they didn't necessarily embrace Milošević or his ethnic cleansing. Before 1989, many of them had regarded the Yugoslavian party as more democratic and Western-oriented than their own. And in the 1990s, when the United Nations had imposed an oil embargo on Yugoslavia, some of them allegedly became smugglers to help break it.

No doubt most PSD members of parliament wanted to vote against the war. On the other hand, they all were selected from the party list, not from individual districts. Iliescu had a lot of influence on how they would vote on this issue.

"I'm not sure I can convince them to abstain," he emphasized. Paşcu agreed.

Jim told them he understood.

"How about we leave it this way?" Jim said. "Obviously, we'd much rather you and your colleagues vote for overfly rights. But if you can't, abstaining would be much better than voting no. Let me ask for one more thing. If you decide to abstain, it would be a great help if you did it quietly, without attacking those who vote for overflight permission."

"We'll talk to our caucus," Iliescu said. "We'll see what happens."

On the day of the vote, Jim had to fly to the United States with President Constantinescu for the NATO summit in Washington. He supposed they wouldn't hear the result until they landed.

Then, several hours into the flight, a Romanian official came into Jim's cabin and said he'd just heard the vote results from Bucharest.

NATO had won with 208 votes. Only 29 members of parliament

had voted no, with 97 abstaining.

To Americans, the Kosovo war was far away and largely incomprehensible. The war's politics in the United States were so confused that, on one day, the U.S. House voted both for and against it.

But in Romania, it was the war next door. Fortunately, no NATO bombs were dropped by mistake in Romania, as they were in Bulgaria and on the Chinese embassy in Belgrade. Still, it was like living in Des Moines if a big foreign power was bombing Chicago—much too close for Romanian comfort.

"LIVE FROM BUCHAREST!"

RELATIVELY EARLY IN THE war, Cris Constantinescu, our extraordinary radio and TV expert in USIA, told Jim that Pro TV, the country's biggest private network, was planning a late-night talk show on the war in Kosovo. A studio audience would listen to four talking-head experts. The network was asking the Yugoslav ambassador and Jim to participate in the first five or ten minutes to make some statements and then leave. Cris wanted to know if Jim would participate.

The four talking heads were to be Mihai Răzvan Ungureanu, the deputy foreign minister, a young historian from Iaşi and a protégé of Pleşu; Cornel Codiţă, who had been national security aide to Iliescu during his first presidential term and was then a professor at the successor institution of the old Communist Party higher school; Octavian Paler, a well-known writer for one of the newspapers; and historian Dan Berindei.

Jim said yes.

He asked Cris when the show was supposed to start. Cris checked and told Jim it was around 11 or 11:30 p.m. The start time was a little like the end of *Nightline*, when Ted Koppel used to say, "We may go over a little bit tonight." As this was Romania, that sort of flexibility was multiplied, if not squared.

As Jim prepared for the show, he learned that his deputy, Mike Einik, who had been the top U.S. diplomat in Croatia when Yugoslavia broke up in the early 1990s, knew Yugoslavia's ambassador to Romania. His background was interesting. Evidently, he was not a hardcore Milošević guy—he had been sent to Romania so he wouldn't be in Yugoslavia. Though he was working for the Milošević government, he was not an insider. Jim wasn't sure whether that was good or bad, but at least he had some sense of who he'd be debating.

Then we learned that the Yugoslav ambassador would be speaking in Romanian, rather than using a translator, as Jim would. Jim's Romanian was not nearly good enough to debate war and peace on live television.

Ugh! Jim was getting more and more nervous.

Cris, Sheilah, and Jim showed up at the studio a little before 11 p.m. Surprise number one was that a news camera greeted us as we got out of the car and walked in the door. They filmed us walking up the stairs and into the studio, then took us into the waiting room, continued filming us, and interviewed Jim. Then the Yugoslav ambassador came in. He was a big man with thick hair and a bushy walrus mustache.

It felt, and must have looked on TV, like the pre-fight coverage of a boxing match.

Before Jim arrived at the studio, he had been apprehensive. Now he was scared to death.

While we were in the waiting room, Cris said to Jim, "I need to speak to you privately." They moved out into the hallway.

"The producer tells me the Yugoslav ambassador has agreed to stay beyond the five or ten minutes—maybe a half hour," he said. "He wants to know if you'll do the same."

If Jim participated for ten minutes and then got up and walked out on live TV, he'd look as if he was running away, and he'd leave the Yugoslav ambassador there to level unanswered charges—not a real option. Cris and Jim agreed that he had to stay the full half hour, and Cris told the producer.

A few minutes later, all of us were escorted down to the studio. The Yugoslav ambassador and Jim were put on raised platforms on opposite sides of the stage behind Corinthian columns. In the center of the stage were the four talking heads, surrounded by the studio audience. The host, Mihai Tatulici, sat on a raised chair with a microphone in his hand, kind of like on the old *Phil Donahue Show*.

Sometime after 11 p.m., the show started. The host introduced the subject and allowed Jim and the Yugoslav ambassador to state their countries' respective cases on the war. As the Yugoslav ambassador spoke, Jim had simultaneous translation in his ear, but Sheilah was sitting nearby with no translation.

Suddenly, the host interrupted the Yugoslav ambassador.

"Excuse me, Mr. Ambassador," he said. "Viewers are having trouble understanding your Romanian. Would you be willing to switch into Serbian and we'll translate from there?"

Yes! Jim thought. *Am I lucky or what?*

It was great that the Yugoslav ambassador wasn't going to be speaking Romanian. It was great that his Romanian was weak enough that he had to switch. And it must have thrown him off his game. Jim didn't exactly relax, but his confidence got a big boost. He might survive this show after all.

They took some more questions. Then, at a commercial break, Cris came over to Jim.

"The Yugoslav ambassador has agreed to stay longer," he told him. "They want to know if you're also willing to stay."

What a surprise! Jim couldn't walk out now. The only question was when the show was going to end. Apparently, the show's producers were as flexible about when they finished the show as when they'd start it. After a while, they didn't even ask—they just assumed both ambassadors were going to stay.

At some point, the host solicited opinions from the talking heads. Then the talking heads started asking the Yugoslav ambassador and Jim questions. Then the studio audience started asking questions of the talking heads and the ambassadors.

Years afterward, a Romanian told Caroline Carver, who was living in Aiud, about one exchange he remembered from the show. A member of the studio audience asked Jim how someone could, at the same time, be both pro-Serb *and* support NATO's action. It was a very relevant question for Romanians.

Jim answered by talking about his father, Joe, who was born in Italy and was a naturalized American. In World War II, he helped the United States overthrow Italian dictator Mussolini. Joe loved Italy enough that he thought it ought to have American-style democracy. Deposing an Italian dictatorship didn't bother him. Romanians could be friends of Serbs *and* be anti-Milošević. Serbs had a right to democracy, Jim said, just as the Americans and Romanians did.

Near the end of the show, a young woman in the studio audience said she was a Romanian Serb living in Romania. She asked Jim how he felt watching the United States bomb Serbs, who sang folk songs as they held positions on Yugolsav bridges. A great question. All Jim remembers saying is that he, too, likes Serbian folk music. Not his best work.

At 1:45 a.m., two and half hours after we had started, the host thanked us all and the show ended. Sheilah and Jim went home, and to sleep.

For the next several days, the show was the talk of the chattering classes. Clearly a lot of people, including all the key policymakers, had watched it.

Pleşu, Roman, and other government leaders were obviously glad Jim was visibly defending American policy, taking some of the heat off them to explain the war to the Romanian public. This was important to the United States, because we needed to keep the Romanian government on board with our policy.

About a week later, the ambassadors to Romania from NATO countries convened one of their monthly meetings in Bucharest. Several of them said they'd seen Jim and complimented him on his performance.

He thanked them, but added, "I've been out in the media almost every day defending what NATO is doing in Kosovo. But I don't think I need to be alone in this. I'm not trying to hog the spotlight here. Feel free to get out there yourselves."

Remember, this was NATO's war, and these were NATO-country ambassadors in Romania.

Their reactions were diverse—and interesting.

The French, British, and Canadian ambassadors, and several others, volunteered to get out front with the media, and they subsequently did so. The Hungarian ambassador said he'd be happy to go public, but he didn't think that would be helpful—a correct analysis. The Greek ambassador's support, they all agreed, would be helpful, but he couldn't inject himself into the debate because the war was much more unpopular in Greece than it was in Romania.

In contrast, two reluctant NATO ambassadors argued that they should not be out publicly explaining and defending what NATO was doing in Kosovo. One explained that he didn't have instructions from his capital to do it, and therefore wasn't going to. OK.

The other said he wasn't qualified to do it because he didn't have the specific facts to answer questions he would get from the media about this bombing of that bridge, or the bombing of the train yesterday. These things were timely and related to the specifics of the war. He said Jamie Shea, the spokesman at NATO headquarters in Brussels, was the only one with the right information who could speak authoritatively for NATO. Ambassadors in Bucharest shouldn't get into something they didn't know about.

Jim agreed with his point on the specific day-to-day coverage of military activity, but it was not true on the larger questions—why NATO was at war in Kosovo, why it was the right thing to do, and why it was good for the Romanians to be working with us on this. On these questions of values and interests, the ambassadors of the NATO countries in Romania were the *world's experts* on how Romanians were thinking about the war in Kosovo. The poor guy in Brussels had no idea how to address a Romanian audience and didn't have the responsibility or capability to do so. His message had to work worldwide. But focusing on specific Romanian issues was exactly what NATO ambassadors in Bucharest were paid for. They were there to speak up and explain their countries' positions.

Jim didn't persuade the reluctant ambassadors, but it still seems odd to us that they disagreed.

About a month after the war ended, U.S. Secretary of State Madeleine Albright came to Bucharest to thank Romanian leaders for their support. She was heading directly back to Washington, and Jim needed to be there, too, for the opening of the Romanian exhibition at the Smithsonian Folk Life Festival, so he flew back on her plane.

Sitting next to one of her press staffers for part of the trip, Jim told him the story of the two-and-a-half-hour TV debate with the Yugoslav ambassador. At the end of it, the press secretary laughed.

"If you'd asked us for permission to do the show," he said, "we almost certainly would have told you not to do it."

"Why?" Jim asked.

"We're risk-averse," he said. "The focus in Washington is always on avoiding mistakes, not gaining yardage. Good thing you didn't ask!"

JOE BIDEN IN BYZANTIUM

A FEW MONTHS LATER, then-U.S. Senator Joe Biden, the ranking Democrat on the Senate Foreign Relations Committee, visited Romania to thank officials for their help in the war. He also planned to pick their brains on the prospects for unifying the Yugoslav opposition and replacing Milošević, which became the top U.S. priority after the war ended in early June.

Our thirty-minute meeting with Petre Roman, president of the Romanian Senate, was like most of the rest. But as Biden and Jim came out of the meeting, Biden said, "That guy looks the way I felt when I chaired my last Judiciary Committee meeting."

He was referring to 1994, when the Republicans won control of the U.S. Senate, relieving Biden of his chairmanship. "He's got some big problem on his mind. Do you know what it is?" Biden asked Jim.

Jim was amazed. Without inside knowledge about Romanian politics, Biden had read Roman's body language and knew he was talking to a politician under great stress.

In fact, Roman *was* under great pressure: Public support was dropping fast for the coalition government of which his party was a part. He was concerned about how he was going to survive the next election. Several months later, he himself brought down the Vasile government, replaced Prime Minister Vasile with Central Bank Governor Isărescu, and took over the foreign minister job himself.

His party survived the next election, though it went into opposition, but Roman himself was deposed as party leader less than two years after the meeting with Biden.

All Jim really wanted to know was: How could Biden tell?

VIOLATING YUGOSLAV AIRSPACE . . . WITH TRUTH

ROMANIANS WERE INTENTLY INTERESTED in assisting the democratic opposition to Milošević. In late 1999 and early 2000, we put together a variety of efforts to help Romanians support their democratic allies in Yugoslavia. The embassy played a part in organizing a visit by the Serbian youth group Otpor to observe how local activists monitored elections during the June 2000 local elections in Romania. Everyone expected Serbia to hold elections later in the year, and we wanted to help the young opponents of Milošević ensure that voting would be fair.

After they had been out around the country at polling places, several dozen Serbian young people met with Jim in Bucharest. He asked them what else the United States could do to help them.

"Get the independent radio and TV back on the air," was the reply. During the war, the U.S. government had aggressively helped keep independent anti-Milošević radio and TV on the air. The government had used transmitters in neighboring countries, including Romania, while broadcasting from planes overhead, but the United States quickly reduced its commitment after the bombs stopped falling.

When Jim cabled Washington for an explanation, he was told that there was wide support in the State Department, USIA, and USAID for keeping independent media on the air, but the State Department's legal office was blocking it. The lawyers contended that if we helped the Romanians continue to rebroadcast independent Serbian media into Yugoslavia, the Romanians could be in violation of international broadcasting treaties.

Jim could never get a satisfactory explanation about why that was true after the war when it hadn't been their position during the war. When he told the Romanian government what was behind the U.S. government's delay, they threw up their hands.

At one point, Jim brought a State Department official to Bucharest to meet with the Romanian officials. He explained to them the lawyers' concern.

"So what's the worst that can happen?" asked one Romanian official. "Milošević is going to sue us?"

To Romanians, who had suffered through a dictatorship much worse than Milošević's, the legalisms of the State Department seemed absurd. They did as well to Jim and to Tom Mesa, USIA's local media honcho who took on this cause with zeal. After all, NATO had been bombing Serbia with explosives less than a year earlier.

Over the next several months, Jim and Tom continued to press the point with Washington. Not much happened. Milošević announced elections for October 2000. Jim argued that we needed to have the radio stations up so voters would have independent information.

The first round of elections took place, and the transmitters were still not on the air. Finally, just days before the runoff election, in which Milošević faced democrat Vojislav Kostunica, the transmissions resumed. As a result, during the crucial two weeks after the runoff, in which Milošević tried to steal the election by appealing to his hand-picked supreme court, Serbian independent media was rebroadcast from transmitters in Romania supported by the U.S. government.

WHY ROMANIA SUPPORTED NATO IN KOSOVO

SEVERAL YEARS LATER, PRESIDENT Constantinescu told us he knew before the first bombs fell on Belgrade that the war would not be popular anywhere—not in Southeast Europe, not in Western Europe, not in the rest of the world, maybe not even in the United States.

"We live in the era of CNN and live TV," he said. "It's one thing to read the communiqué in the paper. It's a completely different thing to see, with your own eyes, the very moment when houses fall down and people die. I realized that the White House needed to give a statement that the biggest country bordering Yugoslavia, and the only uninterested party in this war, supports the decision of the United States. So I addressed a message to the nation where I used a phrase Romanians will not forget until the day I die, and maybe not afterwards: I said that the NATO intervention is 'legitimate and necessary.' These were very tough words for the Romanian people to hear, because the Serbs are the only people in the region we'd had no conflict with from the sixth century until today.

"One hour and forty-five minutes after my message, you could see, on the TV screens, the tracer bullets and the infrared images. And the Romanians got the feeling that it was as if I had pressed the button. The emotional reaction of the Romanians was very tough. I had known that would happen. I also know the Americans, and learned they had very rarely needed allies. But when they do, if the answer comes efficiently, they will never forget it."

So, from one perspective, Romania had a chance to do a favor for a superpower. Romanians have an exquisite sense of how a favor done today can yield a big return tomorrow. But beyond that, Constantinescu spoke of his Kosovo policy as a chance to address something even deeper in the Romanian psyche.

"By taking this position from the very beginning, and being consistent with this policy until its end, making no populist concessions, and offering our complete support for the NATO action—even more than was asked of us—I wanted to fight against a historic Romanian curse. We have quite a strange position. For two thousand years, we have been at the clashing point of all great empires—the Greek, Turkish, Roman, Ottoman, Russian, Austrian, and German empires. If we drew a map, the meeting point of all these empires would be here, between the mountains and the sea, due to the curve of the mountains and the Black Sea."

When great empires clash, small powers suffer unless they figure out how to get out of the way. A proverb we heard often in Romania is, "The bent neck avoids the sword." It seemed to describe a national attitude of, go with the flow, don't make a fuss, keep your thoughts to yourself unless you know they'll be welcome. As President Constantinescu summed it up, "The Romanians, through history, have learned to survive. In a miraculous way, we are a people of survivors."

The "miraculous" method that Sister Mary Rose Christy observed during more than a decade of working with poor families in Sibiu was passive resistance. With her training as a social worker, she concluded, "They resist by doing nothing."

She spoke of it with a mixture of frustration and admiration. "It takes strength," she said. "These people would never have survived Communism under Ceaușescu if they had done all the stupid things he insisted on. [Instead], they didn't pay any attention to the rules.

"The more people don't do, the less people in power can do about it. These people make it almost impossible for people in power to get anything done. It's learned behavior—it's more than an instinct. And it's a strength."

Still, what Sister Mary Rose learned from marginalized families in Sibiu was what Emil Constantinescu wanted the nation to learn as well: that merely surviving doesn't move you forward. Constantinescu saw NATO's challenge as an opening to move Romania beyond generations of compromise—what he called "a collective memory of survival." It was the survival of people with a different language, culture, and tradition than those around them. This type of attitude spilled over into politics, and the attitudes of Romania, both during World War I and World War II, have been consistent with this tradition.

"In 1999," Constantinescu continued, "I saw the opportunity to fight this curse, and to create a basis for a new type of behavior—that of decisions being taken in the first moment and consistently and inflexibly maintained to the end. Of course, there are enormous risks to doing that. And when, after the war ended, I took the decision to cancel rights to Russian planes flying over Romanian territory, it was extremely risky. But it was the first time in the Russian-Romanian relationship that the Russians observed Romania's sovereignty. At that point, I realized how important it was to earn their respect. I learned that whenever you affirm your position, everybody will respect you."

MILOŠEVIĆ ON TRIAL

WHILE HE WAS ON the subject of the value of staking out a position and holding it clearly, President Constantinescu noted that western nations did not always meet that standard.

"The establishment of the international penal court during the Kosovo War, and the announcement that Milošević was being charged, were good signals," Constantinescu said, "first for the democratic movement in Southeastern Europe, and mainly for those in Serbia, because it showed these peoples, and the Serbs in particular, that the United States and the Western allies had decided not to strike any more deals with people committing crimes in order to have an alleged peace.

"That was in stark contrast with the Dayton agreement [in 1995]. The Dayton agreement sent a very confusing signal to the region. On the one hand, Milošević had been demonized, and on the other hand, he was considered the only valid interlocutor. These mixed signals extended the life of Yugoslav Communism quite a lot, just as the myth of Ceauşescu's independence from the Soviet Union extended the agony of Communism in Romania."

ROMANIANS OUTSIDE THE COUNTRY AND INSIDE THE CULTURE

ONE OF THE GREAT conundrums of geopolitics is that so many people live outside the borders of the countries of their ethnic heritage. In addition, particularly since the nineteenth century, the worldwide trend has been toward nation-states that seek to combine political borders with the population concentration of a majority ethnic group.

In America, we think mostly in terms of immigration. We have Chinese, Italian, and African minorities because they or their ancestors moved here. And our national identity is based on our civic values—freedom, equality, and opportunity—not common ethnicity or religion. In spirit as well as in law, anyone can become an American, as long as he or she signs on to our civic values.

That's not true most places in the world. Many other nations have free speech, democratic elections, openness to immigration, freedom of religion, and respect for minorities. But it's not nearly as easy to "become" a German or a Romanian as it is to "become" an American.

That's because most nation-states were not conceived, as the United States was—as a political, rather than ethnic, innovation. At the time of the American Revolution, the nation was already quite multiethnic, with substantial German, English, and Scottish populations. At the conclusion of the Revolution, the major political change, besides our independence from Great Britain, was the division of English-speaking North Americans between the United States and what became Canada. Politics trumped ethnicity in America from day one.

Most nation states have different histories. Iran is for Persians. Germany and Italy were unified in the nineteenth century to create states for their majorities. Norway has a state religion, Lutheranism. Japan is a language and a culture, not just a state. In the United States, we don't have a state religion or a unique language (just ask the British!). We speak something we call "English," and it isn't even the official national language.

Other countries combine their identity with the ethnicity of their majority population, while accommodating the minorities who live within their borders. And most of the time, it works—actually, it works more frequently than we think. Understandably, CNN covers ethnic conflict more often than ethnic harmony. Until we went to Romania, we knew nothing of its Serbian, Polish, and Tartar minorities, just as we knew nothing about the tribulations and triumphs of the Swedish minority in Finland. We didn't know about the Romanians in Ukraine, either. A lot of people in this world belong to ethnic minorities who have lived in the same communities for generations, even as political boundaries have moved and the people's status has shifted from being part of the majority to being part of a minority—or vice versa.

That's the story of today's Hungarians in Romania and of today's Romanians in northern Bucovina in Ukraine. No matter where they live, Hungarians know they're Hungarian primarily by their unusual language and their unique history. Romanians can live anywhere, too, but their language and culture define them. And even more than the Hungarians, they are defined by religion—the Romanian Orthodox Church is the one institution that has held them together through the centuries, both when they were top dogs and when they were underdogs.

Before 1918, Transylvania was part of Hungary and Bucovina was part of Austria. The Hungarians were a minority in Transylvania itself, but were part of the majority of the larger—Greater—Hungary. The Romanians, while a majority in Transylvania, were a minority in Greater Hungary. In Austrian-controlled Bucovina, Ukrainians and Romanians together made a majority, but were minorities in Greater Austria.

But then the Austro-Hungarian Empire lost World War I and the border cards got shuffled. Romania, which had its troops on the ground in both Transylvania and Bucovina, enjoyed relatively good relations with the winners—the British, the Americans, the French, and the Italians. Out of the Paris peace talks came the idea of Greater Romania, folding in Transylvania and Bucovina, as well as other border areas. In essentially one stroke—the Treaty of Trianon in 1920—Romania's land area expanded substantially, as did its population, by acquiring Ukrainian, Serbian, and, most important, Hungarian minorities.

But that was not the end of the story. Through the 1920s and 1930s, Romania worked hard to integrate the new territories into their new state, while the Hungarians in particular kept alive their hope of reversing the decision of 1920.

Early in World War II, the Nazis' Hungarian allies invaded Transylvania, occupying the northern half. Hungarians and Romanians expected that, if the Axis powers won the war, Transylvania would revert to Hungary. But they didn't, and Transylvania remains part of Romania, with a Hungarian population of nearly 1.5 million people.

In Bucovina, the story is more complicated. After the Ribbentrop-Molotov Pact, which allied Hitler and Stalin, Russian troops occupied the northern counties surrounding Cernăuţi. Bucovina was a major battleground of the war, with Romanian troops recapturing Cernăuţi, and then losing it again. At the end of the war, the Soviets forced Romania to give up the northern counties surrounding the city. The result was a somewhat smaller Greater Romania, and a Romanian minority population of several hundred thousand in what was then the Soviet Union, and now is Ukraine.

LEAVING MOLDAVIA, ENTERING MOLDOVA

AMERICANS OFTEN COMPARE ROMANIA to Poland, and sometimes positively. Like Poland, Romania has a strong military tradition. And like the Poles, Romanians are overwhelmingly pro-American.

But in one important way, the two Eastern European nations are quite different. The largest number of Poles living outside Poland— probably nine million today—is in the United States. That bond has been of immense value to Poland, as well as the U.S., both before and after the fall of Communism. For Poles, it has meant continuing access to American ideas, money, and political support.

Where is the largest number of Romanians living outside the country? In Moldova, a small, poor, landlocked nation squeezed between Romania and Ukraine. Its approximately 4.5 million people are mostly Romanian, but there is a substantial Russian minority, and a region, Transnistria, which remains under the control of the Russian army and organized crime. Moldova has its strengths, including a highly educated population and its soil, which has produced wines and brandies that are among the most popular in the former Soviet Union. But the Romanians in Moldova are not like the Poles in the United States. They are the poor cousins, not the rich ones.

Why Moldova is Moldova is an interesting lesson in the changing borders of Central and Eastern Europe. For hundreds of years, what is now Moldova (sometimes called Basarabia, after a Wallachian prince named Basarab) was part of what was then called Moldavia. Moldavia, along with Wallachia, which is now southern Romania (and includes Bucharest), was one of two Romanian principalities under the political domination of the Ottoman Turks. The Romanian language and Orthodox religion—in other words, the defining characteristics of Romanians—were freely practiced, and the big landowners could run local affairs largely as they pleased. But the economy was tightly regulated to profit the Turks, not the Romanians. The peasants were forced to pay heavy taxes to the Sublime Porte in Istanbul. High tariffs and other restrictions guaranteed that the benefits of trade flowed to Turkey as well.

As Russia expanded westward in the seventeenth and eighteenth centuries, it repeatedly clashed with the Turks. Moldavia was right in Russia's path. By 1792, the Russians had won control of what is now Transnistria in Moldova. Twenty years later, at the end of another war with the Turks, Russia took the rest of present-day Moldova. The rest of Moldavia—the part that is now the Moldavian region of Romania—remained a principality under Turkish domination until later in the nineteenth century, when it merged with Wallachia to form the independent nation-state of Romania.

Fast-forward to the end of World War I. Romania was in a strong position; Russia, still gripped by civil war following the Leninist take-over, was weak.

In a moment similar to the collapse of the Soviet Union in the early 1990s, Basarabia declared its independence from Russia early in 1918. But less than two months later, in a move not to be repeated in our time, the new government invited in Romanian troops. By the spring of the following year, Basarabia was officially incorporated into the Romanian state.

For two decades, while Russia controlled Transnistria, and hundreds of thousands of Romanians remained in Russian territory, most Moldavians were reunited in Romania. Then came World War II. The

Soviets saw the opportunity to take back Basarabia, and they used it.

For the next forty-five years, today's Moldova was part of the Soviet Union. Attempting to solidify their control, the Russians deported and killed Romanian-oriented leaders and intellectuals. Russians were moved in, particularly into Transnistria, to shift the population balance. The Cyrillic alphabet was substituted for Latin to promote a "Moldovan" language. Carrying out the repression was not easy. When Leonid Brezhnev, later head of the Soviet Communist party, was the local party boss in Soviet Moldova in the early 1950s, he faced resistance from ethnic Romanians.

That brings us to 1991, when history repeated itself—sort of. The Soviet Union was falling apart. Moldova declared independence. But Romanian troops did not march across the Prut River. Part of the reason was that the world has changed a lot in seventy years. The forty-year peace NATO and the EU brought to Europe gave the borders of nation states more legitimacy than they ever had before. In the industrial and knowledge-based economies of our time, seizing territory, particularly where the local residents are poorer than you are, doesn't make the same sense at it did when agriculture and natural resources paid the bills. And, of course, Russian troops were still on the ground in the country.

Today, Romania's relationship with Moldova is in some ways like America's with Canada. They seem like nice people. We have a lot in common, starting with geography and language. We wish them well. But do we really need to annex their country?

Politically, though, Moldova's relationship with Romania and with the rest of the EU is more difficult. Because of the Russian troops in Transnistria, Moldova continues to be the scene of one of the "frozen conflicts"—another is South Ossetia in Georgia. They are the unfinished business of the Soviet Union's breakup, and periodically erupt, as Georgia did in the summer of 2008.

Moldova had its own political excitement in 2009. When the Communists won re-election in the spring, the pent-up frustration of Moldova's Twittering yuppies, many of whom had studied or worked in Romania, drove them to briefly take over public buildings. Power didn't shift immediately, but the event signaled generational conflict to come and helped bring about new elections that the opposition won.

Romania reacted to the spring conflict in Moldova with solidarity for the ethnic Romanians, an offer of accelerated Romanian citizenship for those who could prove their roots, and no military action.

Because Romania belongs to the EU and Moldova does not, one wag suggested Romania's citizenship invitation to Moldovans represented a policy of EU expansion—one Moldovan at a time.

Moldova has the largest, but not the only, population of Romanians living outside the country. There are some in Hungary, Serbia, and Bulgaria. The second largest concentration is in Ukraine, many of them in northern Bucovina.

Bucovina is a region, now split between Romania and Ukraine, which has been fought over for centuries. It's a Slavic word that means the "land of beech trees."

Poland, Turkey, Romania, and Russia have all governed Bucovina at one time or another. From 1775 until 1918, it was Austria's turn.

Just as Romania took the opportunity of Russia's collapse at the close of World War I to incorporate Basarabia, it did the same with the defeat of Austria-Hungary, bringing Transylvania and Bucovina into Romania. Bucovina's population was predominantly Romanian and Ukrainian, with significant German, Polish, and Jewish minorities. Today, half of Bucovina is in Ukraine, half in Romania.

The Jewish community was especially prominent in Cernăuți, the regional capital, an hour's drive north of the Romanian border. Cernăuți, or Czernowitz in German, was the town where, in the early twentieth century, the big debate among the Jewish intellectual community raged between those promoting Hebrew and those advocating Yiddish.

Many Jewish Americans trace their roots here. Former U.S. ambassador Max Kampleman, a top aide to former vice-president Hubert Humphrey and then a top Reagan administration arms control negotiator, was born in Czernowitz. Felix Rohatyn, the New York investment banker who was U.S. ambassador to France when we were in Romania, told us he lived in Cernăuți for a few years between the wars when his father, who was from Vienna, ran a brewery there. But by 2001, the census counted just 1,300 Jewish people in Cernăuți's population of 236,700.

TRAVELS WITH RADU

ANOTHER JEWISH AMERICAN WHO began life in Czernowitz is John Klipper, president of the Romanian American Enterprise Fund (RAEF). The family later moved to Bucharest, where John's father developed his successful lumber business, and where the Communists arrested him in 1950. He was diabetic. His jailers caught him writing a letter to his wife, his son told us, and withheld his insulin as punishment; he died within a few days in the basement of the Communist Party headquarters—the building where the Romanian Senate met after the Revolution.

In 1960, John emigrated to Israel, and then to Vienna to finish his engineering degree. He was twenty-four when he came to the United States in 1962. One of the first engineering jobs he applied for was in New Jersey; he told us the interviewer looked at his résumé, looked up at him, and asked, "Where the hell is Vienna?" Klipper said he laughed, and didn't get the job.

But he did find engineering work at a French firm operating in the United States and forged a business career here. After he retired, he served on the original board of the RAEF, then as CEO.

John told us that he had never been back to the city where he was born. We were already interested in visiting Cernăuți because of its close ties to Romanian history, and because today it has such a concentration of Romanians.

The month after Jim left his job as ambassador, John proposed we visit the city with his older cousin, Radu Comșa. Radu was born in Cernăuți in 1925, after it became part of Greater Romania, and lived there until he and his parents fled in 1940 as German troops invaded.

He had not been back to Cernăuți in all the ensuing decades. Seeing the old city through the cousins' eyes seemed like a wonderful opportunity. We said yes.

Unlike John, Radu Comşa had stayed in Romania throughout the Communist period. He earned a degree in chemical engineering, but with his strong language skills, went to work right out of college in the Foreign Ministry. His first overseas assignment was during the Korean War. Most of the Communist countries kept their diplomats in China, but Comşa and one other Romania diplomat, his boss, were stationed in North Korea. He told us the food shortages were so severe, they did long-term damage to his stomach. In the 1950s, he was posted to Belgrade.

Romanian diplomats would sometimes drive to nearby Trieste for shopping, he told us, but they were a bit apprehensive when one of the embassy drivers headed to Trieste on his own. After all, he spoke only his native tongue. "No problem," he told them when he returned. "Everyone there in Italy speaks Romanian. They speak very bad Romanian, but still . . ."

In the 1970s, as the Securitate came to dominate the Foreign Ministry, Comşa left to work in the Department of Chemical Engineering in the Ministry of Trade. From his perspective, the new job was less political. After the Revolution, he was appointed ambassador to Germany, his last government assignment before he retired.

We met Comşa in Suceava and drove north, a group of three Americans and two Romanians, including Richard Popa, the driver provided by the RAEF.

At the border, the Romanians were very friendly and cheerful. But when we got to the Ukrainian side, we were held up for almost two hours, then directed inside an office to fill out forms. We knew we needed visas, and had gotten them ahead of time, but now they asked for a payment in lieu of medical insurance, citing our failure to have Ukrainian medical cards. On the merits, it didn't seem unreasonable, although we couldn't remember such a fee being charged in any other country we had visited.

Comșa talked with the border officials at great length in both Ukrainian and Russian. When he finally came back to our car, he was angry. "Who holds you up two or three hours and sends you to different checkpoints, insisting that you pay this and pay that?" he said. "We paid a lot of things, and then they charged us again."

We asked if they wanted to charge extra because we were foreigners.

"Yes! I protested, of course."

"What did they say?" Sheilah said.

"'The Americans have to pay more because they are Americans,' they told me. I said, 'You cannot make such a difference between people. Romanians, Americans—we are all the same. We are all foreigners here. You cannot treat us differently.'"

In the face of Comșa's indignation, the Ukrainian officials ultimately backed down.

"I think they wanted something—cigarettes, money, or something like that." Comșa said, fuming. "It was outrageous. You can see yourself the difference between Romanian border police and what happened to us on the other side of the border. Beginning with that moment, I became very sad. This was a different world we were coming into. Yes, a different world."

The road to Cernăuți was lined with farmland. The drive was less than an hour, but it was almost dark when we arrived at our hotel—a tall, 1960s-vintage building.

"It was built by the Hungarians under the Comecon," Comșa told us, "which didn't exist when I was a child."

Under a high ceiling, the lobby looked almost empty. Later, when we checked out, the front desk clerk made sure we had a receipt so we could show the border police where we had stayed, and that we had checked in and checked out.

We went out to dinner that first night at a fancy restaurant that featured, for no apparent reason, a Napoleonic theme. A Napoleon-era military costume festooned the wall, and the waitresses were dressed as if they had just stepped out of the French army, circa 1800. They handed us elaborate bound illustrated menus listing many entrees, but the kitchen had only two dishes available to serve.

The next morning, Comşa took us on a tour of his birthplace city. It looked much different than the Romanian cities we had visited. The grand, nineteenth-century public buildings downtown were clean, and had been painted bright colors, so they looked to be in better condition than many buildings of comparable age, even in Bucharest. We were told they had not been privatized and that the mayor wanted his buildings to look good. And they did.

*In Cernăuţi, Ukraine in front of statue of Mihai Eminescu,
the great Romanian writer: Jim, a local Romanian professor,
John Klipper, Radu Comşa, and Richard Popa*

But the rest of the commercial area looked much poorer than Romania. A couple of restaurants we stuck our heads into—not fancy ones like the Napoleonic one—were threadbare. There seemed to be little food, few customers, and less maintenance.

Napoleon may not have slept in Cernăuți, but Potemkin would recognize one of his villages.

A friend of Radu Comşa, a Romanian professor who taught at the Ukrainian state university, joined us for part of our tour. We walked around the high school Comşa had attended—the same one where the beloved Romanian poet Mihai Eminescu studied a century earlier.

"I was a student in the so-called power middle school," Comşa explained. "After four years of primary school, I was supposed to go on to eight years of lyceum—altogether, twelve years of schooling. It didn't matter, though. In the fourth year of my lyceum, the Russians came in. It was over."

Comşa took us to the apartment building where his family had lived. It looked like any pre-war apartment building in New York or Bucharest.

"We lived on the higher basement and had six big rooms there, well-furnished. As far as I remember, I was born in this apartment."

He showed us a synagogue, now converted into a movie theater.

"Not only synagogues were converted, but churches, too—they were transformed into stores," Comşa said. "It's a big pity. Sixty years earlier, Czernowitz was a beautiful city with a great sense of the centuries."

We visited the Romanian Orthodox cathedral.

"A big church, with many beggars around," Comşa noted.

We passed the opera house, where a program was playing. We were invited in, but Jim was madly—and successfully—trying to avoid the opera.

John Klipper was born in Cernăuți only because it had the closest good hospital to Vatra Dornei, the small town in what is now northern Romania where he and his family lived. Afraid of deportation because they were Jews, his family moved to Bucharest when he was a toddler. That's where John grew up.

Comşa lived in Cernăuți until he was fourteen years old. About one-third of Cernăuți was Jewish at that time. We visited the Jewish cemetery to see if we could find any references to family names of American Jews who trace their roots in one way or another to Cernăuţi.

Comşa remembered anti-Semitism as rampant in Cernăuţi.

"There were rallies and some Jews beaten up. Of course we were afraid, and we knew what the end would be if the Iron Guard came to power."

We asked how that anti-Semitism compared to the prejudice of Vadim Tudor, former Mayor Funar of Cluj, and other Romanian nationalists of today.

"Not the same," Comşa replied. "It was very different and very dangerous. The anti-Jewish education didn't start with the Iron Guard [in the 1930s]. Anti-Jewish legislation started years before."

So, we asked, why did Jewish people stay in Cernăuţi?

"They had no choice," Comşa replied. "You could not move in three days. Couldn't get an American visa. Israel hadn't yet been created. I don't know where the Jews could go. In Romania, seven hundred thousand Jews had to decide where to go, how to go, how to get money to go.

"My parents didn't have Zionist ideas. They were assimilated people," he said. "My father was a medical doctor. For more than one hundred years, until 1914, Bucovina had belonged to Austria. So my father had studied in Vienna." Dr. Comşa's patients were Romanians, Ukrainians, and Germans, gentiles as well as Jews.

"There's a very small mountain next to Cernăuţi where we skied. I remember my father saying, 'I cannot find such a place in Israel.'"

We asked Radu Comşa what Cernăuţi was like when he was a child.

"It was a wonderful city, with Austrian influence, as you have seen from the buildings, and with a population which spoke mainly German. Of course, there had been 120 years of German influence."

He learned to speak Romanian in school.

"My parents had learned some Romanian. I went to kindergarten and learned Romanian. At home, we spoke German. That went on until 1939, when this unfortunate Ribbentrop-Molotov Pact was signed. Basarabia and the northern parts of Bucovina were forcibly taken over by Russia.

"And that was the start of a new era in Romania. A year later, the northern part of Transylvania, because of the Hitler-Mussolini dictate, became Hungarian. Parts of Dobrogea were given to Bulgaria. That was the start of the Antonescu dictatorship. Romania became a satellite of Germany, of Hitler.

"I left in 1940 with my mother. My father was already in the Romanian army. At that time, many, many reservists were called into the army. As a doctor, my father was made a captain in the Romanian army."

We asked what would have happened if he had stayed in Cernăuți.

"I don't know what would have happened, but we were afraid," he said. "In my family, we were not great Russian sympathizers. And my father—he was somewhere in Romania, we didn't know quite where. My mother had two brothers who lived in Bucharest. So we left everything but what we could fit into small luggage. The Russians gave us three days. Whoever wanted to leave had three days.

"I knew a lot of people who left," Comşa recalled. "But it was very hard, because trains were overfull. The army was evacuating official buildings, institutions, and their archives. It was terrible."

Sheilah's language teacher, Gertrude Ştefan, also spent her childhood in Cernăuți. She remembers the evacuation very clearly.

She was about ten years old when her father, a Romanian citizen who was a lawyer and a veteran of the Austrian army, got word that Romanians who wanted to leave the Russian territory should register. Gertrude remembers adults discussing whether the offer was a Russian trick, then registering, and then waiting for permission to emigrate.

The permission didn't come until Gertrude's father visited a well-connected official who extorted a bribe, Gertrude told Sheilah.

"She said, 'Do you want to leave? I give you the permission in

twenty-four hours—but you give me the apartment, as is, furnished.'"
On the spot, her father agreed, Gertrude said, and "we were jumping
to the ceiling with happiness. We wanted to leave. We were scared to
death.

"We were not allowed to take valuable things. Only the wedding
ring was allowed. My father had a diamond in a crown, in a tooth. And
we were hiding a watch with diamonds. No money, of course, because
there was a search at the border—yes, I remember, they searched even
the pillows. They opened the pillows with a blade. And of course, if
they found something, they took it away."

They left Cernăuți in March 1944. Gertrude said she remembers
the moonlit night, the wooden archway at the Romanian border, and
the slender blond Russian soldier standing near it who laughed at the
emigrants huddled on a truck. Gertrude could still mimic his sneer.
"Hah, hah, hah, you are leaving. We are coming after you."

Gertrude's family is gentile. Jim asked Radu Comşa, "Did Jewish
families react differently than other Romanians?" and got a heated
reply.

"There are in Romania some people who want to restore the
Antonescu reputation. They say that one of the reasons Antonescu
ordered the Jews to be deported from the northern part of Bucovina
was their behavior toward the Romanian army, when the army left for
those three days. That's their argument. I must say to you it's not true,
because I was there. Of course, there were people who saluted the
incoming Russians. Maybe there were some Jews, too.

"But of the fifty thousand Jews who were in Cernăuți, forty thousand were anti-Russian. Because in Cernăuți, people were rather rich.
They had a good life. They owned stores, they were trained in the pro-
fessions, they were intellectuals. They had nothing in common with
the Russians. And the best proof of this is one year later, three or four
weeks before the German-Russian War started, when the Russians
deported a lot of Jews to Siberia—including one of my aunts.

"So it is a lie. But they wanted an explanation for why Antonescu
deported to Transnistria two hundred thousand Jews from Basarabia

and the northern part of Bucovina. Most died from typhus and hunger and cold. That, I think, is important to stress, because it is a big lie. And it has no reasonable support. Because more than in Romania, maybe, the Jews in Cernăuţi were not pro-Russian and not pro-Communist."

What was the Jewish community like in Cernăuţi?

"One-third of the population of Cernăuţi was Jewish," said Comşa. "There were some Germans, of course. There were Poles and Ukrainians and Romanians. Cernăuţi was a very, very cosmopolitan town, and there was very good communication between all those ethnic communities. I remember my father and my mother having friends who were Romanian, and also German. Maybe you can find the same thing today in Timişoara, where you also have such a mixture of populations. But Cernăuţi was a very special case."

Was the Jewish community in Cernăuţi affected in the 1930s by the Iron Guard?

"Of course. I remember it very well. I was the only Jew in my class. It was the best school in Cernăuţi, by far the best school. And I wanted to speak good Romanian. I had in mind that maybe later I would study in Bucharest."

He remembered his child's-eye view of the Iron Guard and fascism.

"I saw it personally in school, in the attitudes toward me, by students, not teachers. 'You, Jew, must leave. What are you doing in this school?' And so on. But, as I told you, I was an ambitious young man and I insisted on staying. And at the end, I had some friends. In 1939, the prime minister Armand Călinescu was assassinated. Afterward, the police came to the school and arrested several of the young people who were members of the Iron Guard, which had big support, by the way, in the northern part of Bucovina, because Codreanu, the chief of the Iron Guard, was born in Bucovina."

Visiting his hometown for the first time since he was fourteen years old, Comşa was not pleased with what he saw.

"It is a big pity what happened to Cernăuţi," he said. "Sixty years earlier, it was a very beautiful city with a very high level of cultural life. It is a pity to see that nothing has happened in the city since, and that a lot of strange people came from different parts of the Soviet empire, having nothing in common with the old Cernăuţi.

"My second feeling is that they have not yet been touched by any democratic sense. Remember our discussions with the Romanian professor there, and with the Romanian guide we had—they were very afraid of having too much public contact with us. They were afraid of repression by Ukrainian authorities. They told me how difficult it is for them to have a Romanian newspaper, to learn Romanian, or even to *speak* Romanian.

"But that's history. We can't change it. Maybe there will be a better time, but I don't think so. It's too late."

CARING FOR THE JEWISH HERITAGE

LEAVING UKRAINE WAS LESS onerous than entering. At the border, we were directed to several different buildings to pay several different fees, present proof that we'd settled up for our hotel stay, and have our passports deeply scrutinized. Then we crossed into Romania, and were struck by a sense of hospitality and disorganization—no one could tell us where to park ourselves.

"I feel a little depressed," Ambassador Comşa said solemnly. "In Ukraine, we had so many papers. Now, I have only my passport. I feel naked."

It was a quick drive to Rădăuţi, a lovely old town of about 25,000. Tanya Gruenberg, the secretary of the tiny Jewish community, showed us the synagogue, which was built and dedicated in 1886.

Before World War II, she said, 8,000 Jews had lived in Rădăuţi. Only three were spared deportation to Transnistria—a lawyer, the gynecologist, and the distiller. Only a few returned from Transnistria. "Now, there are 76 Jews here," she told us, most of them elderly.

We talked about her efforts to get back from the government Jewish properties that had been seized, to rent them out and use the income to support the community. But Tanya herself died a few years after we spoke with her, setting back efforts to restore the synagogue and the Jewish cemetery.

About fifteen miles away, in Siret, we heard a similar story—a rich Jewish heritage, but no one to care for it. John and Radu showed us the three cemeteries that testify to generations of Jewish life and faith here. Rows of stones march across a plateau and up a hill like soldiers breaking ranks. Intricately carved lions of Judah stand proud, and gracefully sculpted hands rise in perpetual blessing. In the oldest of the three cemeteries, high on the hill, the epitaphs are all in Hebrew, some dating to the sixteenth century.

Back in Bucharest, the president of the Federation of Jewish Communities in Romania, Dr. Nicolae Cajal, told us that more than 700 Jewish cemeteries are located in Romanian towns without a single remaining Jew.

Cajal called the situation "catastrophic." More than seven out of ten Jews in Romania are over the age of 65. True, he said, since the Revolution, more young people have been identifying themselves as Jewish, though their parents carefully ducked the designation during Communism. But that's not enough, Dr. Cajal told us.

"If the situation continues like this—two, three hundred deaths a year and no births, no new children—we will have no Jewish communities in Romania in 15 or 18 years."

That's possible. But Romania has seen a surging Jewish presence in Romania since 1989. Israelis and others are coming back to invest, trade, vacation, and even gamble. In spite of the horrors and struggles of Jews in Romania's history, many return—at least as frequent visitors. How many will plant roots and raise families in Romania, no one knows.

Dr. Cajal and his wife Bibi worked tirelessly to find the resources the Jewish community needed. He told us he couldn't have done as much as he did without The American Jewish Joint Distribution Committee, often referred to simply as The Joint.

Dr. Cajal was in his 80s when we knew him, still working almost daily at the Institute of Virology, which he had headed since 1966, and as a professor at the University of Medicine and Pharmacy. He came from a family of doctors—his father Marcu Cajal, early in the twentieth century, was one of the first pediatric specialists in Romania, And none of the many scientific honors Nicolae Cajal earned during his long life gave him as much pride as his granddaughter Catherine, a surgeon in Los Angeles.

He began medical school before World War II in Cluj, and then was forced out because he was Jewish. Just as the war was ending, he finished at the medical school his father had organized for Jews. A year later, he got a prestigious fellowship to work at the Pasteur Institute in Paris. When he left, with Bibi at his side, even his father-in-law assumed he would not return to Romania. But he couldn't see leaving his family, and he told us decades later he was glad he'd come back. "I did what I can to be useful," he said in his gentle way.

In 1994, Dr. Cajal was chosen to succeed the legendary Rabbi Moses Rosen, who, as head of the Jewish federation had helped Romanian Jews emigrate for forty years. The Jewish community that remained was small. Dr. Cajal focused on helping the elderly, preserving cultural monuments like the cemeteries, and promoting understanding of what Jews had contributed to the country.

Jim asked him, a year and a half before his death at age 84, whether he thought the attitudes of Romanians toward the Jewish community had changed over that sweep of time. His answer was characteristically moderate.

"I don't speak about anti-Semitism, I speak about anti-Semites. Romania is not a country of anti-Semitism, because the majority of people are not. But we have a lot of anti-Semites—stupid young people who don't know, like Vadim Tudor," he said, naming a notoriously nationalist politician. Still, Dr. Cajal's hunch was that only about 10 percent of those who voted for Vadim Tudor were anti-Semitic. Most, he said, were just voters looking for change.

For his part, Dr. Cajal wanted to focus on promoting what he called Semitism, and the 700-page book he compiled detailing the contributions of Romanian Jews to science, culture, and civilization.

To us, he sounded like Dr. Norman Vincent Peale. For a beleaguered, shrinking community of Eastern European Jews, positive thinking can be a powerful force in the twenty-first century.

Good Fences, Good Neighbors, Good Borders with Ukraine

When Constantinescu visited the White House in 1998, President Clinton was sitting on the edge of his chair, gripped by the story the Romanian president was telling about Ukraine.

It was a story Constantinescu told many times.

"I was confronted with this matter three days after I became president," Constantinescu told us. "I had to represent Romania at the OSCE conference in Lisbon in December 1996. I left just after I took my oath in Albă Iulia. People still were in the streets and applauding. I went to Lisbon in a military plane, a propeller plane. The trip was quite long and terribly noisy, so I had time to read all the documentation prepared by the intelligence services. The Ukrainian delegation was prepared to accuse Romania of irredentist policy and territorial claims. There had even been the idea of holding military exercises on Snakes Island [in the Black Sea], but President [Leonid] Kuchma had postponed that until after the summit in Lisbon.

"I asked the foreign minister to arrange the first bilateral meetings, which were going to be in this order: first with President Kuchma and second with Vice President Gore. I was newly elected and on the front page of Western papers, so this was not hard to arrange.

"When I met Kuchma, I told him we can do one good thing together, and that is to sort out this problem. We can create stability in Central Europe. Ukraine needs recognition. For Romania, it is important to have a neighbor in Ukraine which is independent, sovereign, and strong. But this agreement should also guarantee the rights of the Romanian minority."

He described the dispute as less about the land—the parts of Bucovina and southern Basarabia that he said were historically Romania's—than about the human rights of the Romanian minority there. He said he told Kuchma that if they didn't move quickly, they might lose control as conflicts flared up. Constantinescu's plan was that he and Kuchma would tackle it personally, with the goal of signing a treaty before the NATO conference planned for Madrid—just six months away.

"This was not an argument for Romania's integration into NATO at Madrid, because that wasn't likely—it was too late anyway," Constantinescu told us. "Also, I didn't want Romania to be perceived as using the conflict as blackmail to assist our effort to join NATO. Blackmail on an issue like that is very dangerous. I told Kuchma, this is a matter of confidence. If we trust each other, we can bring our countries to trust each other.

"He agreed. He met Vice President Gore and told him about our decision. And then I met Vice President Gore. I felt that Gore was really happy about this, but it seemed almost impossible for him to believe that, in so short a time as six months, such a thing could be achieved. But I told him that you have to use the beginning of your term of office to do important things, and not the ending of office. And I also told him that a leader of the right, such as me, could conclude this kind of treaty, because those who have the moral right to question it support me. And this is how it happened."

With TV cameras rolling at the Black Sea resort of Neptune, Kuchma and Constantinescu signed the treaty in June 1997, a month ahead of their self-imposed deadline. At their White House meeting, Clinton was particularly interested in how Constantinescu had won political and public support for the treaty.

"I went on national TV, together with a well-known, respected historian. I explained how I saw things," Constantinescu recalled. "I said we have a burning problem on our hands. We have three options. One option is to sort out this problem, the second option is not to sort out this problem, and the third is to pretend there is no problem."

He dismissed the last option and, like the professor he is, compared the first two.

"The problem has two components for us: the historical rights on the territories of Bucovina and southern Basarabia, and the Romanian minority from Bucovina and southern Basarabia. Which is more important—the land or the people? If we should decide it is the land, there are no chances at all of winning it back, now or later. But we can consider making an appeal to history—and at a certain moment, which might be more favorable, we could claim that we never gave those territories up. The land lasts forever.

"But people don't. Under the new circumstances of history, minorities lose their identities very rapidly—TV and modern civilization can destroy the patriarchal nucleus of the traditional family, the church, and the school.

"So I quoted a young Romanian, originally from Ukraine, who was a student at the University of Bucharest. He was watching a debate of some intellectuals about the region, and said, 'It's very interesting to hear you discuss all this. But if you keep on talking, even if you eventually sort something out, we won't be here anymore.'

"And I believe people understood. Because when the nationalist parties strongly opposed the treaty, they didn't find any popular support for their position.

"Now, in Ukraine, the Romanians have schools and they have magazines. When I was president, I went up to Kiev to talk to the leaders of the Romanian minority in Ukraine. And from the scarce resources of the university, we took books to Ukrainian villages."

Several years after he left office, he told us about a conversation he'd had when he and the former president of Hungary congratulated each other on reconciliation between their two countries. With a wry smile, Constantinescu told us they agreed that Nobel Peace Prizes tend to be awarded to leaders who start dangerous conflicts and then make a peace deal. The Nobel committee doesn't seem to consider it a similar success to rapidly reach an understanding that heads conflict off. "But," he said, "it is a great success for the good of the people."

ARE THE RUSSIANS COMING—ON MONDAY MORNING?

One Saturday morning, soon after the war in Kosovo ended, the phone rang at home. Jim answered it in the bedroom. It was Andrei

Pleşu, the foreign minister.

"Good morning, Jim. Sorry to call you at home, but we have problem," he said in the ironic tone that is his specialty.

"Shoot," Jim replied.

"The Russian ambassador just contacted me. They are asking our permission to fly planes over our airspace on Monday morning."

Just as the war in Kosovo was ending, Russian troops had sprinted from Bosnia to Priština to capture control of the airport. They had arrived ahead of U.S. and U.K. troops.

The Russians had been helpful in getting Milošević to throw in the towel, and we wanted to cooperate with them. But we didn't want them to set up a major, separate military force or base in Kosovo.

Jim was on high alert, but he searched for just the right diplomatic words. "What did you tell them?" he asked.

"That we would discuss it and get back to them," Pleşu continued. "Of course, we want to discuss it with our NATO friends."

Right answer! Jim thought. "Did they tell you why they want to fly over Romania?" he asked innocently.

"Why? Do you doubt their good intentions?" Pleşu replied. Whenever Pleşu would discuss Russia with Jim, he'd suggest, in the nicest possible way, that Americans were a little naive about Russian intentions.

"Just a thought," Jim said, "but perhaps they want to reinforce their troops at the Priština airport." Russian control of the Priština airport was not part of our game plan.

And a Russian airlift of reinforcements across Romanian airspace was not part of our game plan, either.

"Perhaps you're right!" said Pleşu.

"Perhaps *you're* right," Jim said. "I'll talk to the folks in Washington and get back to you ASAP."

The folks in Washington were already aware of the problem, because the Russians had asked Bulgaria and Hungary for the same permission. And we clearly didn't want any of them to grant it.

Jim called Pleşu back.

"Well, we'd like you to deny overflight rights," Jim said.

Pleşu replied slowly.

"I've talked with President Constantinescu and the prime minister about this," he began. "We've talked about our desire to help our friends in NATO. And we've talked about what could happen if the Russians decide to proceed anyway . . ."

This wasn't sounding like a *yes* answer.

". . . and it would be our *pleasure* to stand with NATO," he said.

Whew!

Like all of us, Pleşu knew this was a scary situation. The Russians might defy Romania's decision and enter its airspace without permission, and that could lead to a military confrontation.

But he also knew that, because they'd be doing it at NATO's request, we'd stand by the Romanians militarily as well as politically. And for a country that had suffered so much because of Russian military domination, standing up to the Russians, with backing from the United States, seemed like much more of an opportunity than a threat.

That weekend, Romania denied Russia overfly rights, and no planes flew.

The following week, in consultation with NATO, Romania negotiated a schedule for Russian planes to fly to Priština over its territory.

Some months later, General Constantin Degeratu, Chief of Defense and head of the Romanian armed forces, told Jim his version of these events.

The first day the Russians were allowed to fly, they entered Romania an hour too early. Gen. Degeratu ordered a Romanian MIG-29 into the air to escort the Russian plane out. And he invited the Russian defense attaché over for a chat. The Russian asked Degeratu what the Romanians would do if Russian planes again flew outside the approved schedule.

"First, we'd radio them that they are illegally in our airspace and must turn back. If they didn't, we'd send up our fighters again to escort them out of our airspace," he told the Russian.

"And if they didn't leave then?" he was asked.

"The fighters would be under orders to escort the planes out of our airspace," Degeratu said.

"What if our planes do not turn back, even after these warnings?" the Russian asked. "Will they be fired on?"

"Under our rules, no," Degeratu told him. "But, after all these disputes, the pilots may be tired and frustrated. No one can know what they might do."

The Russian persisted. "What if they didn't follow orders and fired on the Russian planes?"

"They'd be subject to very firm discipline," Degeratu said, "and be punished. Of course, they'd also be national heroes. And we don't want to risk that, do we?"

From then on, the Russians stuck to the approved schedule, and NATO consolidated its control in Priština.

CHAPTER 14
WHY ROMANIA WORKS

THE ECONOMIC BOOM OF THE LAST DECADE

IN THE HEADY DAYS of the December Revolution against Ceauşescu, Silviu Brucan, the curmudgeonly ex-Communist ambassador to the United States, said it would take twenty years for Romanians to adjust to democracy.

He was too pessimistic—and thus very Romanian.

In the twenty years since the fall of Communism, Romania has become not just a democracy—it did that relatively quickly—but also a fast-growing economy, a full member of the European Union, and an ally of the United States in NATO.

On one visit to Bucharest after our return to the United States, Sheilah and her colleagues were late to a meeting because of traffic.

Their host, Professor Cornel Codiţă, who had joined Jim in the two-and-a-half-hour late-night talk show during the Kosovo War, was understanding.

"It's a busy country," he acknowledged.

Indeed, it is, and has been these past twenty years.

Romania has not dodged the worldwide economic crisis which began in 2008. Globalization means the economic escalator goes down as well as up. But it has come a long way in a relatively short time.

When we first went to Romania in February 1998, the country was in a deep recession. Inflation was running at sixty percent and interest rates a staggering ninety-five percent. Romania had failed to get into NATO at the Madrid summit the previous year. The government was in a state of constant crisis and the prime minister, Victor Ciorbea, lost his job a few months later.

That summer, Russia defaulted on its debt, spooking the holders of bonds issued by other countries in the region. By fall, Romania's financial reserves were dropping, the IMF was pressuring Romania to default, and the war drums were being heard in next-door Yugo-slavia.

So why were we then, as we are now, so optimistic about Roma-nia?

Our impressions are so different from much of the conventional wisdom about Romania that people are often shocked that we think Romania works.

Part of it may just be that we are Americans. Our own experience is that the future is generally better than the past. Given how much Romania had suffered in recent decades, it was hard to see how things wouldn't improve.

Part of it is just looking at the facts in context. Western Europe picked itself up after the horror of World War II and reinvented itself as a potential poster child for Immanuel Kant's "perpetual peace." With the exception of Milošević's tragically wrong turn in Yugoslavia, so far, so good.

The transition from forty-two years of Communism *was* difficult. But was it more difficult than for France and Germany to bury the hatchet after several centuries of conflict and the worst war in history? That seems unlikely.

Most important, as we actually look at what happens in Roma-nia—political disputes resolved peacefully, schools churning out well-educated young people, entrepreneurs building businesses in machine tools and software, ethnic conflicts managed through the political process—it looks pretty good to us.

In March 1999, in the middle of a war in Kosovo and a continuing recession in Romania, Jim gave a speech at the Academy of Economic Studies in Bucharest. "Now is the time to invest in Romania," he said.

More than a few people thought he had lost contact with reality. But, in fact, he had called the bottom of the markets, both economic and political. (Unfortunately, given the ethical requirements of his job, we couldn't invest our own money in Romania then, and our market calls since have not been nearly as good, whether in Romania or anyplace else.)

In less than a year, Romania was invited to negotiate to join the European Union. By the end of 2000, Milošević was out of power in neighboring Yugoslavia and, as former President Constantinescu liked to point out, for the first time in history, the Balkans were a hotbed of democracy. The economy bottomed out, leading us to tell friends that, as soon as we left Romania in early 2001, the crops came up, the sunflowers bloomed, and the economy began its eight-year boom.

We've been back to Romania often in recent years. Jim's investment business takes him to Europe several times a year for board meetings. Whenever he can, he visits Romania, checking in with friends as well as portfolio companies.

In Bucharest, the biggest differences from when we lived there are the traffic—there's much more—and the abandoned dogs—there are a lot fewer. When Jim visited Sibiu in 2007, Mayor Johannis told him that so many Western European companies, particularly manufacturers, had invested there that unemployment had dropped almost to nothing. Employers couldn't find enough workers to hire. Within two years, the "masters of the universe" on Wall Street, in London and in Zurich, had created the worldwide financial crisis, thereby solving much of that problem for employers and creating new difficulties for workers.

Today, Romania is what Romanians like to call "a normal country." Shopping centers line the roads outside most cities, middle-class families vacation in Greece and Turkey, students work and study in London and Paris, and credit cards, mortgages, and consumer loans are the coin of the realm.

By 2008, the country had become more "normal" than is good for it. With foreign banks taking over the financial system—something former president Iliescu had worried about—and rising incomes driving expectations, Romania had its own real estate bubble. Because the government did not follow all the foreign advice about how to deregulate, the financial fallout has been less severe than in the United States—no sub-prime mortgages in Bacău. By 2009, mortgage debt in

Romania was 4 percent of gross domestic product; in the U.S., it was 104 percent, with a lower home-ownership rate. In the second quarter of 2009, the Romanian stock market bounced back—up forty-three percent, the best performance in Europe and emerging markets—and much better than in the U.S.

But problems remained. When seventy percent of Romania's exports go to the EU, a recession in Germany means a recession in Romania. Also, the boom in foreign investment drove up the value of Romanian currency, and too many Romanians borrowed in Euro and Swiss francs. Even though the stock market surged back from the worldwide lows of March, the real economy hit a brick wall in 2009. Welcome to the economic crises of capitalism.

Jim (holding boxes for take-out), Lia and Dorel Jurcovan, and Sheilah, in the Jurcovans' pizza parlor in downtown Timişoara in Western Romania

In Timişoara, when Jim went back to Dorel and Lia Jurcovan's pizza parlor, Lia insisted on taking him on a tour of her freezers to dramatize her outrage about EU rules on cheese storage and preparation.

Still, on balance, the peace and prosperity the EU stood for trumped often inscrutable regulations, she concluded.

In the twenty years since the fall of Communism, Romania has moved from the bottom of the pack of former Soviet satellites in Eastern Europe, in both an economic and a political sense, to the front row of the new Europe. In the five years from 2004 to 2008, its growth rate averaged six percent annually, the highest in Europe. Romania is a vibrant democracy and, because of its size, a significant member of NATO and the EU. After a forty-two-year detour into the Soviet orbit, this country of warm, smart, and creative people has returned to Europe.

But outside of Romania, and sometimes even inside, good news travels slowly. Since 1989, Romania has had one of the highest ratios of bad international press to real achievement of any country in the world.

As we said at the outset, most Americans today know only three things about Romania: there were thousands of abandoned children who suffered in hideous orphanages; dictator Nicolae Ceauşescu was a nut as well as a Stalinist; and Dracula came from Transylvania.

These are facts (even if Dracula had been fictionalized), but they hardly explain what Romania is all about at the end of the twenty-first century's first decade. The truth is that, with all its continuing problems, Romania is a success story in the transition from Communism, and its future is bright. In this book, we have tried to describe the Romania we saw during the years when Romanians dealt with their country's Communist legacy, and to explain why they succeeded.

Before going to Romania as U.S. ambassador, Jim was briefed by a U.S. government official responsible for supporting Eastern Europe's transition from Communism. He showed Jim a scattergram that compared countries throughout the region based on ratings of political and economic "progress." The idea was that, if a country had made enough progress, the U.S. government could end foreign aid—the country would "graduate" from our support.

In one way, that made sense. Americans understandably want to see if countries we're helping become so successful that they don't need our help anymore. But the idea that we could quantify "progress" on a scattergram based on rankings by NGOs and international financial institutions suggested an attraction to quantification and oversimplification that risked missing the most significant aspects of the countries' development.

Compared to Poland, Hungary, and the Czech Republic, was Romania's standard of living low? Yes. Were there still too many abandoned children living in large institutions? Yes. Was there too much corruption and too little privatization? Yes. Did Romania have too many xenophobic demagogues in politics and the media? Yes.

But did all that mean Romania was not headed toward becoming a prosperous, modern, European democracy? Definitely not.

The scattergram analysis tends to overestimate policy and underestimate history, geography, religion, and what Romanians call "mentality"—a lot of which we've discussed in this book. The nations of Eastern Europe have some similarities—in particular, about a half-century of Communist rule. But the differences are not trivial.

Consider two examples at the extreme. Poland is large and borders Germany, and has a large American diaspora, a strong Roman Catholic Church (with one of its own recently in charge of the Vatican), tiny ethnic minorities, and a tradition of private enterprise that survived Communism. After 1989, all those factors made it more accessible, and more attractive, to Western investment, as well as to Western ideas.

Moldova, on the other hand, is small, and squeezed between Ukraine and Romania. It has a tiny Western diaspora, the remnants of a Stalinist economy, a struggle for identity between its Russian and Romanian histories, and Russian troops still occupying part of the country.

Sound monetary and fiscal policy, structural reform, and the rule of law certainly improved conditions in both countries. But measuring both countries against the same narrow policy model misses most of what was difficult, and important, in their transitions.

Moldova, with its potential agricultural wealth and well-educated people, will never border Germany and will never have a large American diaspora. For the foreseeable future, it will have to manage both its identity issues and its relationships with Russia and Romania. To be successful, its strategy will have to be significantly different from Poland's.

Or consider Hungary. One of its greatest accomplishments since 1989 was attracting foreign investment. Part of the reason it did so was policy. Part was its strong diaspora—in the United States, George Soros and the late U.S. Representative Tom Lantos come to mind. But it was not irrelevant that most of that investment was in western Hungary, essentially in the suburbs of Vienna. Geography counts.

Or take a look at Albania, which since 1991 has had one of the fastest-growing economies in all of Europe, Western as well as Eastern. Before 1989, its economy was more isolated than any in the region except Romania. Since 1989, it has suffered war, anarchy, and substantial crime. Why has it grown so fast? Bordering Greece and Italy (across the Adriatic) is a big help. With hundreds of thousands of workers in Greece and Italy, Albanian labor is already effectively in the EU. That makes a big difference.

Similar examples abound. The point is simply that geography, history, and other non-policy factors are key to understanding how these countries in transition are doing, and how they are likely to do.

1989: NOT THE START OF HISTORY

SO BACK TO ROMANIA.

Before 1989, all of Romania's neighbors, including the Soviet Union, were Communist countries. Since then, three of its immediate neighbors—Ukraine, Moldova, and Yugoslavia—have had bigger economic and political problems than Romania. Only one—Hungary—is more prosperous or was an earlier addition to NATO and the EU. Not entirely coincidentally, the most prosperous, Western-oriented region of Romania borders Hungary.

From an economic perspective, Romania started the "race" in 1989 in a deeper hole than countries such as Poland and Hungary.

Ceaușescu had imposed a Stalinist economy of no private enterprise and mammoth, energy-inefficient industrial plants long after that strategy had been abandoned in most of Eastern Europe. He managed to turn Romania from Europe's largest oil exporter before Communism into a major importer. He built a coal-mining industry to feed huge electricity plants, many of which are now unneeded. He spent billions to redevelop much of downtown Bucharest into a monument to Stalinist government architecture.

And he did all this in the 1970s and '80s, when Poland and Hungary had stopped most of their Stalinist economic policies and were opening themselves up to market forces. Thus, some of the biggest economic divergence came a decade or more *before* the fall of the Berlin Wall. Just as history didn't end in 1989, it didn't start then, either.

Politically, Romania emerged from a far more repressive Communist regime than most of the other countries of Eastern Europe. Without the embrace of a major Western diaspora, church, or neighboring nation, outside interest was episodic at best. Compounding these problems was the fact that, in the first six years after Ceaușescu's overthrow, former Communist reformers, not anti-Communists, governed Romania. This was very different from the experience of all other Eastern European countries, except the former Yugoslavia. From Estonia to Bulgaria, anti-Communist forces came to power for at least a short time in the early 1990s. Not in Romania, where the break with the past was not as sharp. The result in Romania was more stability, but slower adjustment to Western democratic standards and market economic forces.

One of the results was that many of the pre-1989 political and economic powerbrokers consolidated their positions and effectively resisted change longer than many expected. A remarkable amount of downsizing was done during this period, much more than is generally recognized, but real competition developed slowly. As late as 1998, state banks still controlled most banking assets, and for too much of the period, they were used to promote special business and political interests. Today, modern, primarily Western European banks control most of the Romanian banking market—for better or for worse.

None of this is to argue that Romania's problems were so deep they cannot be overcome—in fact, quite the reverse. Communism did more damage to Romania's political, economic, and social fabric than it did to many countries, and Romania has not yet climbed past some of the countries that were on a higher plane in 1989. But given the depths to which it had been driven, Romania may well have risen farther and faster than some of the others.

Nor do we mean to imply that Romania's future is largely out of the control of its own people—that geography, history, and similar factors will determine its fate. The point is rather that Romania has made remarkable progress given the difficulties it has faced. A free press, a democratic political system, peaceful relations with its neighbors and among ethnic groups, and an economy that grew rapidly in a prosperous world economy before 2009—these are not accomplishments to be ignored. Romanians have every reason to be confident that continuing progress can and will be made, and that advances, from better health care to more job opportunities, need not wait until Romania gets courts as independent as California's, or government as honest as Wisconsin's.

A dramatic example of the ability to make progress amid all the difficulties is the fact that U.S. investment doubled in Romania during the three years we were there, even though Romania's GDP declined in two of those years. The explanations for this dramatic increase point to the importance of focusing on specific factors about Romania, not the theoretical and general.

First, during this period, the government accelerated privatization of state enterprises. That created a range of large and small investment opportunities that had not existed before. As a result, Americans invested in two of the three state-owned banks that were privatized, and also in the oil industry, the machine-tool industry, and a number of others.

Second, the booming U.S. economy, particularly in information technology, created demand that Romania, by education and training, was well-positioned to meet. Among the best examples are Solectron, the Silicon Valley-based computer and electronics manufacturer that opened up a huge plant near Timişoara, and the more than sixty-five American companies that partnered with Romanian software developers.

Finally, the three-year gains then were the result of more than tripling the number of embassy-related people working to promote U.S. investment. It was simply a matter of doing the work and finding the opportunities, coaching the American companies deal-by-deal, and working through problems with the Romanians as they developed.

IS ROMANIA A DEMOCRACY?

CONSIDERING THE RETURN OF authoritarianism in Russia under Vladimir Putin, it's worth considering the state of Romania's democracy.

As we've traveled around the country, we've heard many, many complaints about Romania's democracy. Critics say that the press writes whatever it wants, true or not. They say that members of Parliament are always arguing with each other. And they say that politicians seem only to be worried about the next election.

If all those charges have a familiar ring to them, it's because they're nearly identical to complaints we Americans voice about our own democracy. The fact is that the Romanian press writes what it wants, whether it's true or not, because it's largely free—particularly of government control.

Legislators appear to bicker with each other in Romania for the same reasons they do in all democracies—because they have policy disagreements and represent different constituencies. Politicians are worried about the next elections because there will be future elections, which are seen as the way one gains or keeps power. In our time in Romania, we rarely heard reference to extra-constitutional means of acquiring or maintaining power. Romanian politicians worry about public opinion polls, press coverage, campaign funds, and coalitions—all things that politicians in democracies, but not autocracies, worry about.

In the last decade, politics have been exciting, even by Romanian standards.

In 2004, Traian Băsescu was elected president, pulling into parliament a center-right coalition made up of his PD-L and the PNL, led by Călin Popescu-Tăriceanu—who became prime minister. In short order, they had a falling-out—Popescu-Tăriceanu threw the Democrats out of the government and impeached Băsescu.

Under Romania's constitution, the president was suspended from his job and a referendum was called to vote on the impeachment. Băsescu won the vote overwhelmingly, and then led his party to victory in the 2008 elections.

All of this is great fodder for political gossip and late-night television, but it seemed to have no discernible effect on Romania's economy or its peaceful foreign policy. The Italian ambassador was right when she said that Romanians share with Jim's Italian forebears a delightful, but hardly dangerous, spontaneity.

Those who criticize Romanian democracy often point to the fact that its first post-Communist president, Ion Iliescu, had been a leading Communist before 1989, and that he and his party came back to power from 2000 to 2004. And that's true. But, as we've pointed out, it's important to recognize that it was also Ion Iliescu who, when he lost his reelection in 1996, accepted the result, like any democratic politician, and went into the opposition. After four years, he campaigned again, and won in an election that was free and fair. His chosen successor lost the 2004 election to succeed him. Sounds like free elections to us.

That's not to say there aren't problems with Romania's democracy, as there are with our own. They have different problems, however. The Romanian press is much more like the nineteenth-century media of Joseph Pulitzer and William Randolph Hearst than what we have become accustomed to in recent decades (save for in America's blogosphere and on cable TV). Indeed, there are over a dozen daily newspapers in Bucharest, most tied to one or another local economic or political interest. Two nationwide TV channels are still state-owned, and the two largest private channels are controlled by local business-men with their own economic and political agendas. Ex-Securitate officials continue to manipulate the political process by blackmailing public figures with their old files, or simply through disinformation techniques learned before the fall of Communism.

Some who yearned for both democracy and EU membership bemoaned Romania's low—twenty-nine percent—turnout in the 2009 European parliamentary election.

"Now that they got into Europe, all they worry about are jobs. It's disappointing," one Romanian told us. We disagree. Across Europe, turnouts for EU parliamentary elections are low and focus on local economic conditions. It confirms that, in the last twenty years, Romania has indeed become a "normal" European country with citizens more concerned about economic progress than political divisions. Jean Monnet and other EU founders are no doubt cheering from their graves.

NINETEENTH-CENTURY INCOMES, TWENTY-FIRST-CENTURY SKILLS

ECONOMICALLY, ROMANIA'S MOST IMPORTANT strength is certainly the strong capabilities of its people. Part of that strength is their work ethic, which we heard U.S. employers repeatedly praise, and which we have seen in our own investments there since returning to the United States. Part is the strength of Romania's family values, which leads to much lower rates of crime and drug abuse than we are used to in America. Part is their creativity, which can be seen in their art, their advertising, their software, and unfortunately, on occasion, their computer-hacking.

But the greatest source of their capabilities is the breadth and depth of their education. Here, to be fair, the Communist period was not all bad. Before Communism, Romania made a major effort to expand literacy as well as to achieve high levels of achievement in higher education. To their credit, the Communists built on that base. They expanded educational access dramatically. Like other Communist societies, they provided an "iron rice bowl" for average people, relieving the pressure on young people, particularly the rural poor, to go to work, and thus allowing larger numbers of children to attend school. Likewise, they created opportunities for the smart, hardworking children of workers and peasants to go to college along with children of the professional classes.

We continue to see these Romanian skills first-hand because all our research assistants on this book have been Romanian college and graduate students—Cristina Iacob, Ana Maria Gordan, and Anca Gonț. They are smart, diligent, and well-educated.

Jim also hired Anda Badiu as a financial analyst for his Washington firm in 2004. They met when she was working for the investment banking firm in Bucharest headed by our late friend Valentin George. One day, when Jim was in their office talking about a project, she mentioned her plan to move to the United States.

"Do you know where you're going?" he asked. "Do you have a job there?"

She didn't, but she didn't seem that concerned about it.

It turned out she had won the worldwide visa lottery, which allows people from approximately fifty countries to get an immigrant visa to the United States. She wasn't anxious to leave Romania—she had a good job, and her family and friends were there. But her family encouraged her to try it. "You can always come back if you don't like it."

If there was one profound change from her parents' generation to Anda's, it was this: the heightened sense of possibility.

Jim saw a win-win situation in the making. "Would you be interested in working for my firm in Washington?" he asked her. He didn't have a specific vacancy, but he knew Anda's abilities and her work ethic. She came to Washington in January 2004 and has been working with Jim ever since.

Finance is not the only field in which Romanians excel.

While much of the forced industrialization of the Communist period was economically inefficient, it dramatically expanded the number of people with technical expertise, particularly in engineering.

For example, Romania graduates software engineers at a higher rate for its population than the United States does. Dozens and dozens of American and European companies have come to Romania because of readily available engineering skills. Jim remembers visiting Wisconsin Machine Tools, which bought machine-tool plants in Romania, intending primarily to use Romanians' manufacturing skills. When they got there, they realized that Romanians had world-class engineering skills, and began using Romanian engineers. We saw the same thing in the farm machinery, auto, and hydroelectric industries.

Indeed, there's almost a happy irony in this: Ceauşescu intended to create a self-sufficient industrial sector, built on the model of the late nineteenth century and early twentieth century. He failed, among other reasons, because the world had moved on, but in the process, he helped create a skilled, multilingual workforce well-prepared to thrive in this century's globalized information economy.

Another example of the economic strength that Romania brings to the new century is the fact that since the Revolution, the number of students in higher education has doubled. Interestingly, that's not because the government has invested more in higher education—it has not been able to do so. It's because the culture of education is so strong in Romania that private, tuition-financed universities have been created from scratch in little more than a decade.

ROMANIAN MODEL OF ETHNIC RELATIONS

INTER-ETHNIC RELATIONS ARE an area in which Romania has had big challenges and big achievements. Romania has one of the largest ethnic minorities in Europe—more than 1.5 million Hungarians, primarily in Transylvania. Shortly after the fall of Communism, forces in Romania, not unlike some of those around Slobodan Milošević in Yugoslavia, tried to maintain power by creating violent divisions between Hungarians and Romanians. Indeed, in early 1990, there were a number of such conflicts in which people died.

What's striking is that, in contrast with the former Yugoslavia, Romania did not go down the road of violence and ethnic cleansing.

Instead, it developed a democratic culture of ethnic relations in which the Hungarian minority is well-organized and active in local and national politics. The political party most supported by ethnic Hungarians has been a member of every Romanian government coalition since 1996.

That does not mean there are no ethnic issues in Romania—in fact, there are serious ones, including use of the Hungarian language in public services, participation of Hungarians in the police force, and the re-creation of Hungarian universities. But ethnic Hungarians in Romania press their concerns in ways familiar to Americans—running for office, writing newspaper editorials, and debating in the Parliament.

In 2000, our embassy sponsored a conference on ethnic relations and commissioned a public opinion survey to better understand why Romania had been successful. One of the most interesting findings was that both Romanians and ethnic Hungarians in Romania identified a key difference between Romania and Yugoslavia (at that time): the fact that Romania was a democracy, and therefore these issues could be debated in a democratic process.

ROMANIA'S EUROPEAN FUTURE

WHY HAS ROMANIA SUCCESSFULLY rejoined Europe? Two of the chief reasons are that it was invited to by the EU and by NATO. In the United States, we tend to think of the EU as a free trade zone and NATO as a defense alliance. We're not wrong, but, particularly to Romanians, these two memberships mean far more than that.

Why did joining the EU generate such enthusiasm in Romania, while the IMF or even the World Bank, which were pushing similar policies, generate indifference at best and fear and hostility at worst? The answer is the difference between a bank and a family. To most of us, a bank is controlled by someone else and is looking out for its own interests. We want to take advantage of its loans, but also to be out of debt as soon as we can. We're happiest when we've paid off the loan and gotten out from under the bank's restrictions.

In contrast, when you make a decision to marry, you are joining a family as a partner, not as a supplicant. You see the relationship as permanent, not transitory, and you see it primarily as a social, not an economic, transaction, though it has substantial economic components. That's the EU. It's a family—and a prosperous one at that.

Visas represent an interesting, practical example of how the EU creates ties that bind emotionally.

On the day before the 2008 U.S. election, Jim was interviewed live by Romanian television on the roof of the U.S. Chamber of Commerce, across the way from the White House in Washington, D.C. The reporters had two questions:

"Are Americans too racist to elect Barack Obama president?" Check that one off as a no.

"If elected, would Obama allow Romanians to visit the U.S. without visas, as they can throughout Europe?" A tougher question.

At that time, only visitors from about three dozen countries, primarily Western European ones, could come to the United States without visas. Romania is not one of them. However, because Romania is a member of the European Union, and a key EU principle is the free movement of people, Romanians can travel all over Europe without a visa.

"Why is it OK for us as Romanians to travel to France, the U.K., and Germany visa-free, but not to the U.S.?" they ask.

Part of Romanians' concern about U.S. visas is practical. Thousands of Romanians want to be able to easily visit their new grandchildren, attend college graduations, work with business partners, and study at colleges in the United States, just as they do in Europe.

But it's also symbolic and emotional. Romanians do not understand why they are treated differently by their American and European allies—why their soldier sons can lose their lives, as they have, serving beside American troops in Iraq and Afghanistan, but can't visit America.

It's a measure of how far Romania has come in twenty years that Romanians are kept out of our country by U.S. visa rules, not

Ceauşescu's border police, who shot those trying to leave the country. The difference in visa rules between the U.S. and the EU dramatizes how effective the EU has been in building a real European community, while the United States, all too often, needlessly alienates our friends.

From the Romanian point of view, NATO membership is about security—military security and, probably more important, psychological security.

This is a dimension that Americans should find easier to understand in the post-9/11 world. Romanians know well that they suffered forty-two years of Communism, not because of a strong indigenous Communist movement, but because Russian tanks "liberated" Romania from the Axis powers at the end of World War II. So whether or not there is likely to be a Russian military threat to Romania in the foreseeable future, or ever, the psychological security that comes from being part of the Western alliance is of enormous importance to Romanians, from the top levels of government to those in the most remote village.

We often heard Romanians argue that NATO membership would also encourage U.S. and other foreign investment. Frankly, we thought that view was mistaken. We rarely heard a potential U.S. investor even ask about Romania's NATO status, and the major increases in foreign investment in Poland, Hungary, and the Czech Republic came before, not after, they became NATO members. Similarly, countries in Western Europe that are not NATO members—Austria, Finland, Sweden, and Switzerland—prospered economically and attracted substantial foreign investment throughout the Cold War, and have since.

On one occasion, Jim argued this point with a well-informed Romanian. Finally, the Romanian became so agitated with Jim's reluctance to agree that he blurted out, "Well, I wouldn't invest in Romania until we become a member of NATO." That, we think, is the real point: that Romanians' confidence in the long-term economic and military security of their country was tied closely to becoming part of the NATO alliance.

The most important argument, however, for Romania joining

NATO was that NATO membership represented integration into the West in all aspects. Thus, by joining NATO, Romania made a broad national commitment to a set of values, institutions, and relationships that are important from the point of view of the United States and those in Romania who wanted Romania to lock in its democratic progress. Joining NATO emboldened the proponents of these policies and demoralized its opponents.

The real guarantor of Romania's continuing progress, though, is the attitude and commitment of the Romanian people. Governments can be cynical or even double-dealing, but ordinary people tend to have more long-term views and orientations. The fact is, according to every poll we've ever seen, the Romanian people are the most pro-NATO, pro-American, and pro-European Union population in Eastern Europe. That's why Romanian leaders across the political spectrum supported NATO and EU integration—the people wanted them to.

Romania is not yet the place most Romanians, or other Europeans or Americans, want it to be. Too many retired people can't support themselves in dignity on their pensions. Too many young people leave to work in Italy and Spain because they can't find good jobs in Romania when they graduate from school. And too many Romanians of all ages worry that they have lost the security of socialism without gaining the prosperity of capitalism.

But few would like to go back to the days of Ceauşescu—of food shortages and secret police, of few choices in the stores and fewer on television and in the press. Democracy and good inter-ethnic relations have taken such root that Romanians have taken them for granted.

Most important, Romania is a nation of well-educated, hardworking people who know where they want to go and have a plan to get there.

That's why we titled this book *Dracula Is Dead*. In the last twenty years, Romanians have proved to the world, and more importantly to themselves, that the myths which oppressed them for centuries (not just during the Communist years) are just that—myths. Assumptions of isolation and powerlessness, which too often defined Romanians' view of themselves and their country, are no more real than Dracula. Today, as they enter the second decade of the twenty-first century, Romanians are free, and they know it.

ACKNOWLEDGEMENTS

This book is the product of many minds, many hands, and many hearts. We cannot hope to thank all those who have helped us create it. But we want to acknowledge all as best we can.

First—the people of Romania. This is their story. We learned from many whom we've met and many we have not. They welcomed us as they welcome all who come as friends.

Many Romanians we learned from are quoted in this book. But many others are not. These include Augusta Anca, Mariana Cernicova-Bucă, the late Harry Morgan and students at Tibiscus University in Timişoara, Simona and Dan Baciu, Judy Bloom, Hermina Budai, Virginia Coman, Marion Day, Baron Bernhard Dominik Hauser, Leslie Hawke, Matei Paun, Grigore Popescu, Gabriela Radley and the late John Robbins Radley, Petru Rareş, Father Cristian Sabău, Dinu Săraru, Dumitru Sechelariu, Dr. Cristian Tăbăcaru, and Mihai Tomescu. We learned from all and thank every one.

During the years we lived in Romania, we learned much from the Americans and Romanians who worked there for the U.S. government. Until we took up our position in Bucharest, we had no idea of the breadth and depth of expertise and commitment which these Americans and Romanians bring to building bridges between our countries.

These public servants span the array of U.S. government agencies, and outnumber those of the State Department, which leads America's relations with Romania. There are so many, from the Customs Service and the C.I.A., to the Department of Labor, the Peace Corps, and the U.S. Army, that we cannot mention them all. But we learned from all of them and they all should make Americans proud.

In particular, the hundreds of Romanians who worked for the U.S. Embassy—as policy experts, consular staff, development and communications specialists, security officers, drivers, and much more—are extraordinary resources for the United States and were our invaluable teachers.

We also want to thank Jim's predecessors and successors, all of whom shared their expertise and their friendship—Ambassadors Harry Barnes, John Davis, Alfred Moses, Roger Kirk, the late Alan Green Jr., David Funderburk, Michael Guest, J.D. Crouch, and Nicholas Taubman.

Likewise, the Romanian ambassadors to the U.S. during our time have been exceptional counselors and friends—Ambassadors Mircea Geoană, Sorin Ducaru, and Adrian Vierița.

During our years in Bucharest and since, we have made many friends in Romania—too many to mention all by name here. Some have been particularly helpful as we prepared this book. John and Radu Florescu, Jr. gave expert counsel, and warm friendship, at every stage. Gertrude Ştefan educated Sheilah in Romania's history as well as its language. Emanuel Tânjală shared not only superb photos but also his passionate hopes for the country of his birth.

Our research assistants in Bucharest—Cristina Iacob, Anamaria Gordan, and Anca Gonț—have been fabulous. In the U.S., Jim's staff— Elena Kuzina, Anda Badiu, and Aga Popeda, as well as interns Kasia Antczak and Evis Rucaj—have helped enormously. Danielle Simms, Francine Moody, and Meikka Cutlip transcribed hours of interviews.

Demonstrating the 21st-century skills we describe in the book, the Romanian-American team at Recognos volunteered to create our website (www.DraculaIsDead.com). Check it out, and learn more about Romania. Daniela Nedelschi of Saatchi&Saatchi Romania helped design the book cover.

A number of friends, many with deep Romanian expertise, graciously read parts of the book when it was a *very* rough draft: Vlad Tismăneanu, Ernest Latham, Vic Fingerhut, Caroline Carver, Gene Counihan, Lisa Sonne, Victor Dorff, Ted and Dee Peck, and Jim's sister Decie Bodwell—saved us from some embarrassing bloopers. Any that remain in the text are our responsibility, and we look forward to hearing about them.

Three publishing professionals—Phil Rezvin, Barbara Pape, and

Will Nothdurft—helped conceptualize the book when we had strong motivation and weak focus.

Our publicist, Meg Parsont, has plunged enthusiastically into spreading the word, understanding that our book is travel literature, history, and current affairs all rolled into one.

Finally, we had four gracious hosts—and cheerleaders—in the summers of 2007 and 2008 when we retreated to the Eastern Shore of Maryland to write—Ted and Dee Peck and Lesley and Fred Israel.

Mulţumim pentru tot!

ABOUT THE AUTHORS

Sheilah Kast is an award-winning journalist, well known to viewers of PBS, ABC, and CNN and to listeners of National Public Radio. For ABC, she reported on the collapse of Communism from Moscow and Tbilisi, and covered Hillary Clinton's first trip to Eastern Europe. She currently hosts AARP's weekly newsmaker cable TV show, *Inside E Street*, as well as her own daily magazine show on WYPR, the public radio station in Maryland.

Jim Rosapepe represented the United States as ambassador to Romania from 1998 to 2001, bringing to the job experience in American government and business, as well as in the former Communist world. He currently heads an investment firm active in the US and Europe and serves the boards of several funds investing in Eastern Europe and other emerging markets. He has written about economic and security issues in Europe in *The Wall Street Journal*, *The Baltimore Sun* and *The Harvard International Review*.

Jim and Sheilah have been married since 1983 and live in College Park, Maryland.

(To reach them, go to their website, www.DraculaIsDead.com.)

EUROPEAN UNION

Today's Romania is a big part of the European Union, and the EU is the roadmap for Romania's future.